CARTOONING FOR FUN & PROFIT

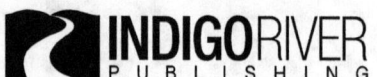

CARTOONING
FOR FUN & PROFIT

OVER 500 STEP-BY-STEP DRAWINGS & DIAGRAMS

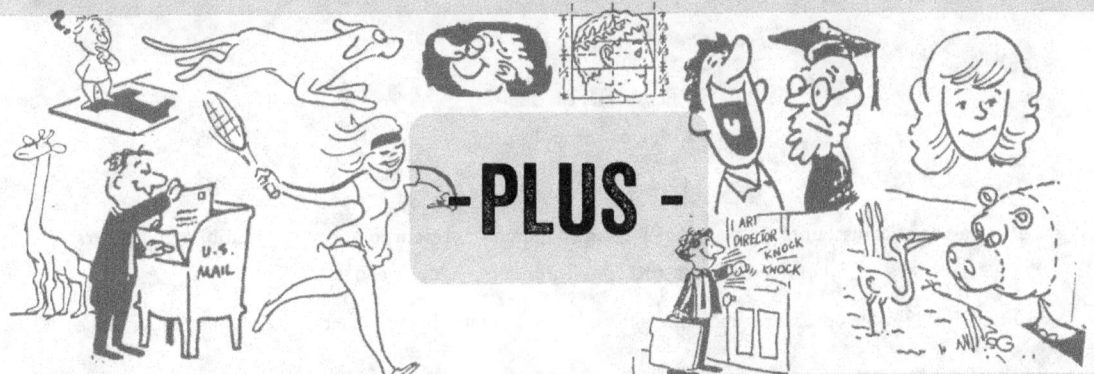

- PLUS -

TIPS ON SELLING TO SYNDICATES, NEWSPAPERS, MAGAZINES, AND ADVERTISING AGENCIES

DON TRACHSLER

Cartooning for Fun and Profit

© 2024 by Danya Clapp

Library of Congress Control Number: 2024915773
ISBN: 978-1-964686-07-3

Although this publication is designed to provide accurate information about the subject matter, the publisher and the author assume no responsibility for any errors, inaccuracies, omissions, or inconsistencies herein. This publication is intended as a resource, however, it is not intended as a replacement for direct and personalized professional services.

Cover Design: Emma Elzinga

Printed in the United States of America

First Edition

3 West Garden Street, Ste 718
Pensacola, FL 32502
www.indigoriverpublishing.com

Ordering Information:

Quantity sales: Special discounts are available on quantity purchases by corporations, associations, and others. For details, contact the publisher at the address above.

Orders by US trade bookstores and wholesalers: Please contact the publisher at the address above.

With Indigo River Publishing, you can always expect great books, strong voices, and meaningful messages. Most importantly, you'll always find . . . *words worth reading.*

CONTENTS

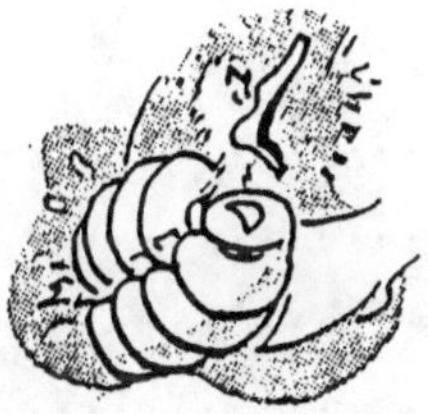

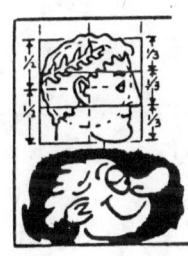
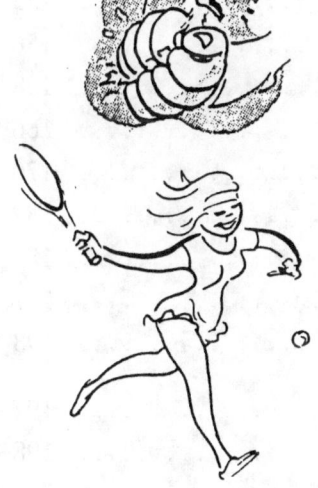
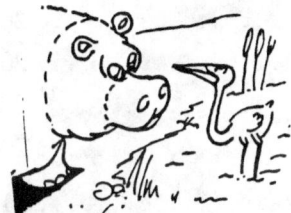

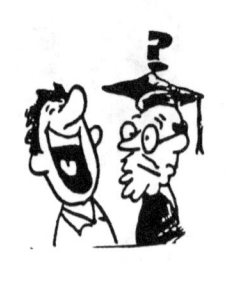
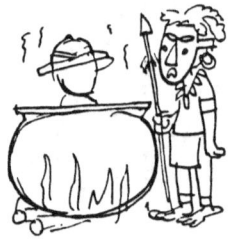
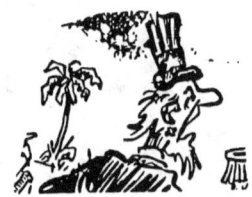
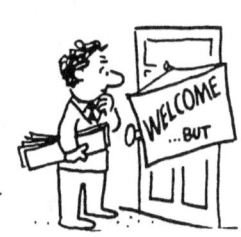
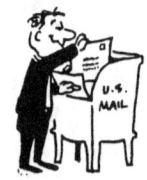

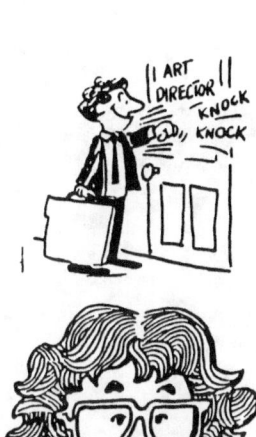

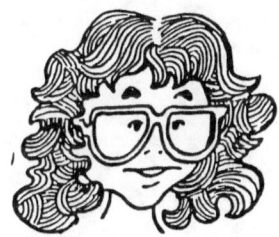

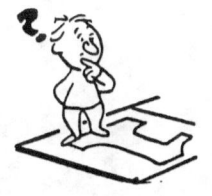

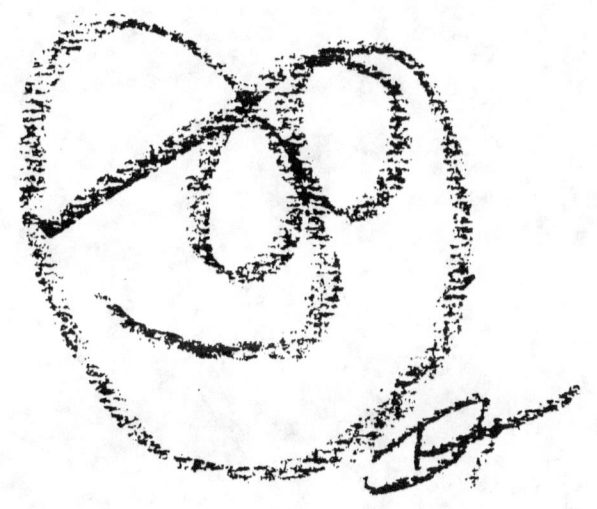

Growing up with Grandpa

Our grandfathers had very special meaning in our lives growing up, you see my father was tragically killed when my sisters and I were very young, so our grandfathers were the men in our lives.

When my sisters and I visited Grandma and Grandpa T's down in West Palm Beach, FL, over the summer months – we knew we were in for an adventure. There were always fun summer projects with Grandpa T. We would wake up and head out to the BIG garage that was grandpa's sanctuary for his work. He was always working on something, but always had projects ready for us every day. We never knew what fun the day held out.

I was always amazed at his talent – he could do anything and did! Painting, plastering, woodworking, sculpting, iron work and of course cartooning.

As I got older, I always appreciated the love and patience he showed to us, teaching us and having fun.

His artistic journey started early and remained until the day he passed on in 2007.

He was a hard worker and always willing to share his talents with others. He set his mind and dedicated many years to sharing with others the knowledge he had in cartooning – and compiled it in the book you have today. Unfortunately, he never got the recognition he deserved for his tireless efforts.

Recently his wife of 45 years, Grandma Lou passed away, she was 95 and Don was the love of her life. When going through what was left of their lives together - we found the complete manuscript he tried to get published back in 1988 - it was returned with an I'm sorry letter. I'm sure he was devastated.

The publishing of this treasure has been a long time coming and although times have changed with computer animation and AI, and may not seem valuable, our hope is that many will appreciate the contents and hopefully learn from his efforts and hard work.

We hope this honors him and his legacy. This is for you Grandpa!

Love and miss you forever,

Your Granddaughters Chris, Danya and Tasha, and Daughter Terri Lou

Introduction

Four or five centuries ago, during the days of the Great European Master Artists, a cartoon was the term used to describe the artists' preliminary drawings and sketches from which the final painting would be developed.

These initial "studies" were often done in pencil, charcoal, or light washes of various colors. Those drawings were quite loose and free-flowing, with much of the finer detailing either lightly suggested or omitted entirely.

Occasionally, after spending weeks, months, even years on the final painting, many artists discovered that their preliminary sketches and rough drawings more successfully captured the intended mood and spirit than did the finished paintings.

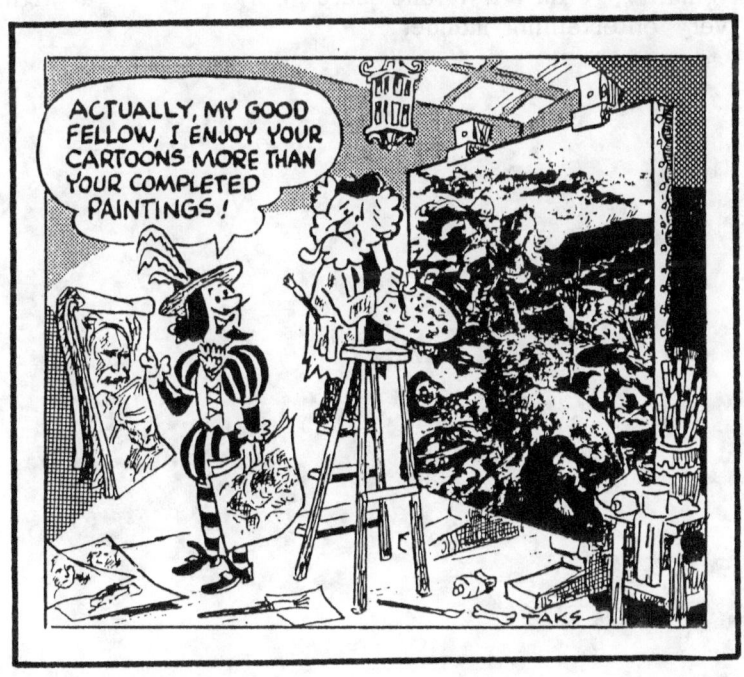

As might be expected, the Old Masters soon learned that the sale of their preliminary rough drawings and "cartoons" offered the opportunity to make extra money for their artistic efforts. Gradually, many of those artists (some of whom perhaps lacked the skill or patience to produce truly great paintings) began to specialize in those "quickie" sketches and drawings. They found that they could demonstrate their artistic skills and convey their thoughts and ideas in this simpler and more direct manner, find a larger market for their work, and still satisfy their creative urge. They gradually replaced the titles on the work with captions and added humor or social statements to the subject matter.

In the natural course of events, those artists became known as "cartoonists" and the era of cartoons was born.

TODAY'S CARTOONIST

In the rush-rush, hurly-burly, madcap world we find ourselves in today, the efforts of our cartoonists are probably more appreciated, and certainly more needed, than ever before. The cartoonist is an entertainer, a philosopher, an observer, and often an educator. Whether he makes his readers laugh heartily or reflect thoughtfully, his role in society cannot be taken lightly.

After reading the manuscript pages and seeing the hundreds of drawings required to produce Cartooning For Fun and Profit, I can give it nothing but FOUR STARS. Further, I sincerely believe it will prove to be the standard by which all other "How to Cartoon" books will be judged. It places the proper emphasis on originality, creativity, and hard work. It is a highly informative book done in a very entertaining manner.

STUDY GUIDELINES

STUDY GUIDELINES FOR CARTOONING FOR FUN AND PROFIT

Producing this book has been a joy for all those concerned, primarily because we were confident that the end result would be a worthwhile product. That is not to say, however, that it has been thrown together in a casual manner. Quite the opposite; every chapter, section, page, and drawing has been carefully planned and positioned with a particular purpose in mind -- much like placing stepping stones across a stream. How one uses those stepping stones is, of course, an individual matter based on individual goals.

THE CASUAL DOODLER

Lots of folks, particularly youngsters, like to draw and sketch and "mess around" with little cartoons. The first several chapters of Cartooning For Fun and Profit offer sound, basic teaching principles that can make doodling more fun than ever.

THE "SUNDAY" CARTOONIST

Many gainfully employed people who are quite happy with their jobs find that part-time cartooning is a fun, and occasionally profitable, hobby. Designing cartoon posters, booklets, and newsletters for local community events and political campaigns can be an enjoyable and satisfying effort. There are many little tips and suggestions scattered throughout this book that should make those efforts much more effective.

THE DEDICATED STUDENT

I don't know that anyone has ever completely explained why some of us, even at an early age, have an inborn desire to communicate through drawings and cartoons. The urge is there, and experience has shown that there is very little one can do about it except nurture it, encourage it, and get it pointed in the most desirable direction. Hopefully, Cartooning For Fun and Profit will serve as a helping hand in achieving the rainbow and its pot of gold.

The reader, or student, will get as much out of this book as he or she wishes. Spend a little time with it and have a little fun. Spend a lot of time with it, follow all suggestions and recommendations, and take the first step toward a very rewarding, and certainly satisfying, career.

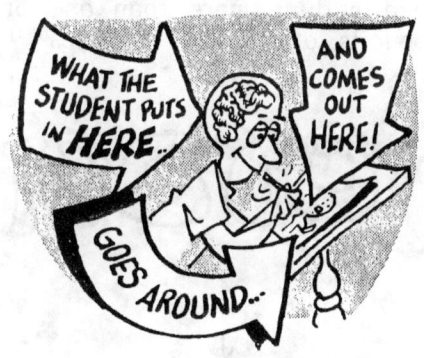

STUDY GUIDELINES

In the final analysis, <u>Cartooning for Fun and Profit</u> is a textbook -- hopefully an amusing and entertaining one, but a textbook nonetheless. For best results, it should be treated as such.

We respectfully recommend that no less than 40 study hours be spent on each chapter. Do the lessons and exercises over and over again before proceeding to the next section or chapter.

The student who has had previous art instruction is not excused from starting at page one, chapter one, since every succeeding chapter is based on information presented in the one before it. Starting somewhere in the middle of the book, or skipping over certain sections, will leave some very harmful gaps in your knowledge of the subject.

REFERENCE MATERIAL

Throughout the book, we stress the importance of originality and creativity. Proper reference material can be the key to those important assets. While copying the work of other artists and cartoonists is a common practice, we discourage it at every opportunity. It will do nothing but stifle your own natural ability.

However, reference material is of the utmost importance. Newspapers and magazines are loaded with excellent photographs of nearly every imaginable subject. These should be clipped and pasted into scrapbooks in as orderly a fashion as possible. Admittedly, this can be a time consuming task, but it is one that friends and relatives are usually happy to help with once they understand that it will be helpful in your studies. But remember, photos only. Do not copy the work (or the mistakes) of other artists and cartoonists.

QUICK SKETCHING

This is another aspect of drawing that is emphasized throughout the book. We do so for many reasons, not the least of which is that it improves drawing skills and strengthens the powers of observation. Additionally, it adds confidence to one's drawing abilities and makes drawing a more enjoyable, less painful and tedious task.

MATERIALS

At the outset, you will need nothing more than one or two good quality sketch pads and a few drawing pencils of assorted "grades" (2B and HB are good for starters).

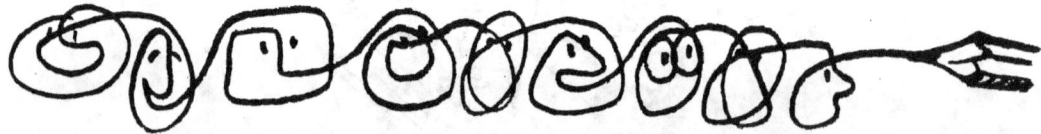

STUDY GUIDELINES

Gradually, other supplies and equipment can be obtained. A small drawing table, T-square, draftsman's 45 and 60 degree angles, a pad or two of drawing bristol board, ink, pen points and holders, and so on. A visit to the local art supply store can be an education in itself. Ask for free catalogs and booklets concerning their supplies and equipment. There are all kinds of neat new things coming out every day!

BASIC PERSPECTIVE

Although it is not always immediately apparent, there is at least a slight suggestion of perspective in just about every cartoon. It might be used in nothing more than a brim of a hat, a coffee cup, or the top of a table, but it will be there. Without it, we could not suggest distance, direction, or shape.

Most of us are familiar with the fundamentals of perspective, but a quick review of the basic principles might refresh our memories.

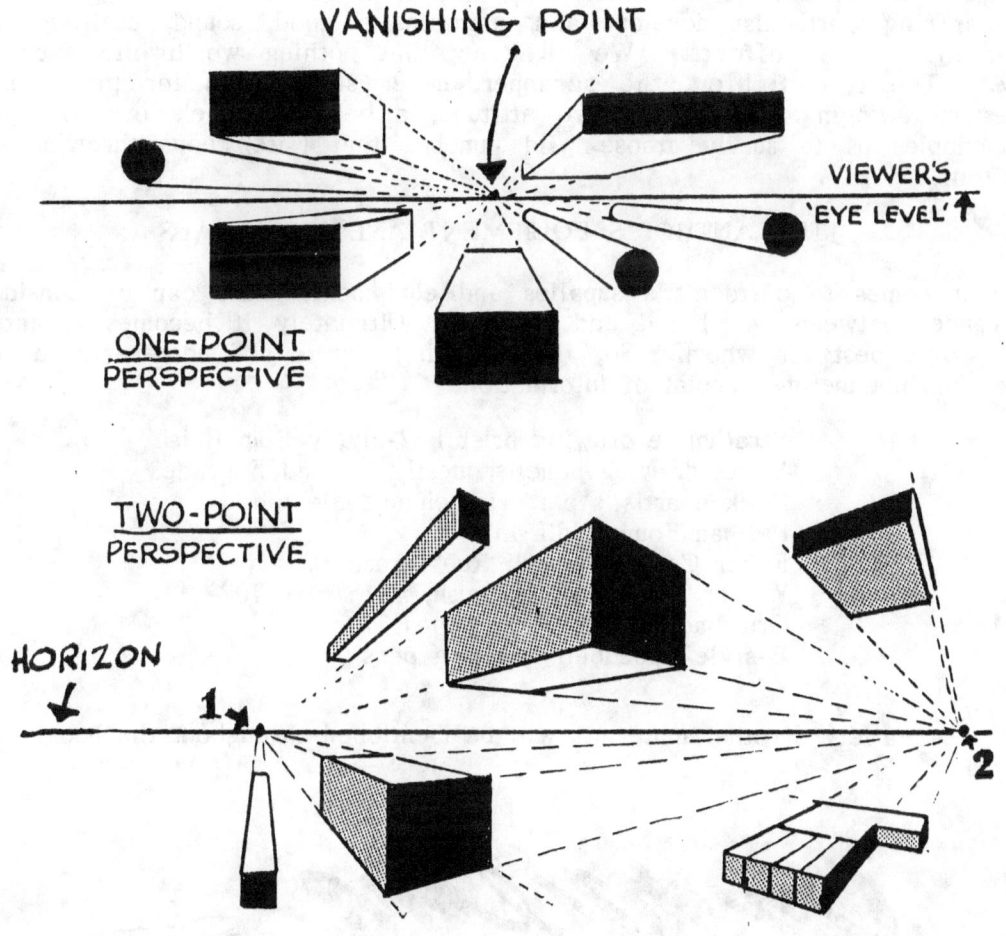

STUDY GUIDELINES

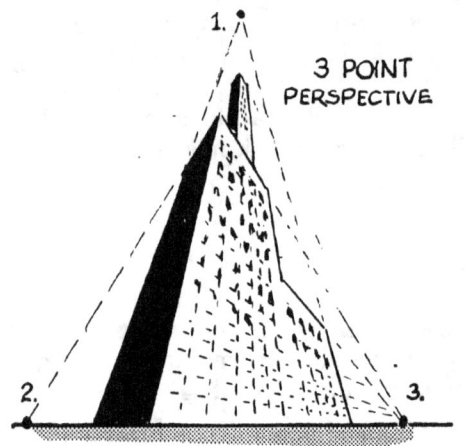

3 POINT PERSPECTIVE

There is also something called "3-point perspective," but it is pretty much an oddball and is rarely used in the ordinary, everyday cartoon.

MENTAL ATTITUDE

Cartooning is, and has been for many years, a very competitive profession, perhaps equal to any of the other arts. So it is of the utmost importance that the aspiring cartoonist develops and maintains a good, sound, positive attitude about his or her efforts. We all know that nothing worthwhile ever comes easy. The true fighter, the scrapper, never stays down for the count, but comes up swinging. It's a positive attitude, a belief in one's own capabilities, that enables us to survive those wild punches that Fate keeps throwing around so often.

THE AUTHOR'S EQUIPMENT AND MATERIALS

When it comes to cartoonist's supplies and equipment, there can be considerable differences between one brand and another. Ultimately it becomes a matter of what works best for whom. So, the following list is not necessarily a recommendation, but merely a point of information.

Strathmore drawing bristol, 2-ply, vellum finish
Venus drawing pencils, mostly 2B and F grades
Pelikan artist's pen with changeable nibs
Pelikan Fount India Ink
Faber Castell "Magic Rub" erasers
Winsor Newton sable brush, #2, series 707
Grumbacher brush, #5, series 874
B-style Speedball lettering pens

A variety of other materials will be mentioned throughout the book.

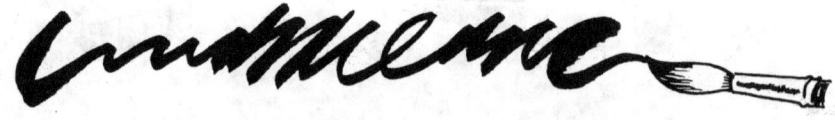

CHAPTER ONE
Heads and Faces

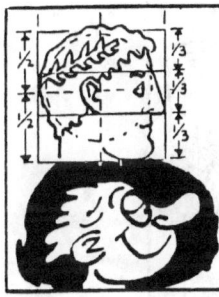

SECTION 1
PROPORTIONS
FROM THE MUSEUM TO THE COMIC PAGES.

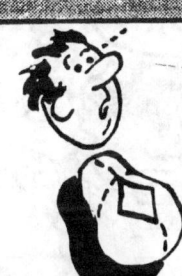

SECTION 2
HEAD LINES
- CREATING DIRECTION
- FACES THAT "DRAW THEMSELVES".

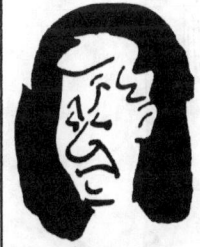

SECTION 3
EXPRESSIONS
- A 'LOOK' IS WORTH A THOUSAND WORDS.

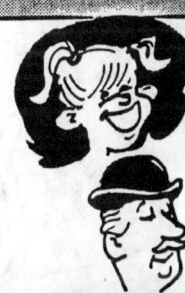

SECTION 4
HAIRDOS & HATS
- HAIR STYLES HELP DESCRIBE PERSONALITY, EMOTION, & ACTION.
- IF THE HAT FITS— PUT IT ON.

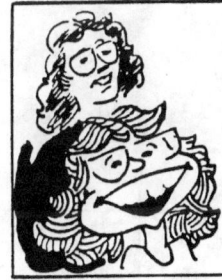

SECTION 5
CAST of CHARACTERS
- SKETCHING FROM REFERENCE MATERIAL.
- BASIC CARICATURE

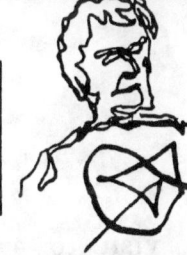

SECTION 6
CREATIVE SKETCHING
- "SINGLE LINE" EXERCISES
- THE 'SCRIBBLE SKETCH'

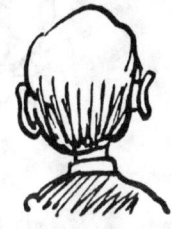

SECTION 7
DIFFICULT HEAD POSITIONS
- WHAT TO DO ABOUT THEM.
- HOW TO AVOID THEM.
- BRIEF REVIEW OF CHAPTER ONE.

* * *   A BRIEF LOOK AT THE CLASSICS   * * *

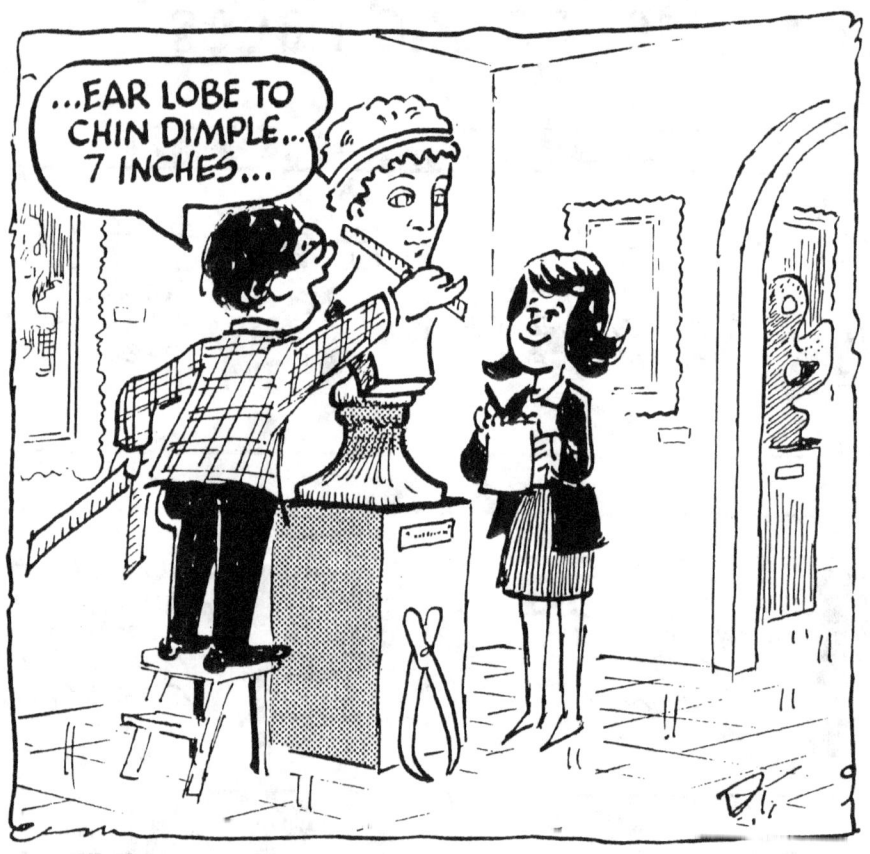

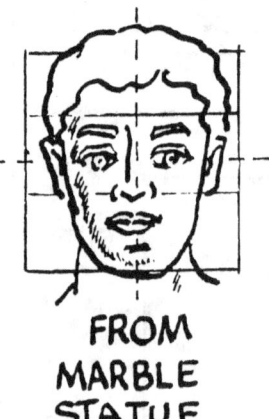

FROM
MARBLE
STATUE

A visit to a museum may seem like an odd way to begin a book on cartooning. However, since this book will be extolling the virtues and benefits of research and originality, we felt it necessary to set a good example right at the very outset.

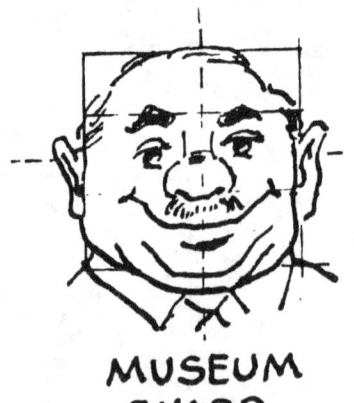

MUSEUM
GUARD

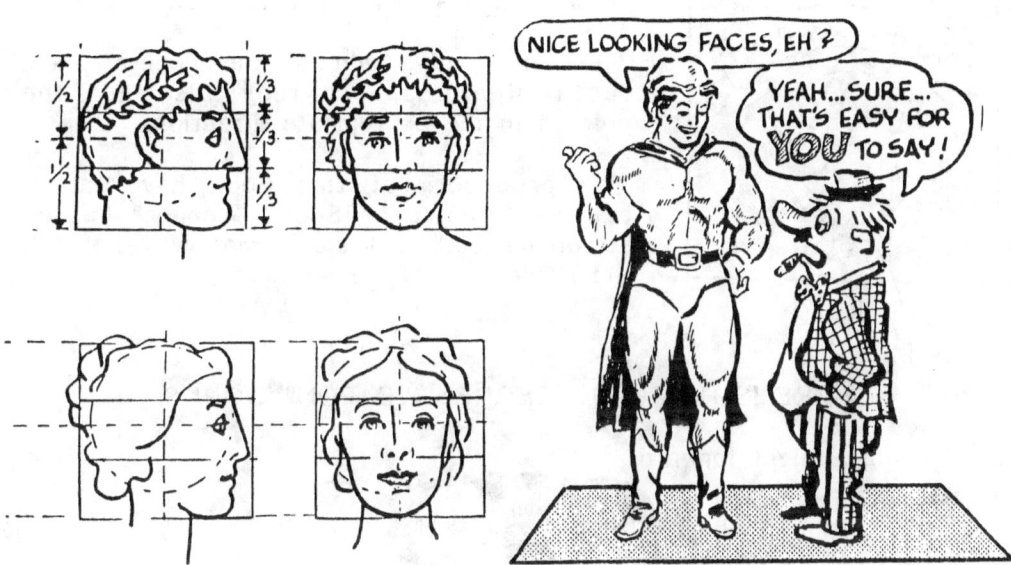

The "Illustrative/Adventure" type of cartoon usually adheres very closely to "classic proportions," but the vast majority of today's cartoons are of a simplified nature, often stylized in a clean, crisp manner.

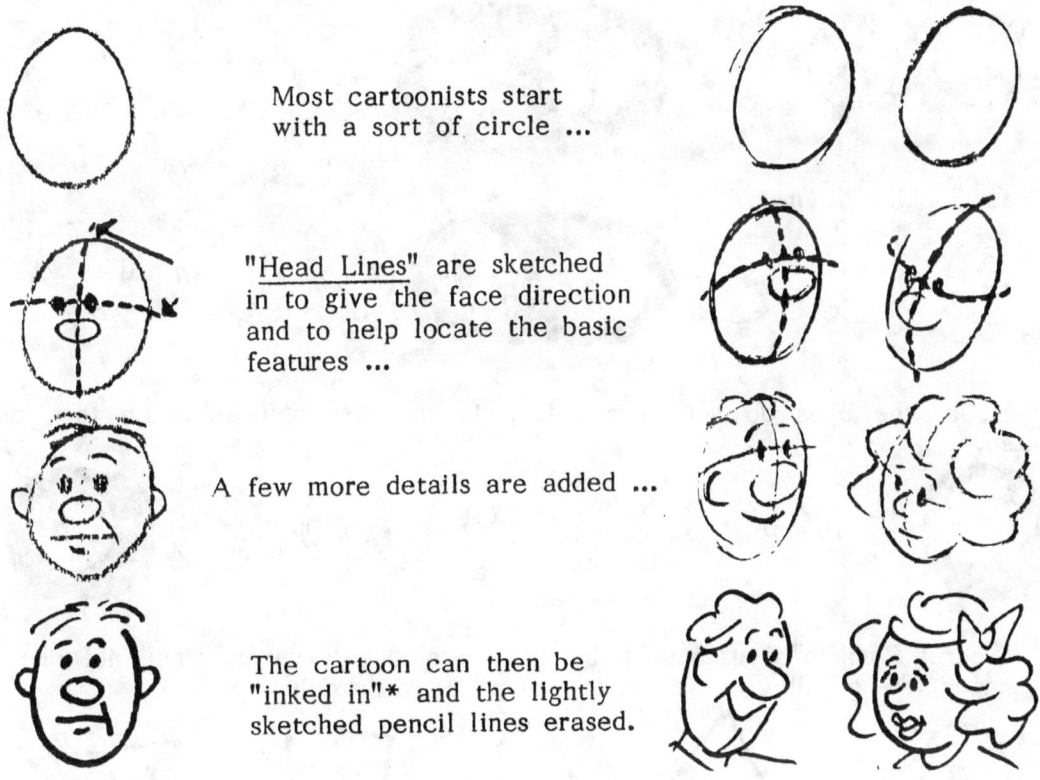

Most cartoonists start with a sort of circle ...

"Head Lines" are sketched in to give the face direction and to help locate the basic features ...

A few more details are added ...

The cartoon can then be "inked in"* and the lightly sketched pencil lines erased.

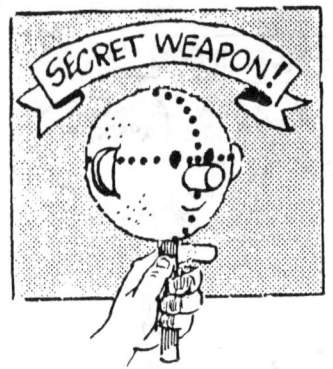

"HEAD LINES" ARE EXTREMELY IMPORTANT!

They not only indicate the general location of facial features, but they also get the head pointed in the appropriate direction.

The producers of this book have, at no little expense, created a "Secret Weapon" (made from a styrofoam ball and stuff) that will help illustrate the proper use of "Head Lines."

HERE IS HOW THE "SECRET WEAPON" WORKS:

° Head looking straight forward:

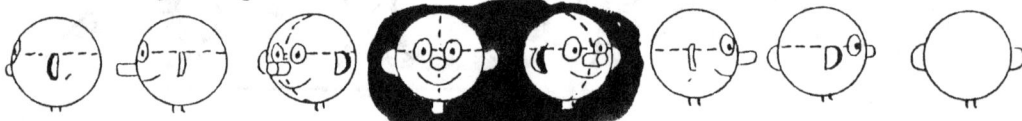

° Head looking upward:

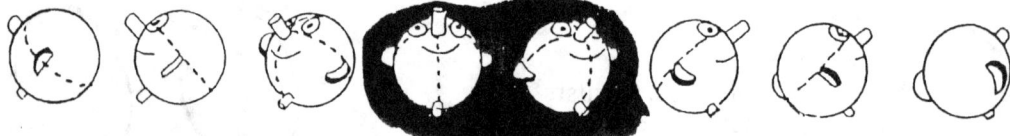

° Head looking downward:

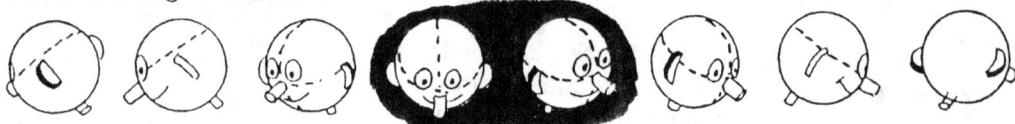

Of course, the eyes do not always look in the direction to which the nose is pointed.

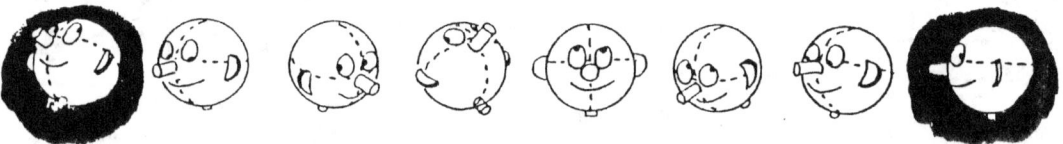

Our "Secret Weapon" runs into a bit of a problem, however, since not all heads are shaped like a ball! Just about <u>any</u> shape can be used.

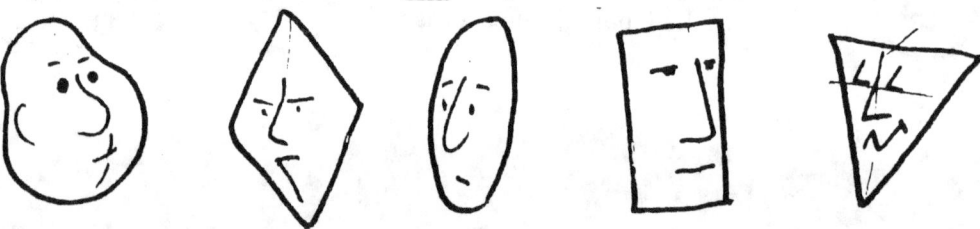

EXPERIMENTING WITH SHAPES AND FORMS

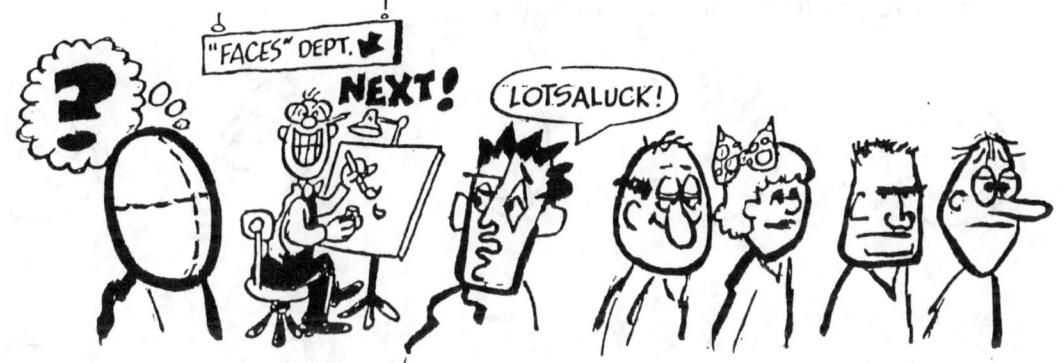

"UNUSUAL" SHAPES CAN HELP CREATE SPECIAL CARTOON CHARACTERS!

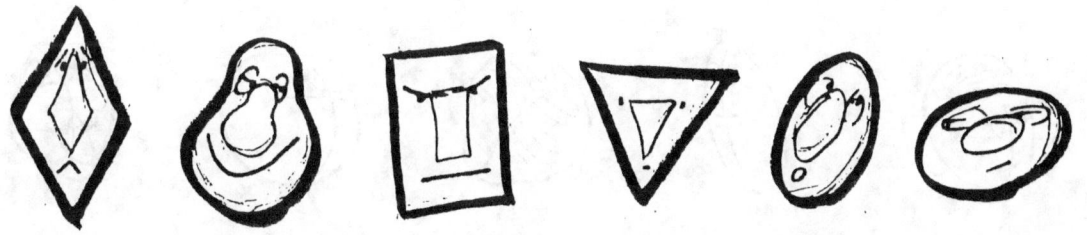

THESE FACES ALMOST DRAW THEMSELVES!

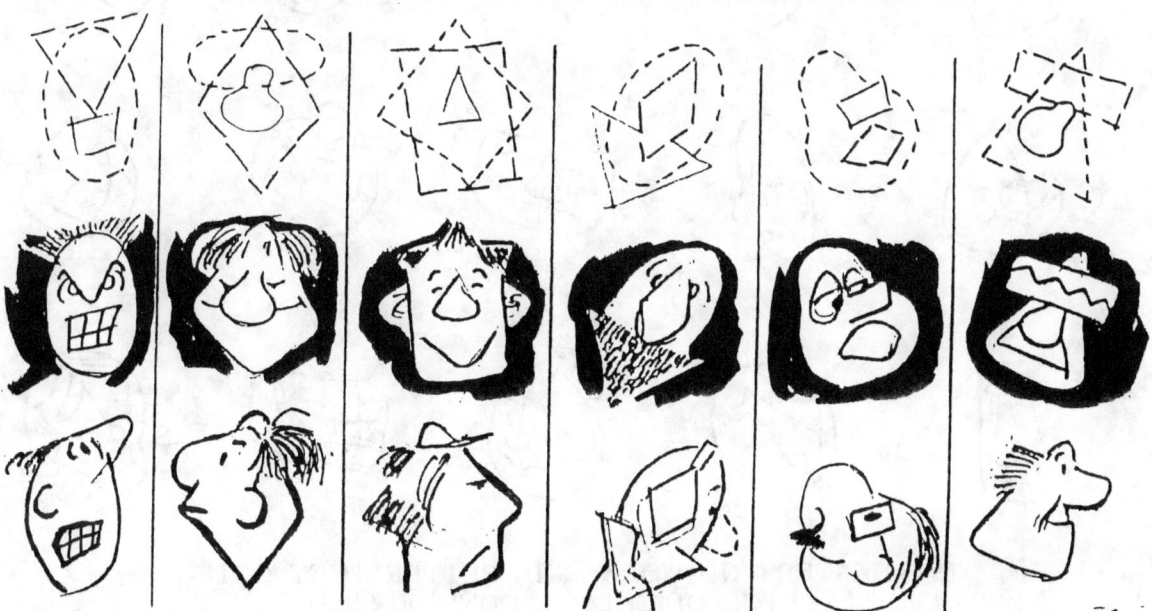

Here are more head lines and shapes. The student should fill several dozen pages of his or her practice sketchbook with quick sketches similar to (or better yet, different from) those shown here.

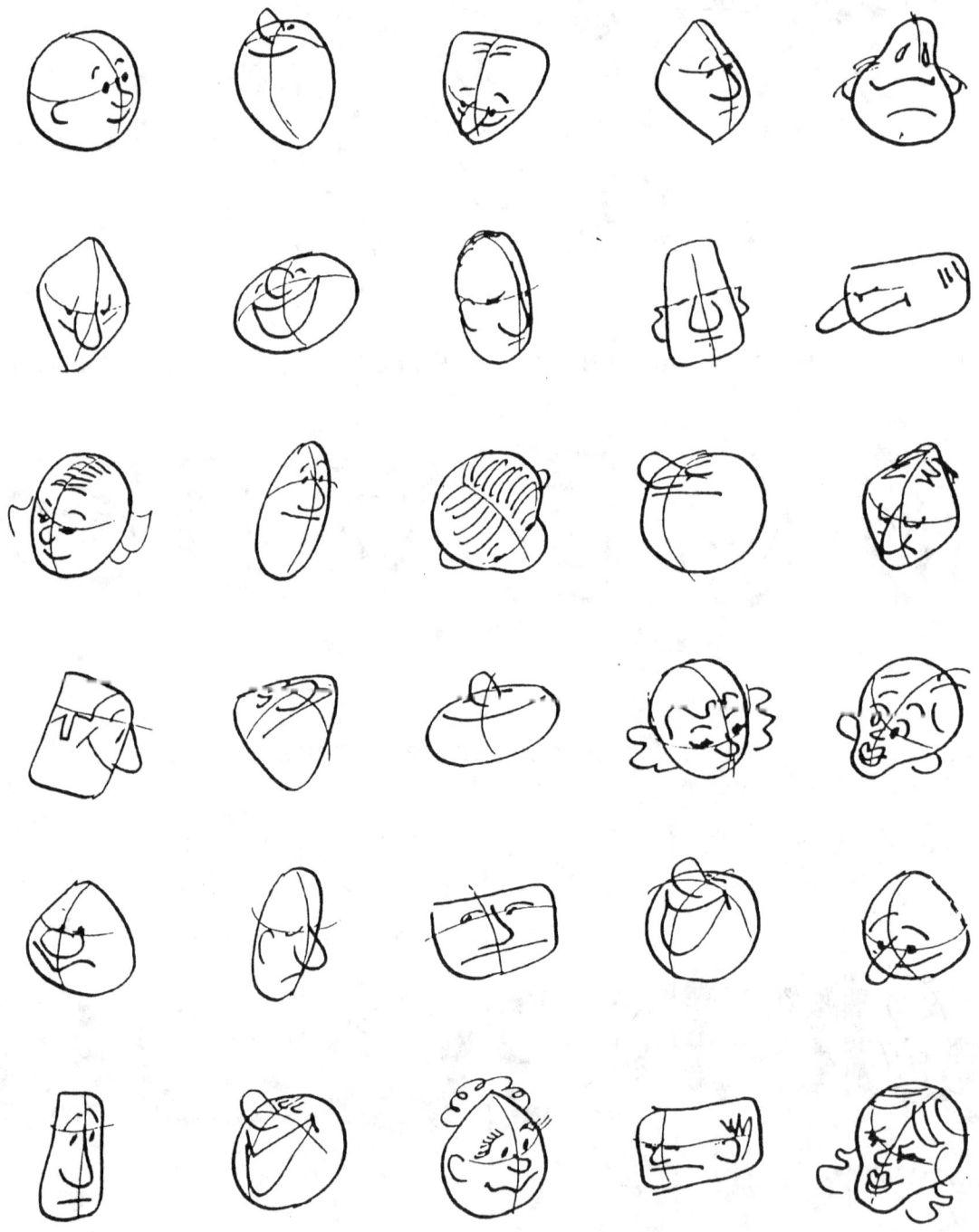

THE FASTER YOU WORK, THE BETTER THEY GET!
SKETCH QUICKLY ... DON'T FUSS.

The old saying, "A picture is worth a thousand words," probably applies more to a cartoon than any other form of art, for it is the cartoonist who, with just a few simple strokes of the pen, can tell a whole story.

"A BIG, STRANGE DOG WALKS ACROSS THE LAWN"

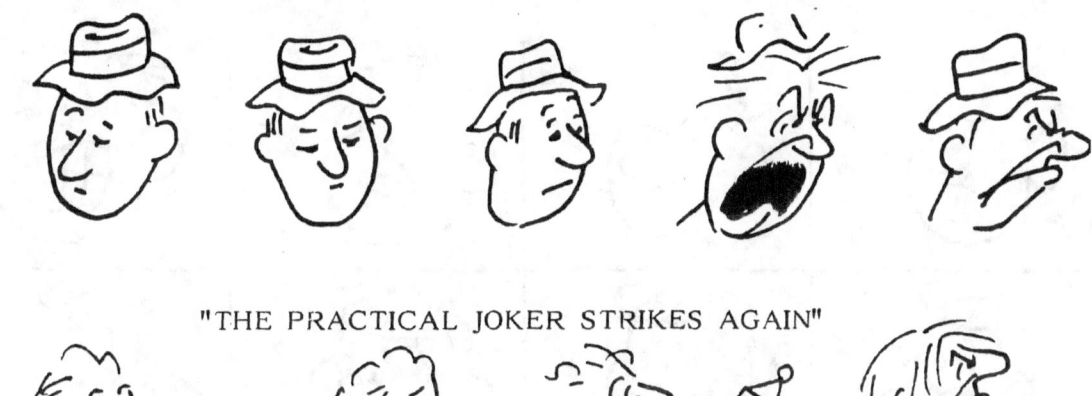

"THE PRACTICAL JOKER STRIKES AGAIN"

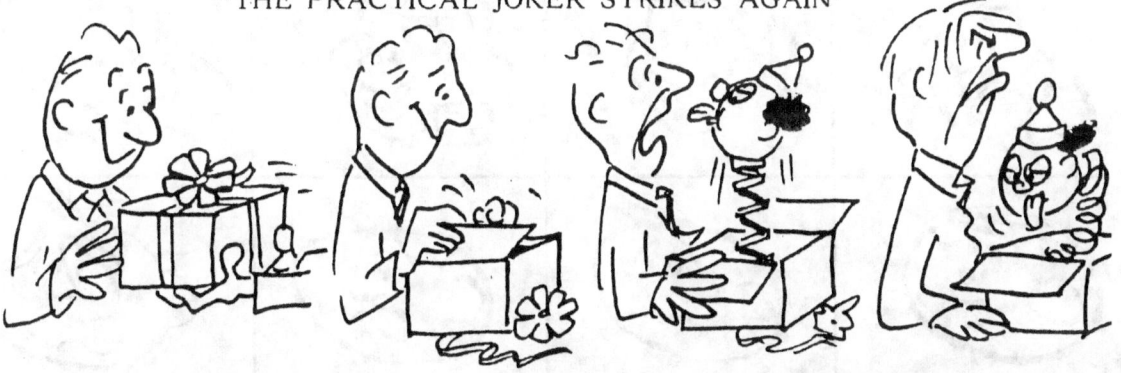

Emotions come in many degrees. We can be mildly annoyed or in a rage, slightly amused or laugh uproariously, a bit surprised or totally astonished.

Choosing just the right degree of expression for a given situation can make or break the cartoon message. For instance, a mild mannered individual is not likely to get as angry as a big, burly person.

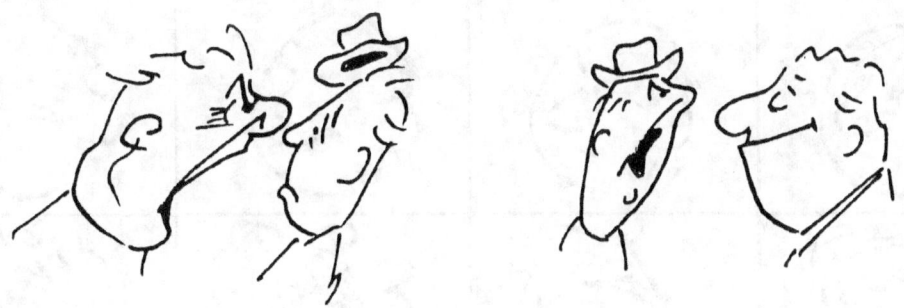

The expressions shown on this page are mostly basic and are only a tiny sampling of the hundreds of variations the cartoonist has, or should have, in his or her mental "inventory."

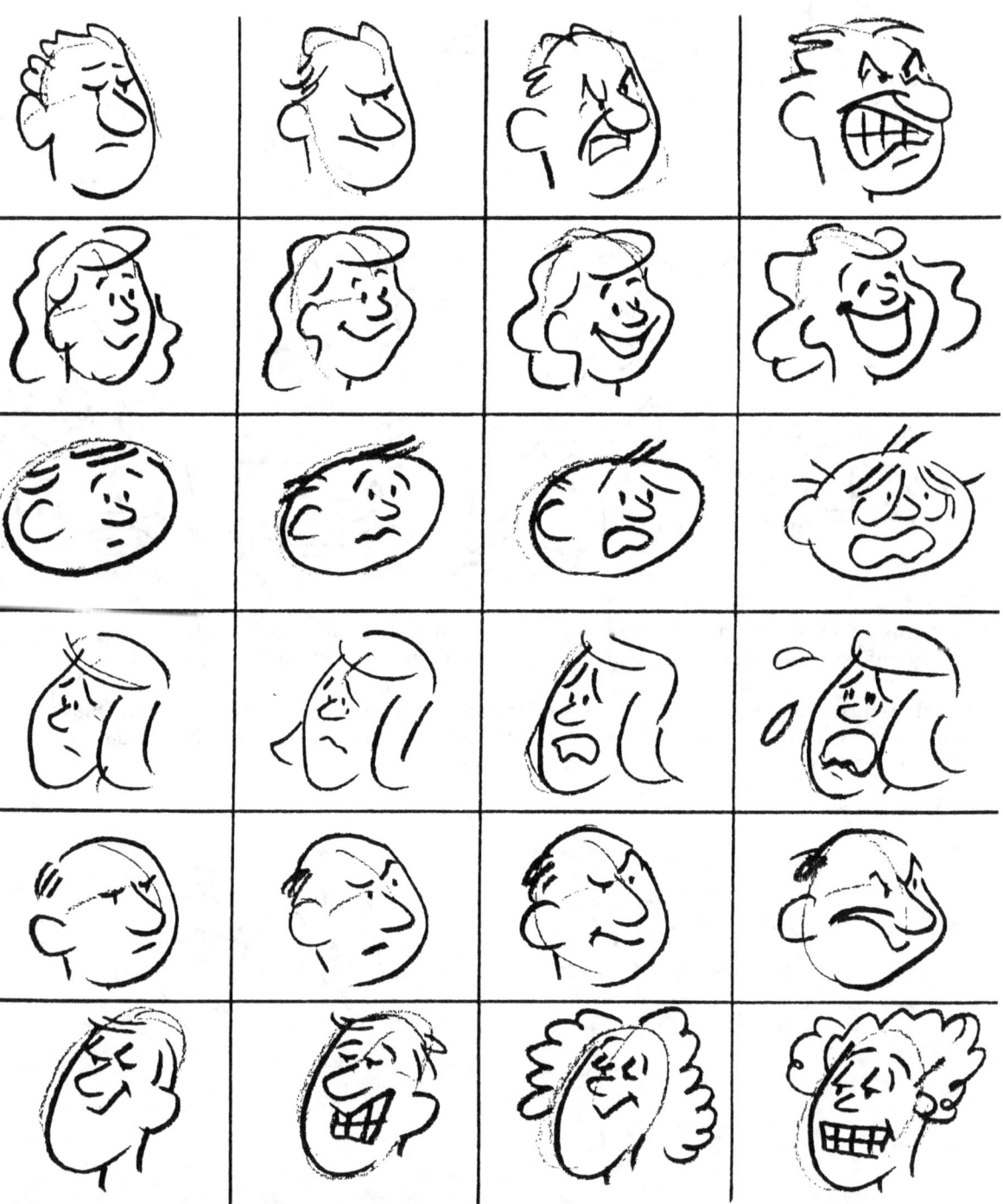

Hair styles are usually kept very simple so as not to detract from facial features and expressions. Occasionally, however, the very latest hair fads or fashions are required, so it is advisable to keep up with the latest trends.

TYPICAL CARTOON HAIRDOS

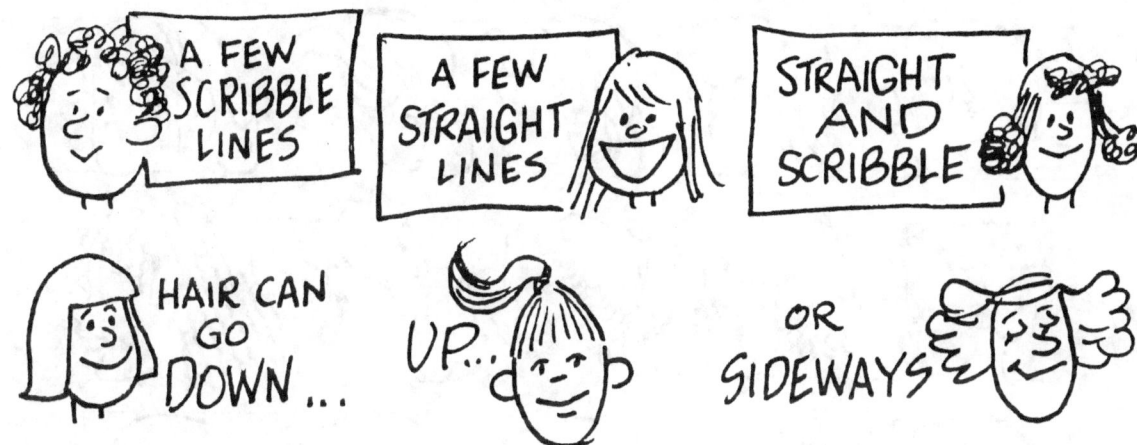

Hair always reflects the MOOD, CHARACTER, or ACTIVITY of its owner.

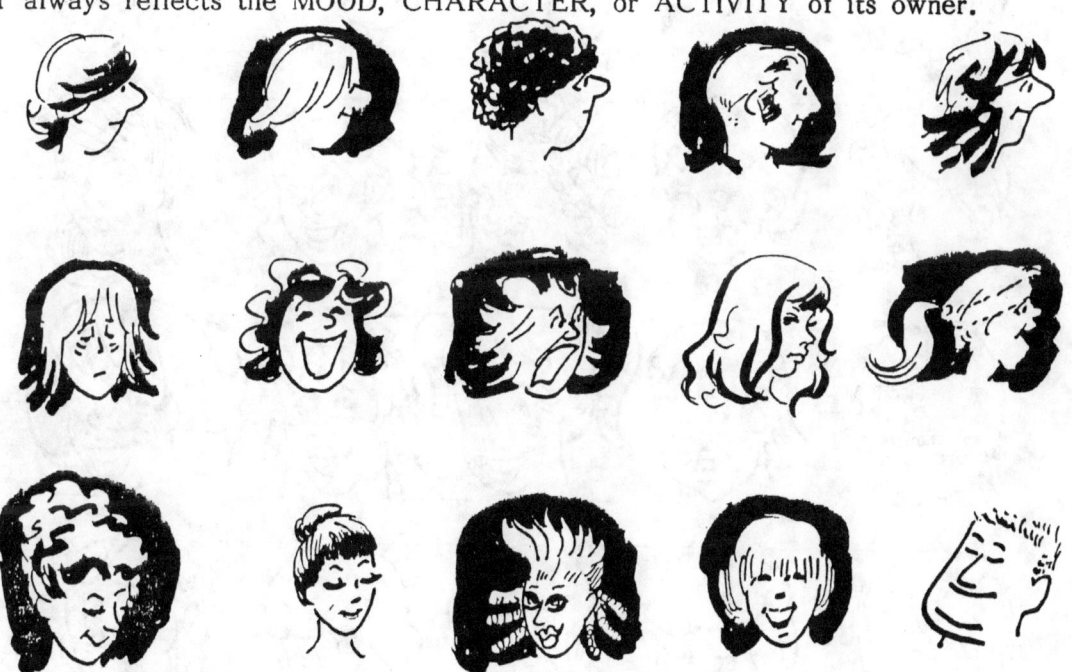

In some cases, a "graphic design" touch is required to indicate hair styles.

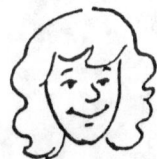 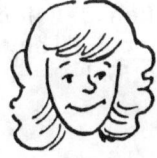 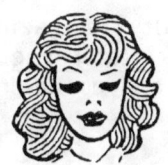 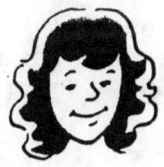 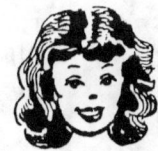

The drawings on this page were based either wholly or in part on clippings from an assortment of ladies' magazines. Most "specialty" magazines (entertainment, fashion, sports, etc.) can be a gold mine of reference material.

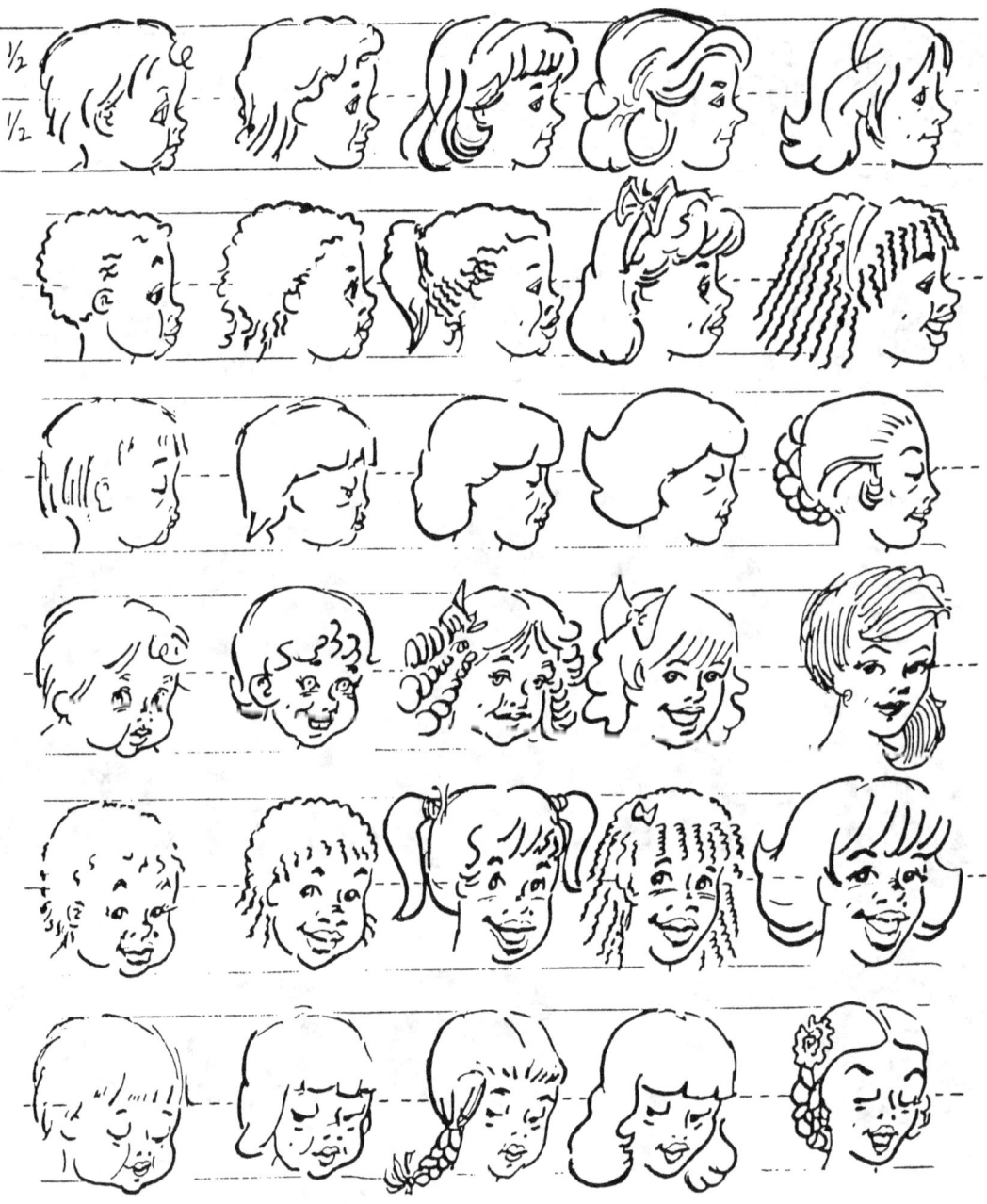

Do not overlook "specialty" magazines when developing your all-important "Scrapbook Reference Library." They often yield tons of important and useful information!

Here are more faces and hair styles, although these were done in a somewhat bolder technique.

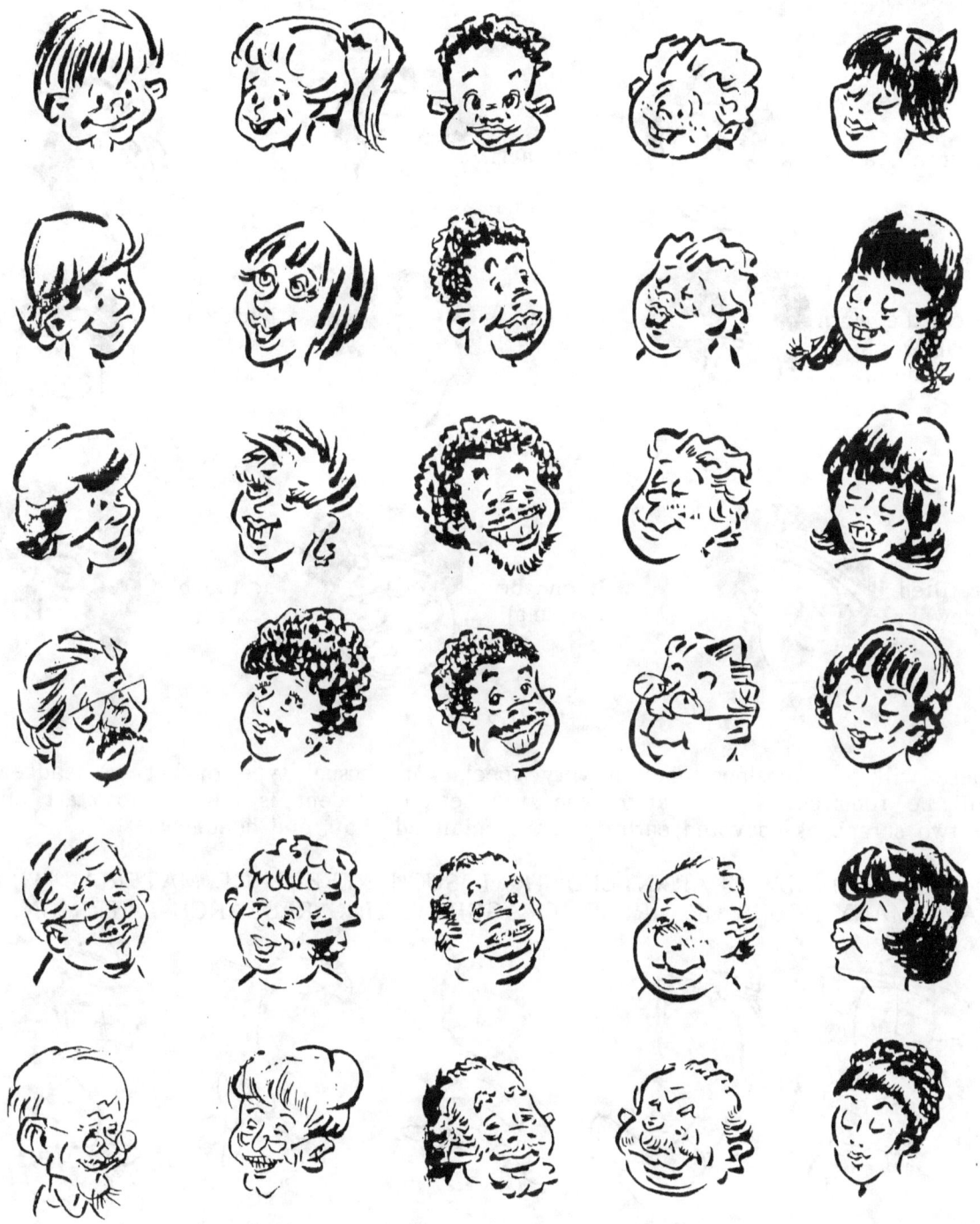

Originally, these heads were drawn about 1½ inches high. They were inked in with a #2 Winsor & Newton sable brush.

Under ordinary circumstances, hats and caps do not present the cartoonist with much of a problem ...

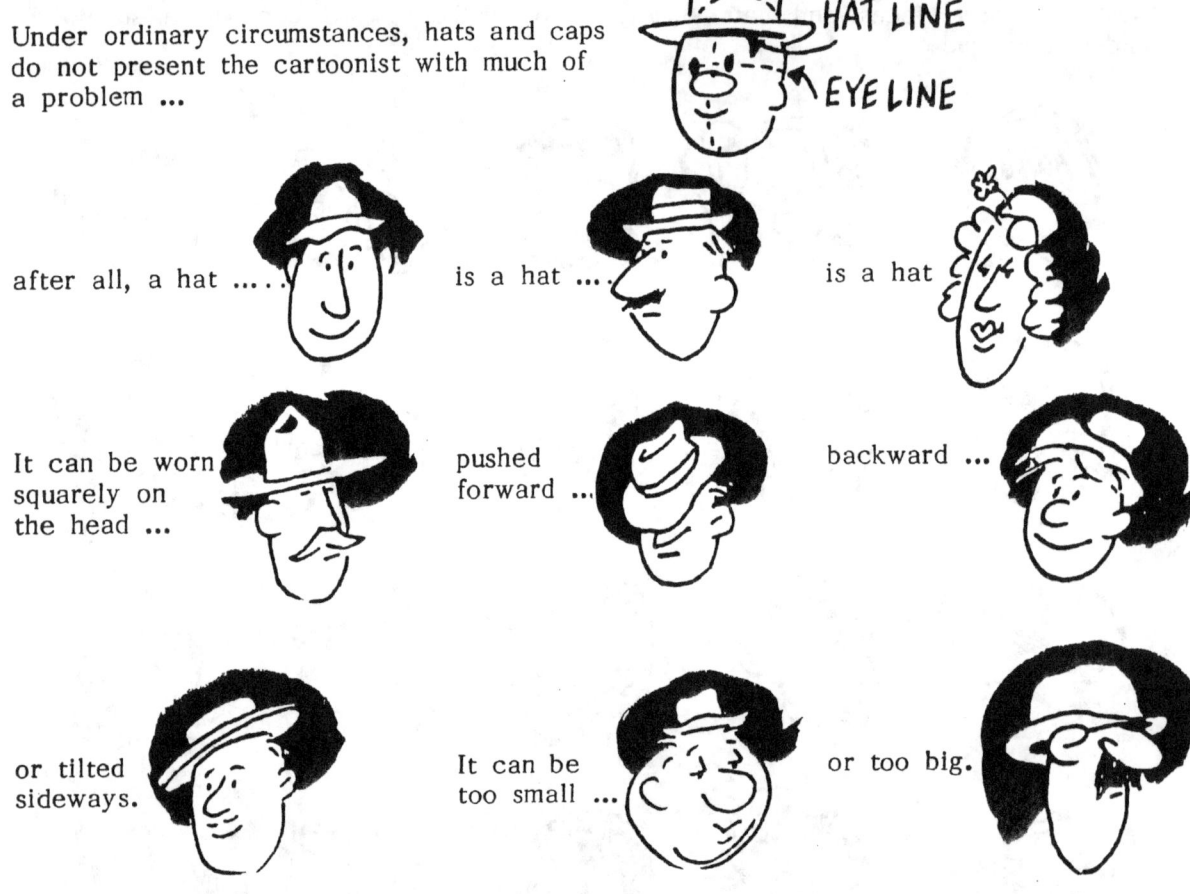

after all, a hat ..... is a hat ... is a hat

It can be worn squarely on the head ...   pushed forward ...   backward ...

or tilted sideways.   It can be too small ...   or too big.

HOWEVER ...

there will be occasions when a very special or unusual type of hat or headgear will be required.   For that reason, the serious student is advised to start one or two scrapbooks devoted entirely to "specialized" hats and headgear.

IT IS POSITIVELY GUARANTEED THAT SUCH REFERENCE MATERIAL WILL SAVE MANY HOURS OF TIRESOME, AGGRAVATING RESEARCH LATER ON.

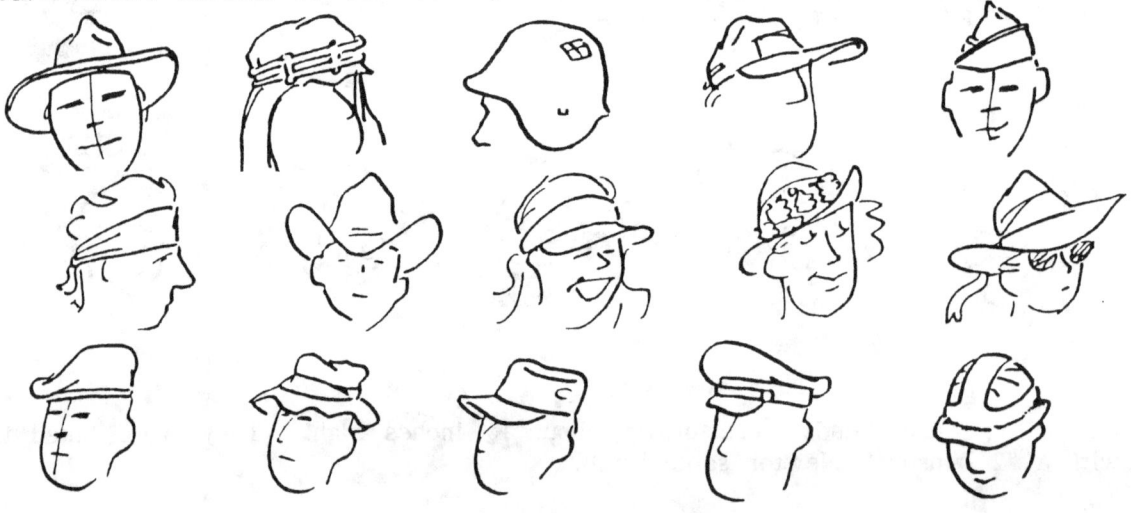

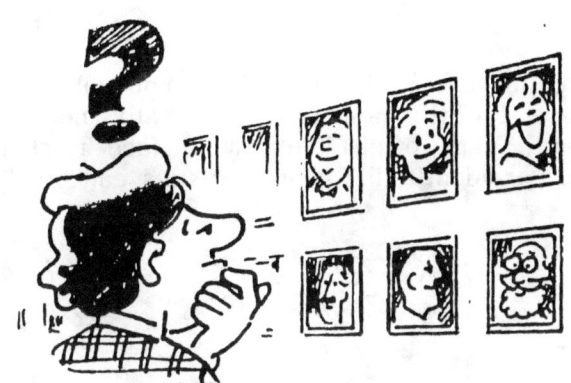

The successful cartoonist wears many hats. Perhaps the most important is the beret of the "Casting Director."

Creating just exactly the right cartoon character for a particular situation can make the difference between a mediocre cartoon and a very good one.

Admittedly, the creative imagination is miraculous thing, but it sometimes requires a little prodding. For that reason, the student of cartooning should observe and sketch "real" people as much as possible. Be on the lookout for photographs of interesting or unusual faces and "quick sketch" them or paste them into a reference scrapbook for future use.

QUICK SKETCHING "REAL" PEOPLE IMPROVES DRAWING SKILLS AND ADDS TO THE CARTOONIST'S MENTAL INVENTORY OF CHARACTERS.

These sketches were all done within a 10-minute period:

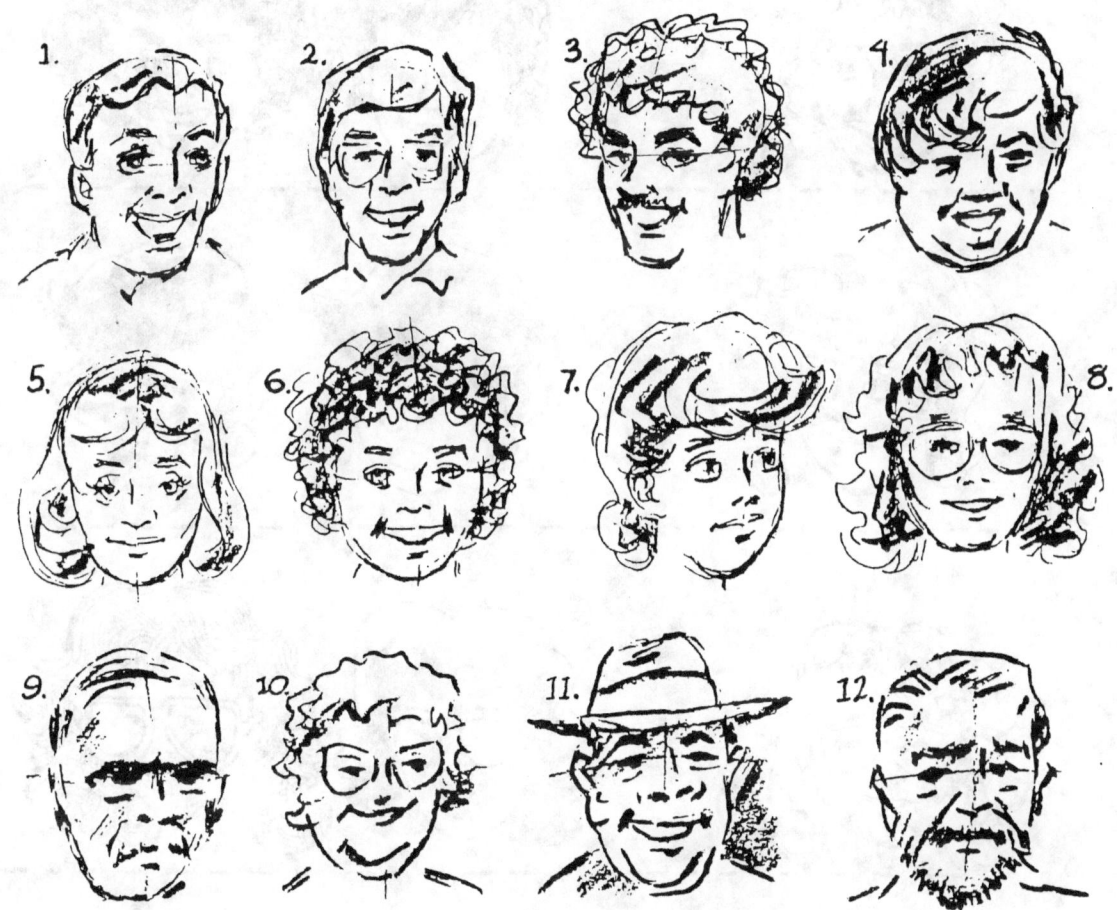

Sketching the "gals" is usually not quite as easy as sketching the men because female facial features are normally not as pronounced or unusual as those of males.   Very often, the female face must be studied carefully before any truly unique or identifiable characteristics can be discovered.

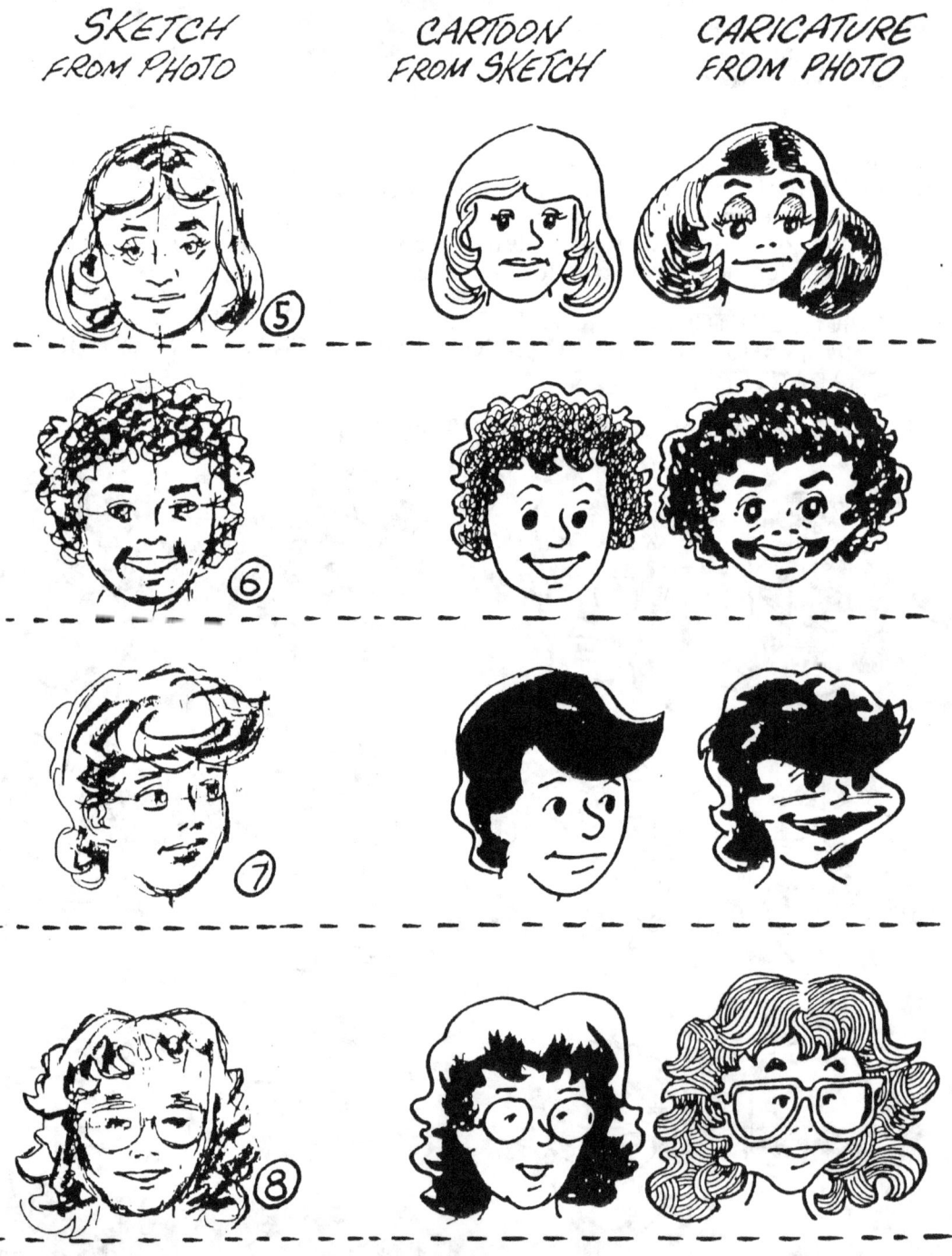

"QUICK SKETCHING" REAL PEOPLE OFFERS THE STUDENT
THE OPPORTUNITY FOR A SPECIAL EXTRA BONUS!

It can serve as a solid foundation for the art of CARICATURING, either as a
specialty or used in conjunction with editorial, advertising, or special feature
cartooning.

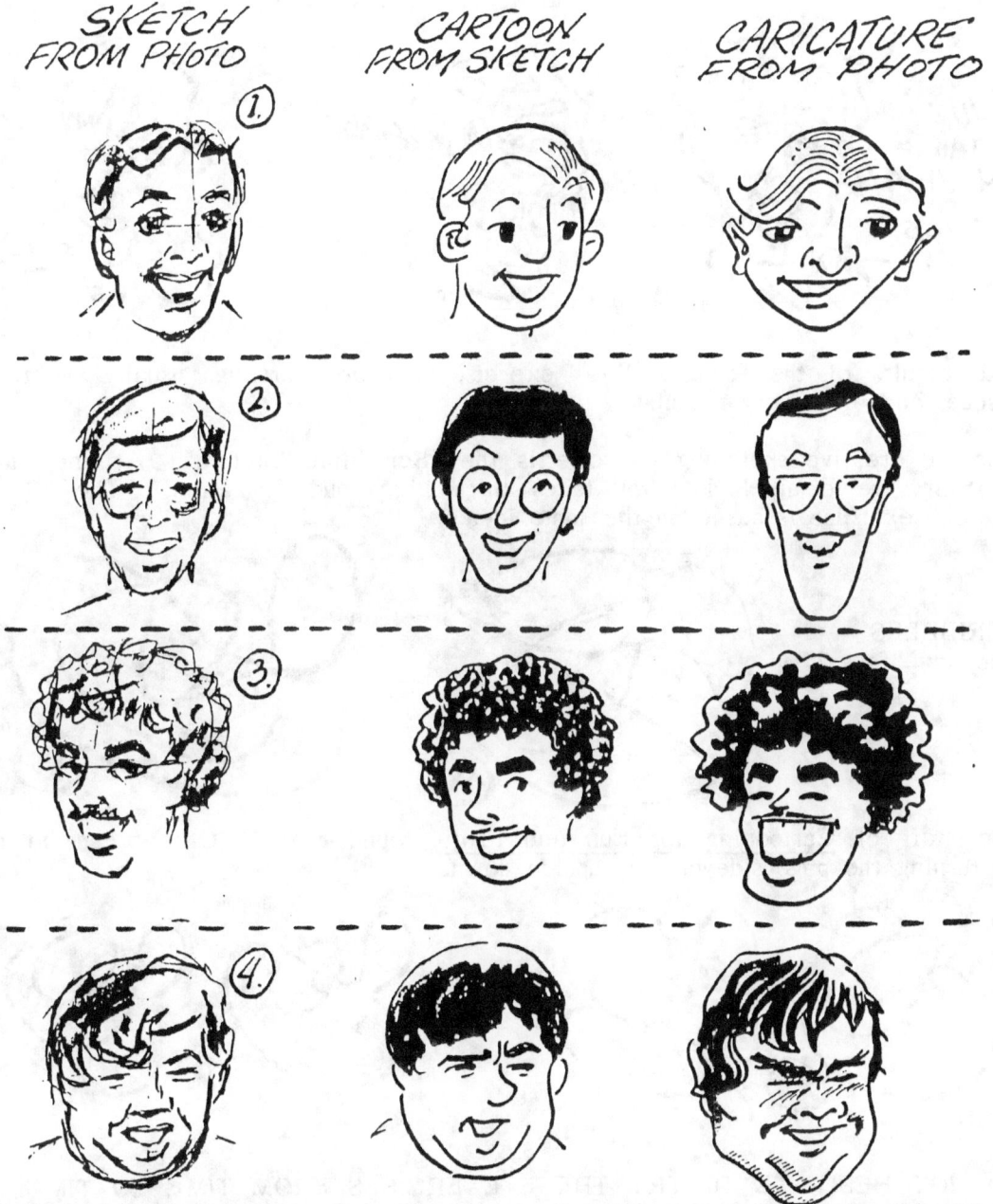

The numbered sketches in this section are drawings of "ordinary" people whose
photographs appeared in local newspapers.

The drawings presented thus far have mostly been based on standard sketching methods where a "foundation" is sketched in and the details added.

There are, however, other sketching exercises that are especially designed to stimulate the mind and enhance natural drawing talents. One such exercise is the "Single Line" sketch where the subject is drawn in one continuous line. The pencil is never lifted from the paper from start to finish.

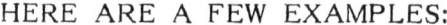

HERE ARE A FEW EXAMPLES:

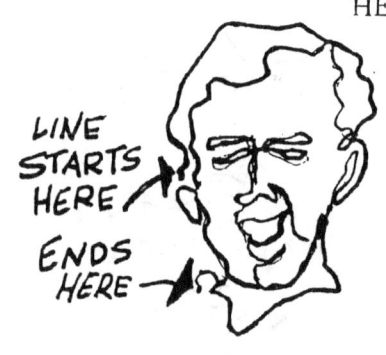
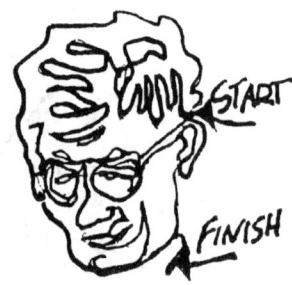
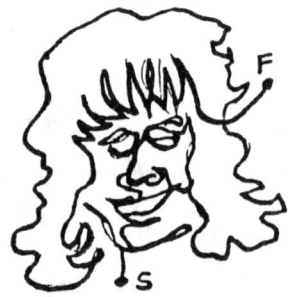

The results of the "Single Line" exercise can be startling, usually a bit grotesque, and often very useful.

Another creative sketching exercise is the "Scribbling Sketch." At one time or another, we've all looked for faces in a big cloud formation. The "Scribble Sketch" exercise is based on the same idea:

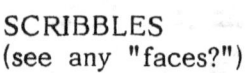
SCRIBBLES
(see any "faces?")

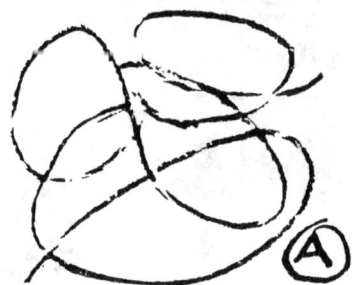
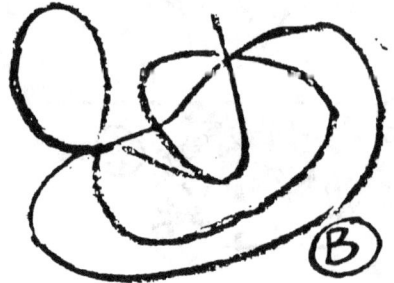

The staff of <u>Cartooning for Fun and Profit</u> found these. Others can be found by turning the page sideways or upside down.

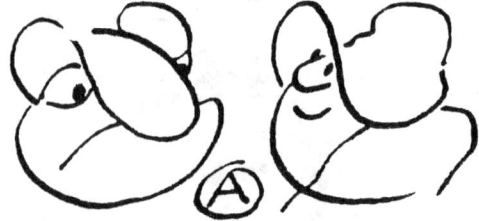
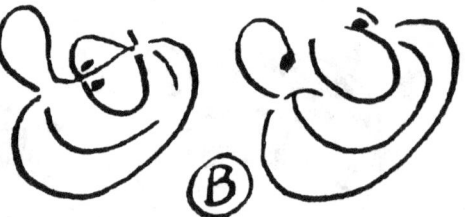

DO NOT HESITATE TO TRY THESE EXERCISES FROM TIME TO TIME. AS LONG AS YOU HAVE A PENCIL IN YOUR HAND AND YOUR IMAGINATION IS WORKING FULL SPEED, YOU ARE IMPROVING YOUR CREATIVE ABILITY AND CARTOONING SKILLS!

There are basically three head positions that give cartoonists (both beginners and professionals alike) some trouble. These are:

1. A back view of a woman's head.
2. A person looking down and to one side.
3. A person looking almost directly away from the viewer.

It's best to avoid those troublesome positions if possible. This can be done by rearranging the composition so that the viewer gets a better look at the cartoon character. If the situation is such that it is not possible or practical to shift the composition, then a little extra bit of shading or detailing may be required.

EXAMPLES:

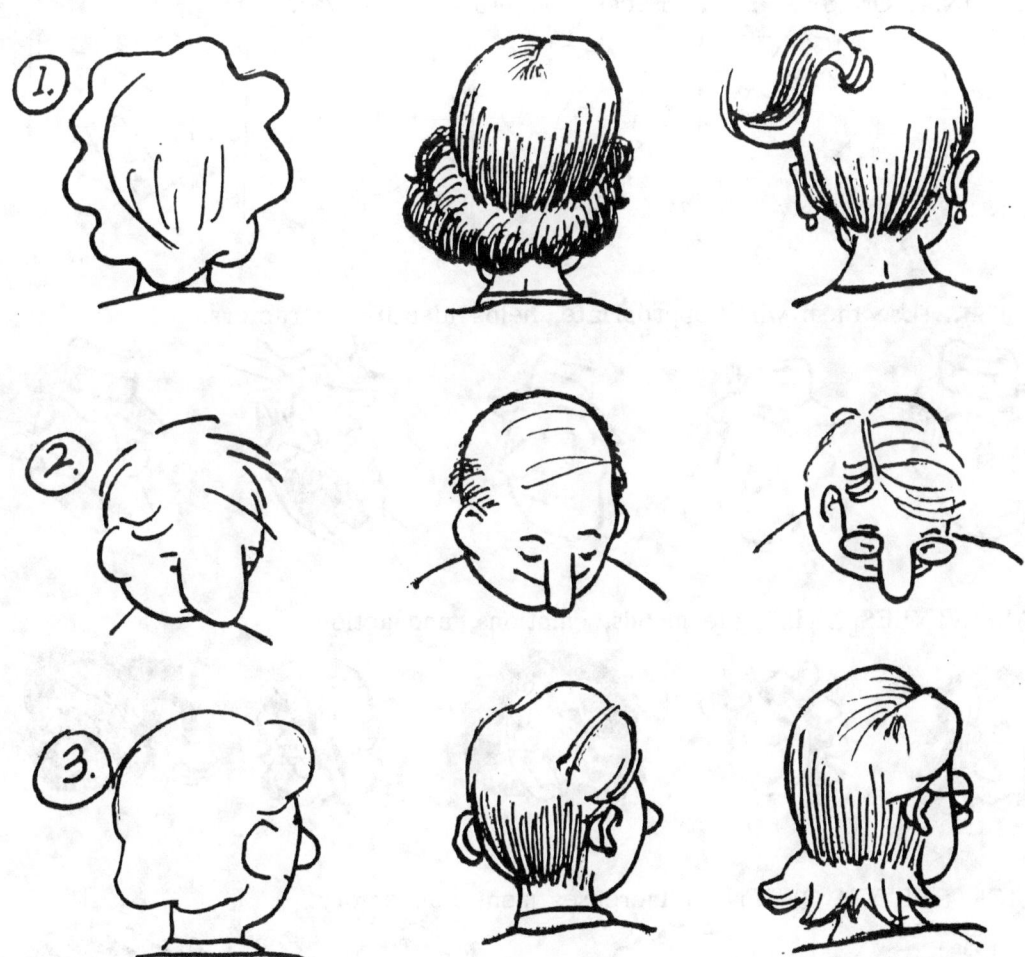

In any event, the student should not be discouraged when running into drawing problems. Sometimes it's best to leave the problem alone for a while and go back to it later.

Quickie Review Chapter 1

HEAD LINES ... Gives the face direction, helps locate facial features.

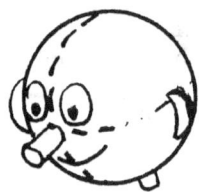 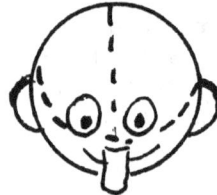 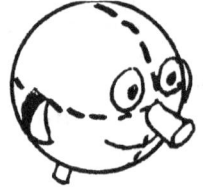 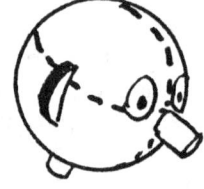

COMBINATION SHAPES ... Faces that draw themselves.

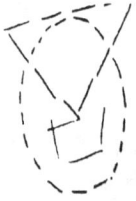 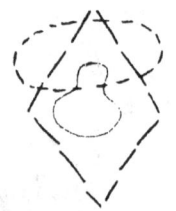 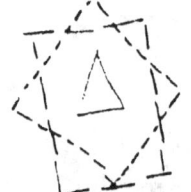 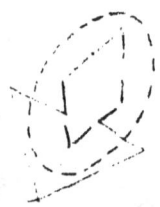 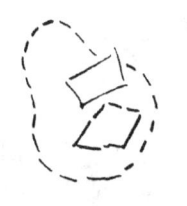

HATS ... Use them when appropriate, helps identify characters.

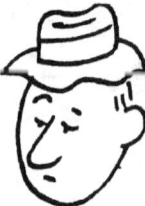 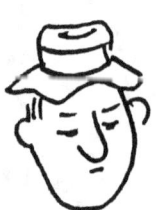 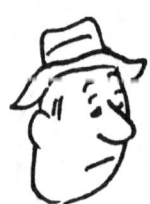 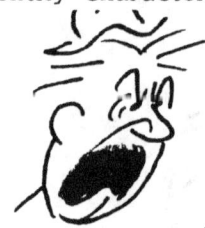 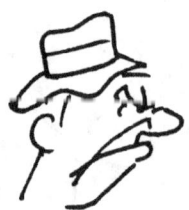

HAIR STYLES ... Indicate moods, emotions, and action.

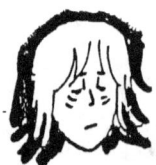 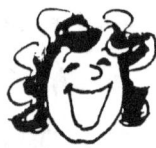 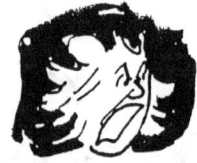 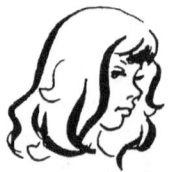 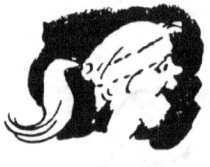

QUICK SKETCH OFTEN ... Increases mental inventory.

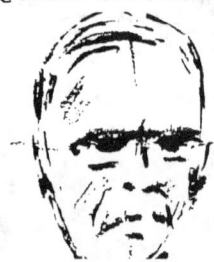 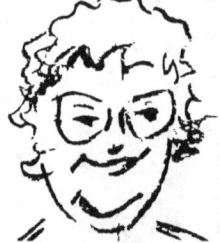 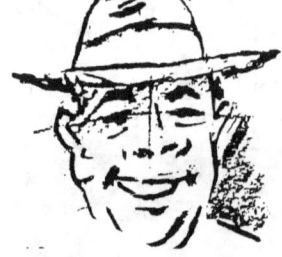 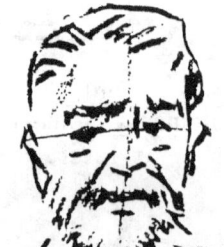

CHAPTER TWO
Hands and Feet

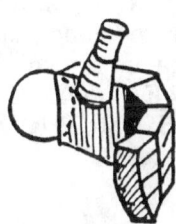

SECTION 1
PARTS OF THE HAND
- *MAJOR UNITS*
- *MOVEMENT*
- *"BLOCK" SHAPING*

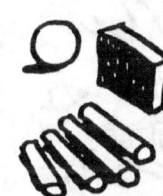

SECTION 2
CONSTRUCTION
- *THE BALL (WRIST)*
- *THE BOARD (PALM)*
- *THE DOWL (FINGERS)*
- *FORESHORTENING*

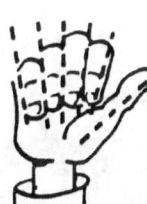

SECTION 3
RADIAL LINES
- *WHERE THEY APPEAR*
- *WHY THEY EXIST*
- *HOW THEY HELP*

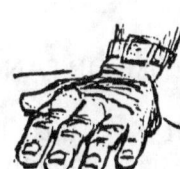

SECTION 4
QUICK SKETCHING
- *FROM LIVE "MODEL"*
- *FROM PHOTOGRAPHS*
- *USING A MIRROR.*

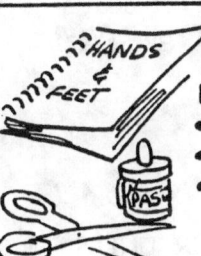

SECTION 5
REFERENCE MATERIAL
- *THE "SCRAPBOOK"*
- *OFTEN SOLVES PROBLEMS*
- *PRODUCES IDEAS*

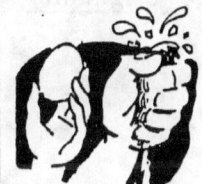

SECTION 6
COMMENTS
- *HOW HANDS PORTRAY CHARACTER & EMOTION.*

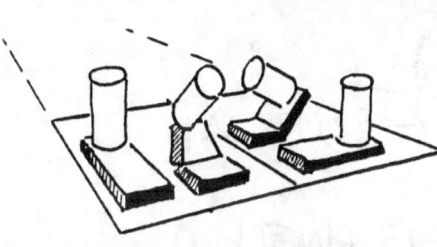

SECTION 7
FEET & SHOES
- *ANGLES & PLANES*
- *FORESHORTENING*
- *STYLES & TRENDS*
- *QUICKIE REVIEW CH. 1 & 2*

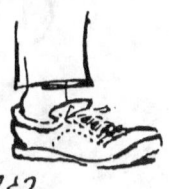

Follow these step-by-step instructions closely and do all of the recommended exercises and assignments. You will soon be able to draw professional looking hands quickly and easily -- a giant step forward to a successful career in cartooning!

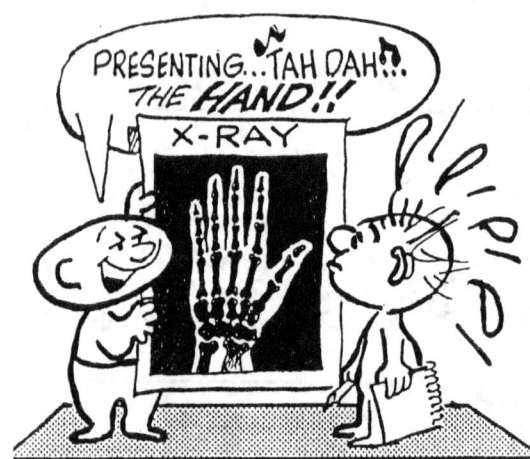

The hand is a very complicated piece of machinery, with more movable parts than the average locomotive! Therefore, hands can often present problems to the cartoonist, whether a beginner or a seasoned professional. You will not have done this lesson correctly until you have drawn at least SEVERAL HUNDRED QUICK SKETCHES USING ALL OF THE METHODS SHOWN.

**** THE IMPORTANCE OF THIS CHAPTER ****

Some students will say this lesson is much more extensive than it needs to be, given the simplicity of most of today's cartooning styles. To a degree, they might be right, except that this chapter has been designed to serve SEVERAL purposes, not the least of which is to help the student improve his or her drawing skills.

Additionally, this chapter is calculated to stimulate the student's creativity, encourage originality, and enhance the powers of observation.

LET'S THINK OF THE HAND AS BEING MADE UP OF FOUR UNITS

(1) The wrist   (2) The palm   (3) The fingers   (4) The thumb

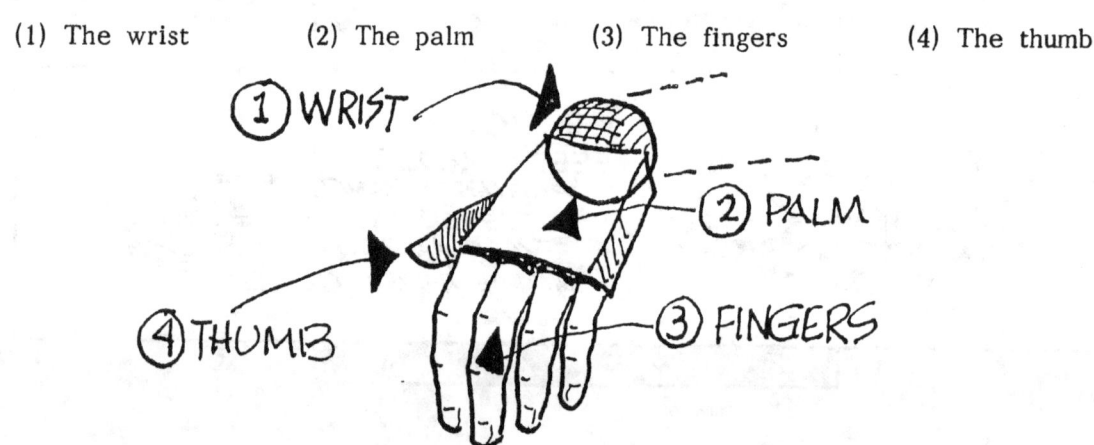

UNIT ONE -- THE WRIST

Here we have a sort of "Ball-Joint" affair that allows the hand to bend and turn in a whole bunch of different directions.

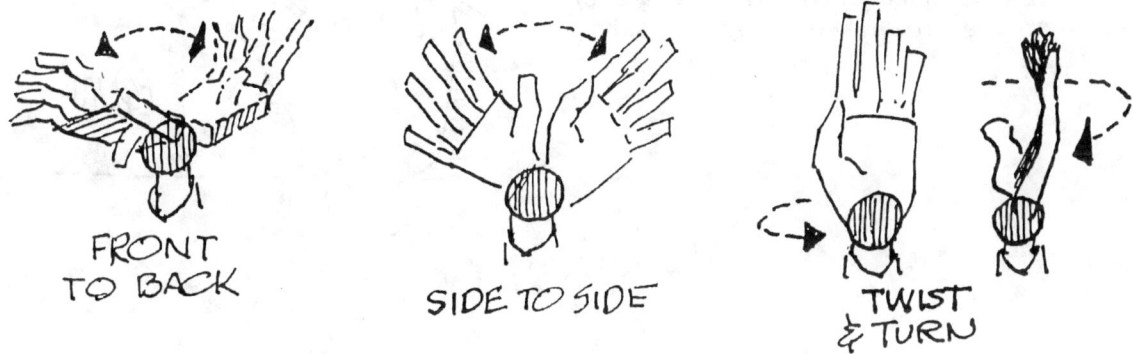

UNIT TWO -- THE PALM

This is home base for the fingers and thumb. It will be useful to note that it can assume THREE different shapes:

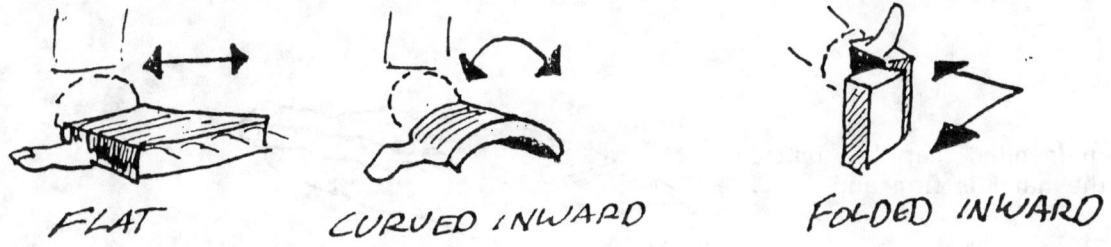

UNIT THREE -- THE FINGERS

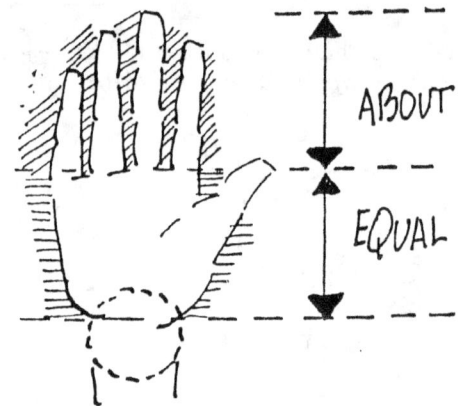

The area occupied by the fingers is about equal to the area taken up by the palm.

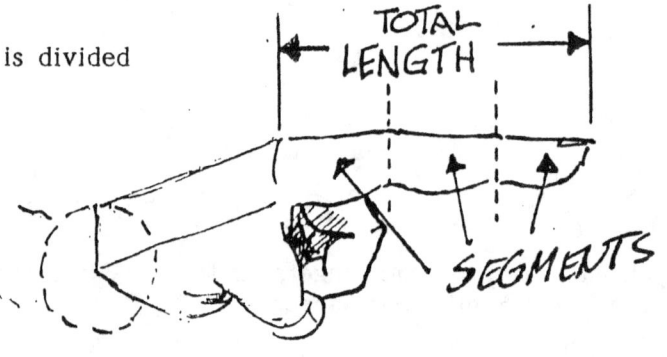

The length of each finger is divided

into three

ALMOST equal

segments

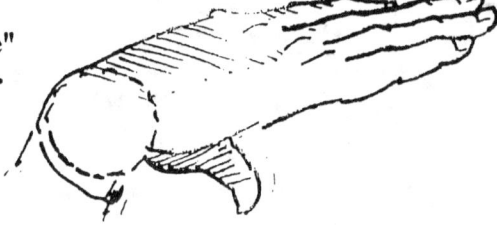

Keep in mind that the "outside" of the hand is firm and flat ...

While the "inside" of the hand is soft and fleshy (padded).

UNIT FOUR -- THE THUMB

This is the "workhorse" of the hand
and differs from fingers in that it
has only TWO segments that are generally
visible.   The third segment is contained
within the palm and appears as a large
roundish muscle.

Also, it starts on the side of the palm,
near the bottom.   This puts it in a great
position to assist the fingers.

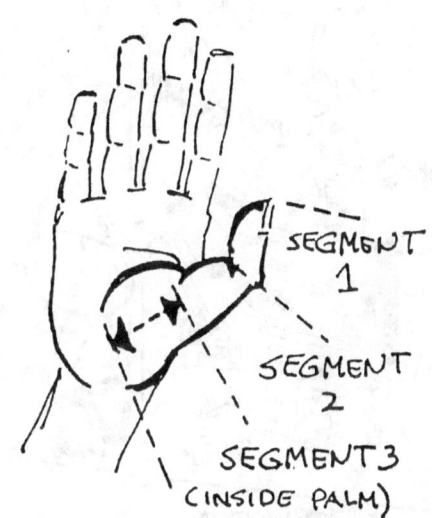

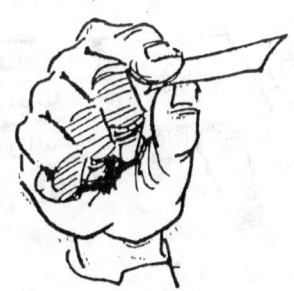

ALWAYS MAKE SURE THE THUMBS ARE POINTED IN THE RIGHT DIRECTION

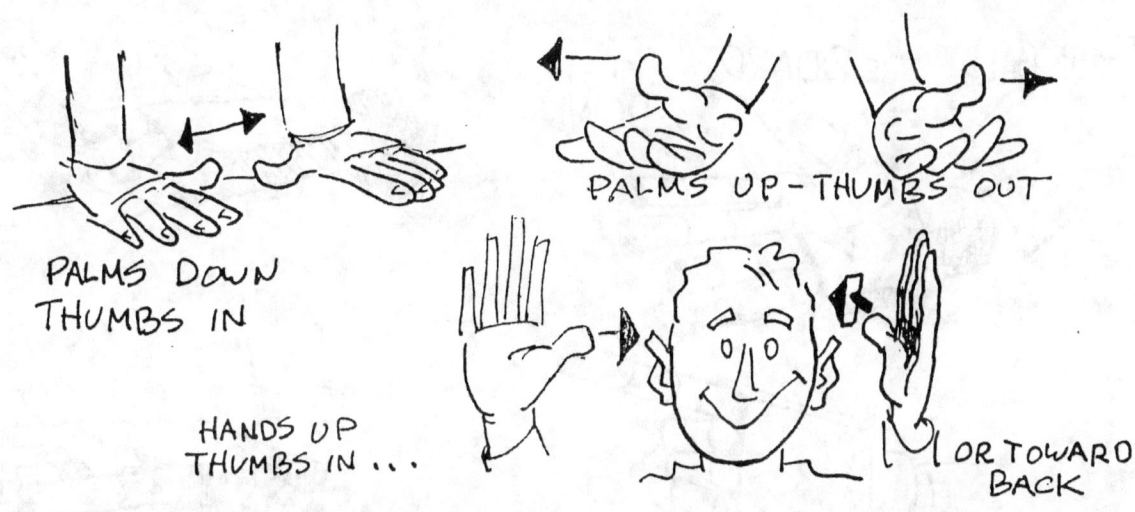

23

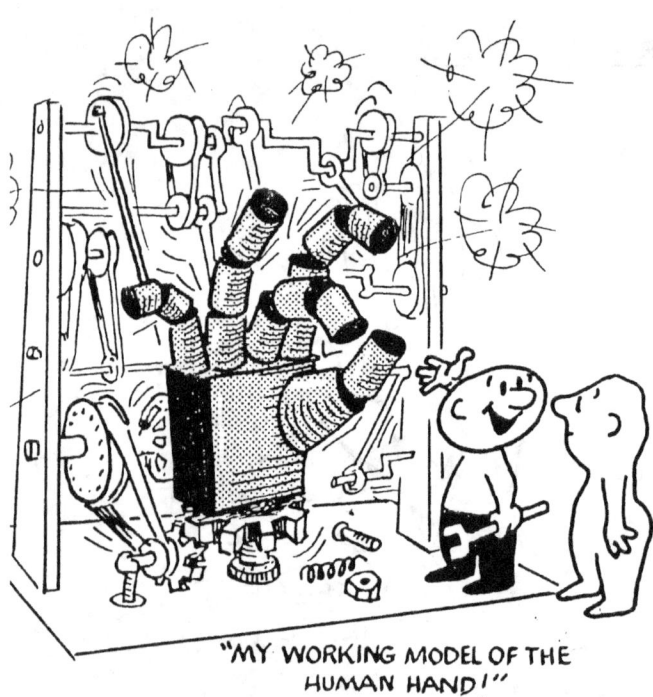

"MY WORKING MODEL OF THE
HUMAN HAND!"

Drawing decent-looking hands would be no problem whatsoever, except that its four separate units sometimes have a habit of going off in all sorts of different directions at the same time. THAT can create some serious drawing problems.

The student is urged to study the "Ball, Board, and Dowel" method as outlined in this section. Doing so will prove to be extremely helpful when drawing hands in all positions.

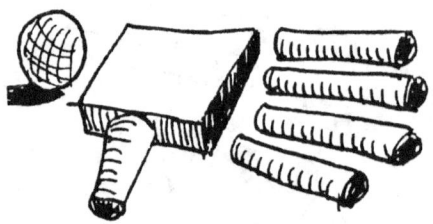

THE "BALL, BOARD, AND DOWEL" SYSTEM OF HAND CONSTRUCTION

This is the easy way to draw hands that have the proper form, action, and direction.

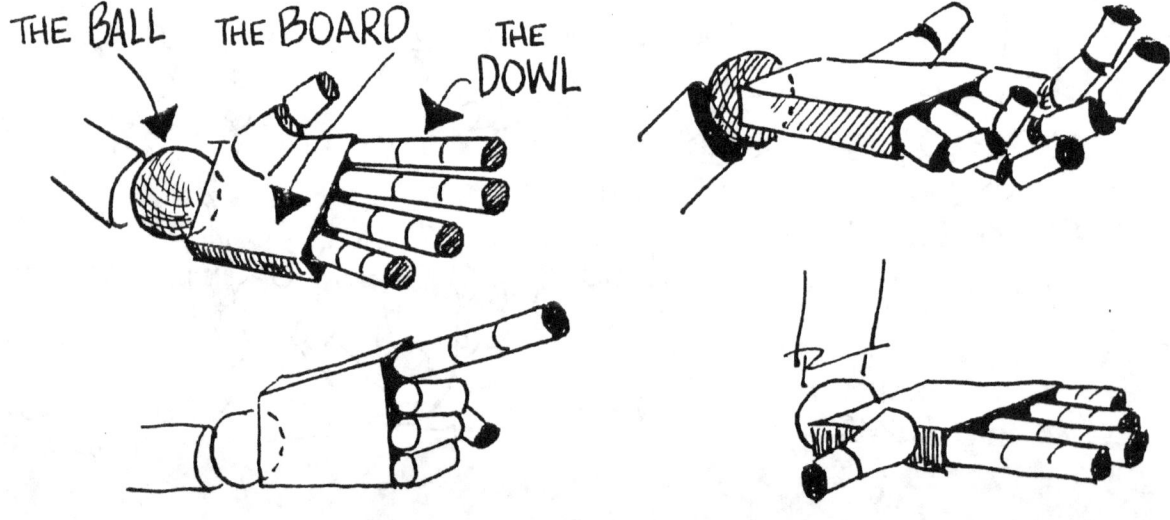

THE BALL   THE BOARD   THE DOWL

THE "B B & D" METHOD IN ACTION!

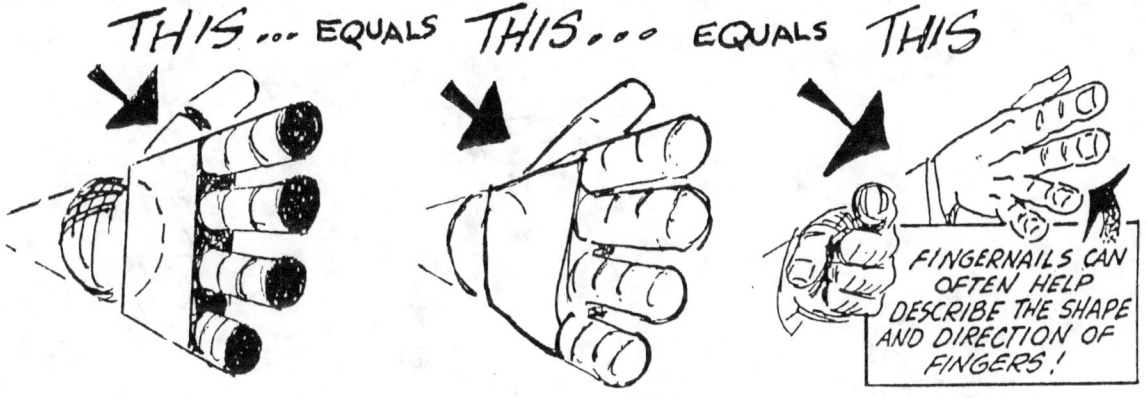

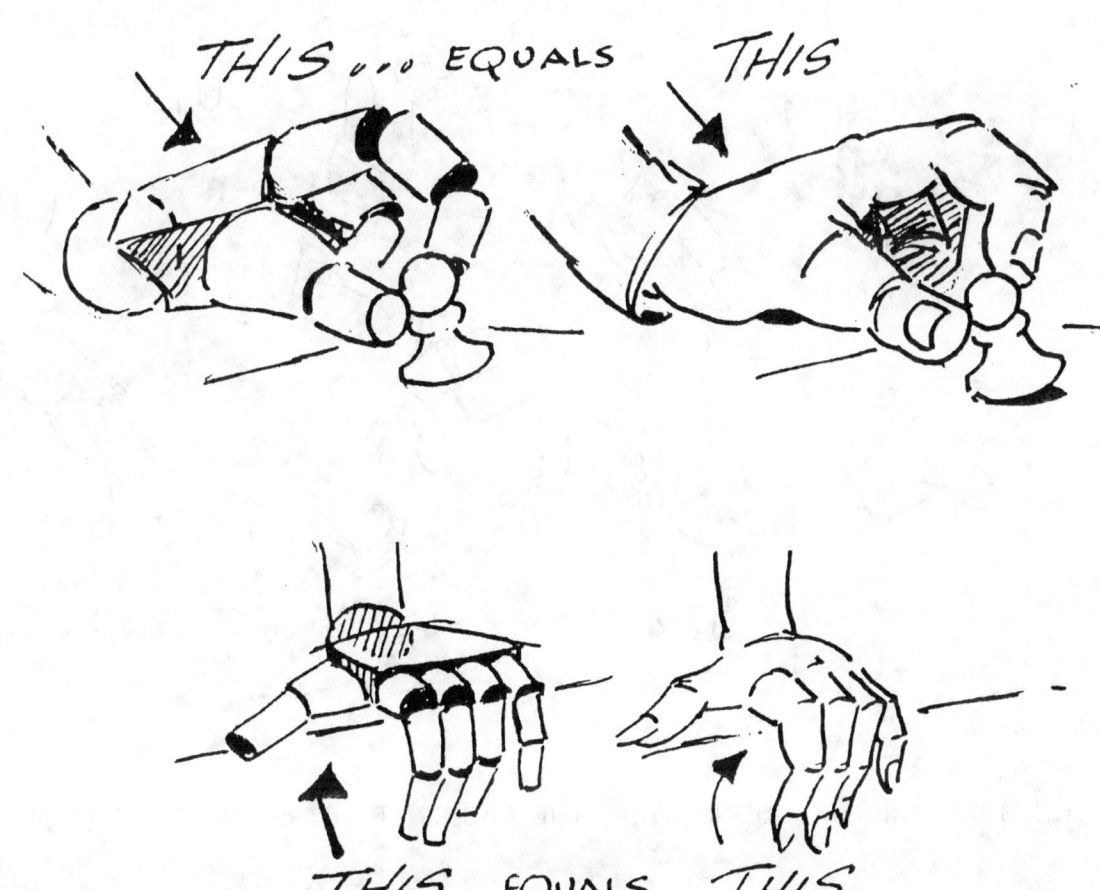

DRAWING AND SKETCHING HANDS IS EASY WITH THE B B & D SYSTEM!

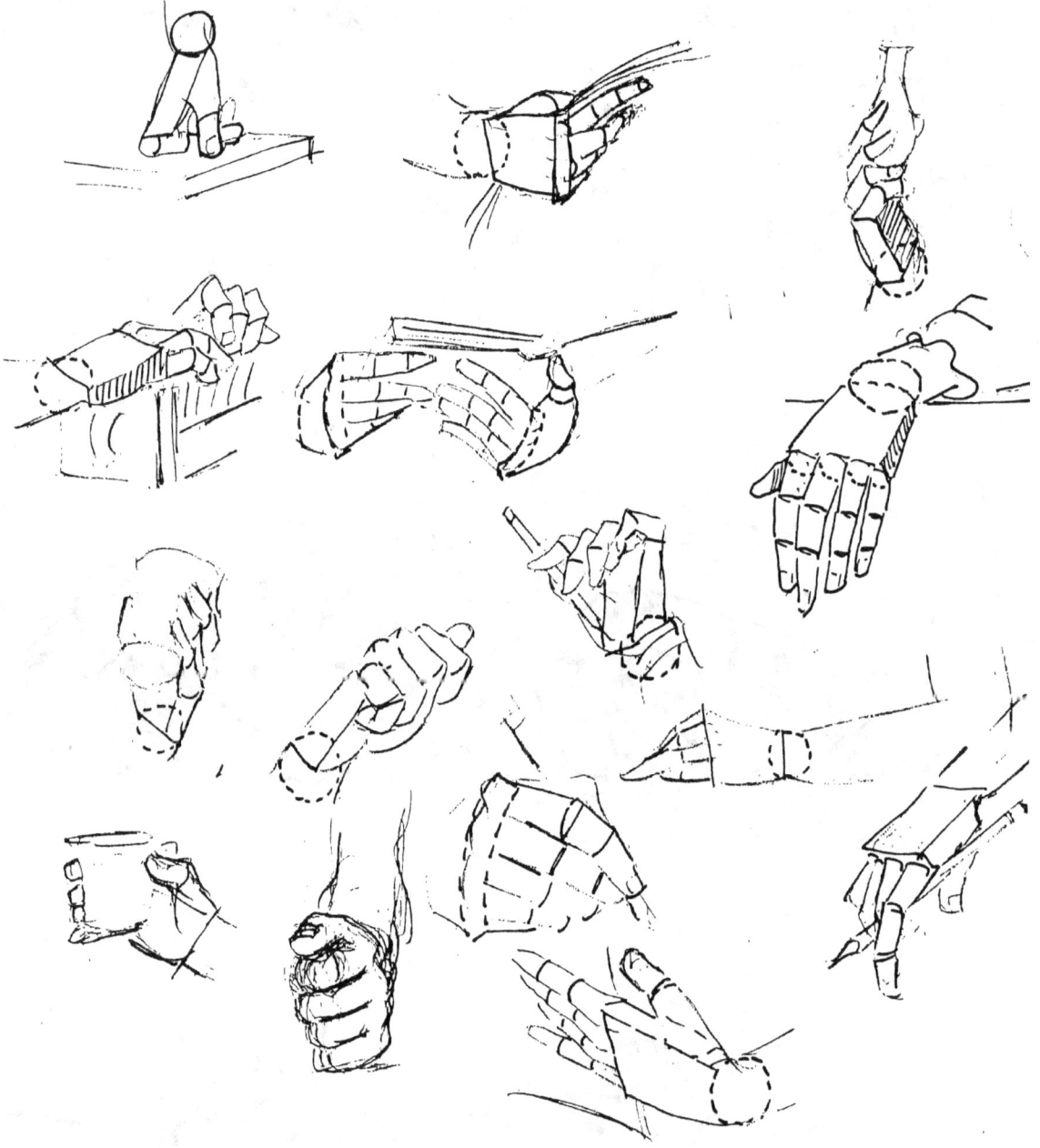

THE MORE THIS METHOD IS USED, THE EASIER IT GETS! PRACTICE IT OFTEN!

THE PRINCIPLE OF FINGER "RADIAL LINES"

Another very important tip to remember when drawing hands!

DUE TO THE SOMEWHAT ROUNDED SHAPE OF THE PALM AND THE TAPERED FORM OF THE FINGERS, CERTAIN BASIC <u>DIREC-TIONAL LINES</u> DEVELOP. WE CALL THESE "<u>RADIALS</u>" AND WILL STRESS THEM THROUGHOUT THIS CHAPTER.

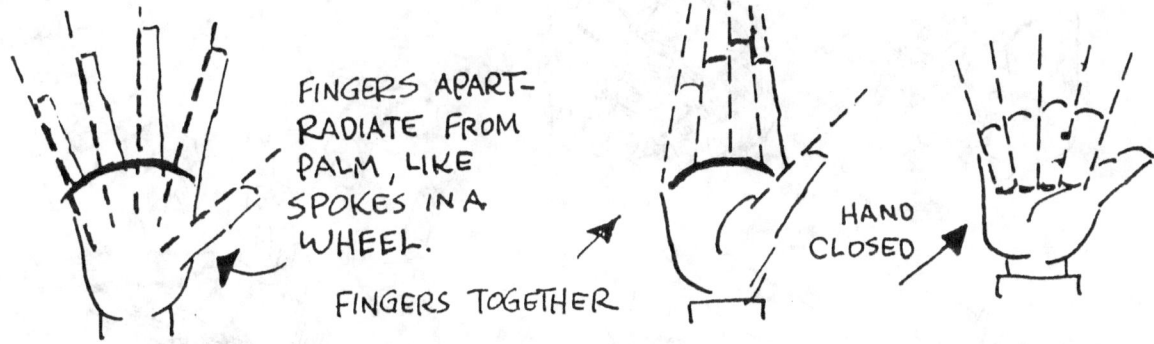

FINGERS APART—
RADIATE FROM
PALM, LIKE
SPOKES IN A
WHEEL.

FINGERS TOGETHER

HAND CLOSED

Study the "radial" lines shown below. Note how they almost describe the hand action without any other detail.

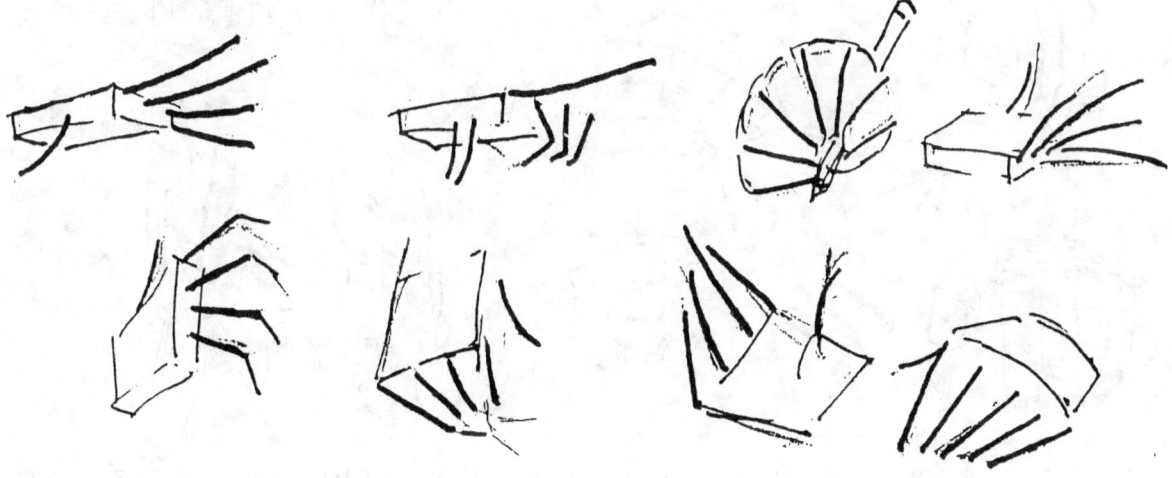

The drawings on this page were all sketched from photographs found in various newspapers and magazines.

The finger radial lines have been emphasized to show how they help in positioning the fingers.

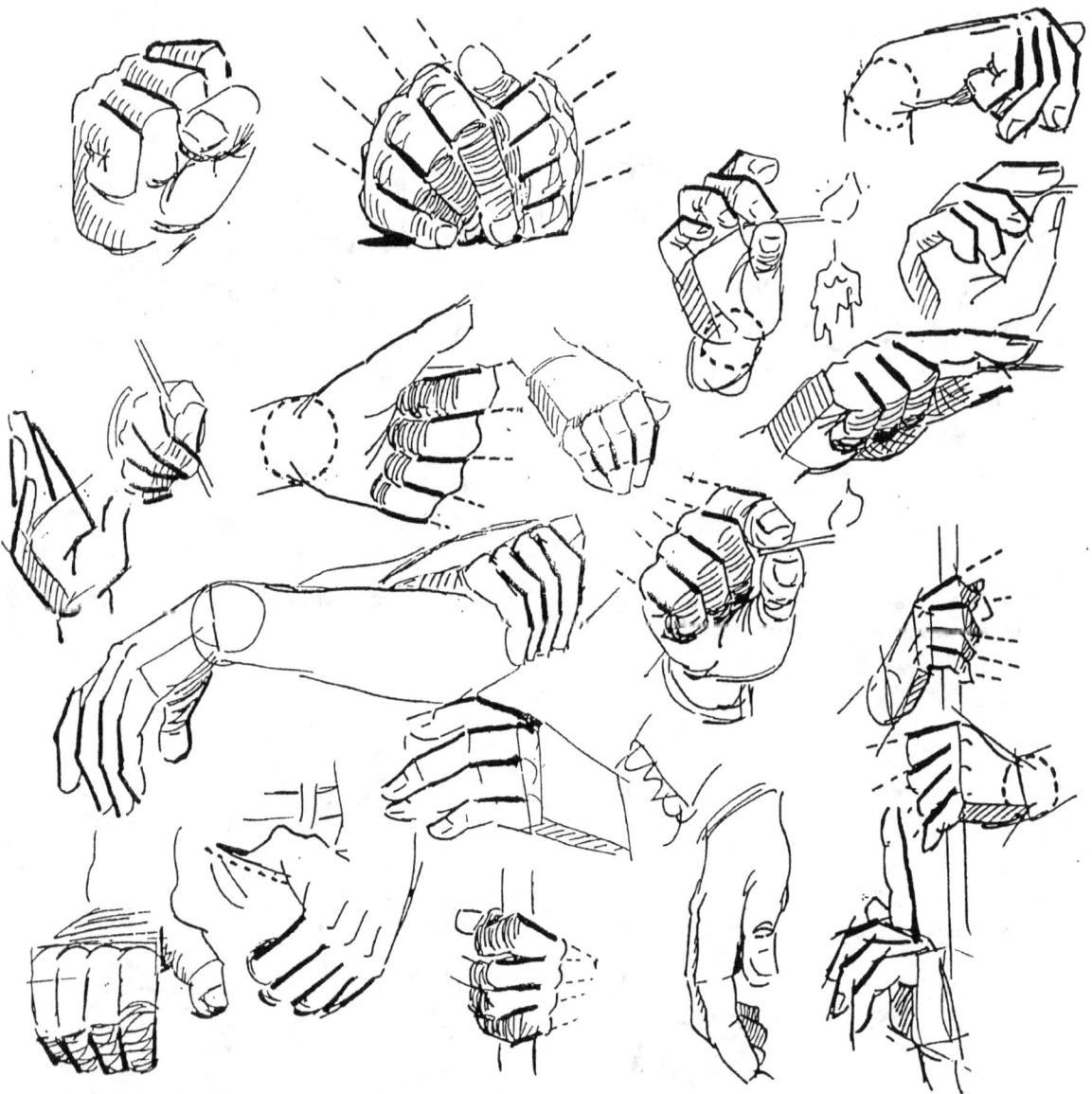

QUICK SKETCHING PROMOTES ORIGINALITY, DEVELOPS SKILLS, AND INCREASES ONE'S "MENTAL INVENTORY"!

Drawing hands can be fun, once you get the hang of it!   Keep your sketche
loose and simple.   Work quickly.

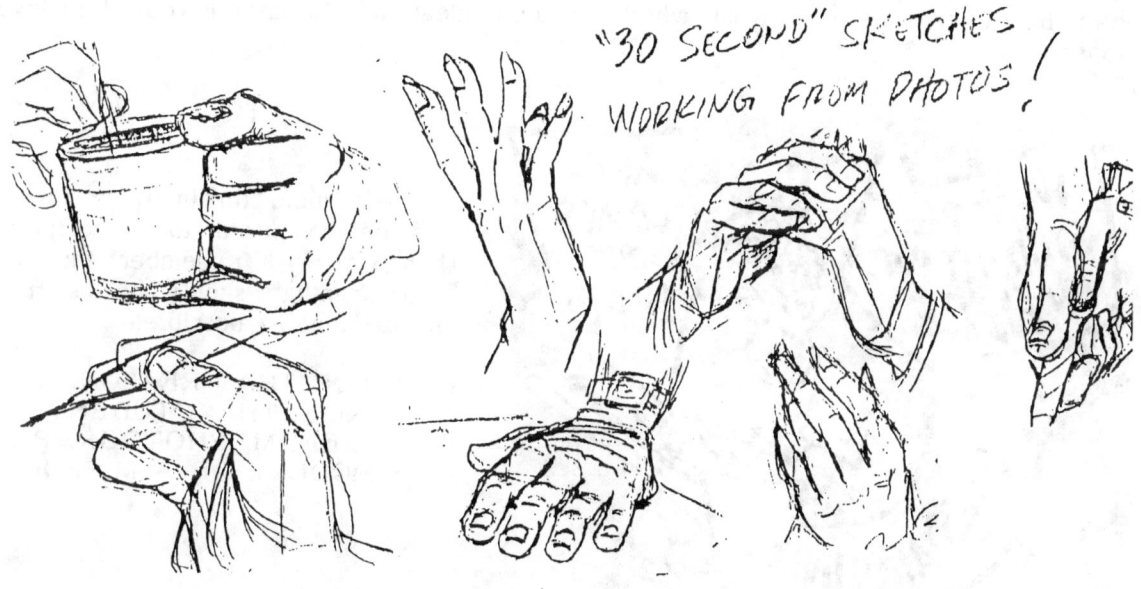

HAND PROPORTIONS

The size of the average hand,
when shown directly alongside
the face, measures approximately
from the chin to the upper
portion of the forehead.   However,
one does not always see the hand
in this position.

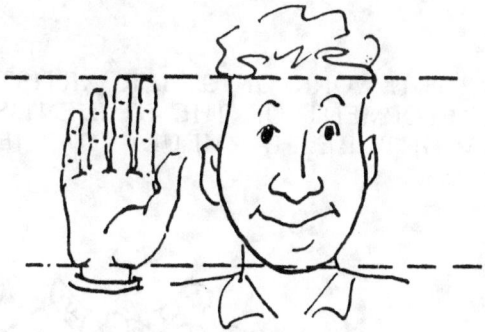

Perspective plays an important part in determining what "size" the hand shoul
be.   When used in figure drawing, perspective is called "FORESHORTENING" an
will be explained more fully in the following chapters.   However, the sketche
below will illustrate the basic principle.

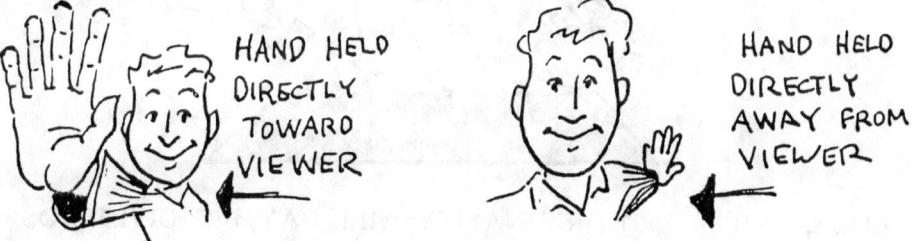

The importance of building a complete reference library will be stressed again and again throughout this book. The student's reference material need not be more than spiral bound notebooks filled with clippings from newspapers and magazines. These scrapbooks will not only save the student time later on, but can be a great source from which cartoon ideas and situations can be developed.

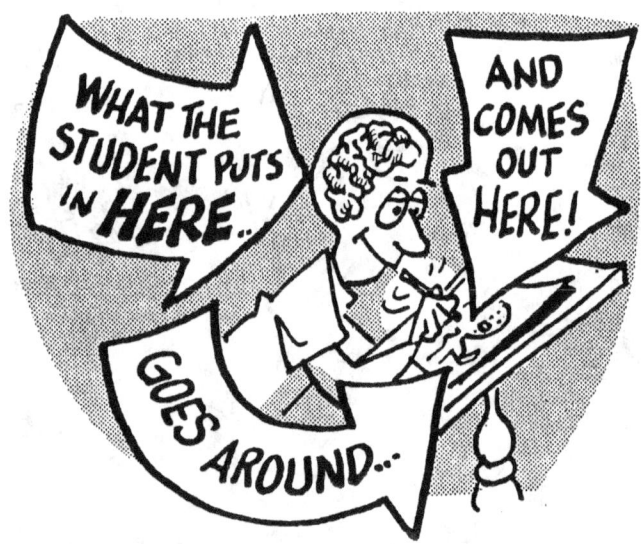

If one's mind (brain if you wish) can be compared to a computer, then we must remember that our "programming" should be as fresh and original as possible!

IT IS FOR THAT REASON THAT WE URGE THE STUDENT TO WORK FROM PHOTOGRAPHS, LIVE MODELS, OR A MIRROR.

COPYING THE WORK OF OTHER ARTISTS OR CARTOONISTS WILL PREVENT THE DEVELOPMENT OF THE STUDENT'S OWN NATURAL ABILITIES AND, IN FACT, MIGHT BE HARMFUL TO THE STUDENT'S SENSE OF "ARTISTIC MERIT."

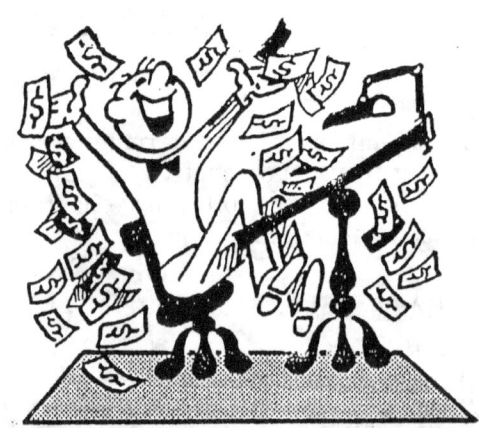

KNOWLEDGE, SKILL, AND ORIGINALITY WILL PAY BIG DIVIDENDS!

**** REMEMBER ****

This chapter has not only been designed to help the student draw professional looking hands quickly and easily. It is also hoped that the drawing methods, as outlined, will improve OVERALL drawing skills and encourage originality, promote creativity, and increase the powers of observation!

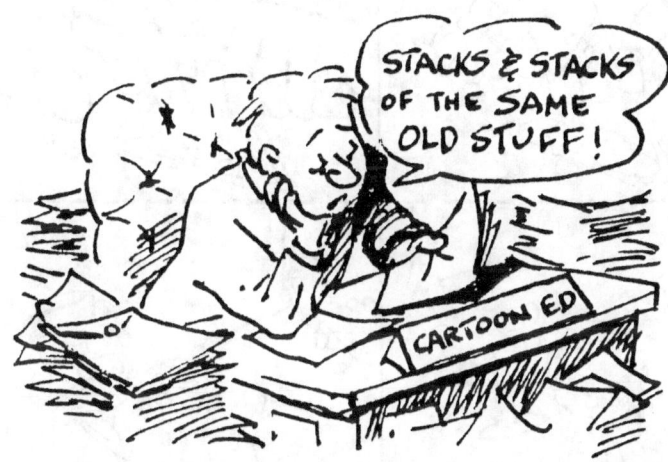

The student must keep in mind that, for the most part, major cartoon buyers (call them Cartoon Editors, Feature Editors, Art Directors, or whatever) do know their business. A new-comer's work will be rewarded with nothing more than a yawn unless it shows CREATIVITY, SKILL, AND ORIGINALITY.

There remains a huge demand for cartoon material but, generally speaking, it must be of a new, fresh variety. It is primarily for that reason that the student is urged to "start from scratch" as opposed to copying the work and material of other cartoonists.

THAT IS WHY AN EXTENSIVE REFERENCE LIBRARY IS SO IMPORTANT! Again, this reference material need not be more than a lot of spiral bound notebooks filled, in scrapbook fashion, with photo clippings from newspapers and magazines.

WHAT SORT OF MATERIAL SHOULD BE COLLECTED?

If the student happens to have a special area of interest in his or her cartooning plans, then by all means collect material relating to that interest.

Also to be collected would be clippings of almost anything that seems to be new, interesting, or somewhat unusual. In addition to the subjects covered to this point, clippings should include such things as clothing, uniforms, buildings, street scenes, special equipment, animals, indoor scenes of all kinds, costumes, and so on.

It's a very good idea to develop a system of categories so that needed reference material can be found easily.

ADDITIONAL TIPS ON BUILDING A COLLECTION OF REFERENCE MATERIAL CAN BE FOUND IN THE STUDY GUIDELINES SECTION AT THE BEGINNING OF THIS BOOK.

"QUICK SKETCHING" FROM NEWSPAPER AND MAGAZINE PHOTOS

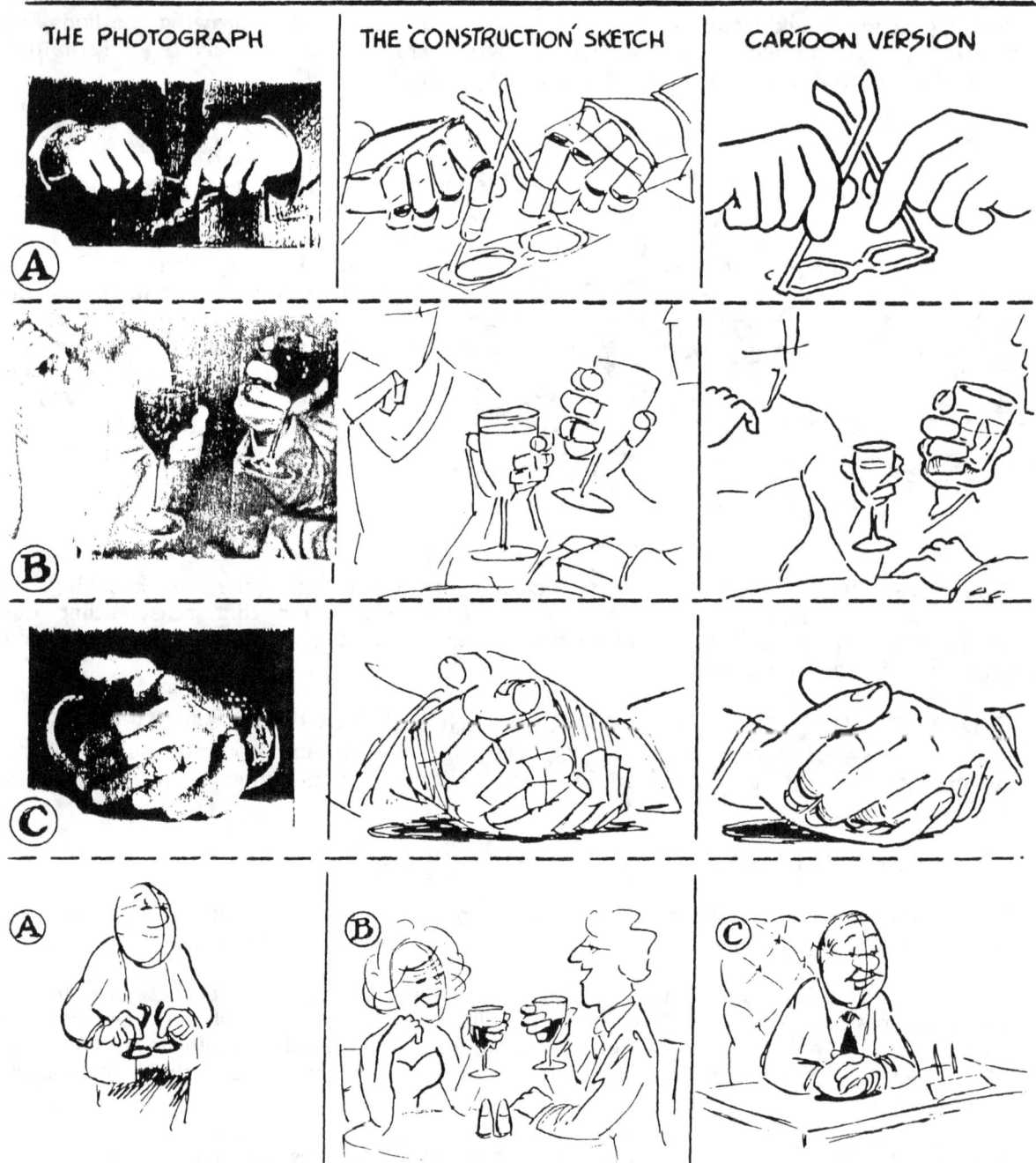

| THE PHOTOGRAPH | THE 'CONSTRUCTION' SKETCH | CARTOON VERSION |

COLLECT REFERENCE MATERIAL!

A "SCRAPBOOK" TYPE OF REFERENCE LIBRARY WILL PROVE TO BE AN INVALUABLE AID IN YOUR CARTOONING CAREER. SUCH MATERIAL WILL NOT ONLY HELP SOLVE CERTAIN PROBLEMS IN DRAWING AND COMPOSITION, BUT CAN BE AN EXCELLENT SOURCE OF FRESH, NEW CARTOON IDEAS.

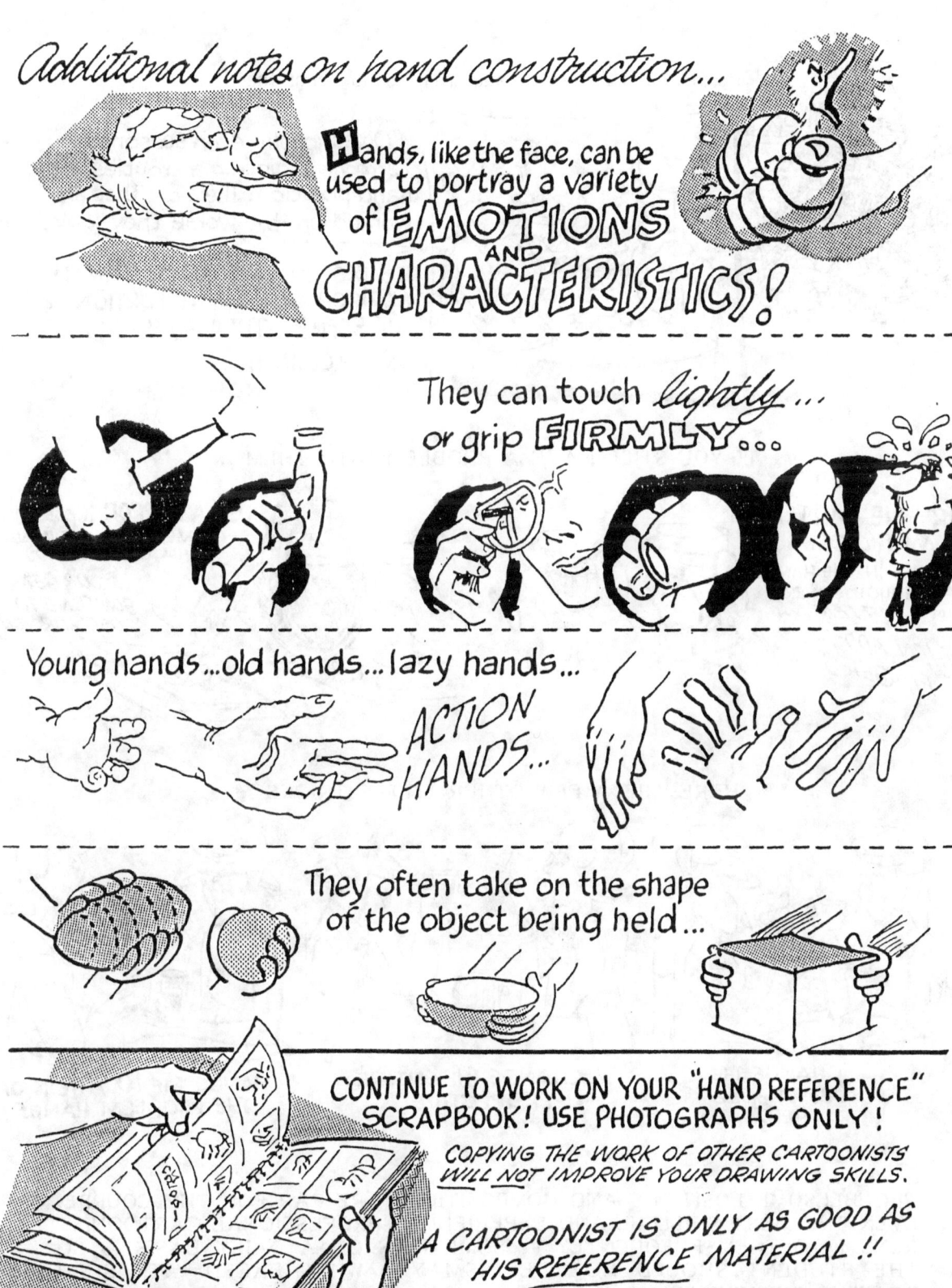

Additional notes on hand construction...

Hands, like the face, can be used to portray a variety of **EMOTIONS** **AND** **CHARACTERISTICS!**

They can touch *lightly...* or grip **FIRMLY...**

Young hands...old hands...lazy hands... *ACTION HANDS...*

They often take on the shape of the object being held...

CONTINUE TO WORK ON YOUR "HAND REFERENCE" SCRAPBOOK! USE PHOTOGRAPHS ONLY!

COPYING THE WORK OF OTHER CARTOONISTS WILL NOT IMPROVE YOUR DRAWING SKILLS.

A CARTOONIST IS ONLY AS GOOD AS HIS REFERENCE MATERIAL !!

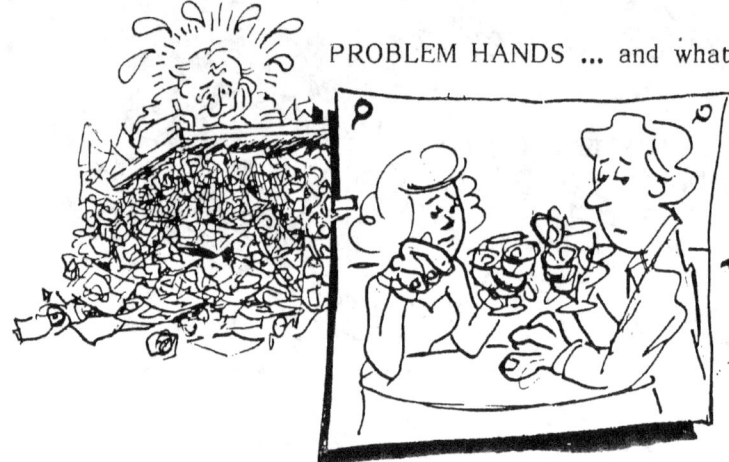

PROBLEM HANDS ... and what to do about them!

Occassionally, even seasoned cartoonists run into a troublesome hand position. The more they are worked on –the worse they look!

IT'S BEST TO LEAVE THEM FOR AWHILE... WORK ON A DIFFERENT PORTION OF THE SCENE ... THEN GO BACK AND TRY AGAIN !!

IF YOU STILL HAVE A PROBLEM WITH THEM ...

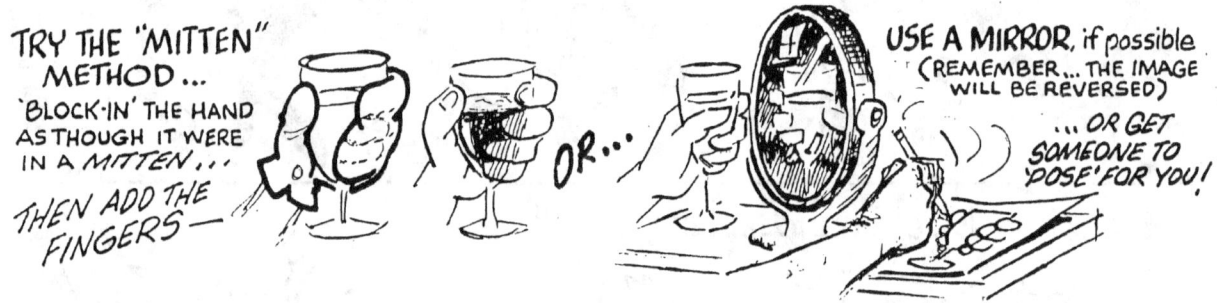

TRY THE "MITTEN" METHOD ... 'BLOCK-IN' THE HAND AS THOUGH IT WERE IN A *MITTEN* ... THEN ADD THE FINGERS —

OR...

USE A MIRROR, if possible (REMEMBER ... THE IMAGE WILL BE REVERSED)

...OR GET SOMEONE TO 'POSE' FOR YOU!

HERE ARE A FEW OTHER LITTLE TRICKS ...

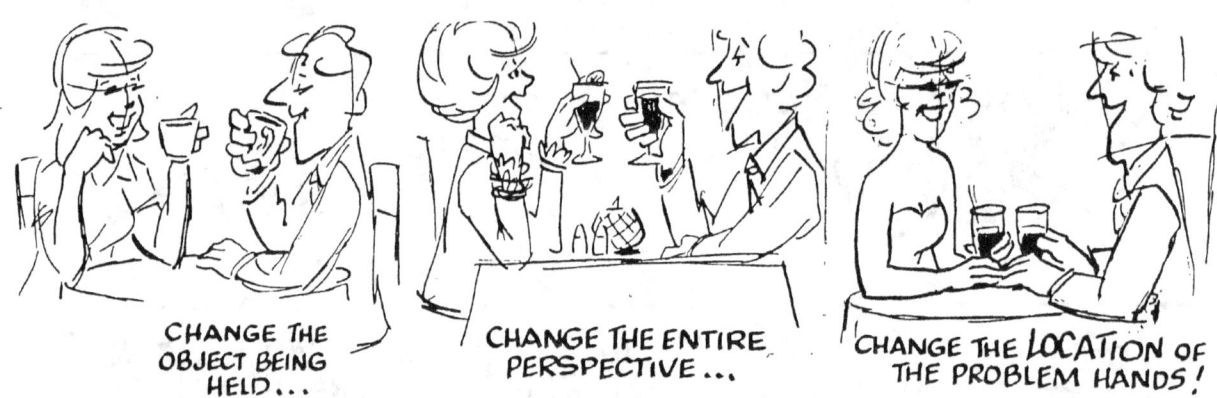

CHANGE THE OBJECT BEING HELD...

CHANGE THE ENTIRE PERSPECTIVE...

CHANGE THE *LOCATION* OF THE PROBLEM HANDS!

TROUBLESOME POSITIONS AND COMPOSITIONS ARE PAR FOR THE COURSE. EVEN THE MOST SKILLFUL AND EXPERIENCED PROFESSIONAL CARTOONIST RUNS INTO THEM FREQUENTLY -- SOMETIMES ON A DAILY BASIS -- SO THE STUDENT SHOULD NOT BE DISMAYED WHEN FACED WITH SUCH DRAWING DIFFICULTIES!

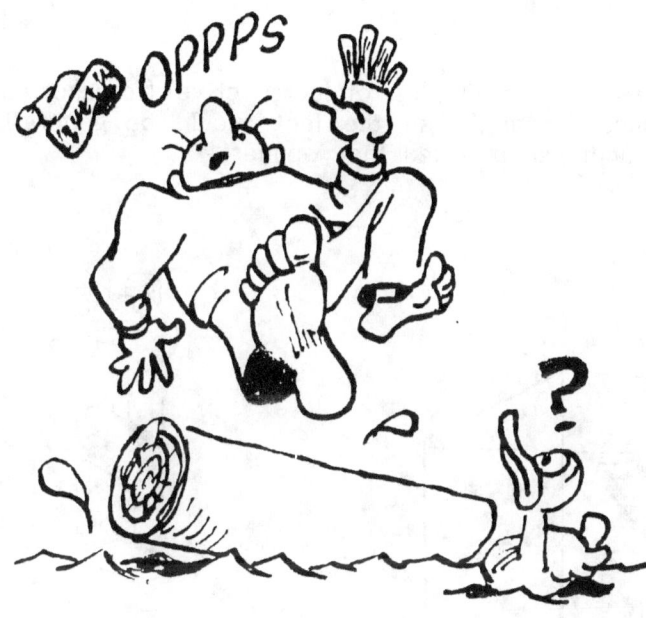

Drawing feet (and shoes, of course) in a masterful, professional manner will be as easy as slipping off a log if the student has diligently done the work as outlined in the previous sections of this chapter.

ACTUALLY, THE FOOT IS SIMILAR TO THE HAND IN SEVERAL WAYS!

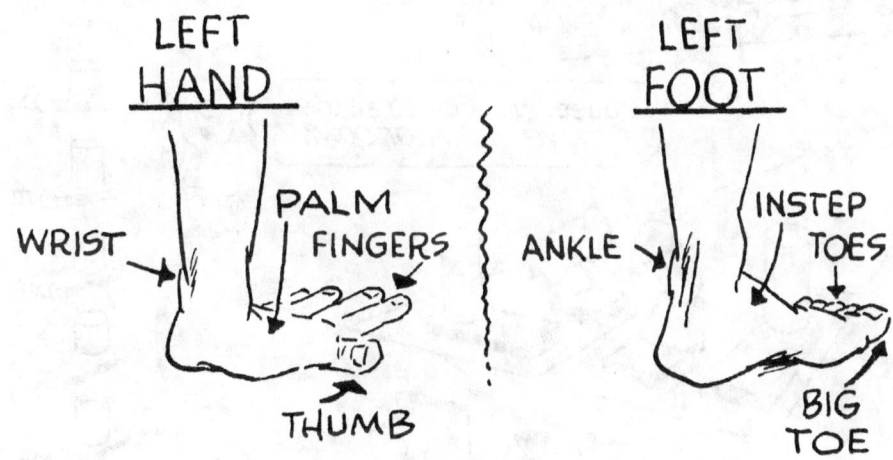

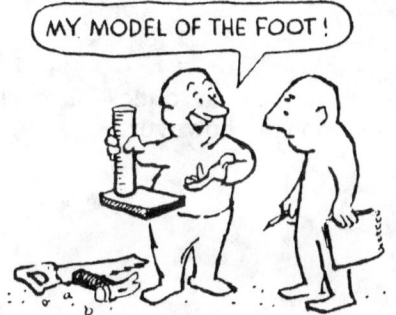

HOWEVER ...

Drawing feet properly requires a slightly different approach.

Once again, we have gone to no little expense to create a special teaching tool to help illustrate some basic rules that apply to this very important subject.

35

It's important to keep in mind the basic principles of perspective (foreshortening) when drawing feet. The "plane," or angle, of the feet should be generally compatible with the surface (or surroundings) in which they appear.

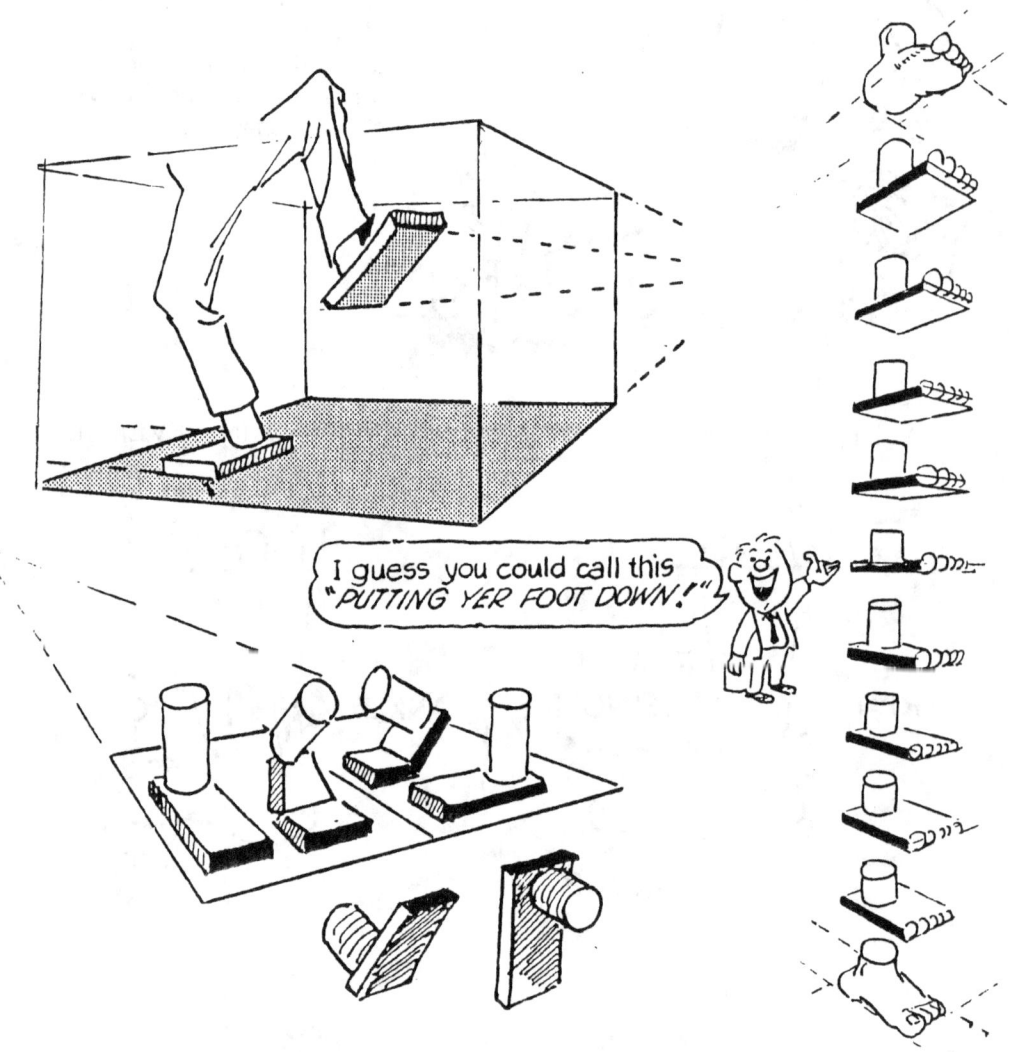

I guess you could call this "*PUTTING YER FOOT DOWN!*"

Occasionally, the use of "T-Square" perspective is needed to check a particular foot position. "Eyeball" perspective is usually close enough, however.

Since form, shape, and direction are important factors in drawing and positioning feet, it is helpful to think of them as shaped blocks of wood.

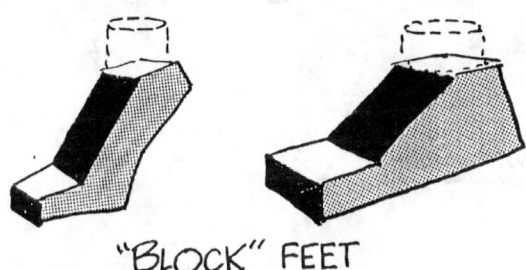

"BLOCK" FEET

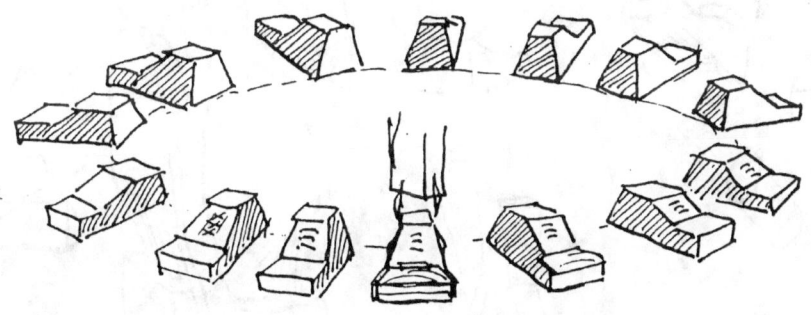

Once the basic shape and direction of the foot is established, it is not difficult to add the details of the shoe style.

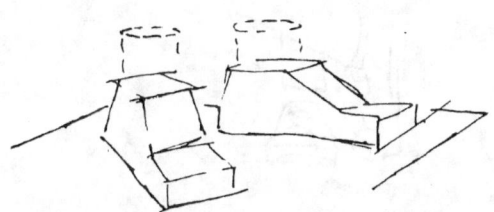
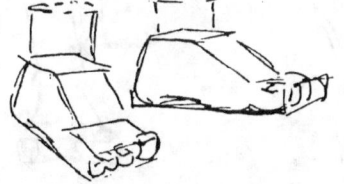
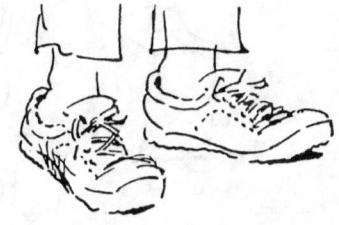

"BLOCK-IN" FOOT POSITION...THINK FEET ..... ADD SHOE DETAIL !

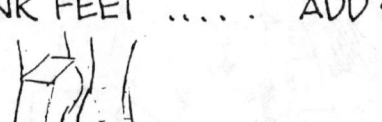
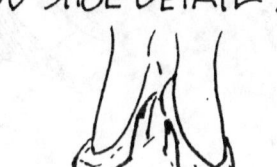

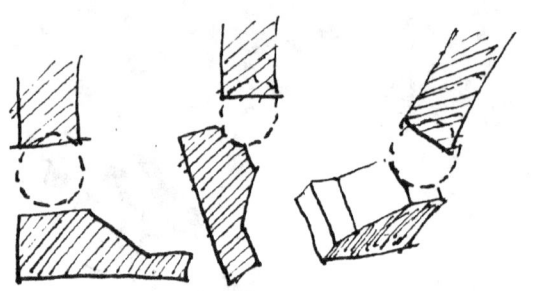

It should be remembered that the foot does not always come out at a sharp right angle to the leg. The ankle is almost as flexible as the wrist and plays just as important a part in overall movements of the body.

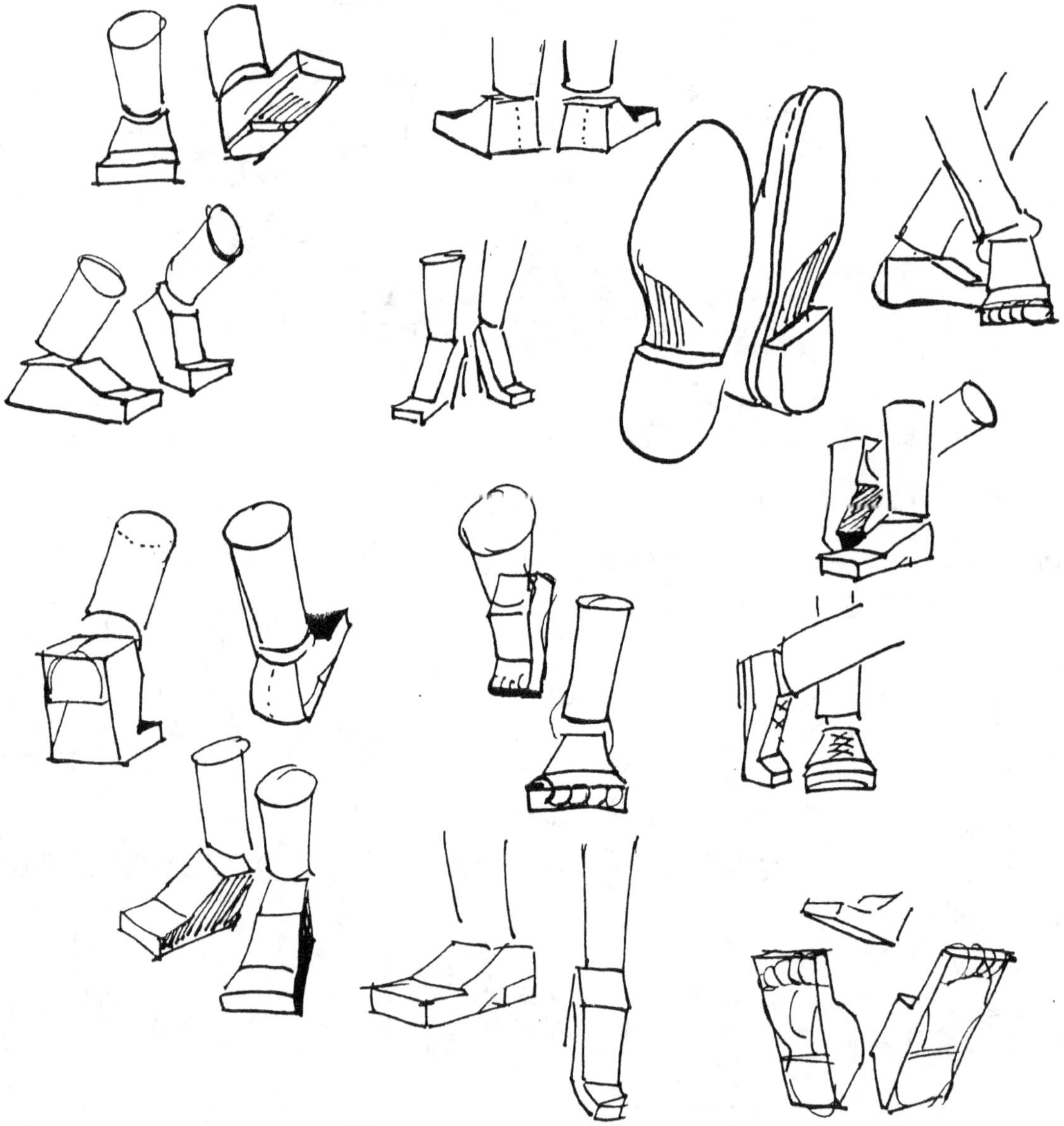

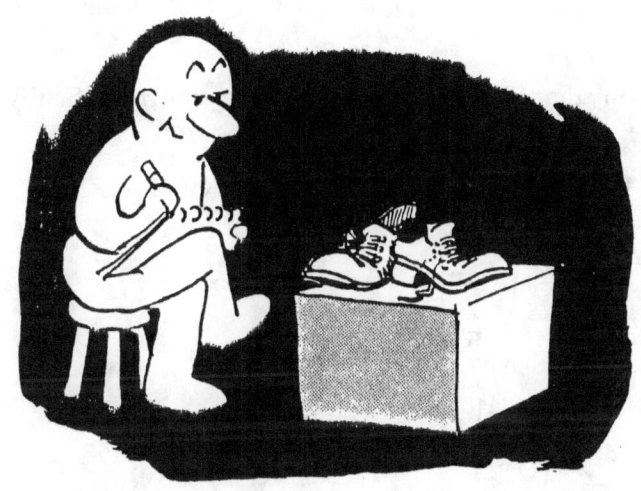

QUICK SKETCHING

This is no time for the student to ease up on the Quick Sketch habit that has, hopefully, been acquired. Nearly every page of the daily newspaper will likely contain a photo of some sort of footwear. Take note of the specialty shoes, including everything from fuzzy slippers to fishermen's hip boots!

Remember, the purpose of your sketches is to capture the basic type and style of the item. Indicate the overall "character" of the shoe. Detail is only secondary!

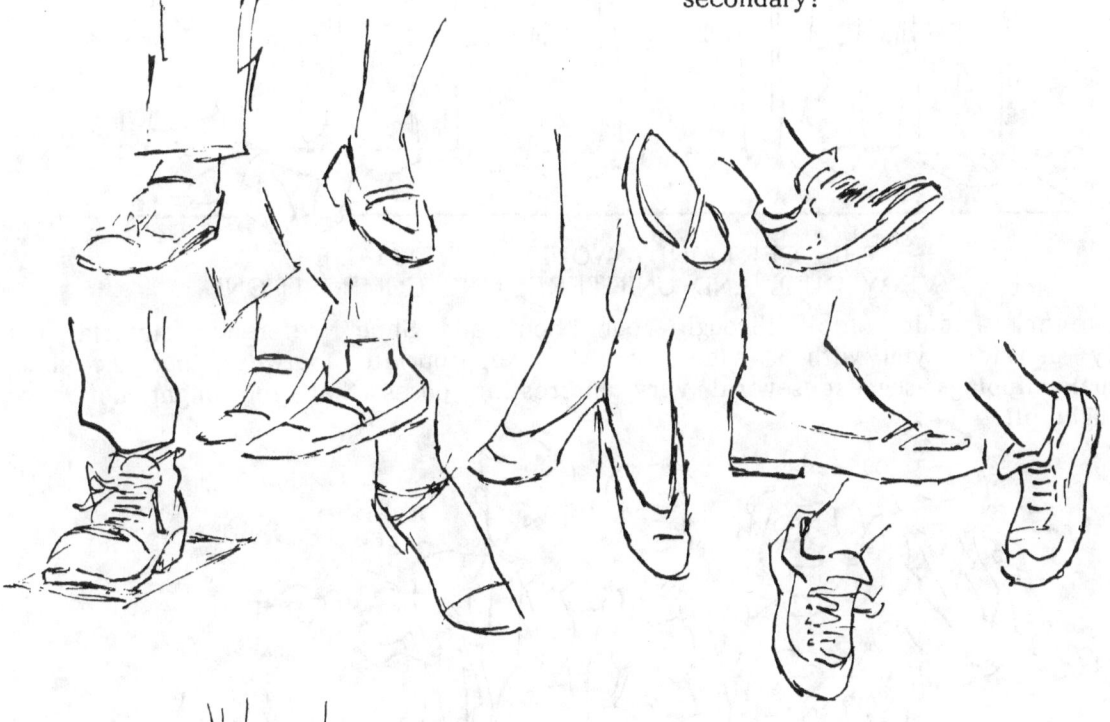

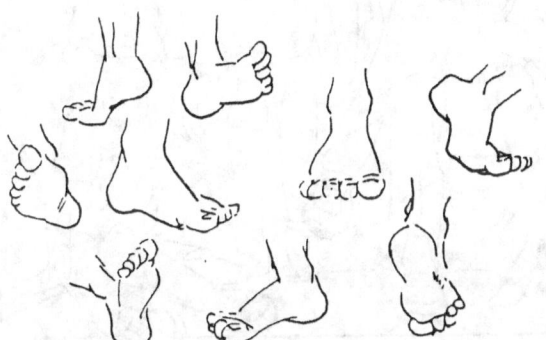

The student's job of putting shoes on cartoon figures will be made easier if he or she remembers that there is a FOOT somewhere in the shoe.

This chapter gives us an excellent opportunity to point out a side benefit of collecting reference material.

Let's say you have a cartoon situation that calls for a somewhat informal family gathering.

YOUR FIRST ATTEMPT MIGHT TURN OUT SOMETHING LIKE THIS:

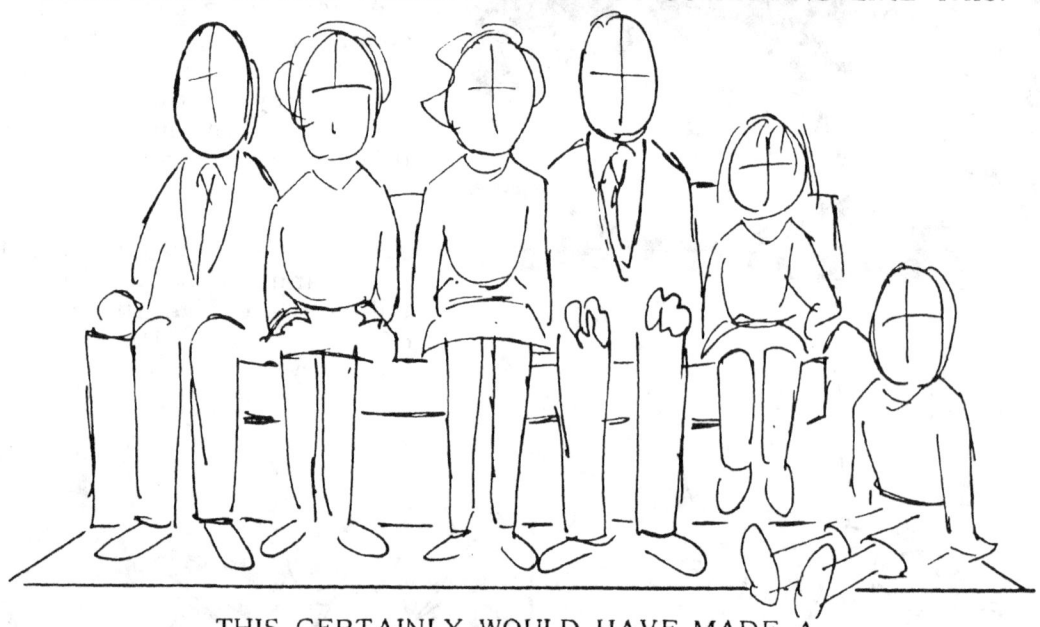

THIS CERTAINLY WOULD HAVE MADE A
VERY DULL AND UNINTERESTING COMPOSITION!

However, a quick look through your "Foot and Shoe" reference material not only provides you with a wide variety of appropriate footwear, but the individual clippings suggest several very interesting poses that you might not have thought of!

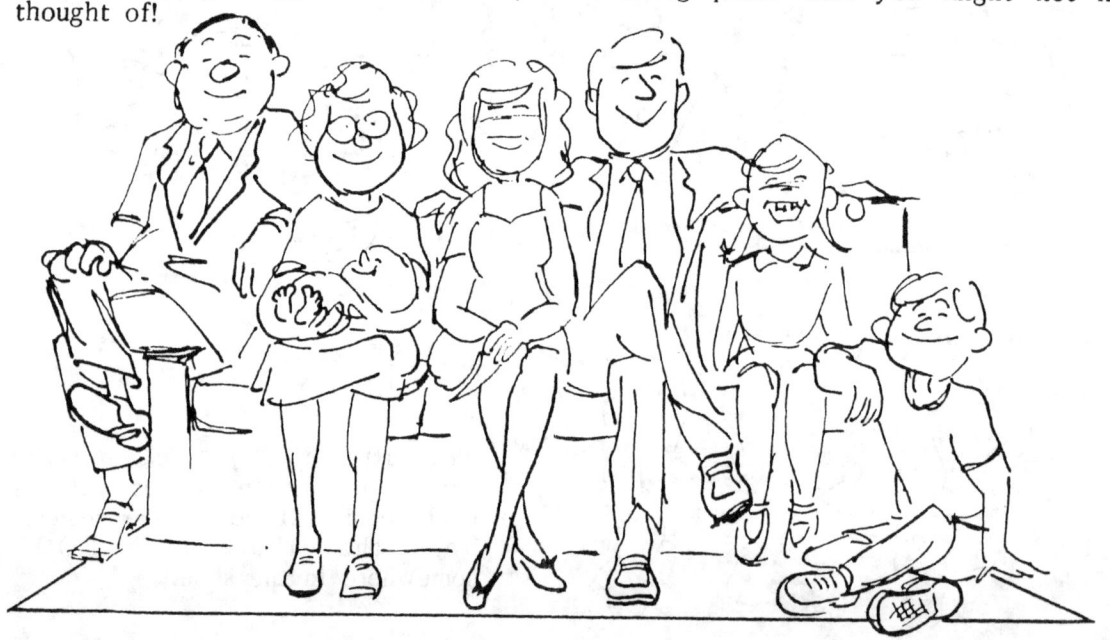

Quickie Review Chapters 1 & 2

EXPERIMENT WITH SHAPES ... create original characters.

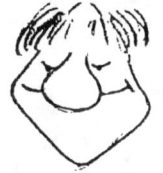 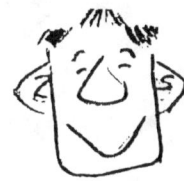 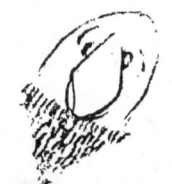 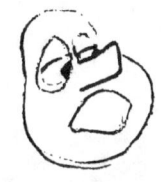 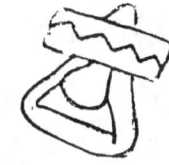

KEEP ABREAST OF HAIR STYLES ... sketch from the fashion pages.

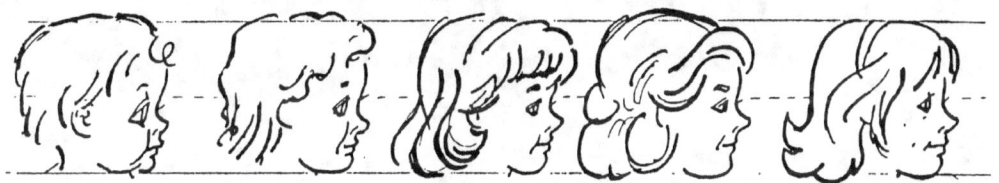

USE HEADGEAR TO HELP IDENTIFY CHARACTERS ...
collect photos of specialty hats.

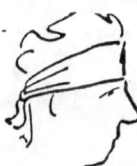 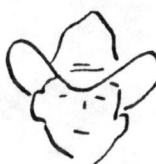 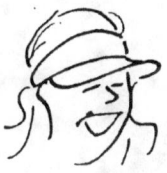 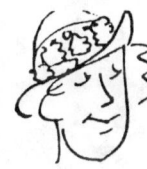 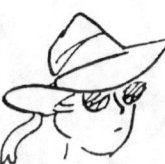

THE BALL, BOARD, AND DOWEL ... gives the hand form and direction.

WORK ON REFERENCE SCRAPBOOKS!

FINGERNAILS CAN OFTEN HELP DESCRIBE THE SHAPE AND DIRECTION OF FINGERS!

CHAPTER THREE
The Cartoon Figure

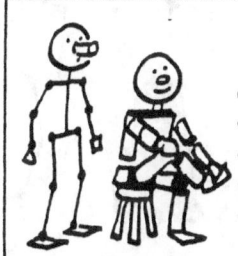

SECTION I
- CONSTRUCTION
- STICKS
- BLOCKS
- SHAPES

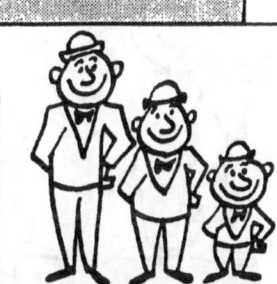

SECTION 2
PROPORTIONS
- CLASSIC
- FASHION
- CARTOON

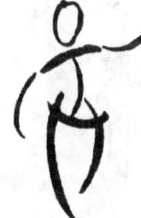

SECTION 3
- BODY LANGUAGE
- GESTURE LINES
- RHYTHM
- OPPOSING CURVES

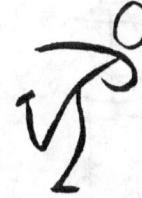

SECTION 4
- BALANCE
- COMPLETE ACTION
- INCOMPLETE ACTION

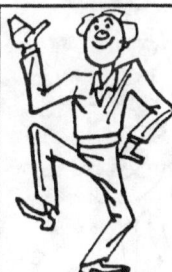
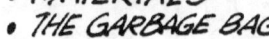

SECTION 5
WRINKLES
- STRESS POINTS
- MATERIALS
- THE GARBAGE BAG

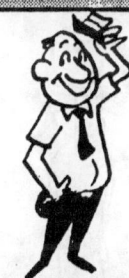

SECTION 6
LINE TECHNIQUES
- BASIC CARTOON "STYLES"

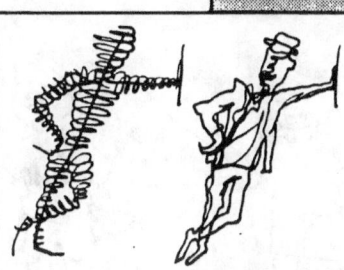

SECTION 7
SKETCHING
- REFERENCE MATERIAL
- "TORNADO" METHOD
- SKETCHING FROM MEMORY
- REVIEW - CHAPTERS 1, 2, & 3

STICKS AND STONES TO SHOW THE BONES

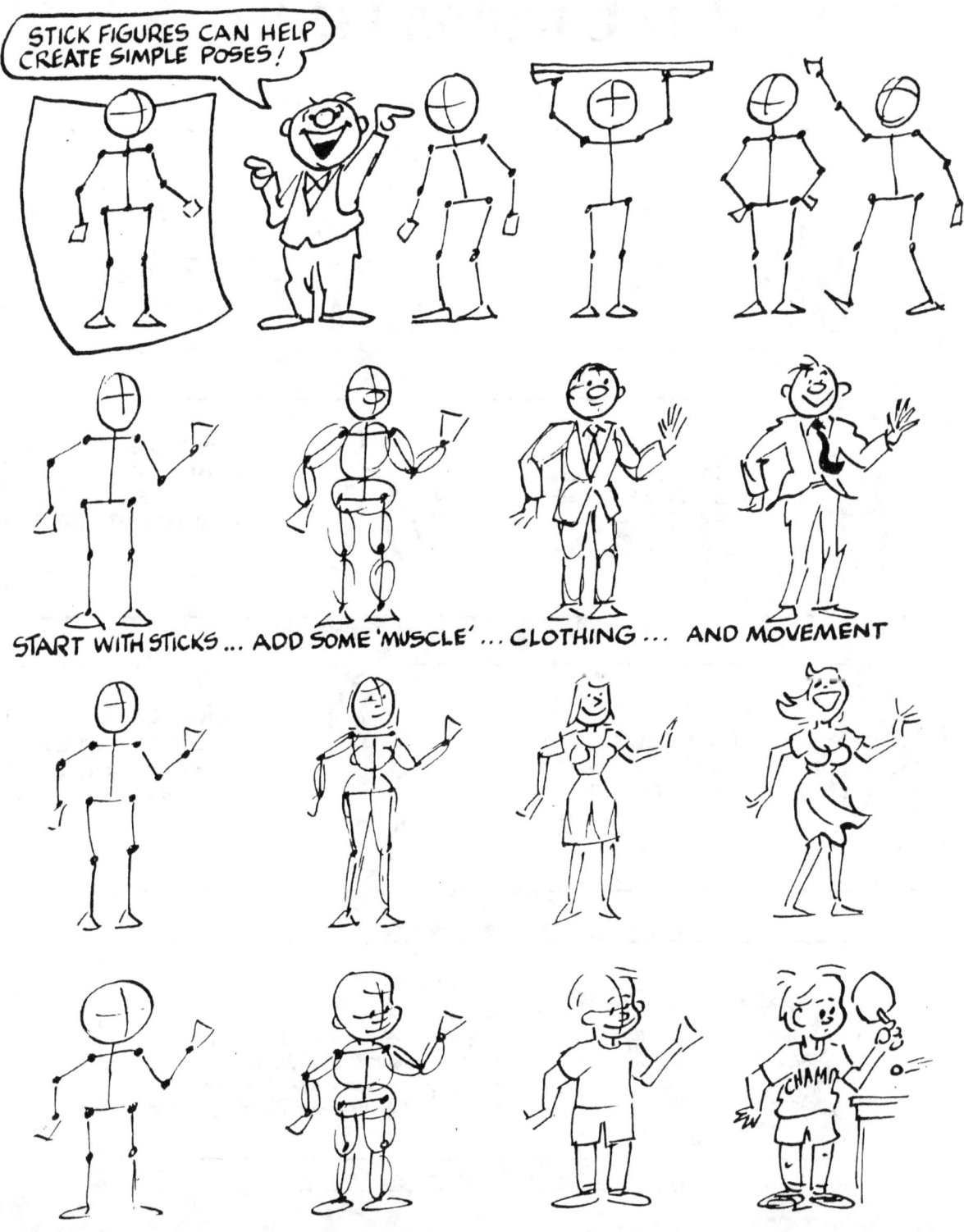

START WITH STICKS ... ADD SOME 'MUSCLE' ... CLOTHING ... AND MOVEMENT

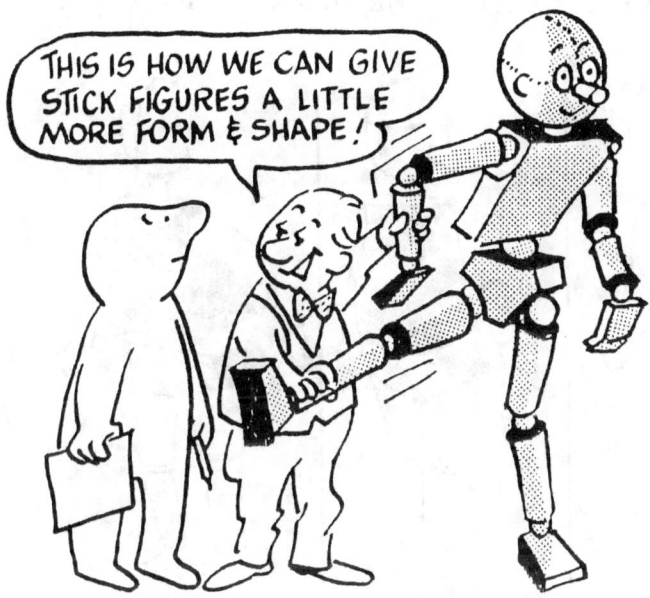

While the stick construction is just fine for relatively simple poses, the sticks have a way of getting all jumbled up when we attempt to create more complicated poses. In those cases, you need to work from the "block" type of construction.

Here are a few examples of how the "block" construction can be very helpful:

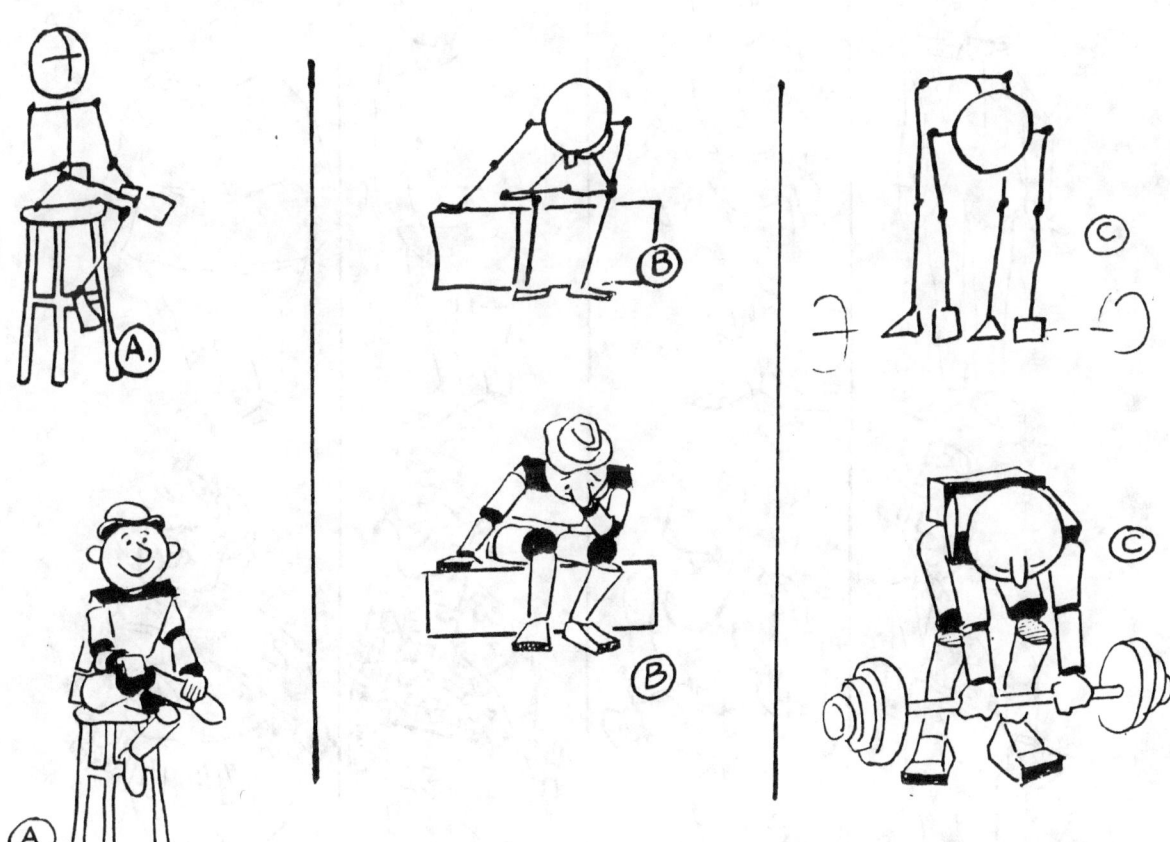

OF COURSE, IT MUST BE REMEMBERED THAT THE HUMAN BODY COMES IN
ALL SORTS OF SHAPES!

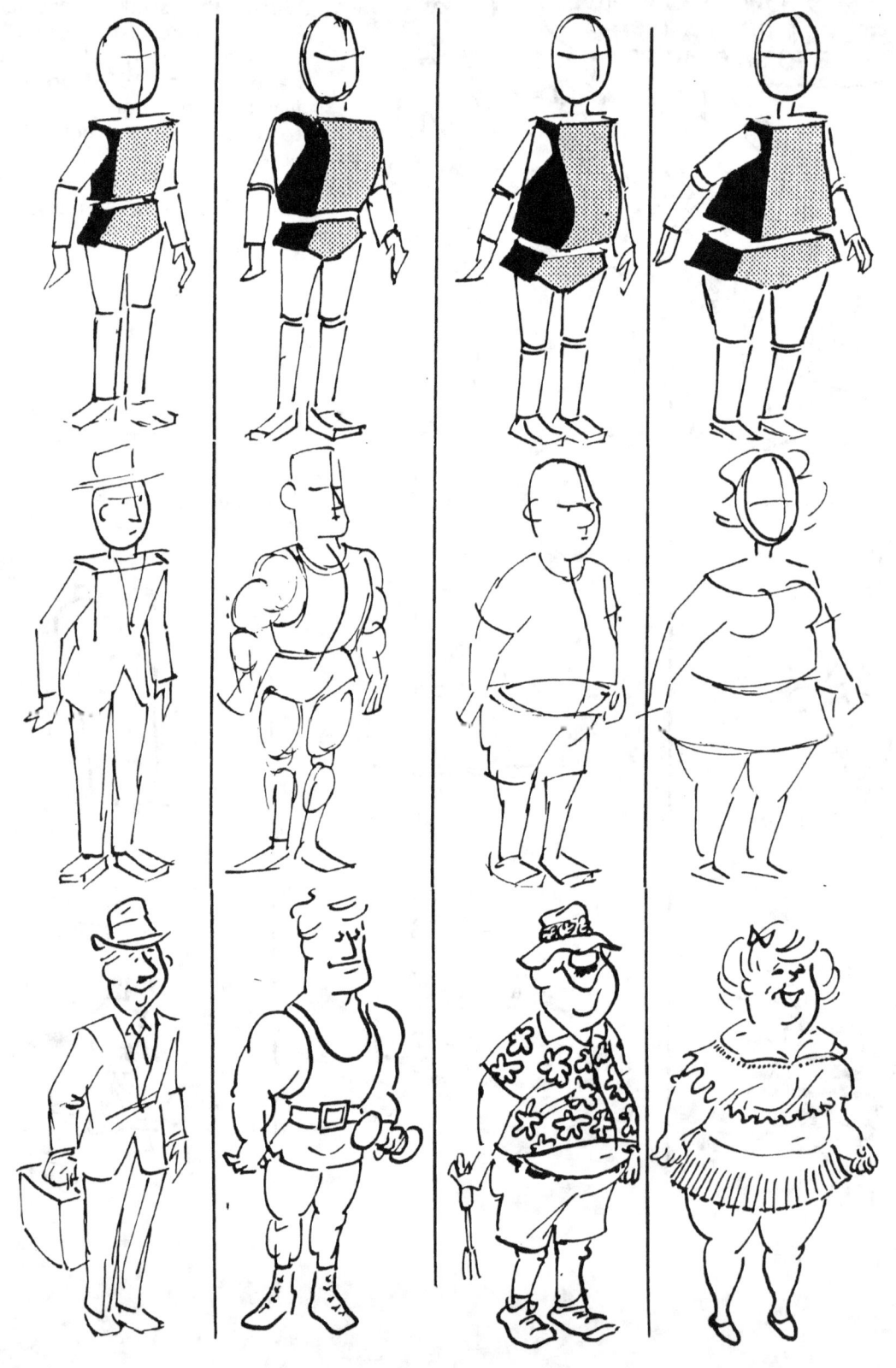

BLOCK CONSTRUCTION IS ESPECIALLY HELPFUL WHEN CREATING UNUSUAL POSES OR THOSE THAT REQUIRE EXTREME FORESHORTENING.

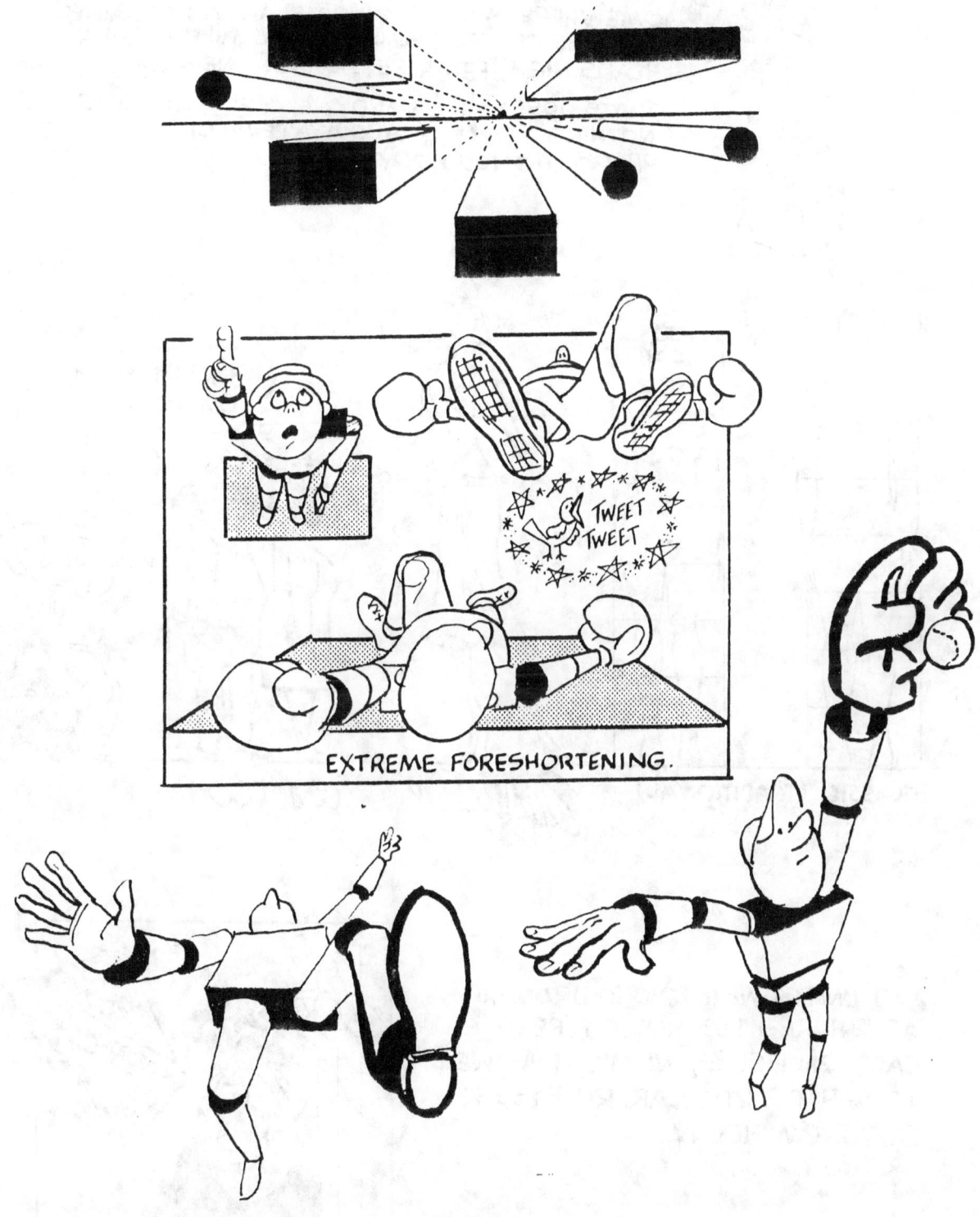

EXTREME FORESHORTENING.

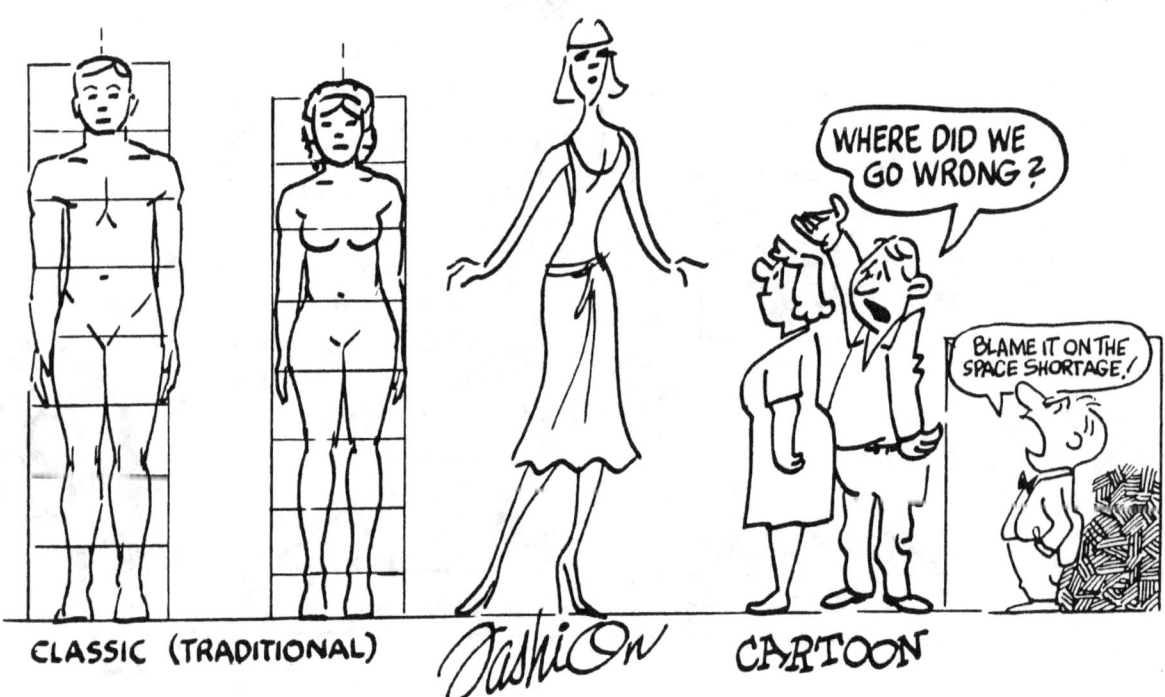

SOMEWHERE, WAY BACK IN TIME, ARTISTS ORDAINED THAT THE PERFECT MALE FIGURE MUST BE EIGHT HEADS HIGH, FEMALES SEVEN & ONE-HALF!!

THAT'S JUST FINE & DANDY, EXCEPT THAT THERE'S NOTHING **FUNNY** ABOUT A PERFECTLY PROPORTIONED BODY!!

CLASSIC (TRADITIONAL)   *Fashion*   CARTOON

WHERE DID WE GO WRONG?

BLAME IT ON THE SPACE SHORTAGE!

SO, UNLESS WE INTEND TO DRAW THE ADVENTURE-ILLUSTRATIVE TYPE OF CARTOON FIGURE, WE MIGHT AS WELL TOSS THAT PARTICULAR RULE BOOK OUT THE WINDOW.

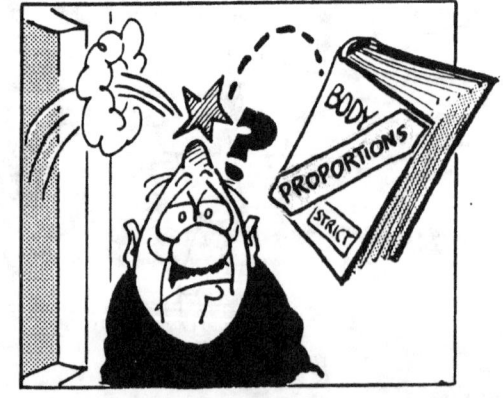

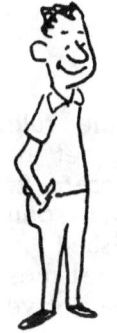 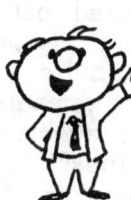

GENERALLY SPEAKING, CARTOON PROPORTIONS ARE GOVERNED ONLY BY THE CARTOONIST'S OWN SENSE OF HUMOR AND DRAWING STYLE !!

A FEW EXAMPLES OF CARTOON PROPORTIONS !

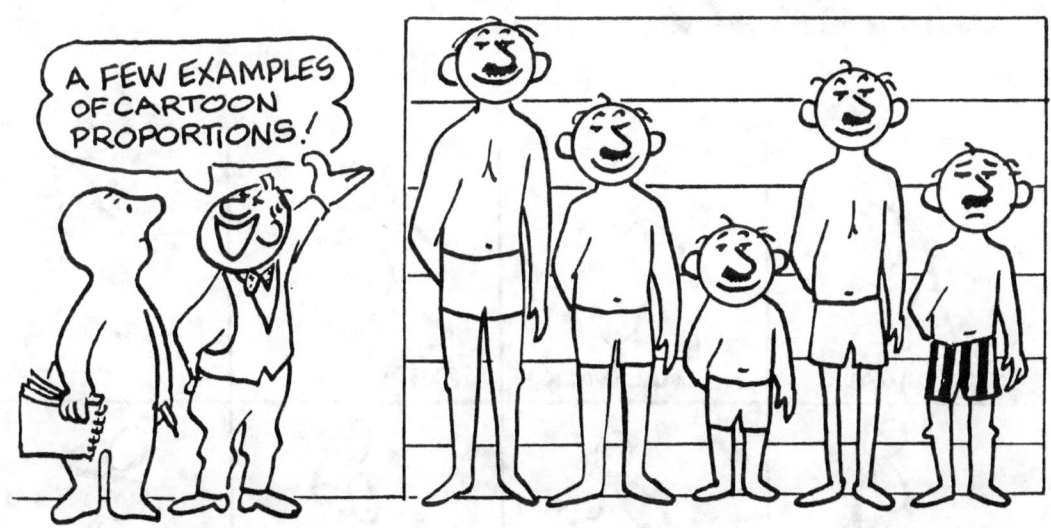

THE GALS ARE ABOUT THE SAME EXCEPT FOR THE CURVES

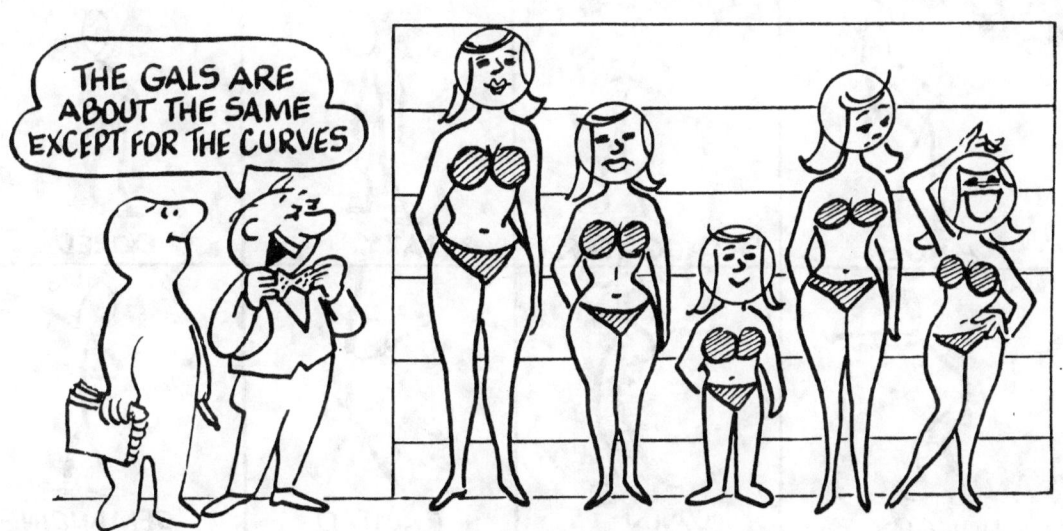

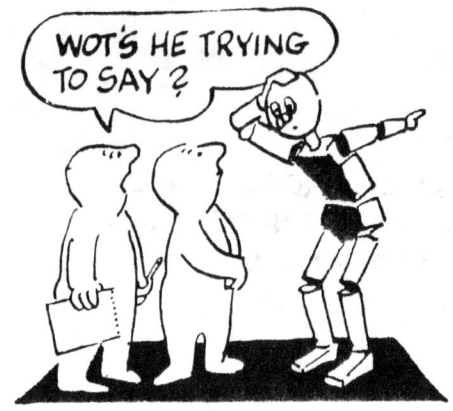

Although we may have tossed out the rule book on proportions, there is one set of guidelines that must be studied carefully. Stance and posture, by themselves, can convey a message. This is accomplished by the use of "Gesture Lines" (sometimes referred to as action lines or descriptive lines).

TIRED WALK	NORMAL WALK	FAST WALK	STRUT
PRIDE	ANXIETY	SURPRISE	FEAR
ANGER	LAUGHTER	LAZY	BORED
HUNGRY	VAIN	EXCITED	DEMANDING

HERE ARE A FEW EXAMPLES OF HOW
GESTURE LINES CAN BE USED TO CONVEY A "MESSAGE"

POOPED!

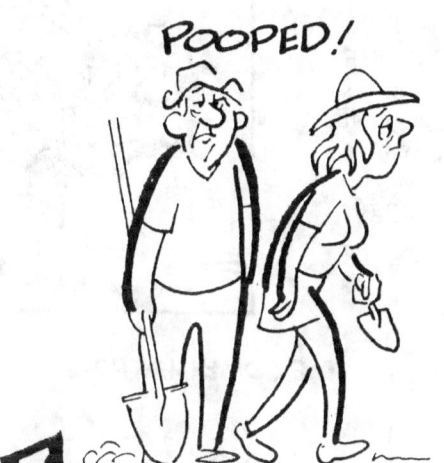

ANGRY!

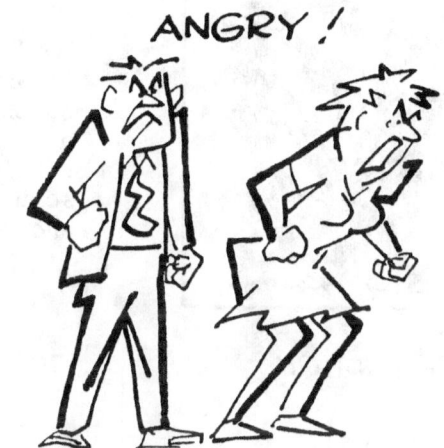

IT IS NOT NECESSARILY DUE TO COINCIDENCE — OR A "COPYCAT SYNDROME" — THAT SOFT, GENTLE LINES ARE ALWAYS USED BY CARTOONISTS TO STRESS CERTAIN MOODS & EMOTIONS...

...WHILE HARD, SHARP LINES & ANGLES ARE USED TO INDICATE CERTAIN *OTHER* CHARACTERISTICS, ACTIONS, AND EXPRESSIONS!

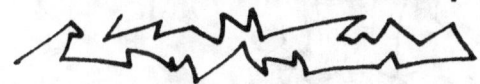

THE MIND "INTERPRETS" LINES AND SHAPES INSTANTANEOUSLY!

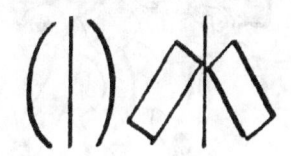

SYMETRICAL LINES
BALANCE OR FORCE

OPPOSING LINES
CREATE MOVEMENT

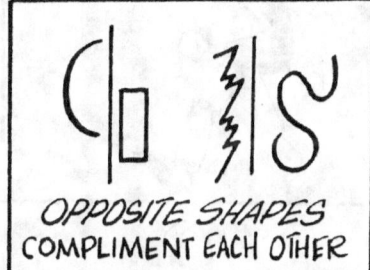

OPPOSITE SHAPES
COMPLIMENT EACH OTHER

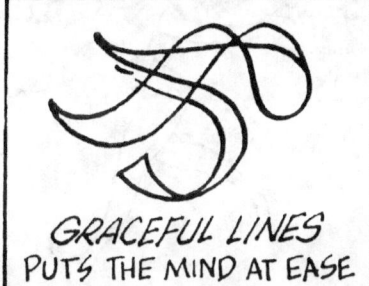

GRACEFUL LINES
PUTS THE MIND AT EASE

HARSH LINES/ANGLES
CREATE ANXIETY, FEAR

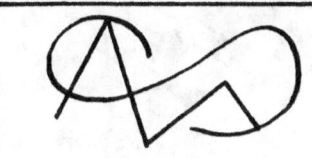

COMBINATION LINES
CANCEL OUT EACH OTHER

In addition to using Gesture Lines to express emotions, they are also used to create body rhythm and to indicate smooth flowing action.

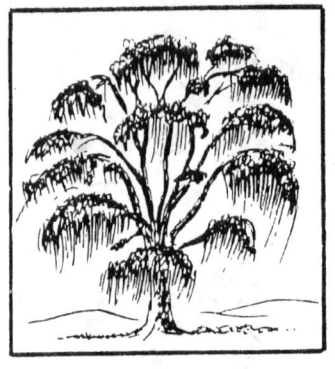

NATURE'S OWN GESTURE LINES. The gentle curves of the willow tree suggest peace and serenity, while the sharp angles of the scrub pine suggest anger and hostility.

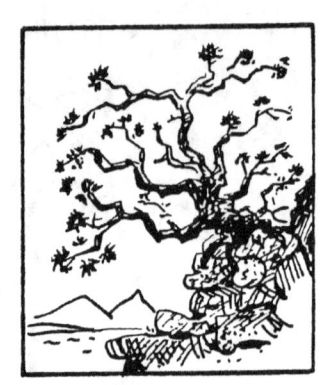

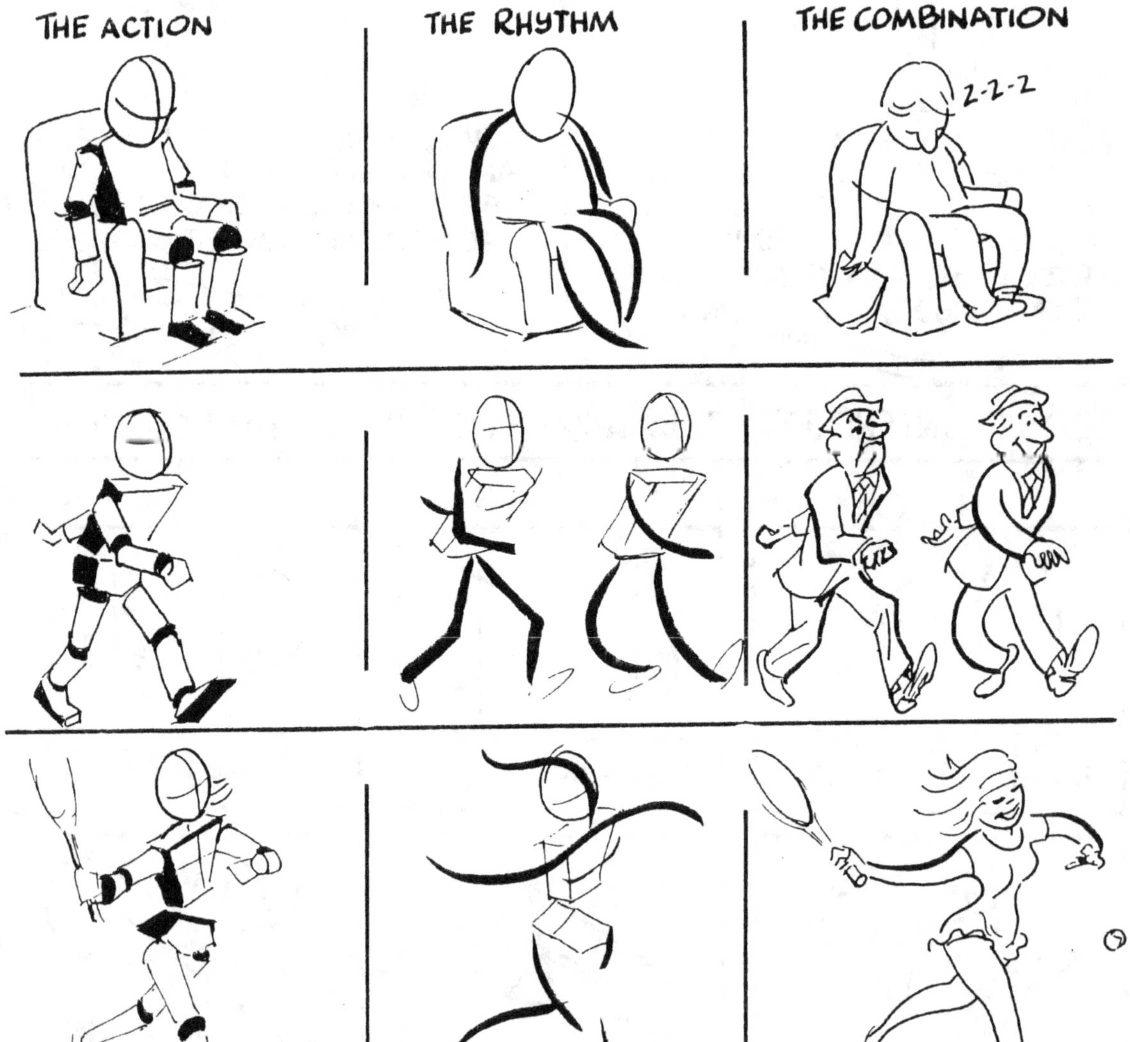

THE ACTION	THE RHYTHM	THE COMBINATION

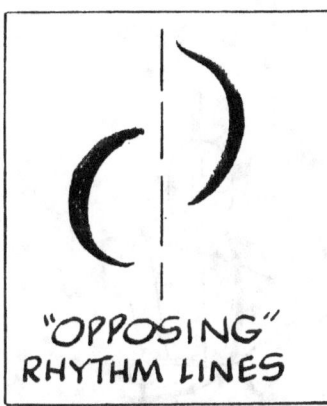

"OPPOSING" RHYTHM LINES

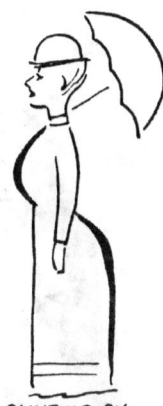

OPPOSING CURVES AND ACTION LINES. The well-established principles of "Opposing Curves" should be used whenever possible, especially when drawing the female figure. It can add an extra element of grace and beauty that might otherwise be lacking. Great artists of another era employed this principle often, with wondrous results.

AFTER A PAINTING BY GEORGES SEURAT.

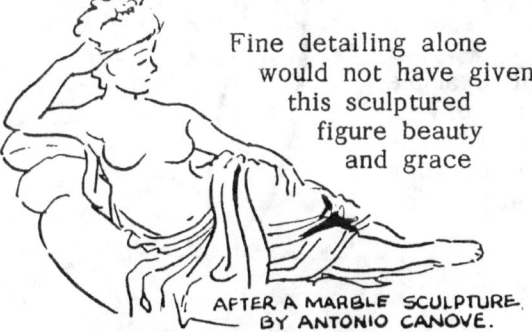

Fine detailing alone would not have given this sculptured figure beauty and grace

AFTER A MARBLE SCULPTURE. BY ANTONIO CANOVE.

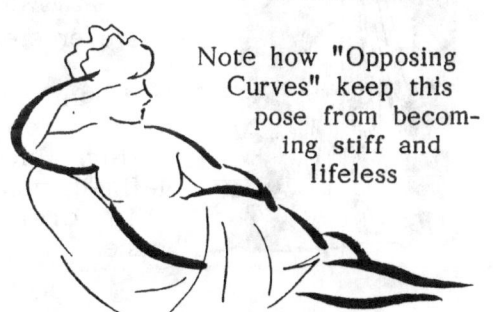

Note how "Opposing Curves" keep this pose from becoming stiff and lifeless

Here, opposing curves emphasize the downward pull of the hair

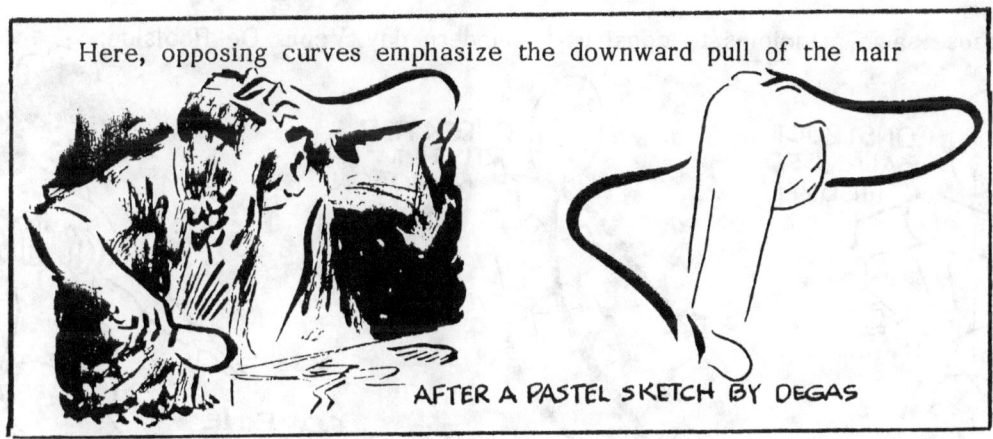

AFTER A PASTEL SKETCH BY DEGAS

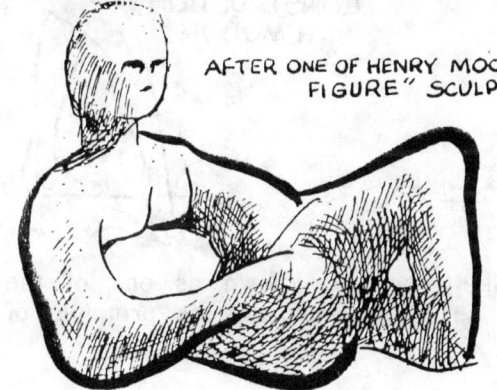

AFTER ONE OF HENRY MOORE'S "RECLINING FIGURE" SCULPTURES.

More recently, artists and sculptors tend to eliminate detail almost completely, depending on gesture lines alone to indicate the figure.

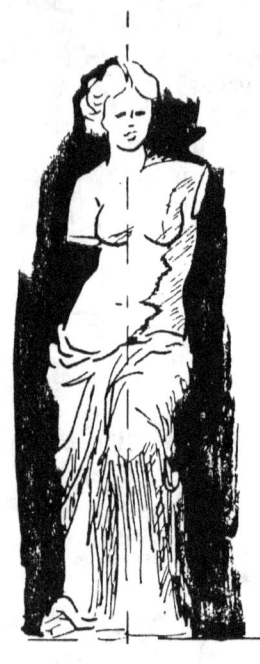

COMBINING BALANCE WITH OPPOSING CURVES AND GESTURE LINES.

The sculptured figure of "Venus de Milo" is probably one of the most widely known works of art that was ever created.

It is an excellent example of how opposing curves, rhythm lines, and a well-defined center of balance help create beauty and grace.

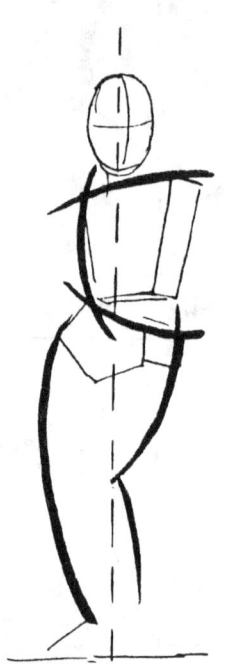

Let's use those same principles to construct a modern day Venus De Poolside:

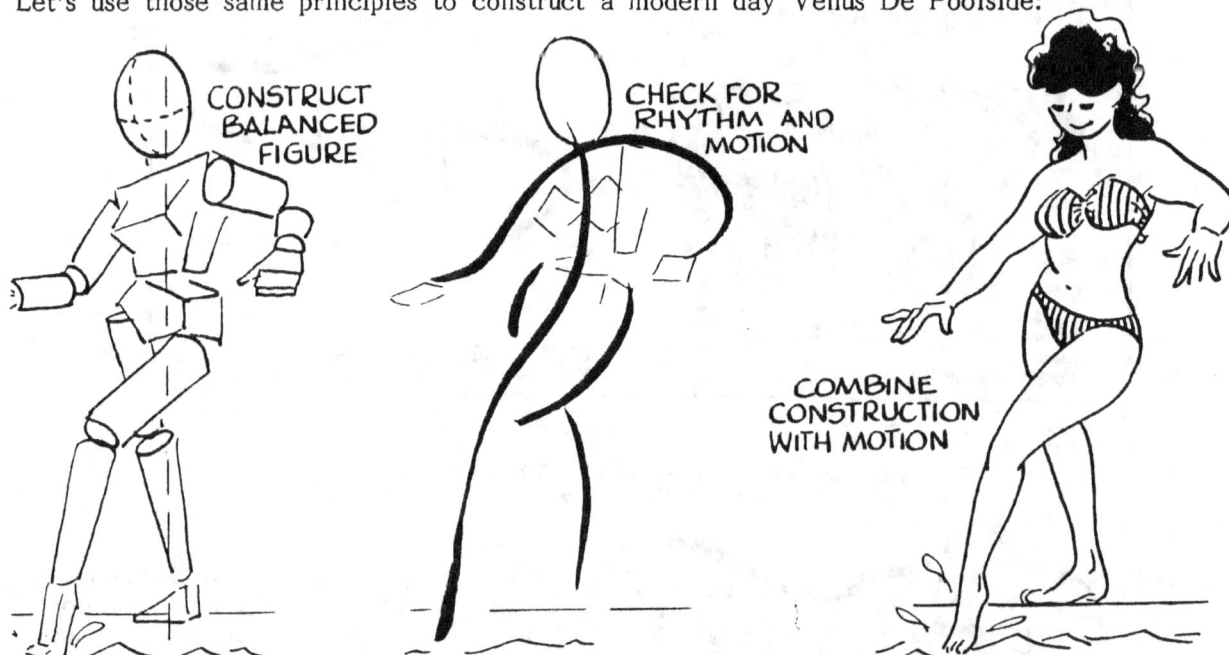

CONSTRUCT BALANCED FIGURE

CHECK FOR RHYTHM AND MOTION

COMBINE CONSTRUCTION WITH MOTION

Admittedly, our bathing beauty will not likely become known as one of the great masterpieces of all time, but she does serve to illustrate the principle of balance and gesture lines.

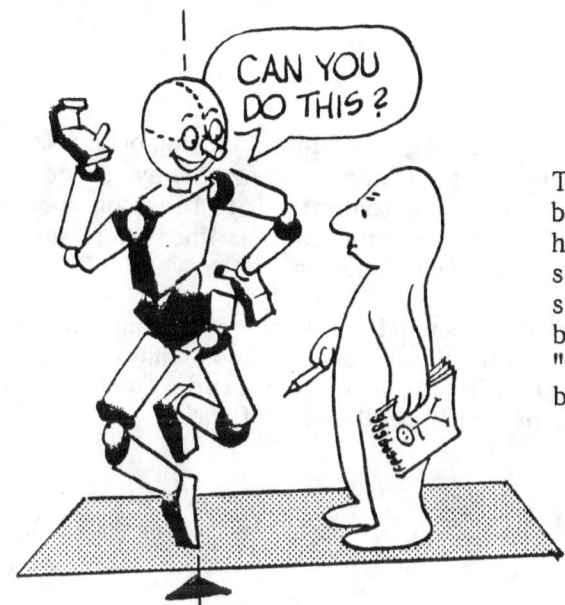

The "Mind's Eye" tends to look for balance in an object, particularly in a human figure. A balanced figure seems to be complete in itself, and suggests no further action. It should be remembered, however, that a "balanced" figure need not necessarily be a perfectly symmetrical one.

n almost all action positions, the arms and legs move in opposite directions left leg forward with right arm forward, etc.)

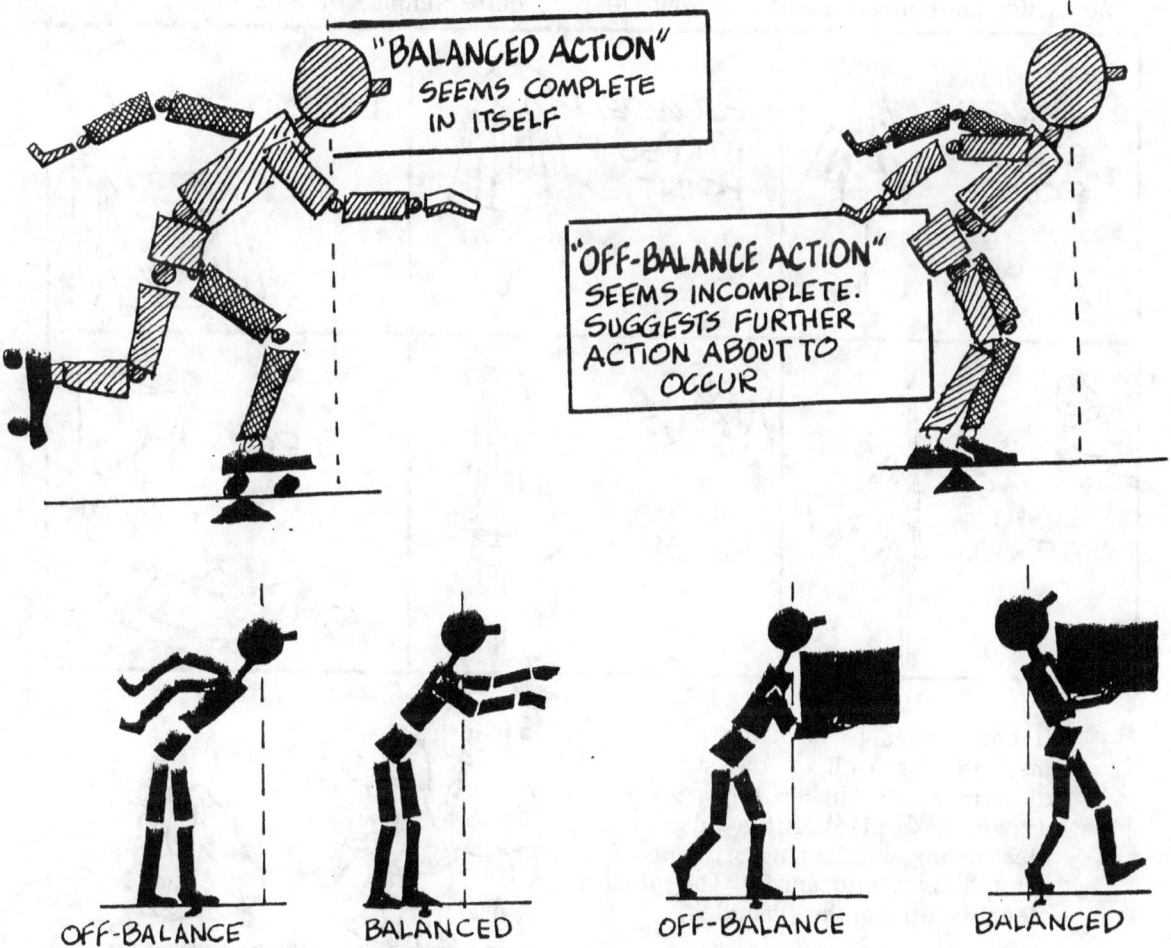

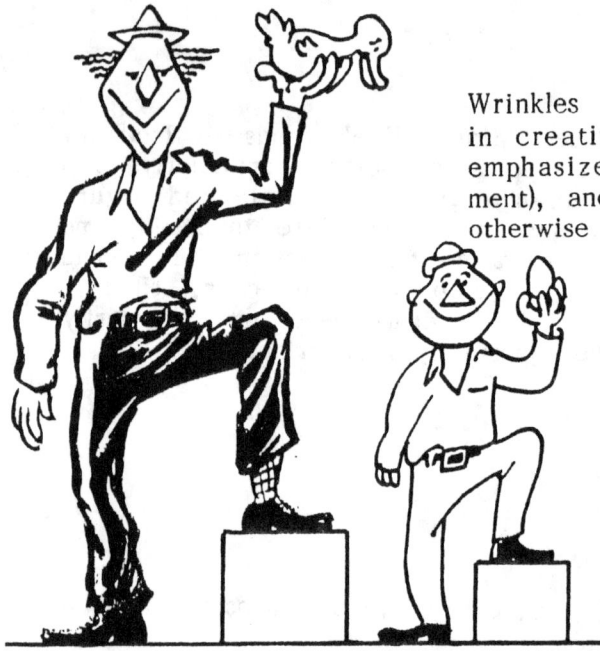

Wrinkles in clothing can play an important role in creating cartoon characters. They serve to emphasize body movements (or lack of movement), and also add interest to lines that might otherwise be somewhat boring.

They should be kept to a minimum and logically placed. Too many wrinkles might complicate and goof up a perfectly well-drawn figure!

The basic guidelines concerning wrinkles are quite simple, of course:

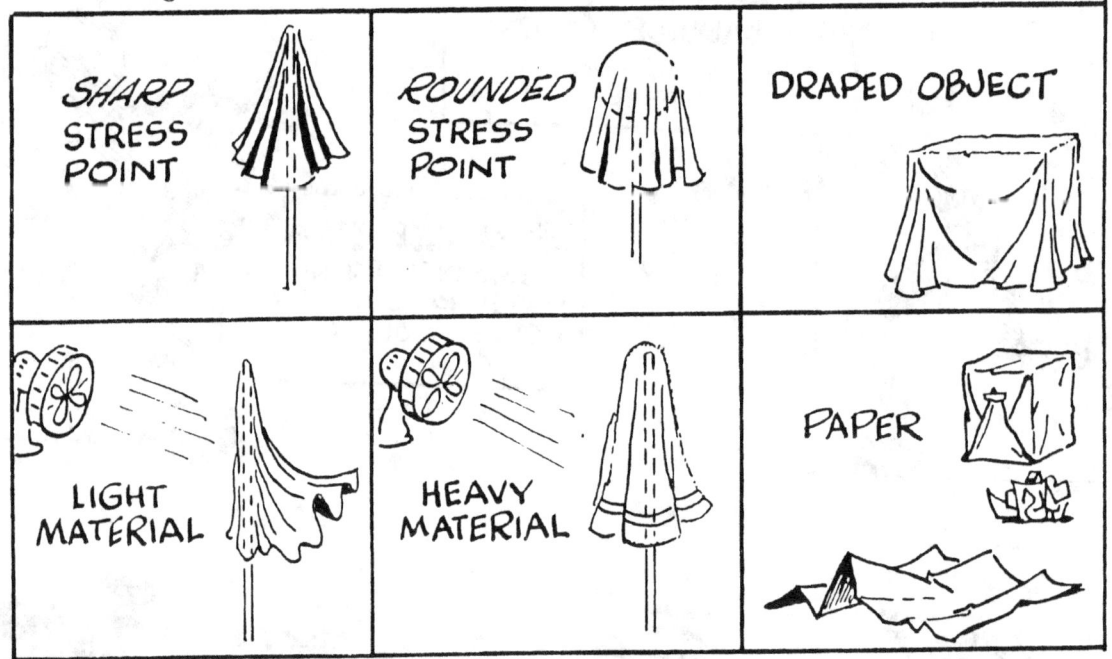

If one wishes to do some real in-depth research on the subject of wrinkles (it makes for a great drawing exercise), fill a large plastic bag with an assortment of empty boxes and stuff. The plastic clearly defines the wrinkles.

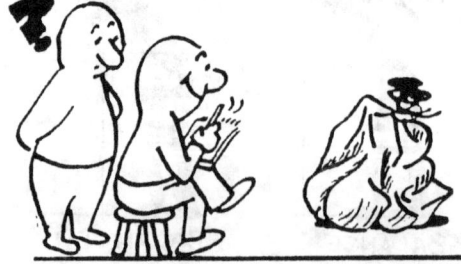

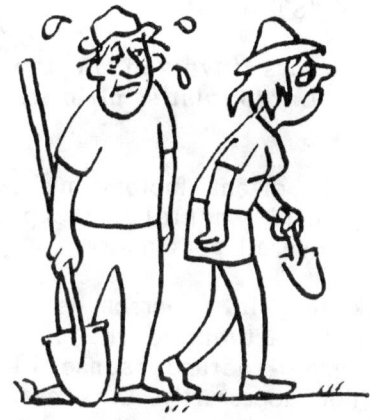

CONSTANT LINE

The manner in which a line is drawn is largely a matter of personal preference and depends, to a great extent, on the type of "tool" that is used to produce the line and the type of material on which the line is drawn.

Basic line structures fall into six or seven general categories, but there are numerous variations of each.

The student is urged to experiment with a wide variety of tools and materials in developing a particular line technique.

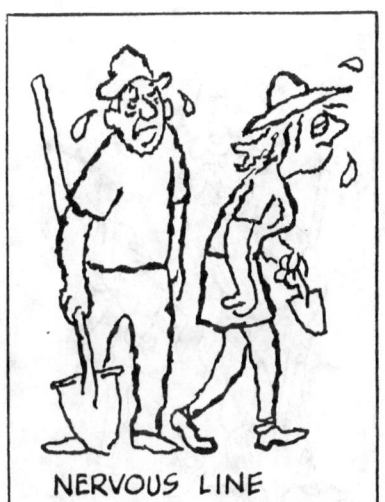

NERVOUS LINE

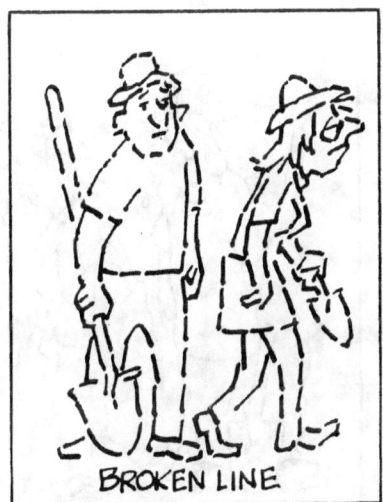

BROKEN LINE

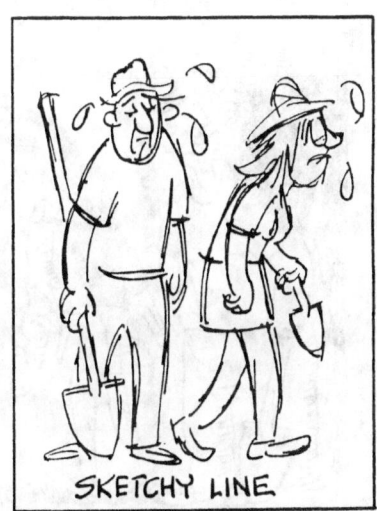

SKETCHY LINE

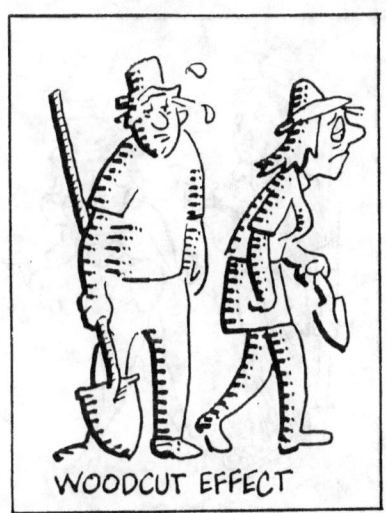

WOODCUT EFFECT

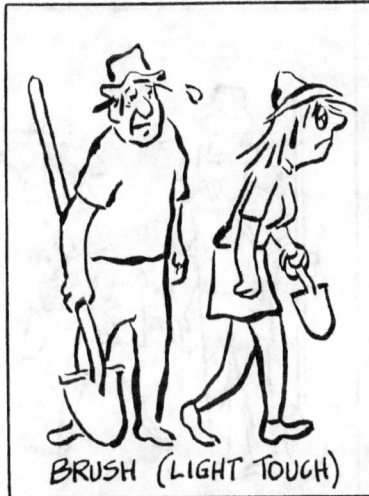

BRUSH (LIGHT TOUCH)

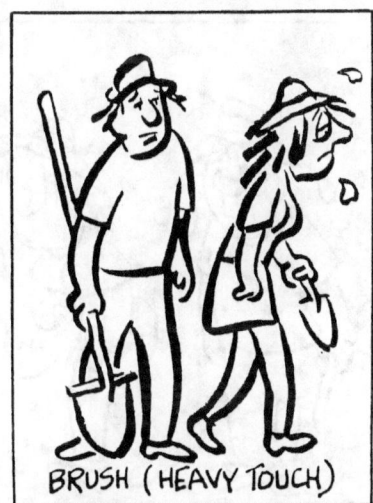

BRUSH (HEAVY TOUCH)

CARTOON "STYLES"

There are many factors involved in the development of a cartoonist's ultimate drawing "style."

Some of the more important factors might be training, background, mental makeup, general interests, and overall personality.

Lots of folks think that if a person is to become a successful cartoonist, the first requirement is a great natural sense of humor. This is not necessarily the case. Most of the consistently funny cartoons we see today are produced by people who are considered to be quite serious-minded.

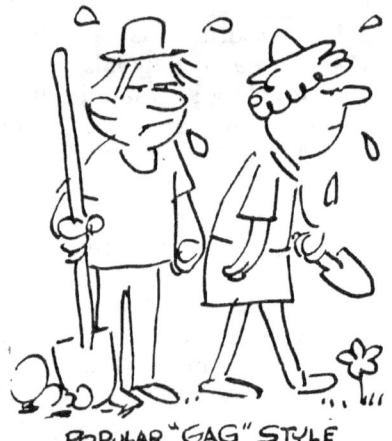

POPULAR "GAG" STYLE

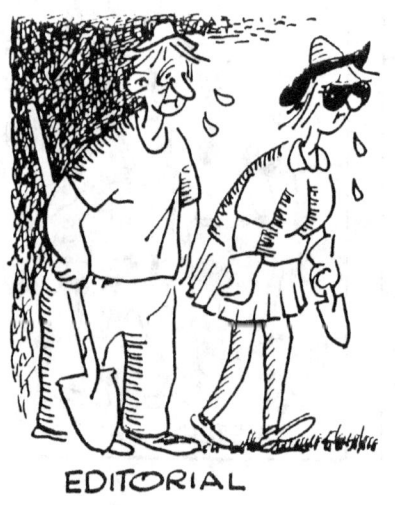

EDITORIAL

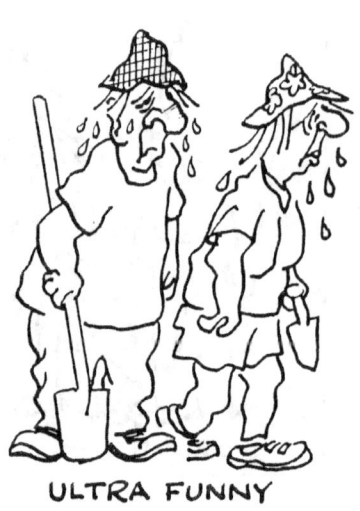

ULTRA FUNNY

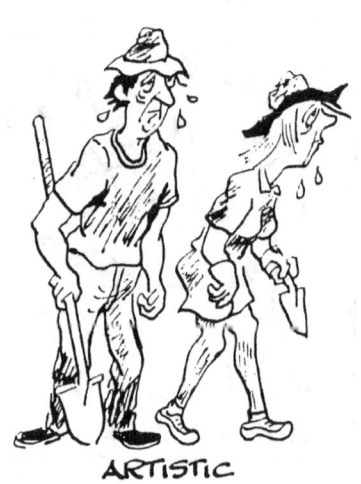

ARTISTIC

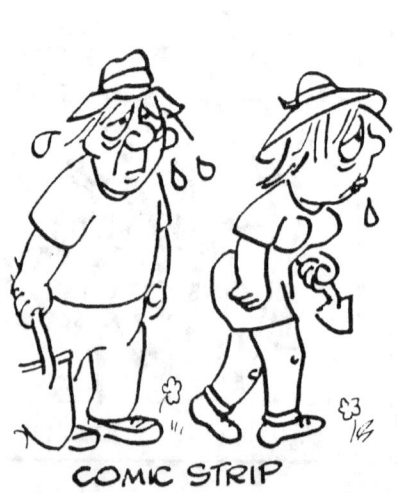

COMIC STRIP

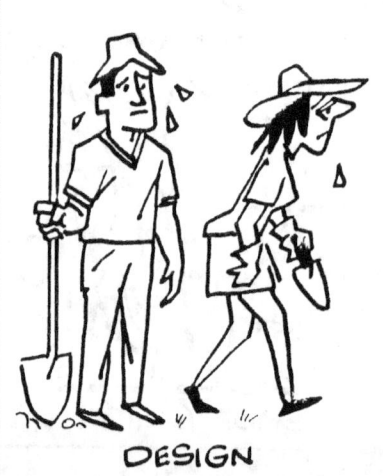

DESIGN

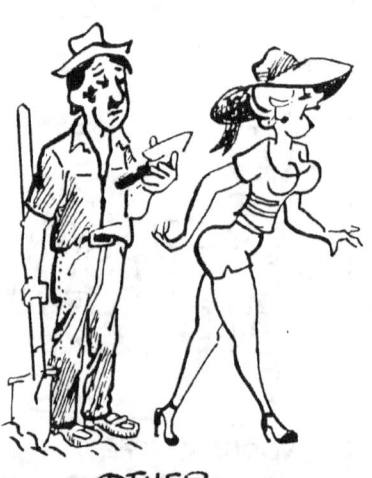

OTHER

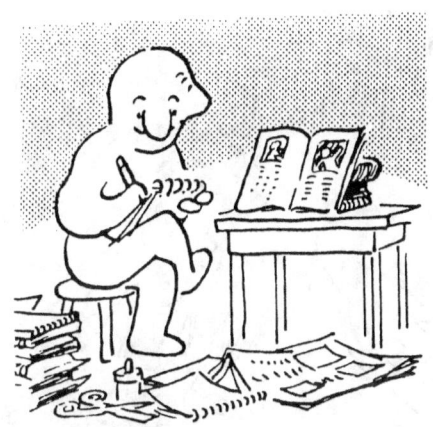

HERE WE GO AGAIN -- HARPING ABOUT THE IMPORTANCE OF DEVELOPING THE SKETCHING HABIT!

This is one topic that will be stressed throughout this book (as you may have already noticed).

We do so because we feel it is the best way for the student to develop the necessary drawing skills and mental "inventory" that are required in the pursuit of a cartooning career.

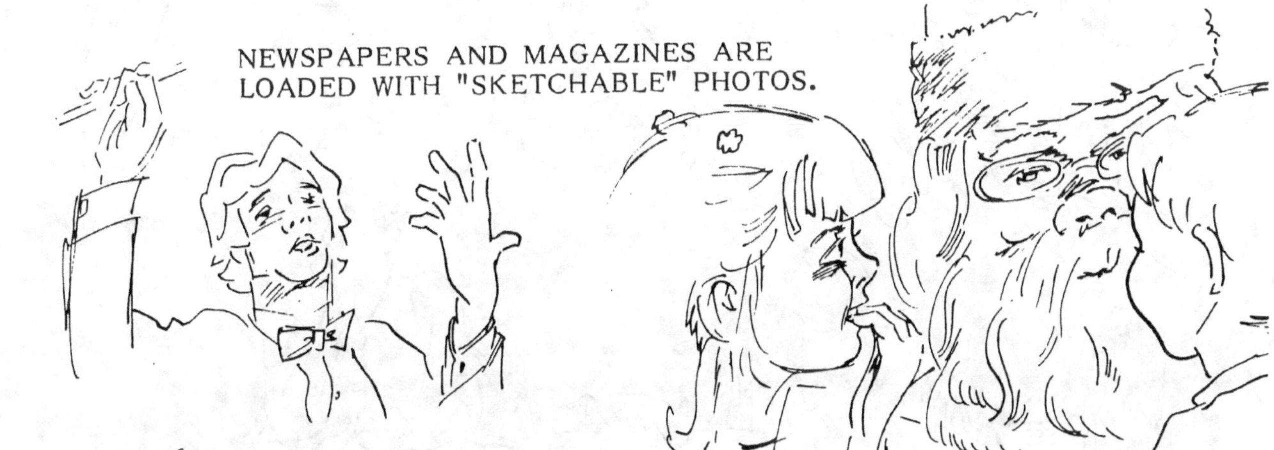

NEWSPAPERS AND MAGAZINES ARE LOADED WITH "SKETCHABLE" PHOTOS.

WORK QUICKLY! DON'T STRIVE FOR DETAIL OR PERFECTION.

NO MORE THAN A MINUTE OR TWO SHOULD BE SPENT ON EACH SKETCH.

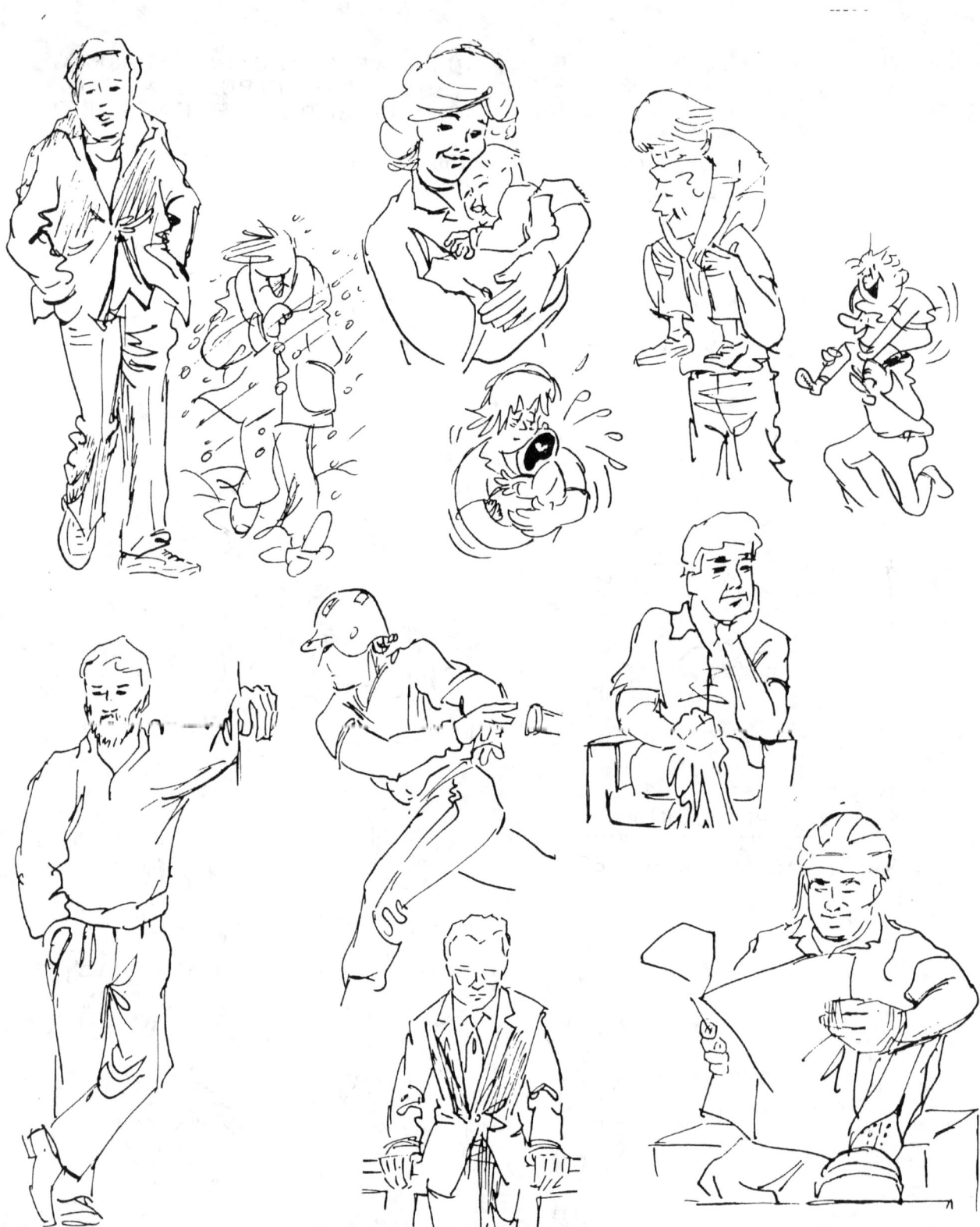

THERE ARE GREAT CARTOON POSSIBILITIES IN ALL OF THESE SKETCHES.
LOAD UP YOUR "MENTAL INVENTORY!"

A CHANGE OF PACE : CREATIVE SKETCHING!

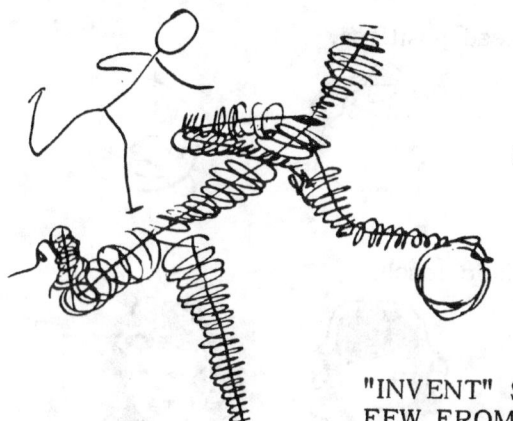

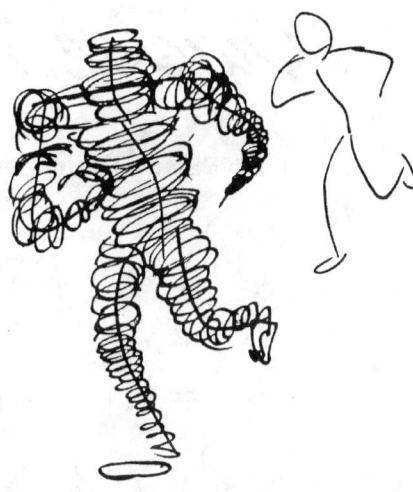

"TORNADO
STYLE"
SKETCHING

"INVENT" SOME ACTION POSES, OR SELECT A FEW FROM REFERENCE MATERIAL. INDICATE THE GENERAL ACTION WITH A FEW QUICK LINES, AND THEN PROCEED TO "WRAP" THOSE ACTION LINES WITH A CIRCULAR MOTION.

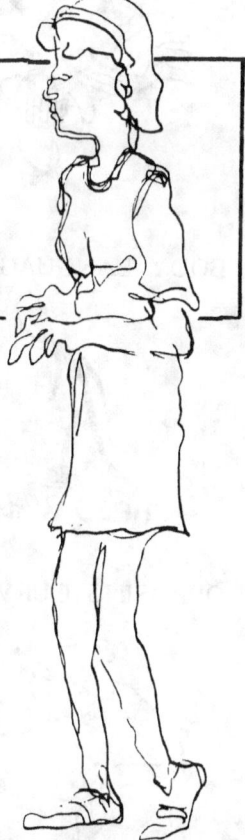

SINGLE LINE SKETCHING.
As recommended in Chapter One, except now do the entire figure! Work from reference material or a live model.　Remember, once you have started, do not lift the pencil or pen from the paper.

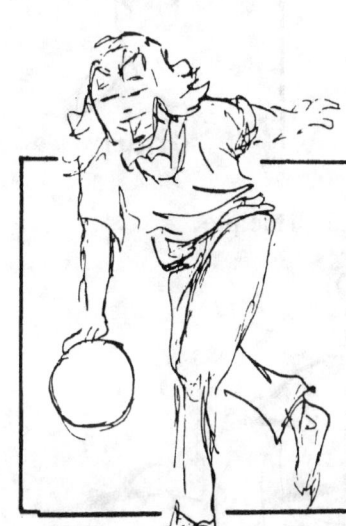

SKETCHING FROM MEMORY.

Here is a real challenge!　Study a photo for one minute, then put it aside and try to sketch it strictly from memory.　You will be amazed at how this will improve your powers of observation!

Quickie Review Chapters 1, 2 & 3

HEAD LINES ... Helpful when drawing difficult head positions.

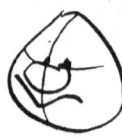 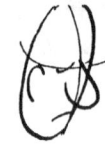 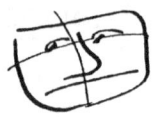 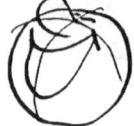 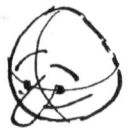

HAIR STYLES ... From squiggly lines to the artistic touch.

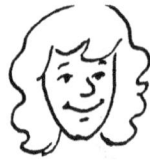 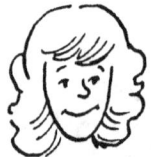 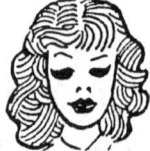 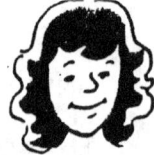 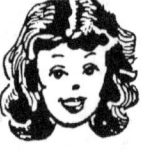

THE WRIST ... An important unit of hand construction.

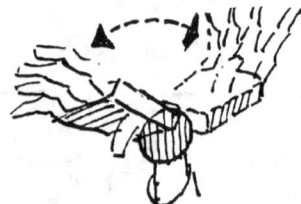 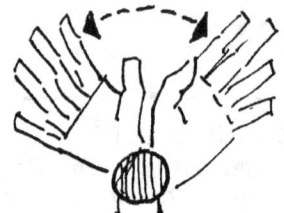 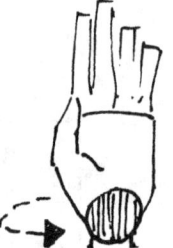 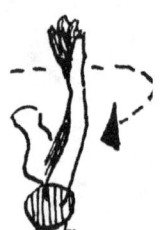

BODY LANGUAGE ... Necessary to convey a message.

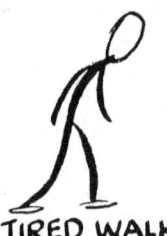 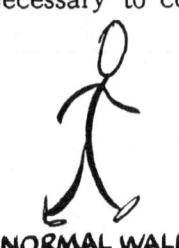 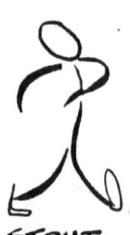

TIRED WALK | NORMAL WALK | FAST WALK | STRUT

OPPOSING CURVES/ACTION LINES ... A well-established principle.

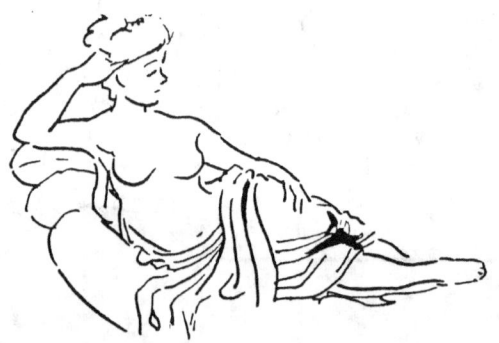 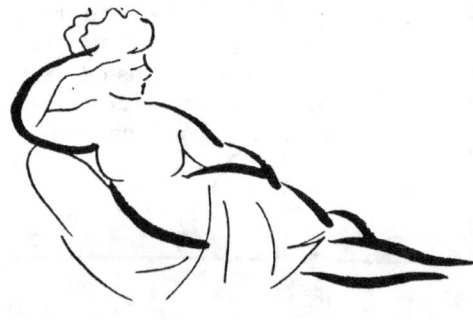

CHAPTER FOUR
Animals

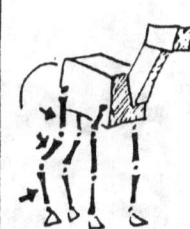

SECTION ONE
LEG STRUCTURE

- HUMAN'S 2 PART SYSTEM
- ANIMAL'S 3 PART SYSTEM
- EXTRA ELBOWS & KNEES
- THE 'FIFTH' LEG

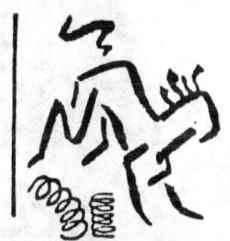

SECTION TWO
TYPES OF ACTION

- THE LEFT ARM / RIGHT LEG PRINCIPLE
- TYPES OF ACTION LINES
- COIL AND SPRING

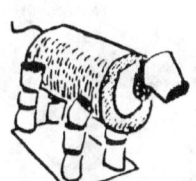

SECTION THREE
BODY CONSTRUCTION

- BUILDING SHAPES --
  LARGE, MEDIUM, UNUSUAL!
- FORESHORTENING
- DON'T LET THEM 'FLOAT'.
- TECHNIQUES

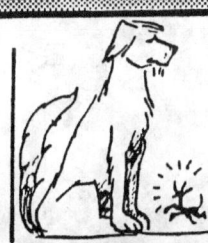

SECTION FOUR
'MAN'S BEST FRIEND'

- BIG AND STRONG
- LIGHT AND SWIFT
- SKETCHES / CARICATURES
- CHECK YOUR PROGRESS

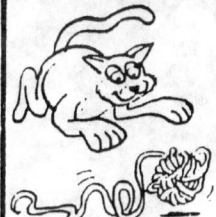

SECTION FIVE
CATS

- SEARCH FOR PERSONALITY
- GETTING ACQUAINTED
- THE 'MULTI-PURPOSE' FACE

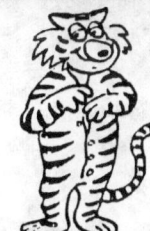

SECTION SIX
'HUMANIZING' ANIMALS

- THE MIND'S 'COSTUME SHOP'.
- RESEARCH + IMAGINATION
- GIVE THEM A ROLE TO PLAY
- BIRDS AND PEOPLE

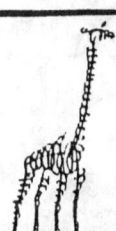

SECTION SEVEN
SKETCHING REMINDER

- FINDING REFERENCE MATERIAL
- 3 SKETCHING METHODS
- ANIMAL ILLUSTRATIONS
- REVIEW CHAPTERS THREE & FOUR

SPECIAL TIP!!
THINK UP LITTLE 'TAG LINES', GAGS,
OR STORY LINES TO ACCOMPANY
EACH OF YOUR ANIMAL DRAWINGS.
IT'S GREAT MENTAL EXERCISE...
AND FUN!

The beautiful nineteenth-century wood engravings used extensively throughout this chapter as examples of excellent reference material are selections from the book 'Animals - A Dover Pictorial Archive Series, Jim Harter.' and are reprinted courtesy Dover Publications, Inc., N,Y.,N.Y.

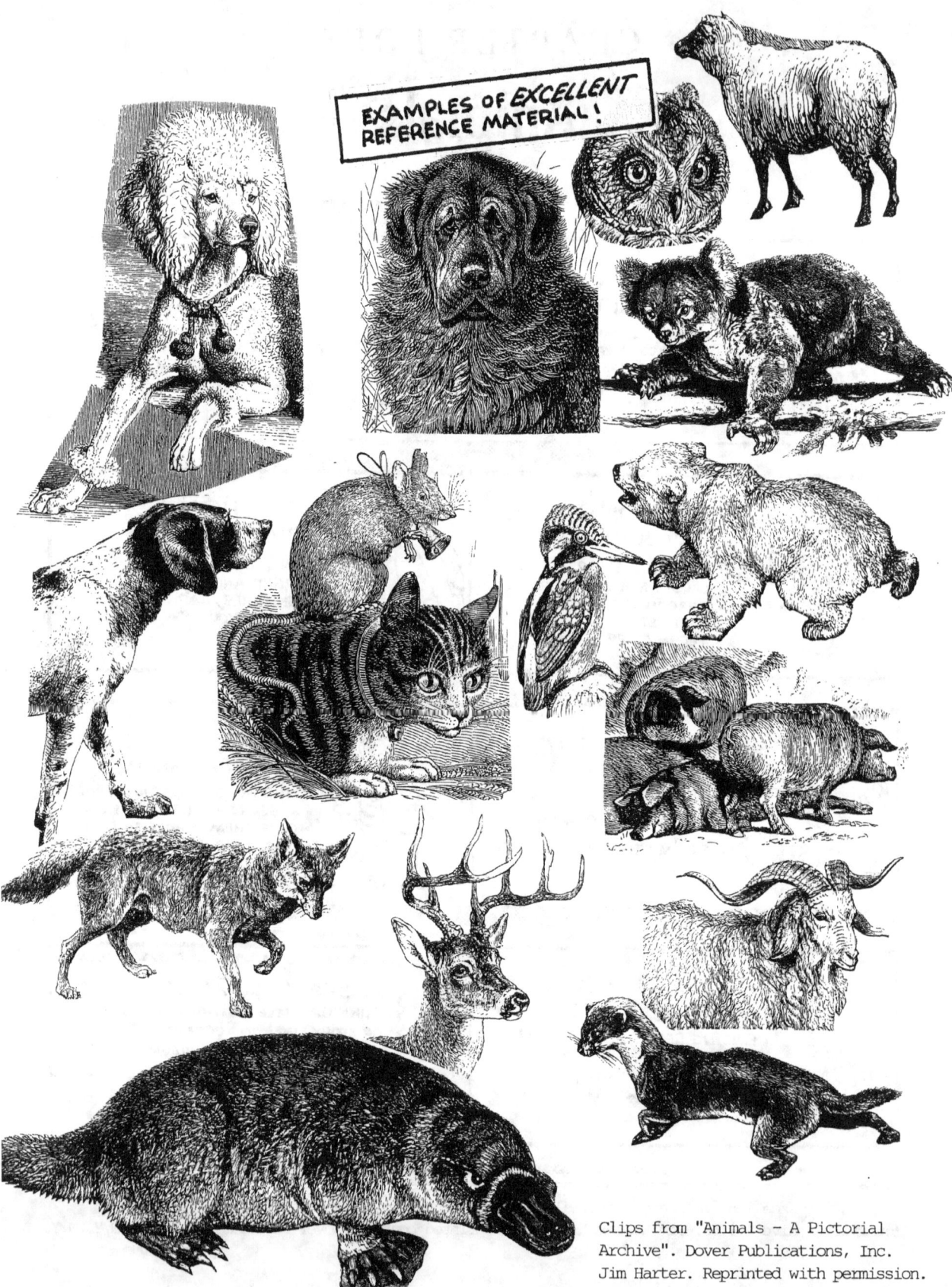

Clips from "Animals – A Pictorial
Archive". Dover Publications, Inc.
Jim Harter. Reprinted with permission.

The cartoon animal has been a universally popular subject for many years and its future looks brighter now than ever before.

Any extra time and effort the student puts into this chapter can pay rich dividends. Cartooning horizons will be broadened, drawing skills will improve, powers of observation will be sharpened, and creativity will be enhanced.

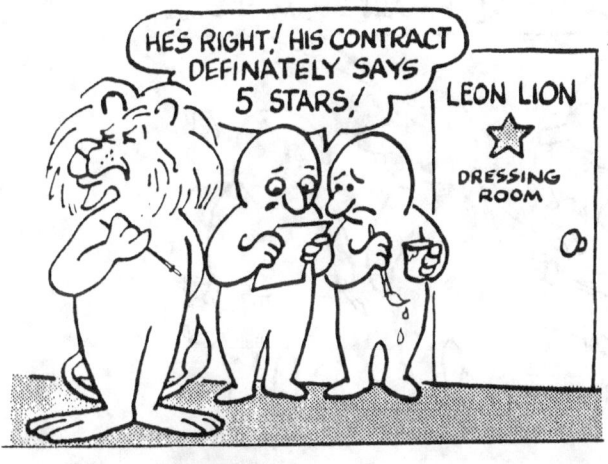

If Mickey Mouse came face to face with Garfield or Heathcliff, it's possible that Marmaduke would come to his rescue.

Krazy Kat might throw a brick at poor Mickey, while Felix the Cat would likely suggest malpractice against the whole bunch.

Ophus would want to referee the proceedings as Snoopy took notes.

Such is the wonderful world of cartoon animals. A universal favorite!

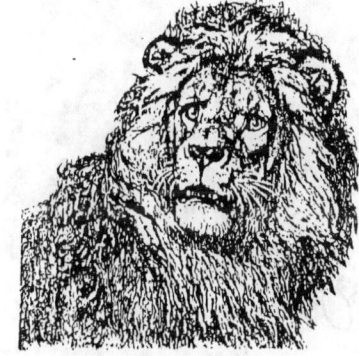

Cartoon animals are usually portrayed in one of three ways:

CARTOONERIZED when used in a minor role.
CARICATURE-IZED when co-starring in a feature.
HUMANIZED when used as a star performer.

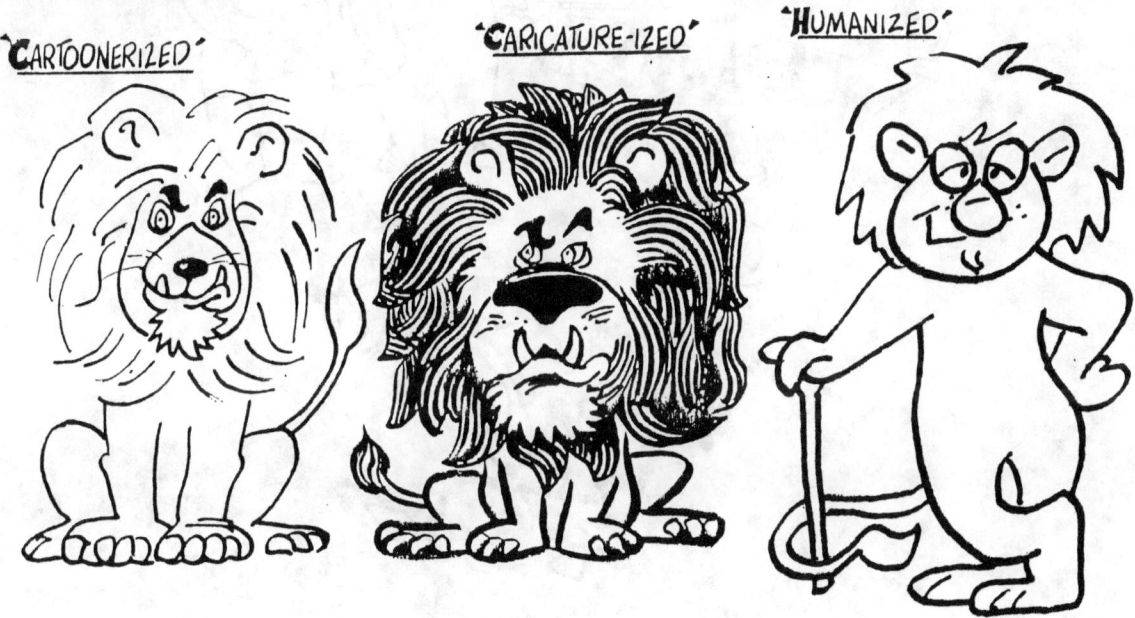

"CARTOONERIZED"   "CARICATURE-IZED"   "HUMANIZED"

ANIMALS HAVE EXTRA ELBOWS, KNEES, AND ANKLES

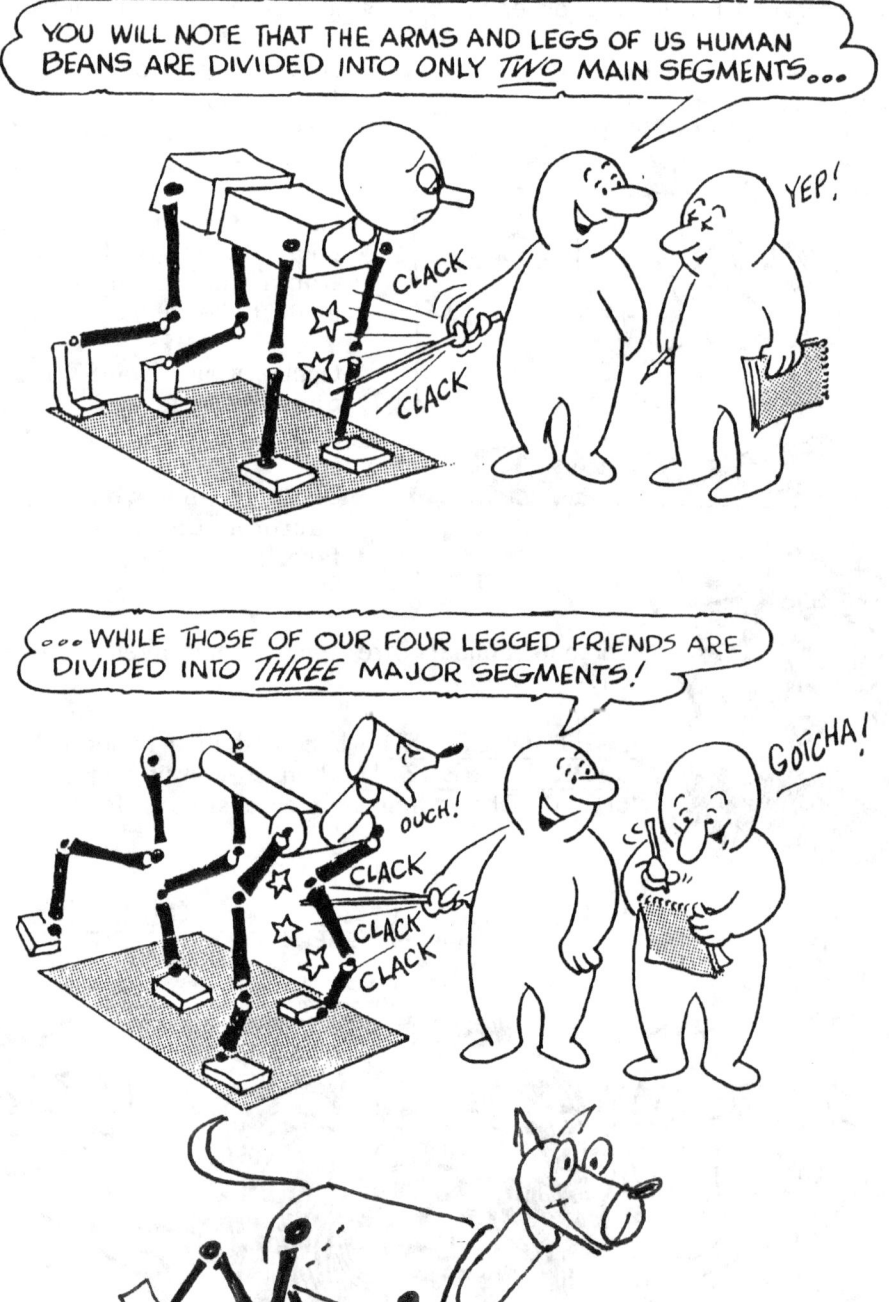

All those "extra" elbows, knees, and stuff are very important to our four-legged friends.

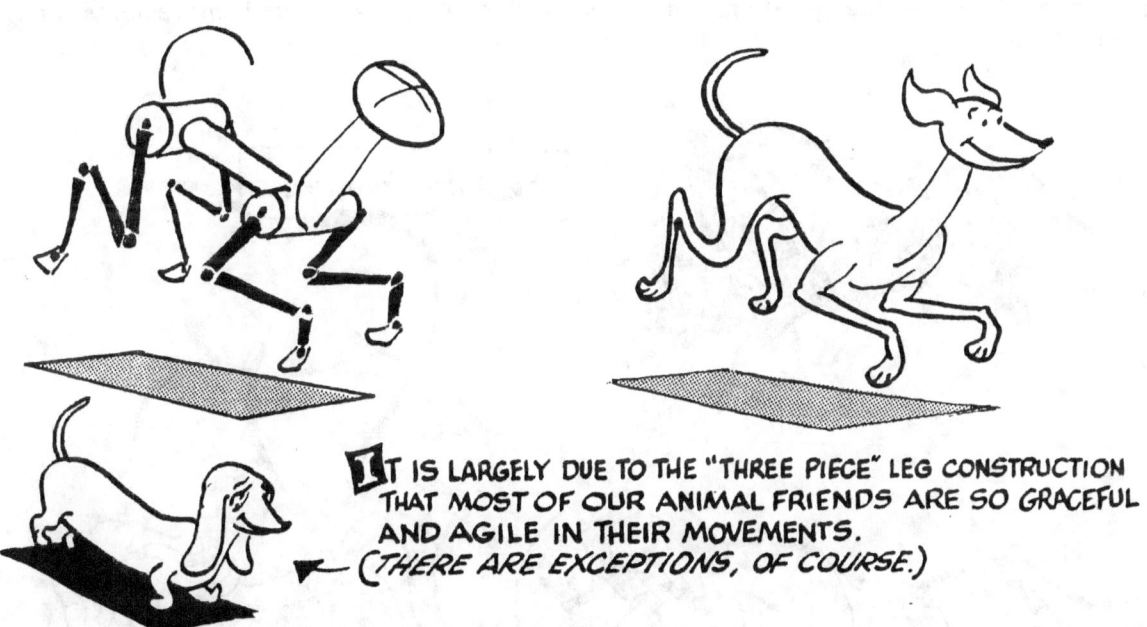

IT IS LARGELY DUE TO THE "THREE PIECE" LEG CONSTRUCTION THAT MOST OF OUR ANIMAL FRIENDS ARE SO GRACEFUL AND AGILE IN THEIR MOVEMENTS. *(THERE ARE EXCEPTIONS, OF COURSE.)*

TAILS CAN FREQUENTLY BE CONSIDERED AS AN ANIMAL'S "FIFTH" LEG!

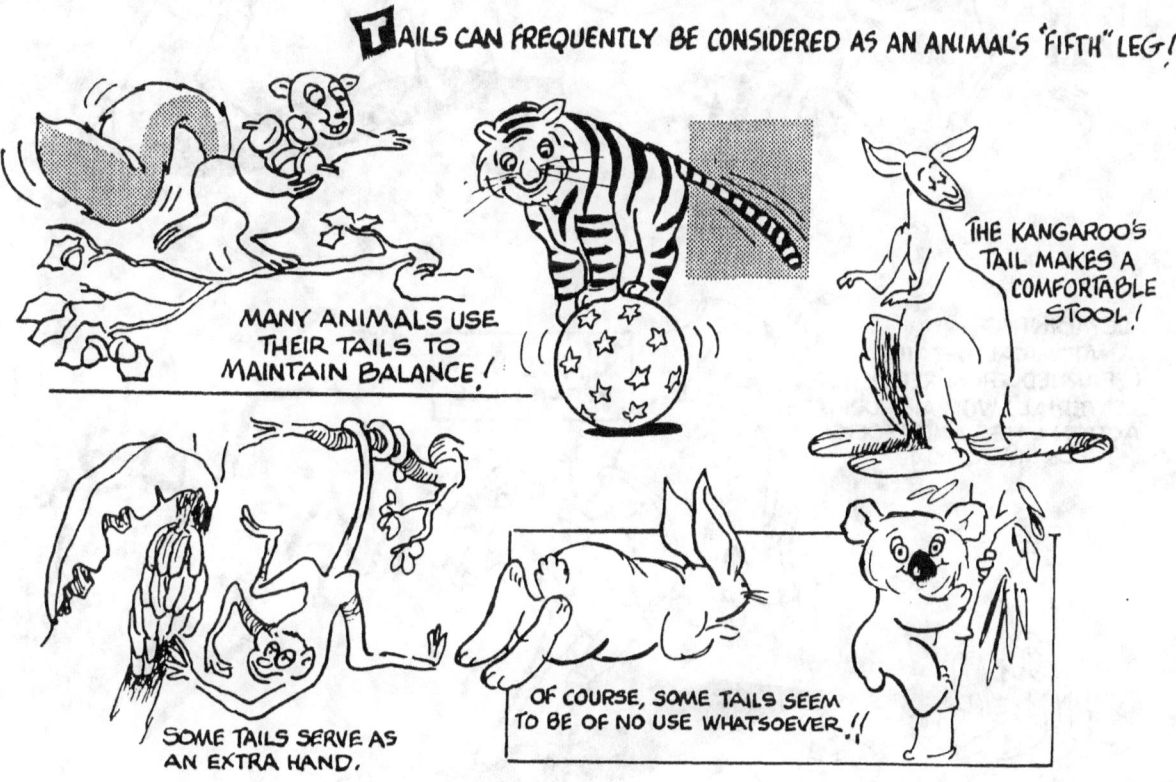

MANY ANIMALS USE THEIR TAILS TO MAINTAIN BALANCE!

THE KANGAROO'S TAIL MAKES A COMFORTABLE STOOL!

SOME TAILS SERVE AS AN EXTRA HAND.

OF COURSE, SOME TAILS SEEM TO BE OF NO USE WHATSOEVER!!

Every species of animal has its own special style of movement and action. Some are heavy footed and move about slowly and deliberately, while others are light footed, swift, and graceful.

Experiment with exaggerations of a particular animal's typical movements and mannerisms.

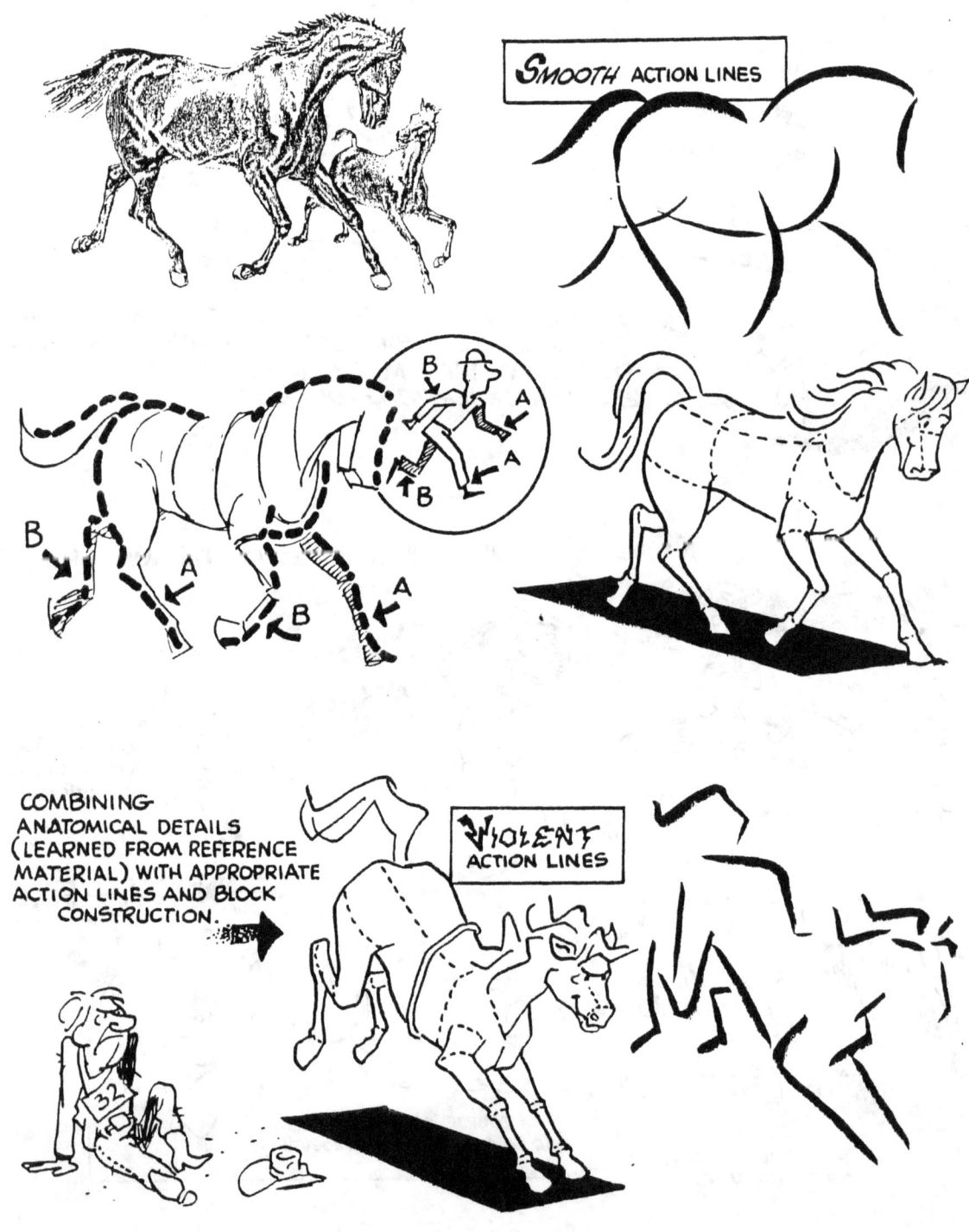

Since most cartoons are supposed to be <u>funny</u>, the cartoonist is not necessarily restricted to nature's rules of balance, motion, and action.   Often, breaking those rules can result in some very humorous effects.   The student, however, <u>should know the rules first</u> before attempting to goof around with them.

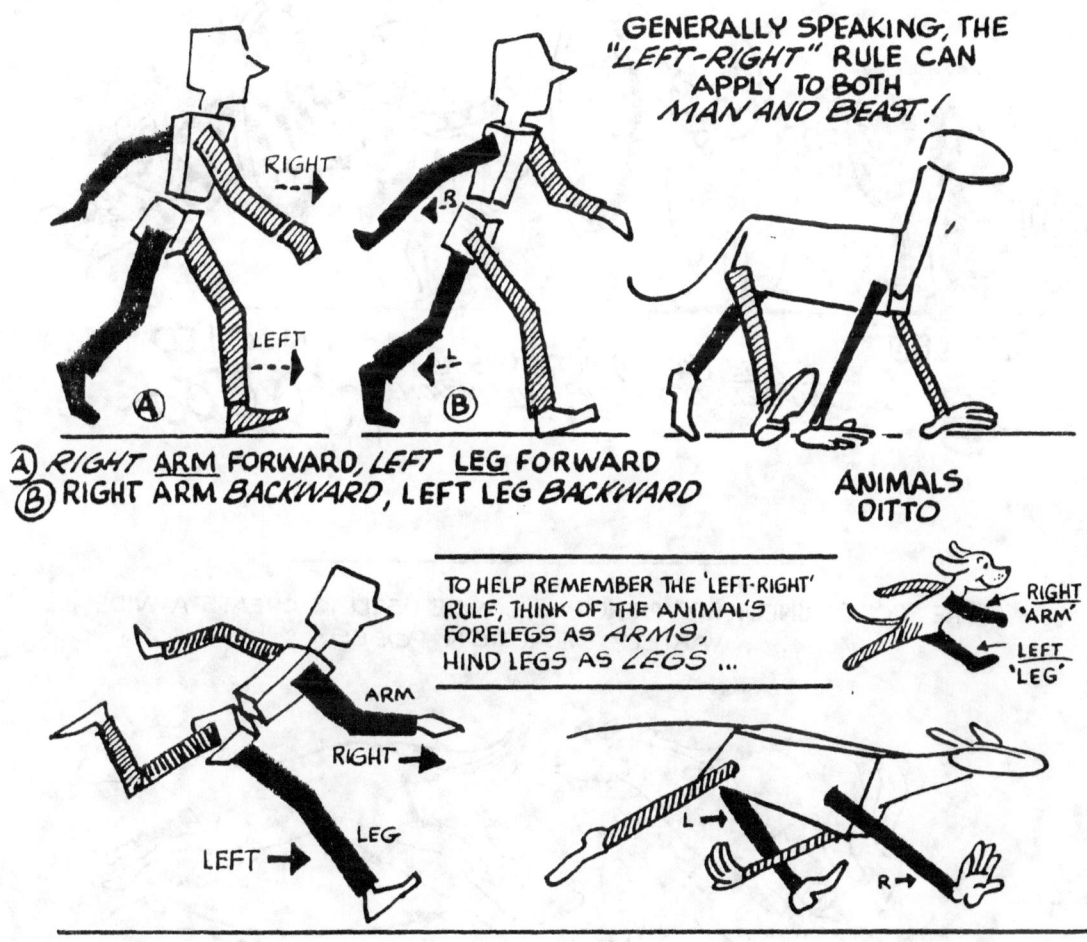

GENERALLY SPEAKING, THE "LEFT-RIGHT" RULE CAN APPLY TO BOTH MAN AND BEAST!

Ⓐ *RIGHT* <u>ARM</u> FORWARD, *LEFT* <u>LEG</u> FORWARD
Ⓑ RIGHT ARM *BACKWARD*, LEFT LEG *BACKWARD*

ANIMALS DITTO

TO HELP REMEMBER THE 'LEFT-RIGHT' RULE, THINK OF THE ANIMAL'S FORELEGS AS *ARMS*, HIND LEGS AS *LEGS* ...

RIGHT 'ARM'
LEFT 'LEG'

ARM
RIGHT ➤
LEFT ➤ LEG

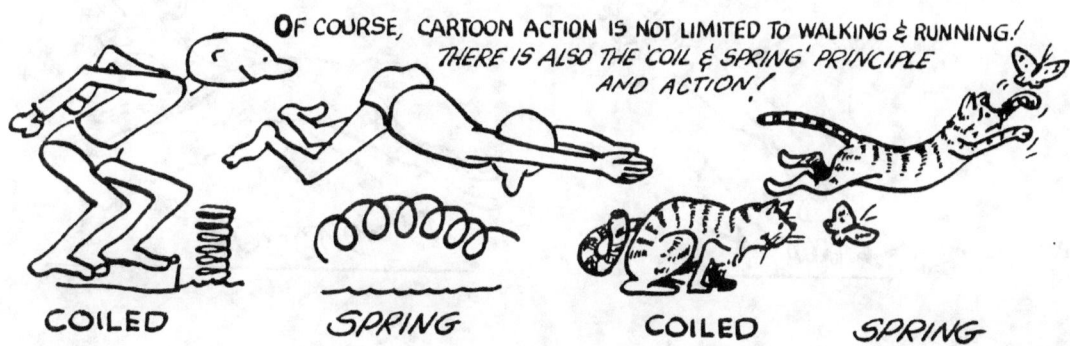

OF COURSE, CARTOON ACTION IS NOT LIMITED TO WALKING & RUNNING! THERE IS ALSO THE 'COIL & SPRING' PRINCIPLE AND ACTION!

COILED   *SPRING*   COILED   *SPRING*

By using the basic principles of movement, action, and construction, the cartoonist can "teach" his or her cartoon animals to do almost anything!

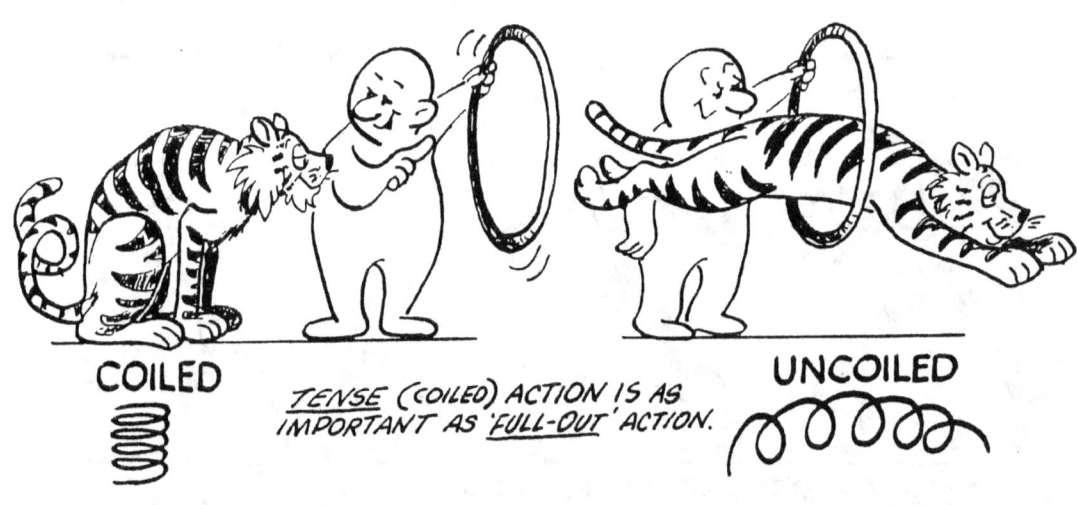

COILED

UNCOILED

TENSE (COILED) ACTION IS AS IMPORTANT AS 'FULL-OUT' ACTION.

THE "COILED-UNCOILED" PRINCIPLE CAN BE USED TO CREATE A WIDE VARIETY OF ACTION POSES!

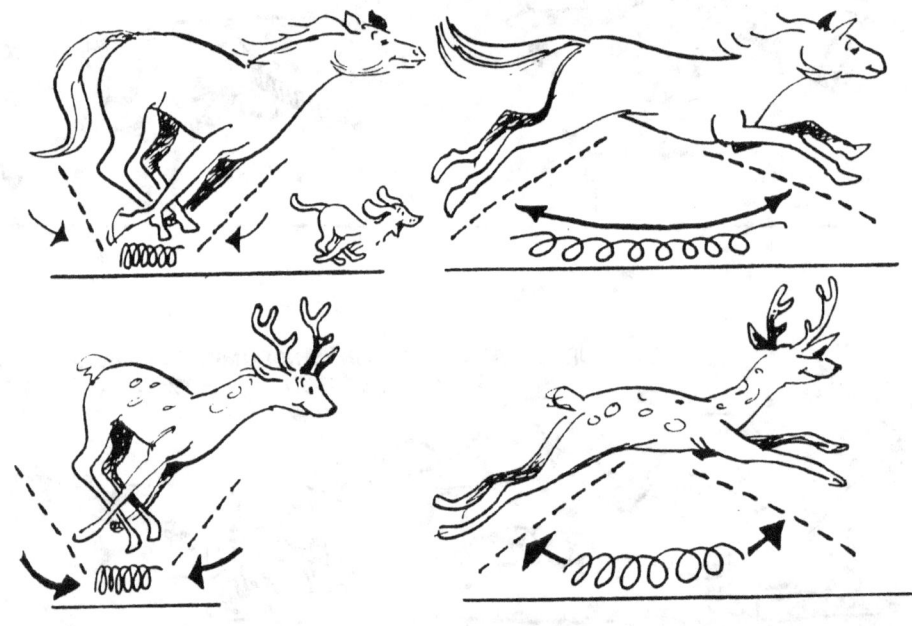

Careful study and consideration must be given to the basic overall shape and appearance of each species of animals. Additionally, an indication of a particular animal's <u>character</u> and <u>personality</u> should be portrayed and exaggerated.

When starting to construct an animal, an effort should be made to determine what the creature is doing, or about to do, what it might be thinking, and how it might feel.

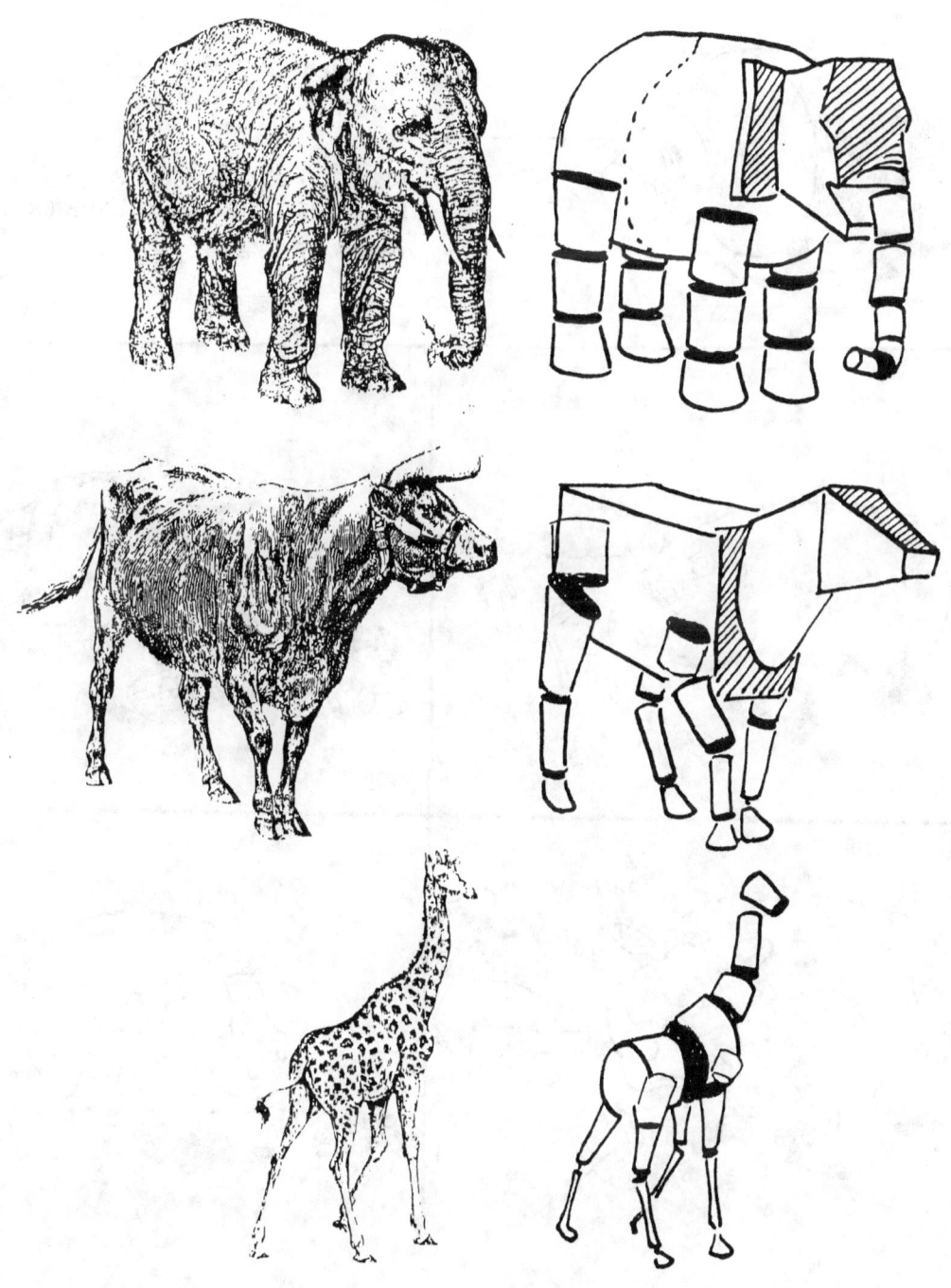

Every animal has its own particular "stance and poise." Those <u>characteristics</u> help determine its <u>personality</u>, much as it does in humans. That is not to say, however, that personalities cannot be switched around. How about a rhino that LOVES people, or a hippo that is addicted to honey.

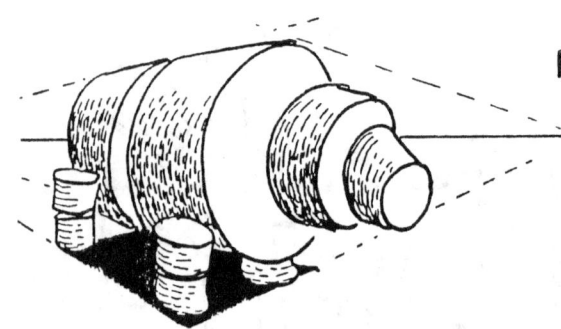

HEAVY BODIED ANIMALS.
THINK BULK!

PROPER PERSPECTIVE & SHADOWS KEEP THEM FIRMLY ON THE GROUND.
DON'T LET THEM FLOAT!

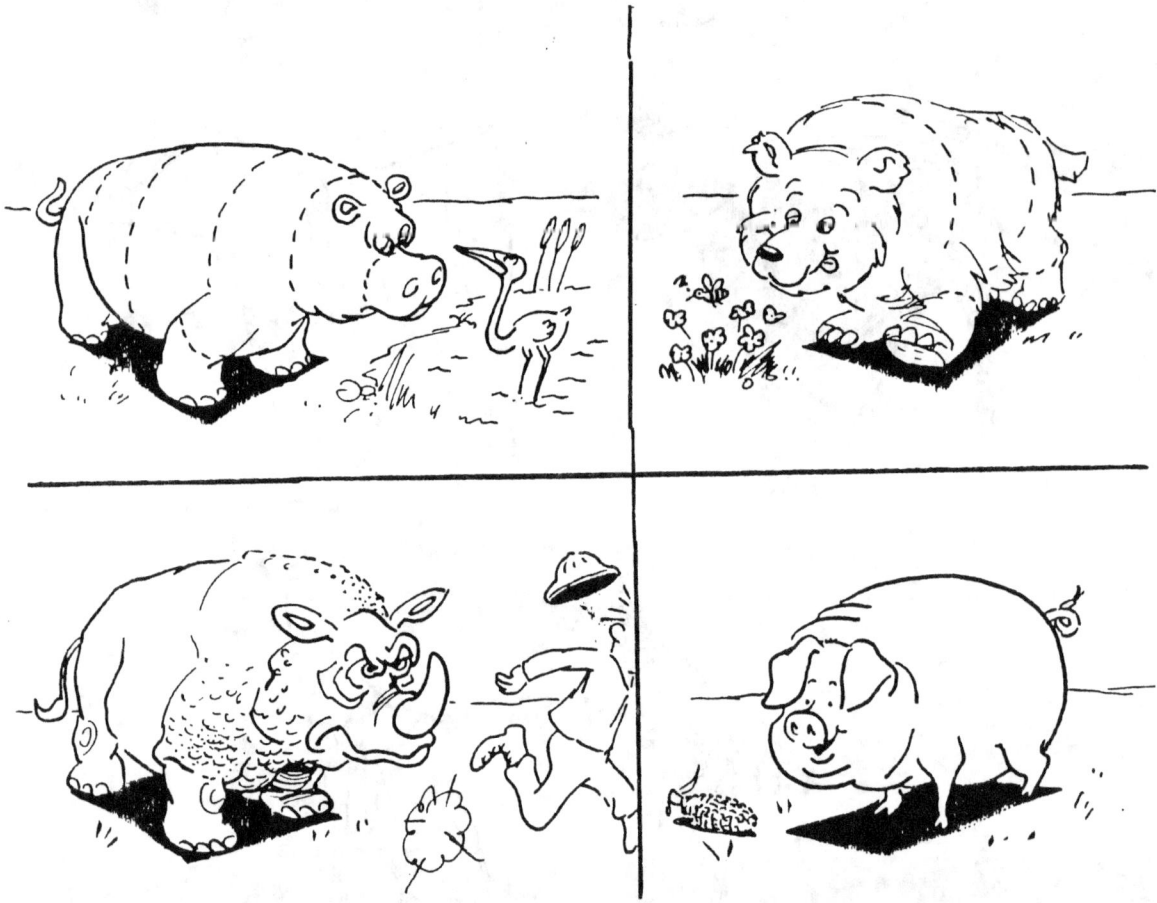

As with humans, animals have their own particular interests and purposes.

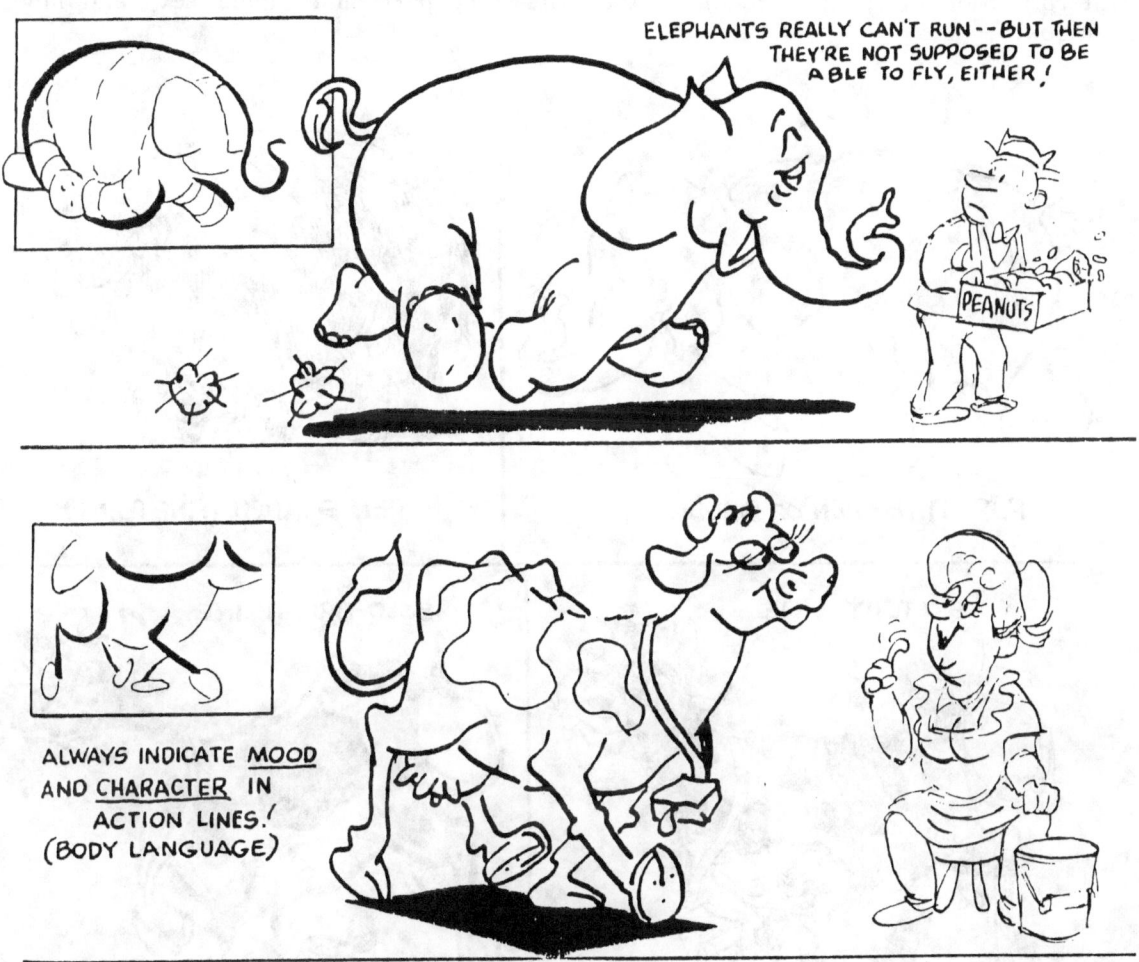

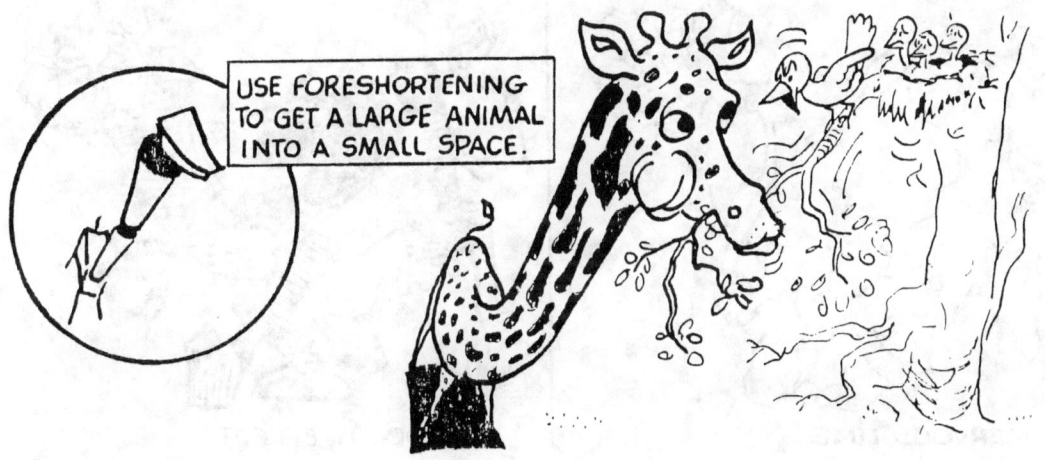

It is important that the student <u>experiment</u> with a variety of line and shading techniques. Doing so will help in the development of <u>individual style</u> and interpretation. Find a technique that fits your particular "mind set" and mental outlook.

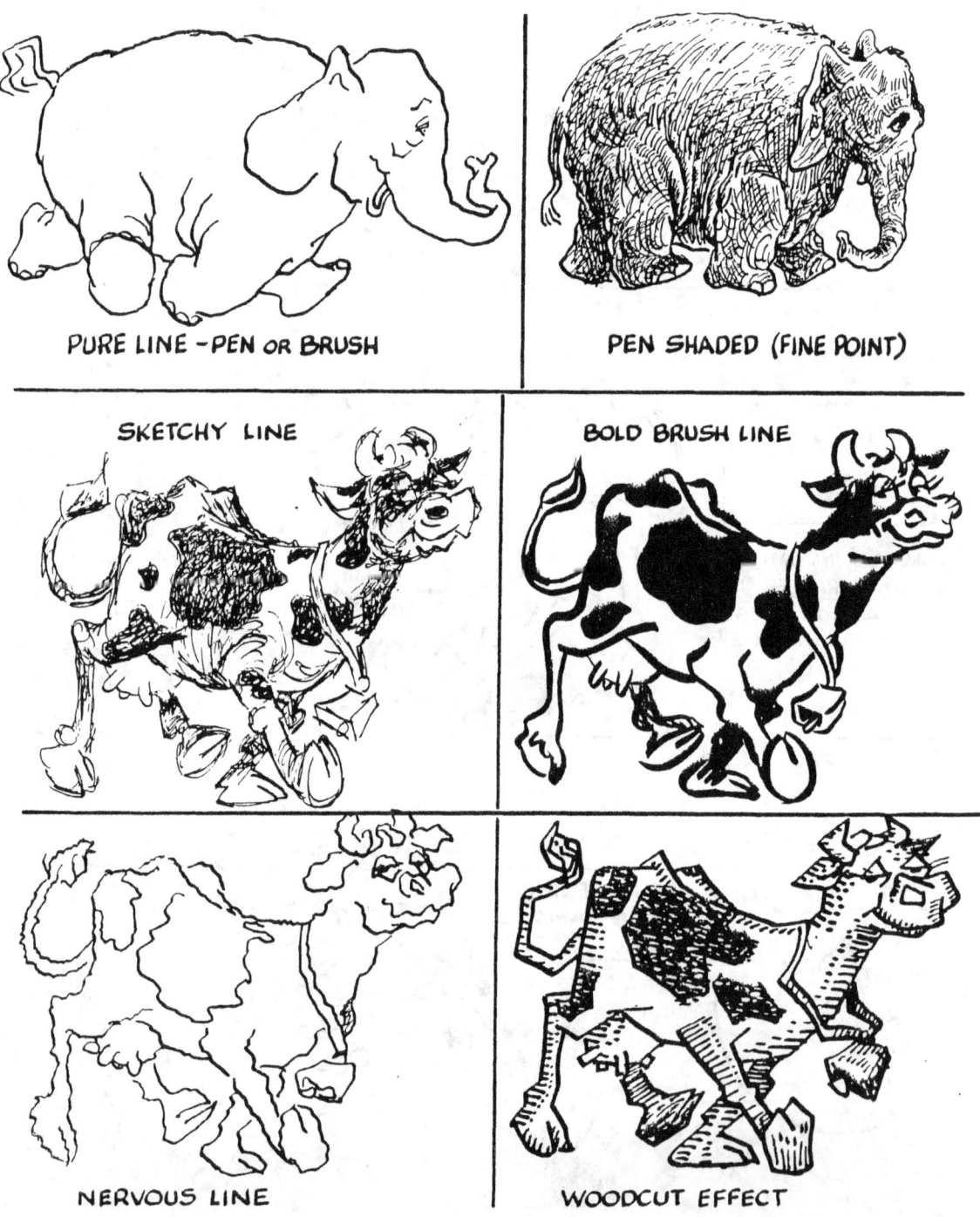

PURE LINE – PEN or BRUSH   PEN SHADED (FINE POINT)

SKETCHY LINE   BOLD BRUSH LINE

NERVOUS LINE   WOODCUT EFFECT

When it comes to unusual shapes, the camel and giraffe top the list! Their unique qualities can provide the cartoonist with lots of material.

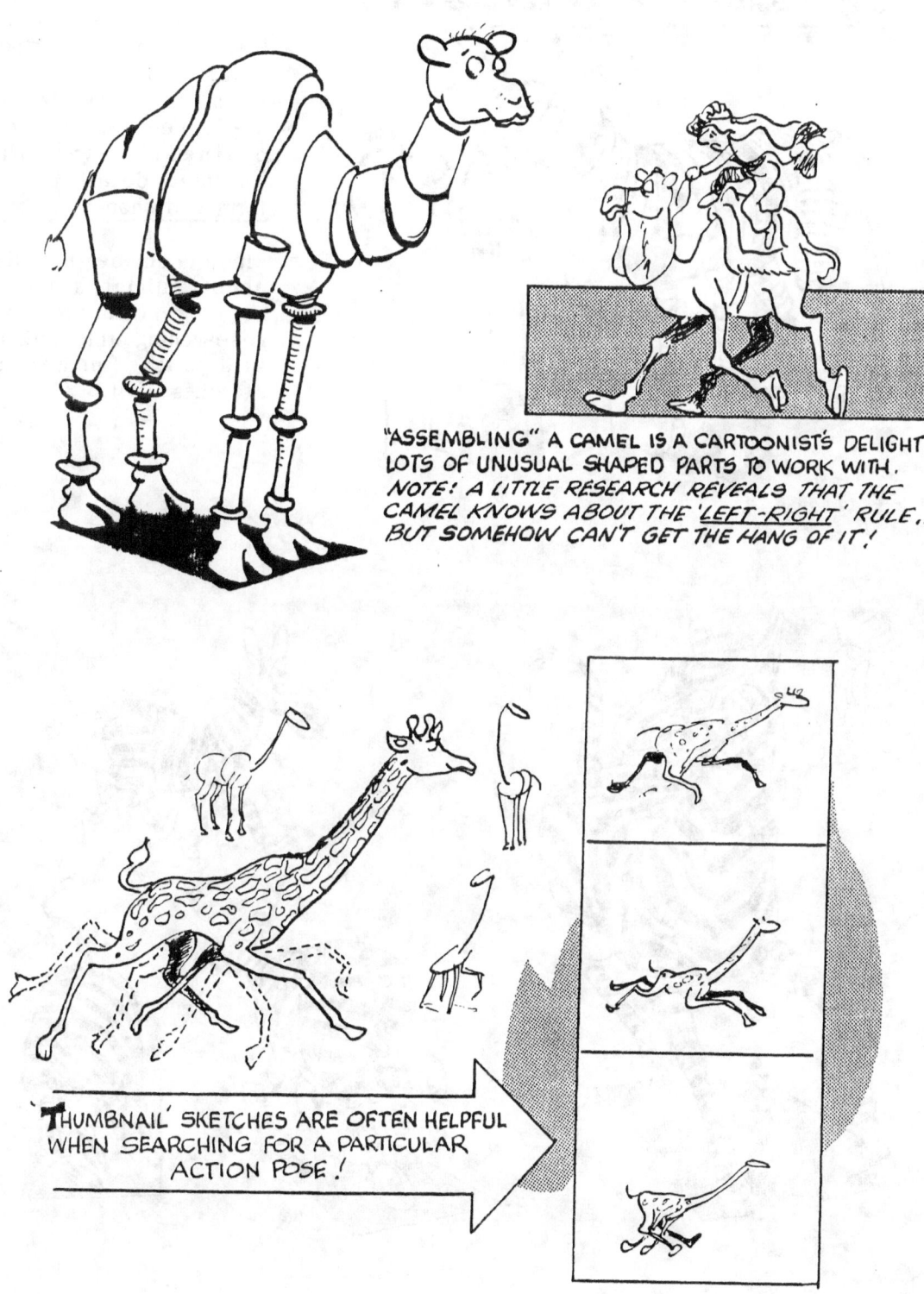

"ASSEMBLING" A CAMEL IS A CARTOONIST'S DELIGHT!
LOTS OF UNUSUAL SHAPED PARTS TO WORK WITH.
NOTE: A LITTLE RESEARCH REVEALS THAT THE
CAMEL KNOWS ABOUT THE 'LEFT-RIGHT' RULE...
BUT SOMEHOW CAN'T GET THE HANG OF IT!

'THUMBNAIL' SKETCHES ARE OFTEN HELPFUL
WHEN SEARCHING FOR A PARTICULAR
ACTION POSE!

NATURE'S OWN DRAWING INSTRUCTOR

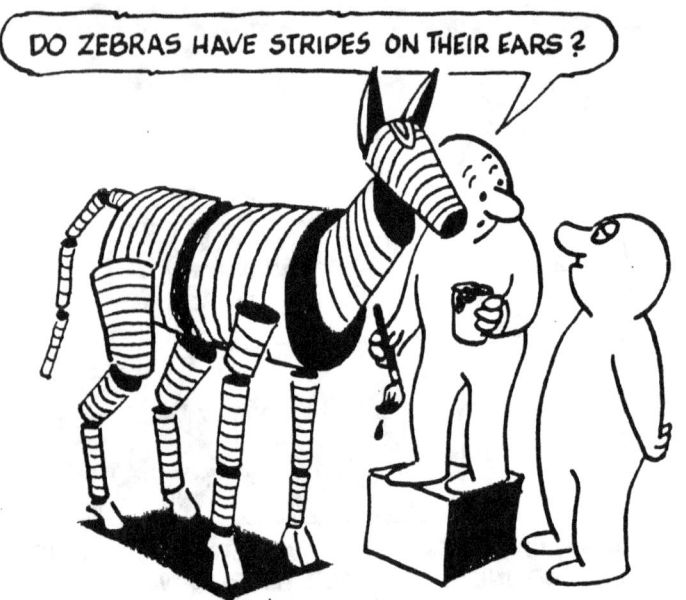

The zebra more clearly illustrates the principles of body construction than any other animal. Its well-defined stripes delineate even the smallest detail of its <u>form and shape</u>.

Much can be learned about animal structure and movement by researching this animal and doing numerous sketches of it.

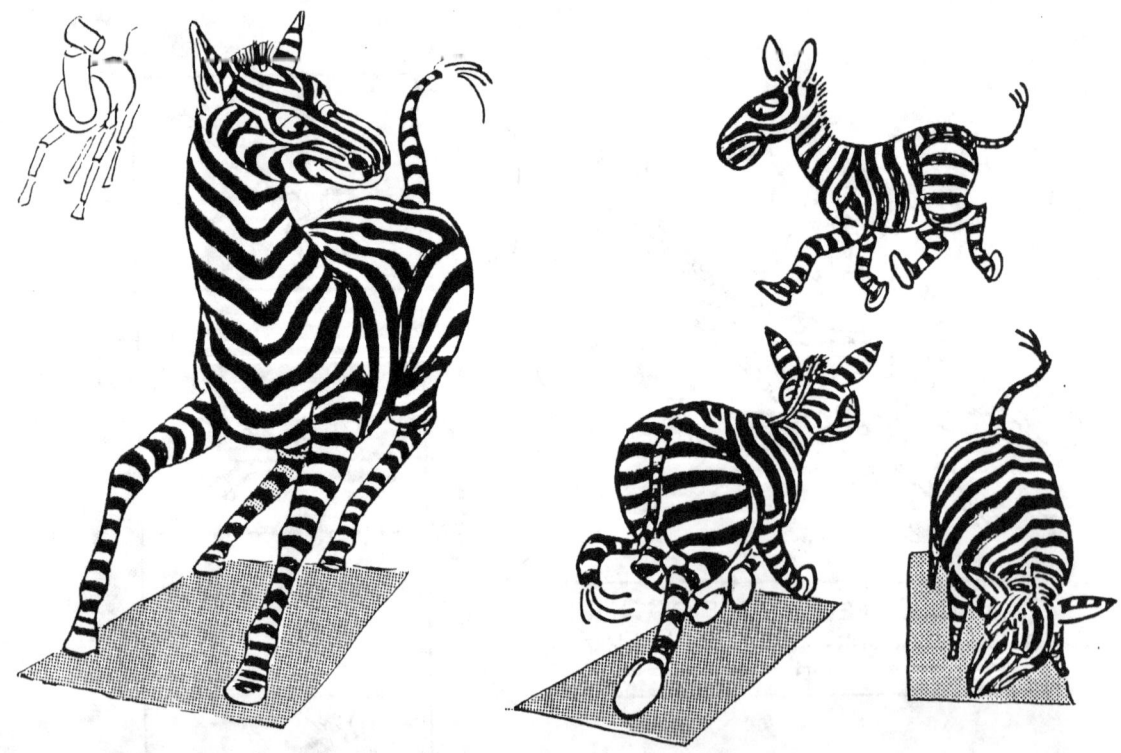

EXPERIMENT WITH LINE STYLES, DISTORTIONS, AND EXAGGERATIONS!

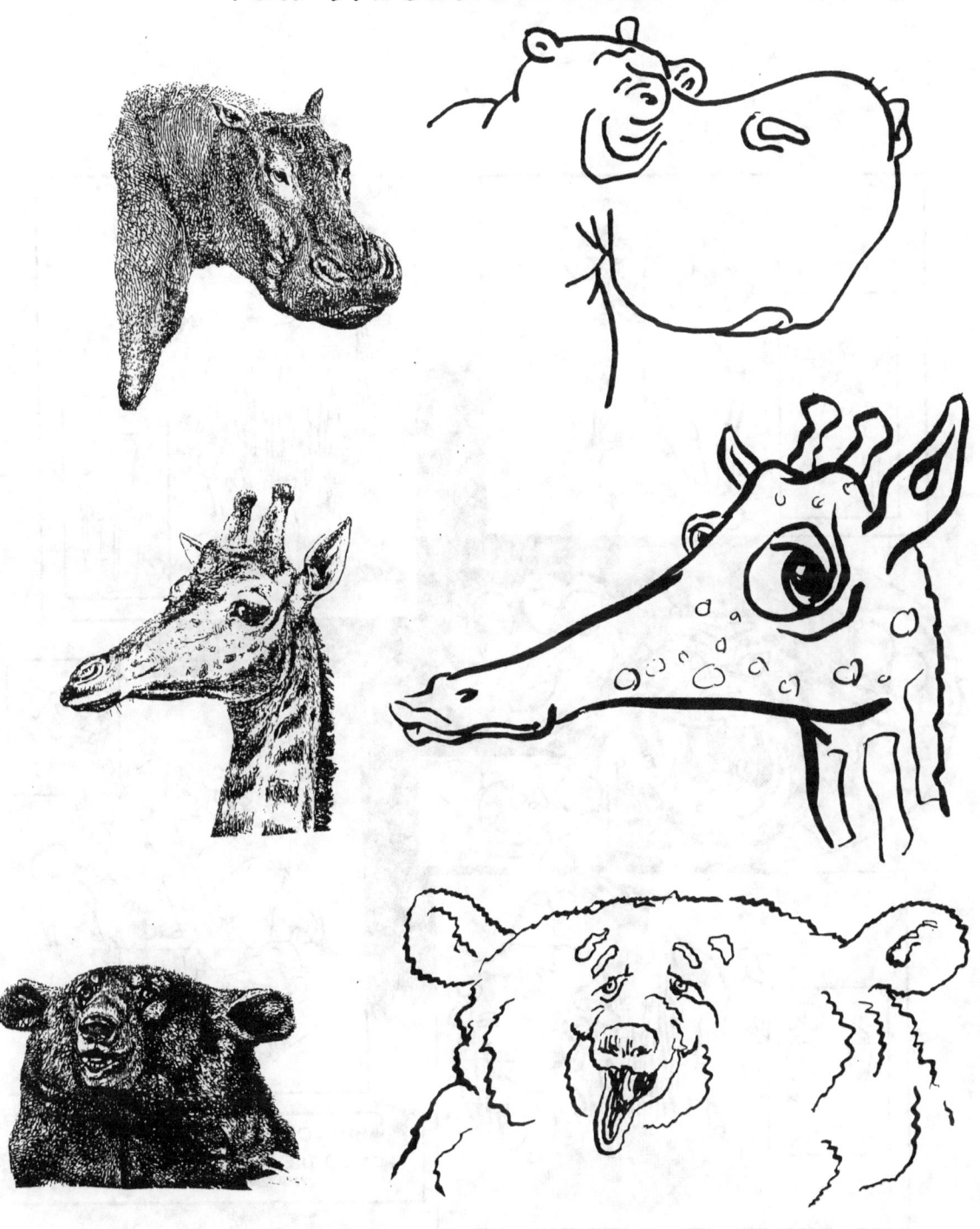

Due to certain space limitations or predetermined page layouts, cartoonists are frequently required to <u>work within a given area</u>. Sketch out a variety of squares, circles, rectangles, and ovals and draw your subject <u>within</u> those areas. Line techniques should be bold and simplified for the small areas, varied and interesting in the larger areas.

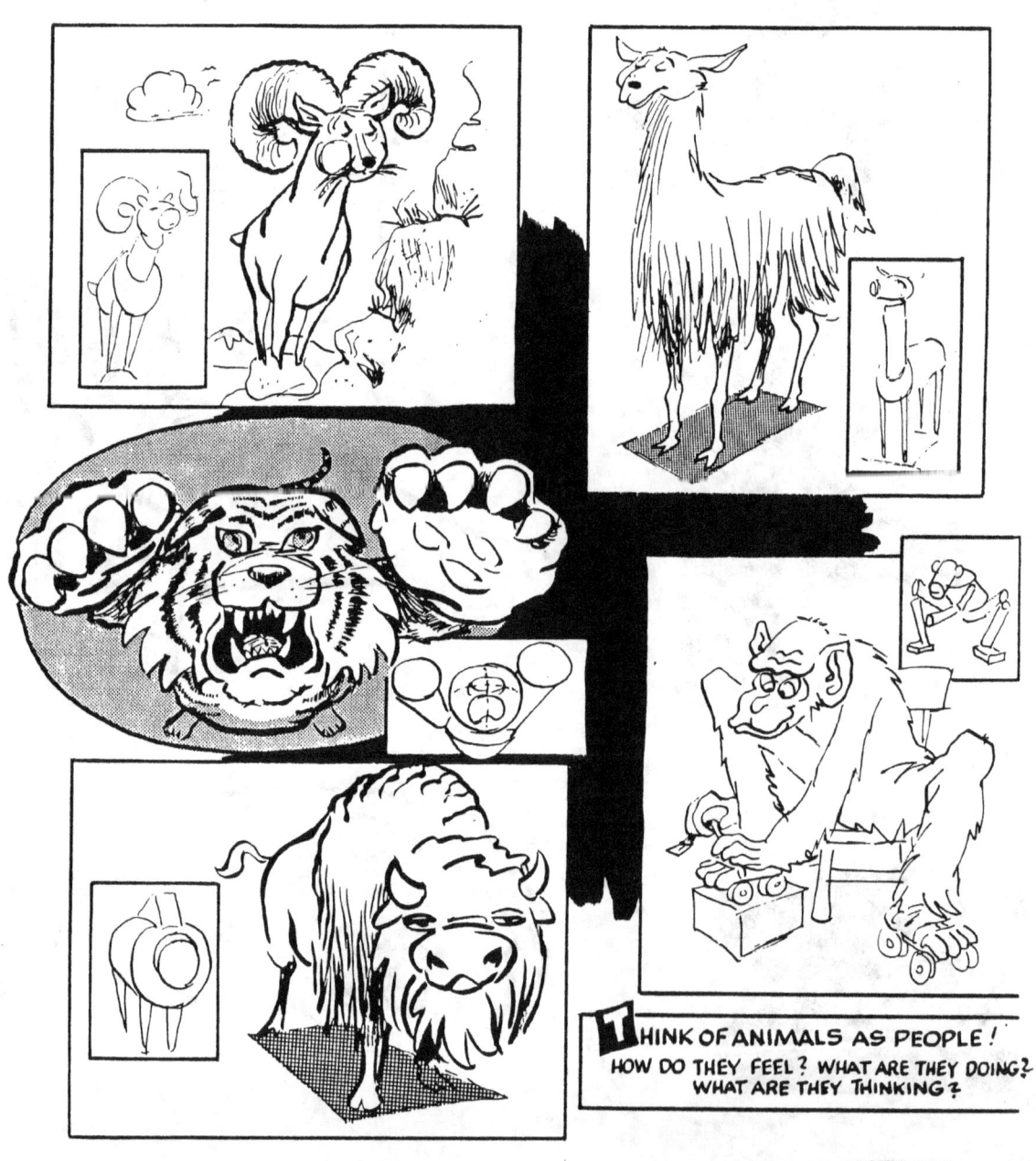

An elephant, for the most part, is an elephant, and a tiger is a tiger. But DOGS ... now they're something else again!

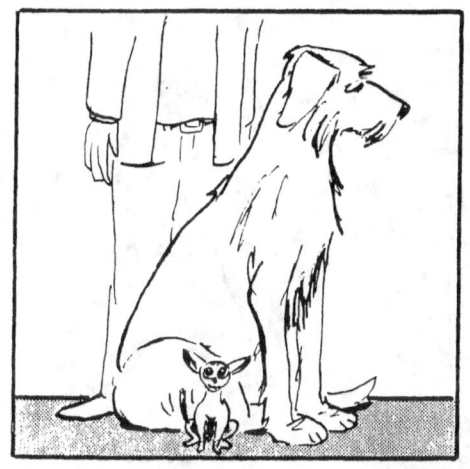

What a tremendous variety to work with! Dogs can weigh as little as a few ounces or as much as a hundred pounds. Some are swift and agile, while others seem to trip over their own feet. Long hair, short hair, or seemingly nude. Happy and lively, or bored and grumpy.

Dogs are truly wonderful creatures and are deserving of a little extra study and research.

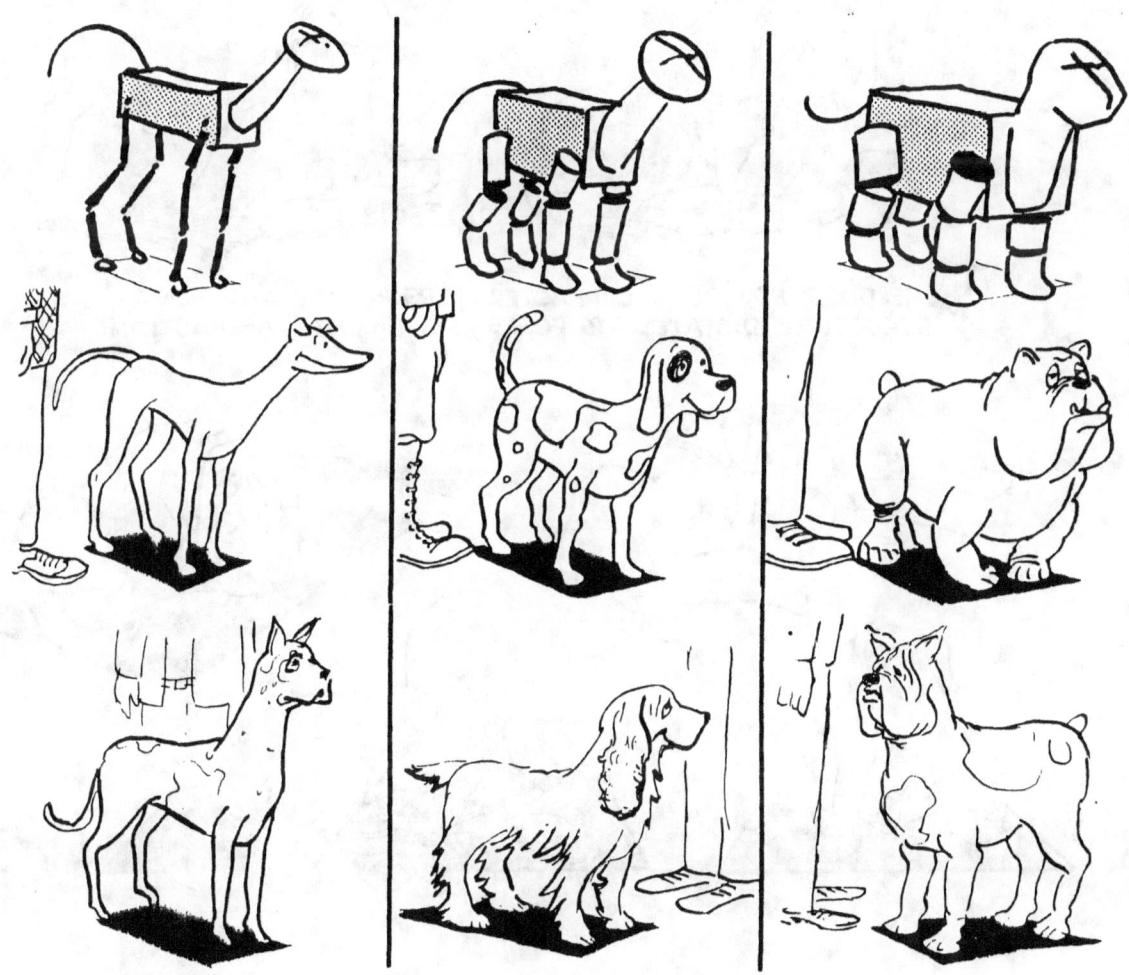

A dog's "pose" will indicate its <u>personality, character, and attitude.</u>   This can, of course, apply to ALL animals, birds, and fish (and insects, too).

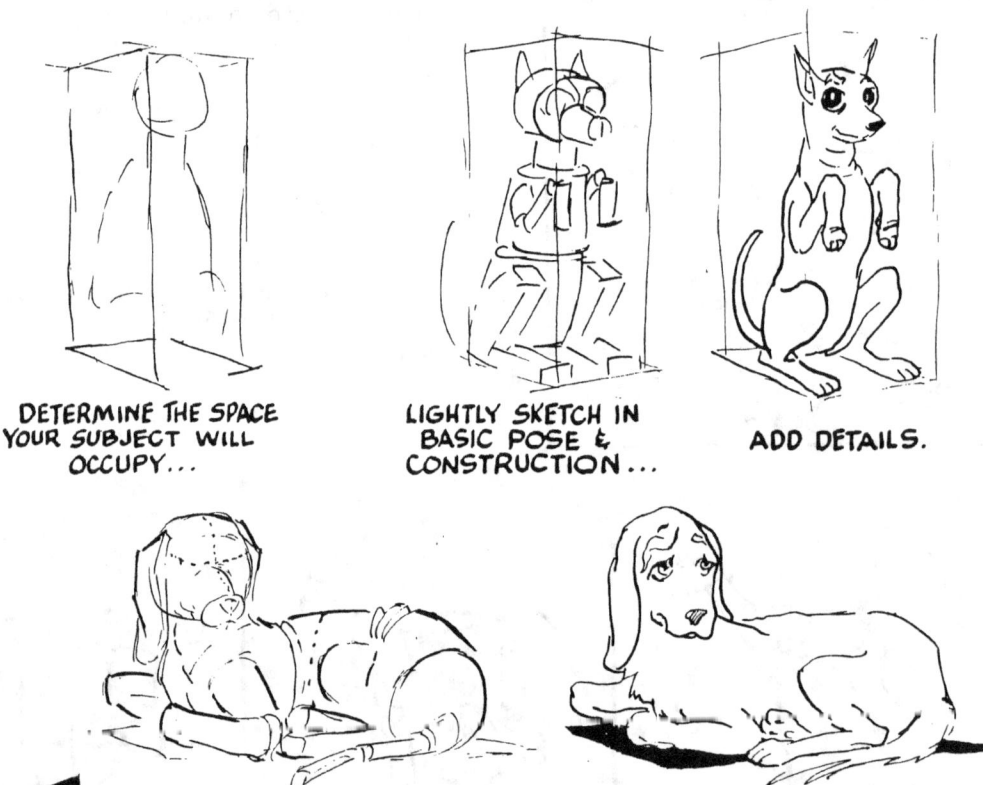

DETERMINE THE SPACE
YOUR SUBJECT WILL
OCCUPY...

LIGHTLY SKETCH IN
BASIC POSE &
CONSTRUCTION...

ADD DETAILS.

THE DOG'S INDIVIDUAL CHARACTER, PERSONALITY AND BODY
STRUCTURE DICTATES ITS POSES, MOVEMENTS, AND ACTION.

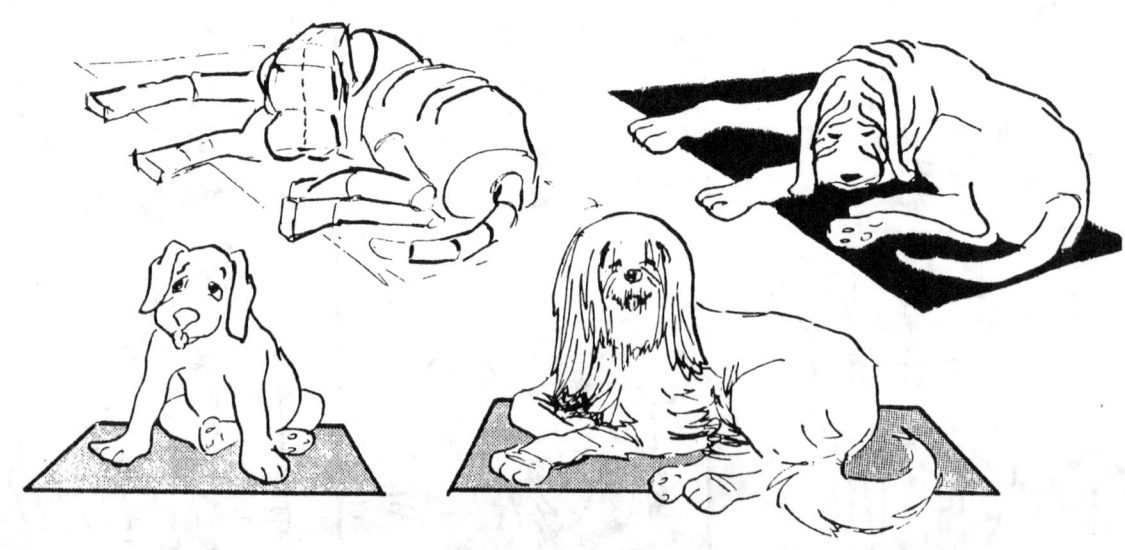

Sketch them! Draw them! Cartoonerize them! Caricaturize them!

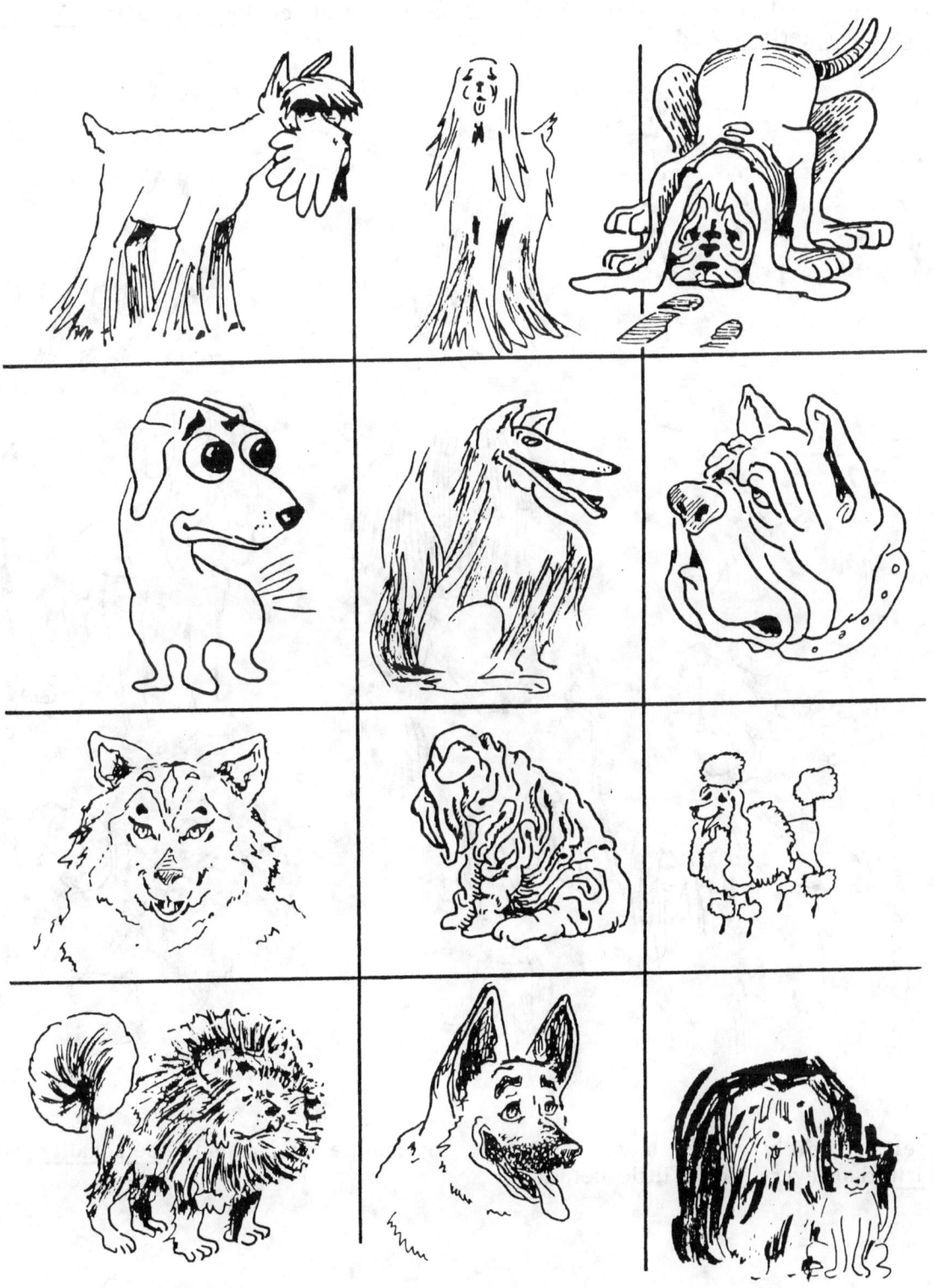

There are literally dozens (if not hundreds) of books, magazines, special publications, and booklets devoted especially to "Man's Best Friend." Most encyclopedias contain numerous pages on the subject. Pet shops often stock excellent booklets about dogs, cats, and birds. Collect <u>lots of information and research material.</u> And sketch, sketch, sketch!

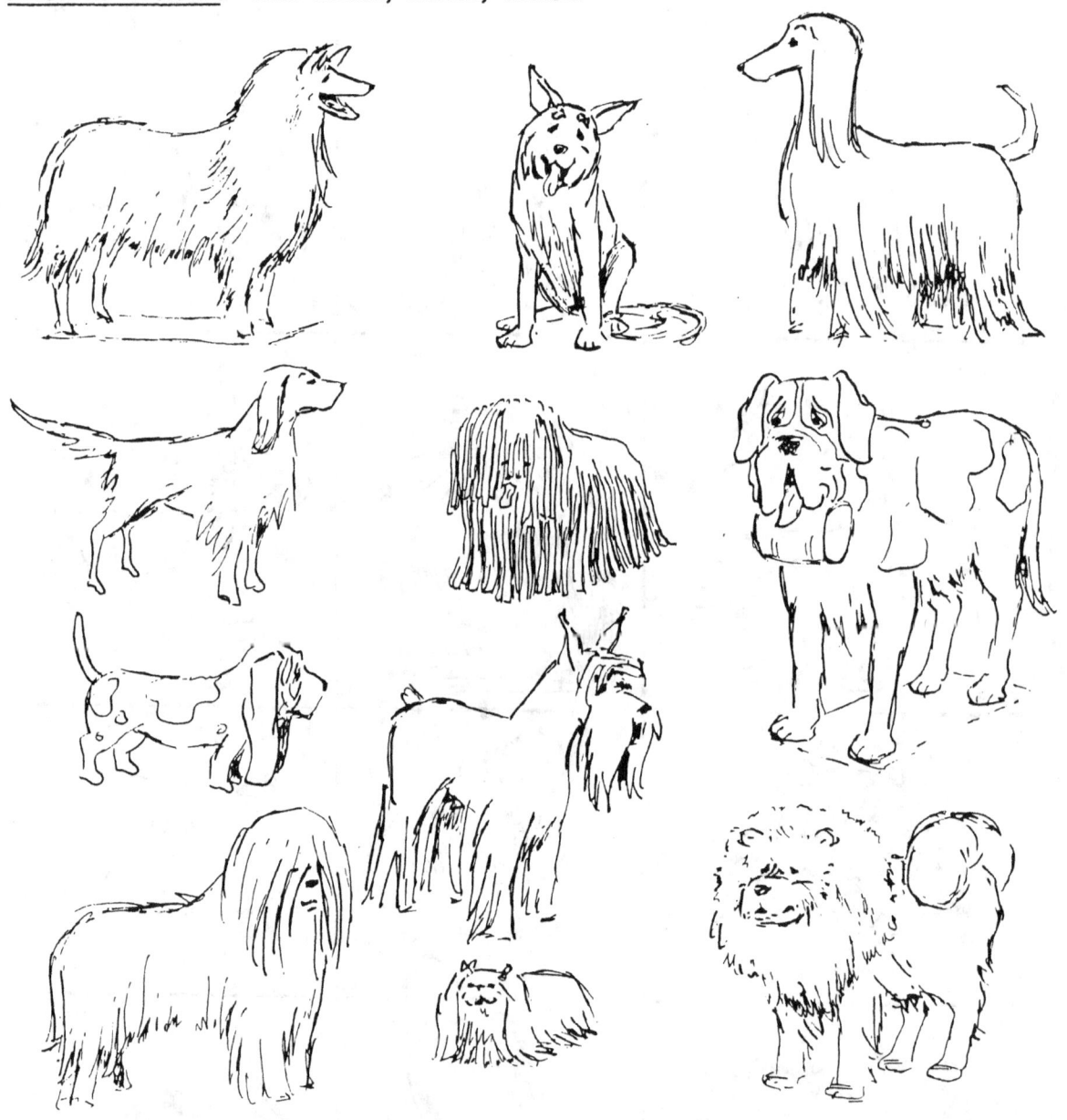

Sketch rapidly. It's more important to capture an animal's <u>personality</u> and <u>spirit</u> than every single little detail.

CREATIVE DRAWING
CHECK YOUR PROGRESS!

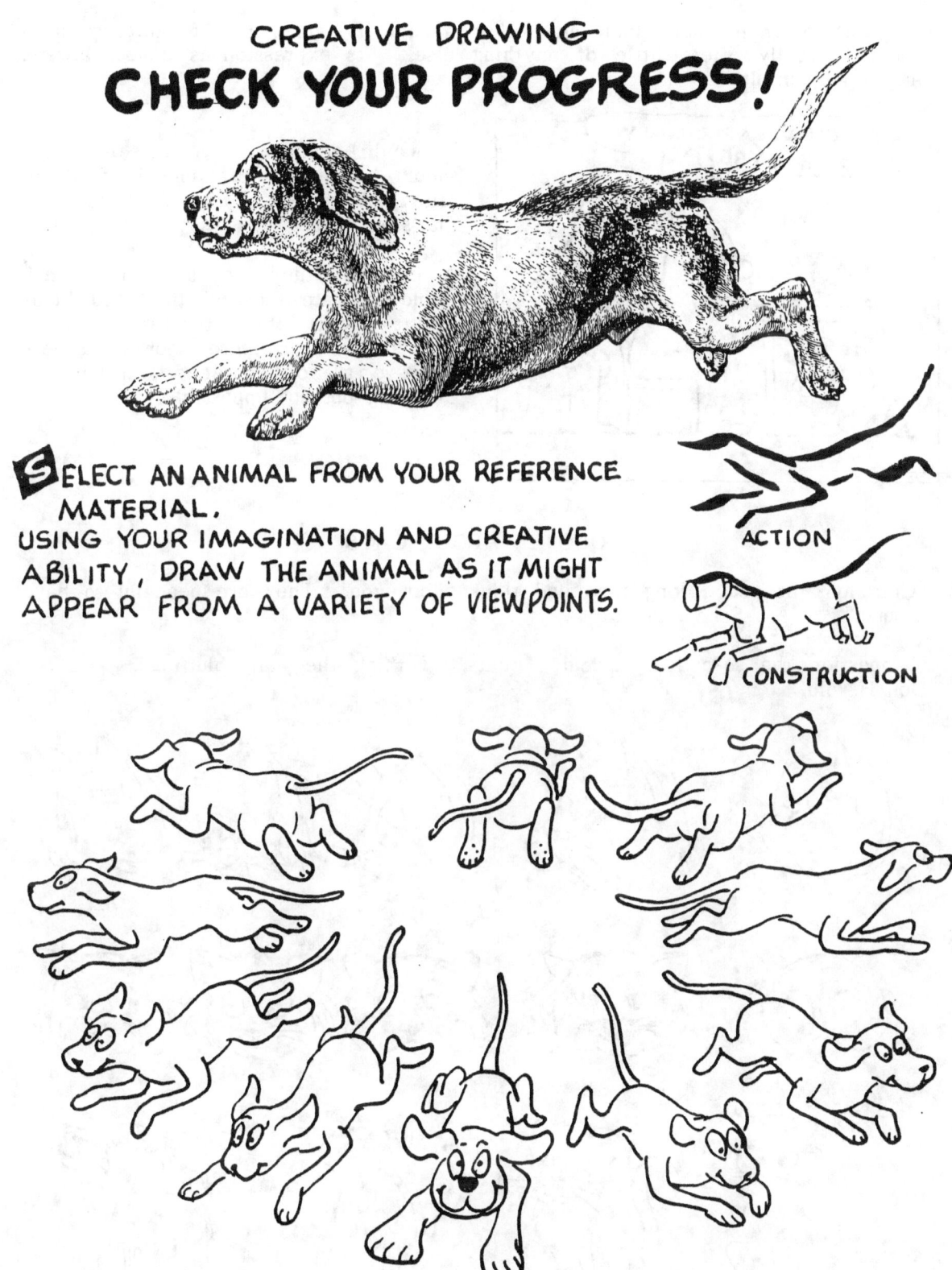

SELECT AN ANIMAL FROM YOUR REFERENCE MATERIAL.
USING YOUR IMAGINATION AND CREATIVE ABILITY, DRAW THE ANIMAL AS IT MIGHT APPEAR FROM A VARIETY OF VIEWPOINTS.

ACTION

CONSTRUCTION

The cat, perhaps more than any other animal, is wide open to <u>interpretation</u> since it usually offers little of anything else.   Its expression is almost always one of thoughtfulness.

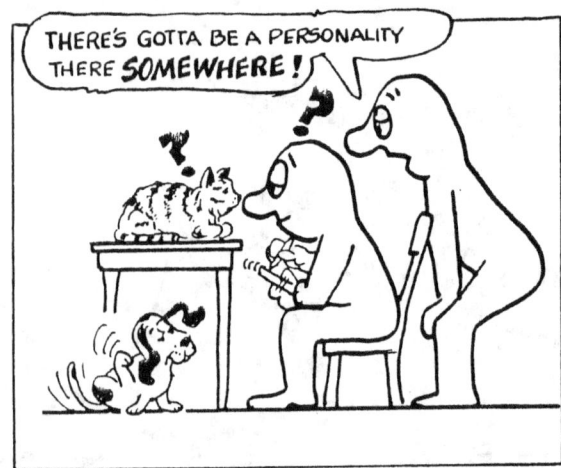

It would seem that a cat or kitten should be the easiest animal of all to draw.   A couple of circles, a tail, and that's it, right?

A careful study of "superstar cats" would indicate that all the good ideas about a cat character are already spoken for.   Is there another "superstar cat" out there somewhere? Doubtful, but not impossible.

QUOTES ABOUT CATS

"Cats look at you a long time and think about you.   They are peaceful to have around." . . . . School child.

"I question the so-called wisdom of cats.   I think they are bluffing."   . . . . Don Herold.

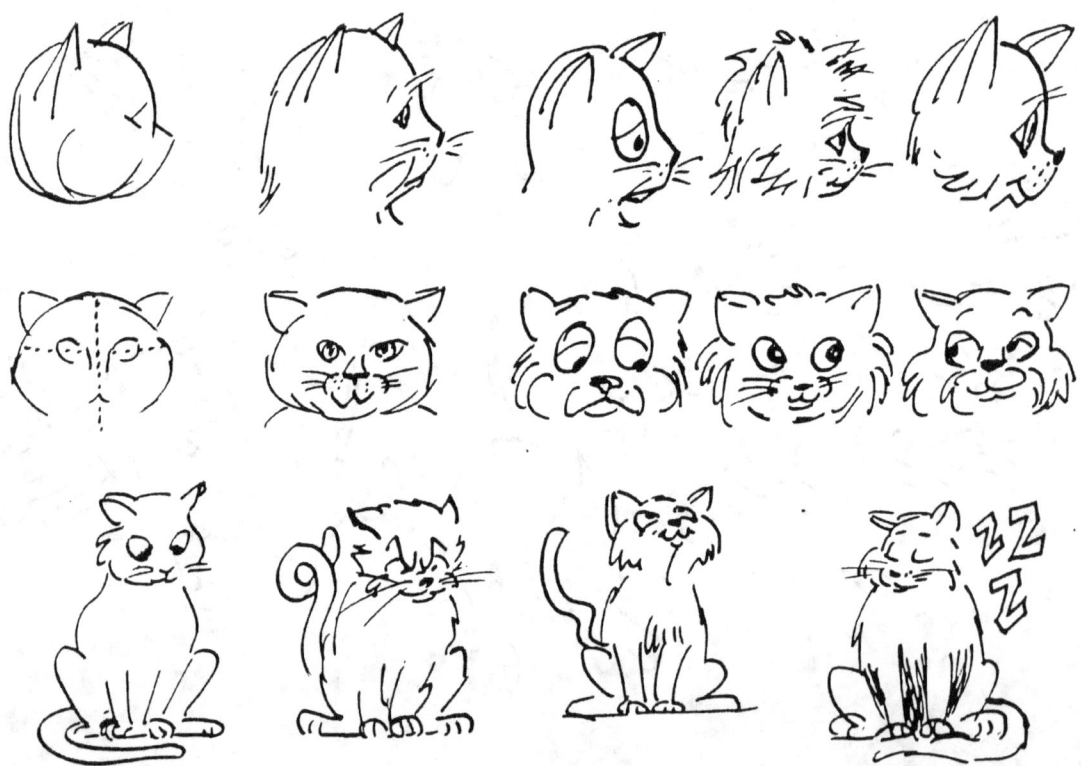

Studying a cat can be a great mental exercise, since it is difficult to determine exactly what they are thinking about or planning. For that reason, a cat can be given almost any sort of personality.

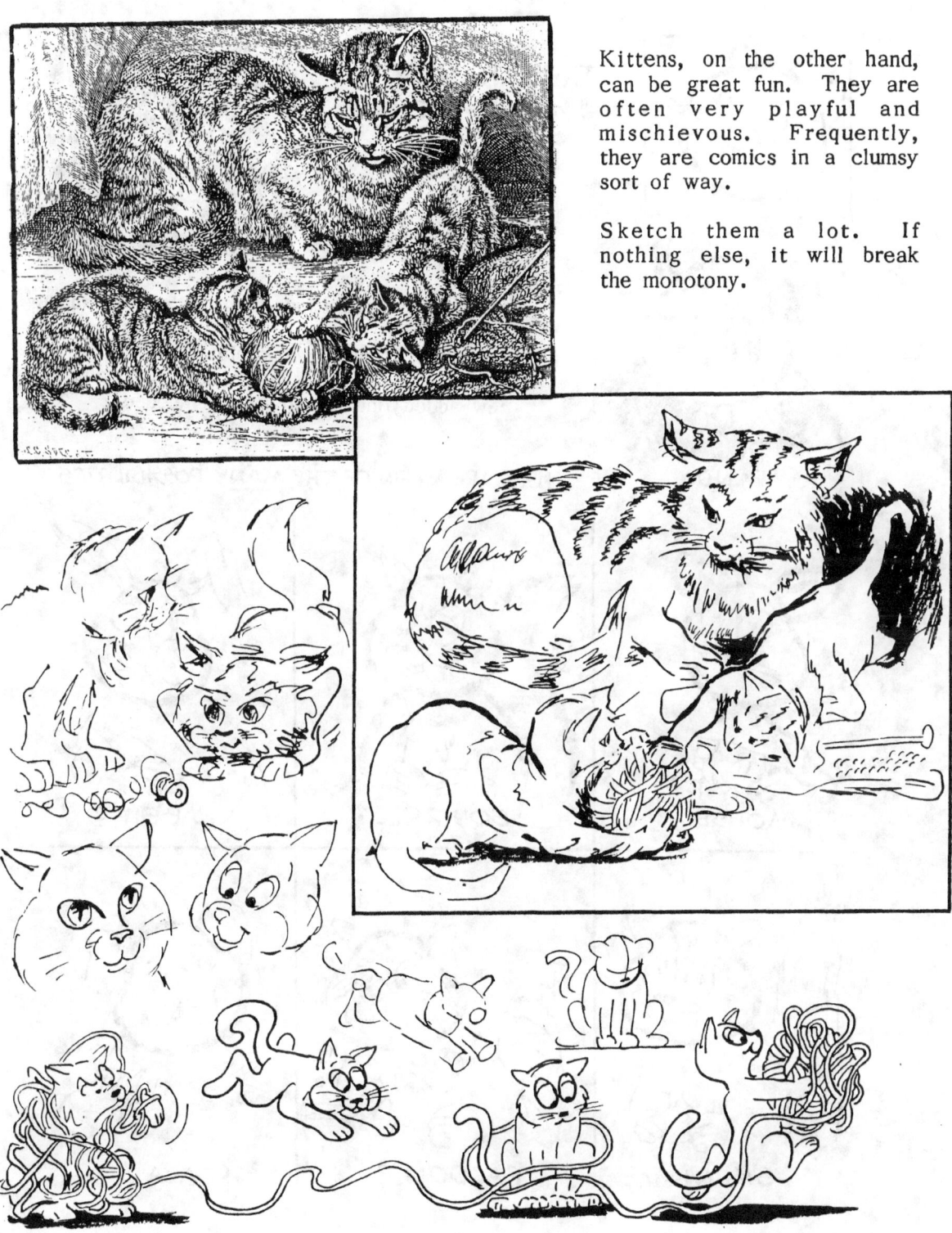

Kittens, on the other hand, can be great fun. They are often very playful and mischievous. Frequently, they are comics in a clumsy sort of way.

Sketch them a lot. If nothing else, it will break the monotony.

KNOWING HOW TO DRAW A CAT CAN HAVE SOME VERY DEFINITE ADVANTAGES!

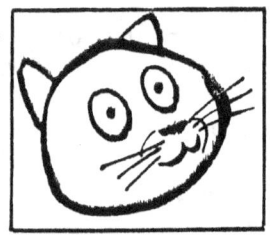

THE CAT'S HEAD...
A MULTI-PURPOSE STRUCTURE!

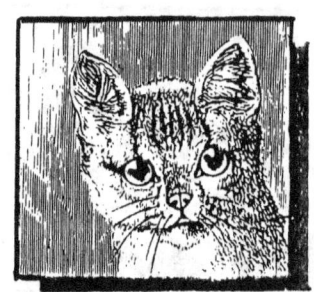

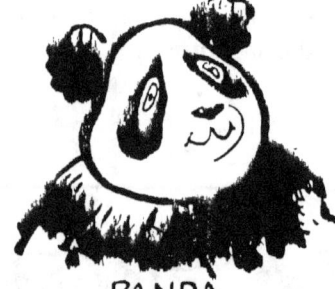

PANDA

Study the illustration of a cat's head (upper right) carefully. Note that it <u>closely resembles</u> that of a rabbit, squirrel, skunk, mouse, racoon, and many other animals. A few added lines is all that is needed.

HERE ARE A FEW OF THE <u>MANY</u> POSSIBILITIES:

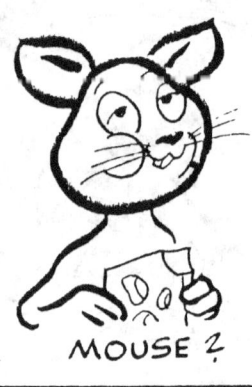

MOUSE ?

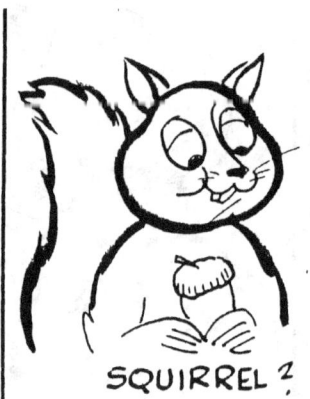

SQUIRREL ?

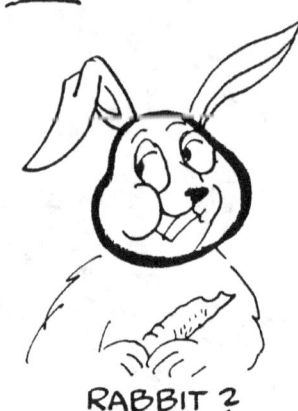

RABBIT ?

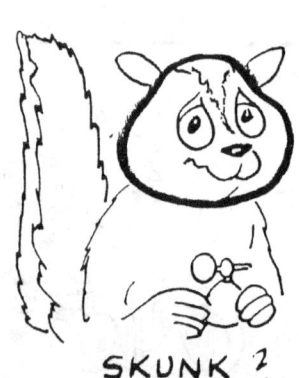

SKUNK ?

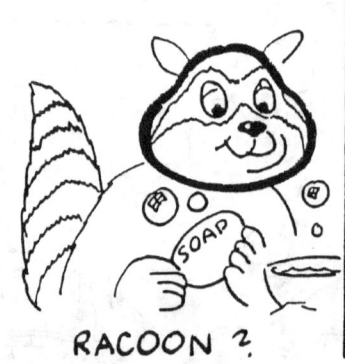

RACOON ?

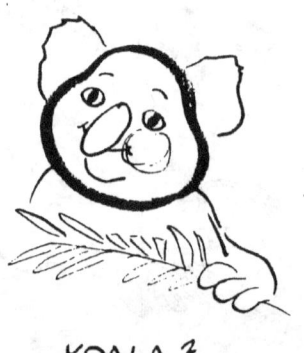

KOALA ?

WHEN AN ANIMAL IS NOT REALLY AN ANIMAL AT ALL!

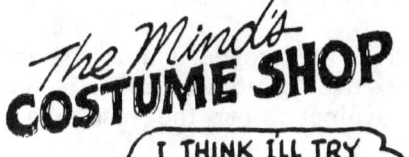

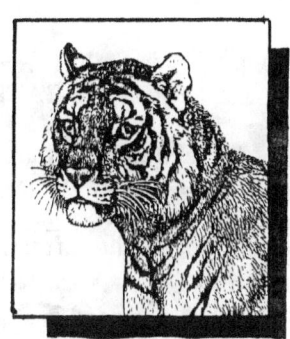

Is this a tiger, or is it someone we know?

I THINK I'LL TRY THIS ON FOR SIZE!

Students of cartooning often have difficulty in transforming a "realistic" animal into a "person-type" character with a particular personality. Perhaps the most effective way to accomplish this transformation is to forget, temporarily, that an animal is involved at all. Simply create a <u>human personality</u> and then add an animal "costume."

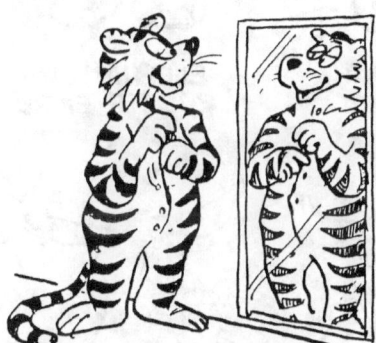

"SEEMS TO FIT JUST FINE!"

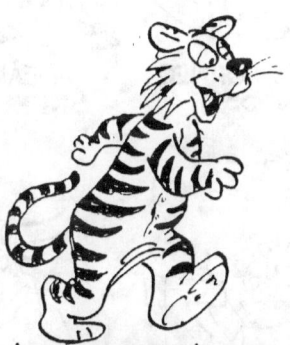

"THIS IS GREAT! LOOK LIKE AN ANIMAL, THINK LIKE A HUMAN!"

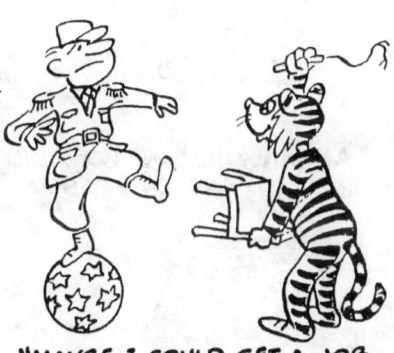

"MAYBE I COULD GET A JOB WITH THE CIRCUS!"

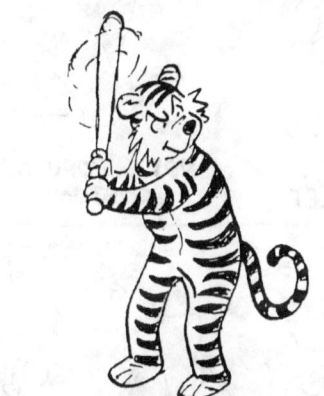

"...OR BECOME A STAR ATHLETE!"

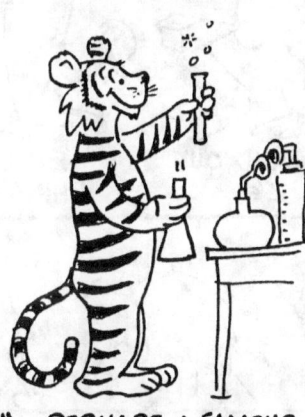

"...PERHAPS A FAMOUS SCIENTIST!"

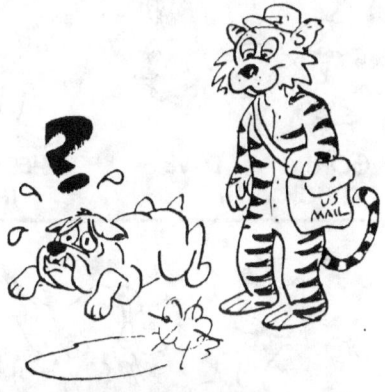

"I COULD BE A MAILMAN. DOGS WOULDN'T CHASE ME!"

THERE ARE NO SHORTCUTS IN THE PROCESS OF CREATING TRULY ORIGINAL ANIMAL CHARACTERS

It is essential that you start at <u>square one</u> (accurate reference material) and proceed from there.   It may require hundreds of trial sketches and doodles before a really <u>unique</u> animal cartoon character is developed, but the results are well worth the effort.

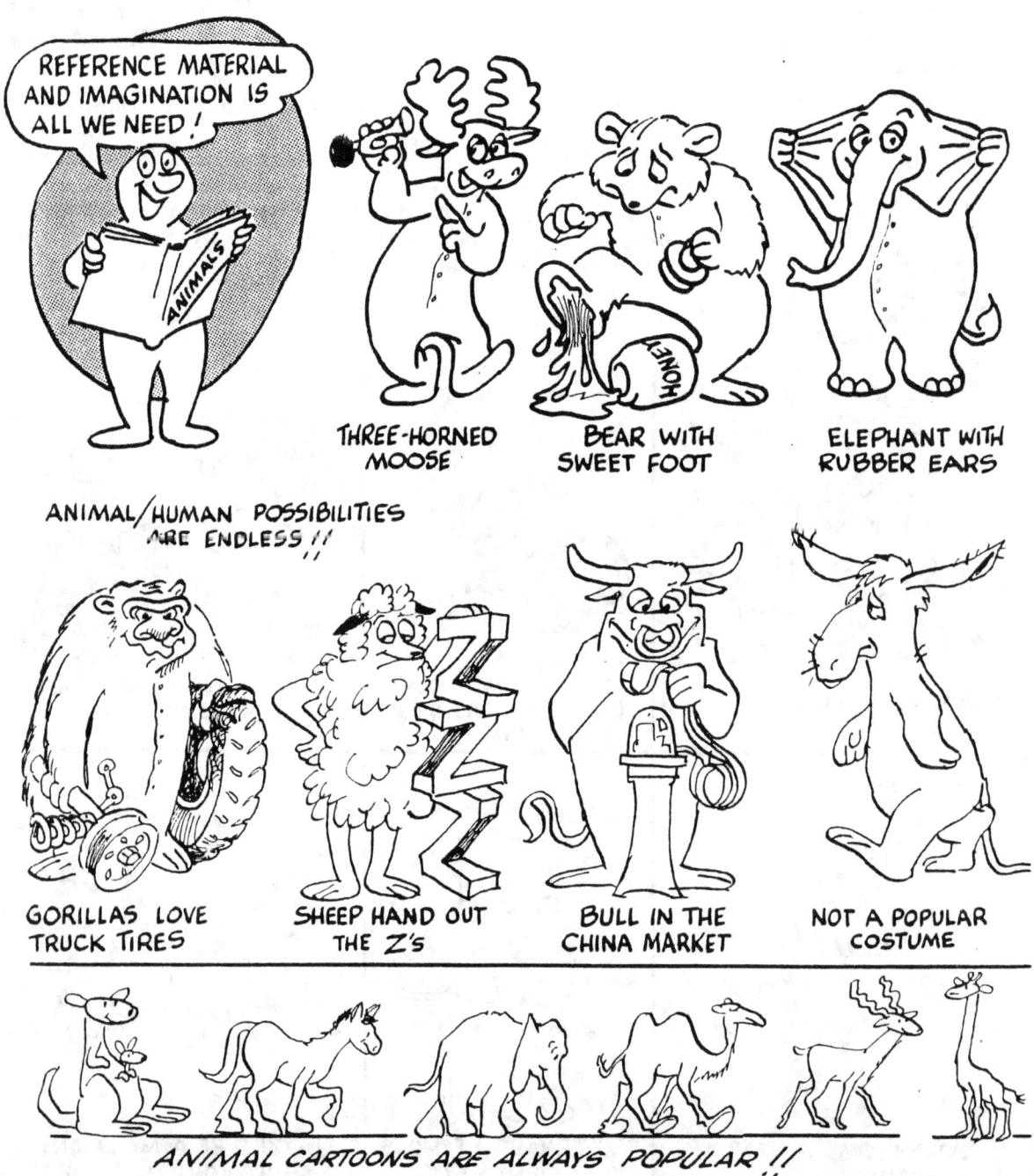

REFERENCE MATERIAL AND IMAGINATION IS ALL WE NEED!

THREE-HORNED MOOSE

BEAR WITH SWEET FOOT

ELEPHANT WITH RUBBER EARS

ANIMAL/HUMAN POSSIBILITIES ARE ENDLESS!!

GORILLAS LOVE TRUCK TIRES

SHEEP HAND OUT THE Z's

BULL IN THE CHINA MARKET

NOT A POPULAR COSTUME

ANIMAL CARTOONS ARE ALWAYS POPULAR!!

Birds make great cartoon characters.   They can also be helpful in your search for originality.

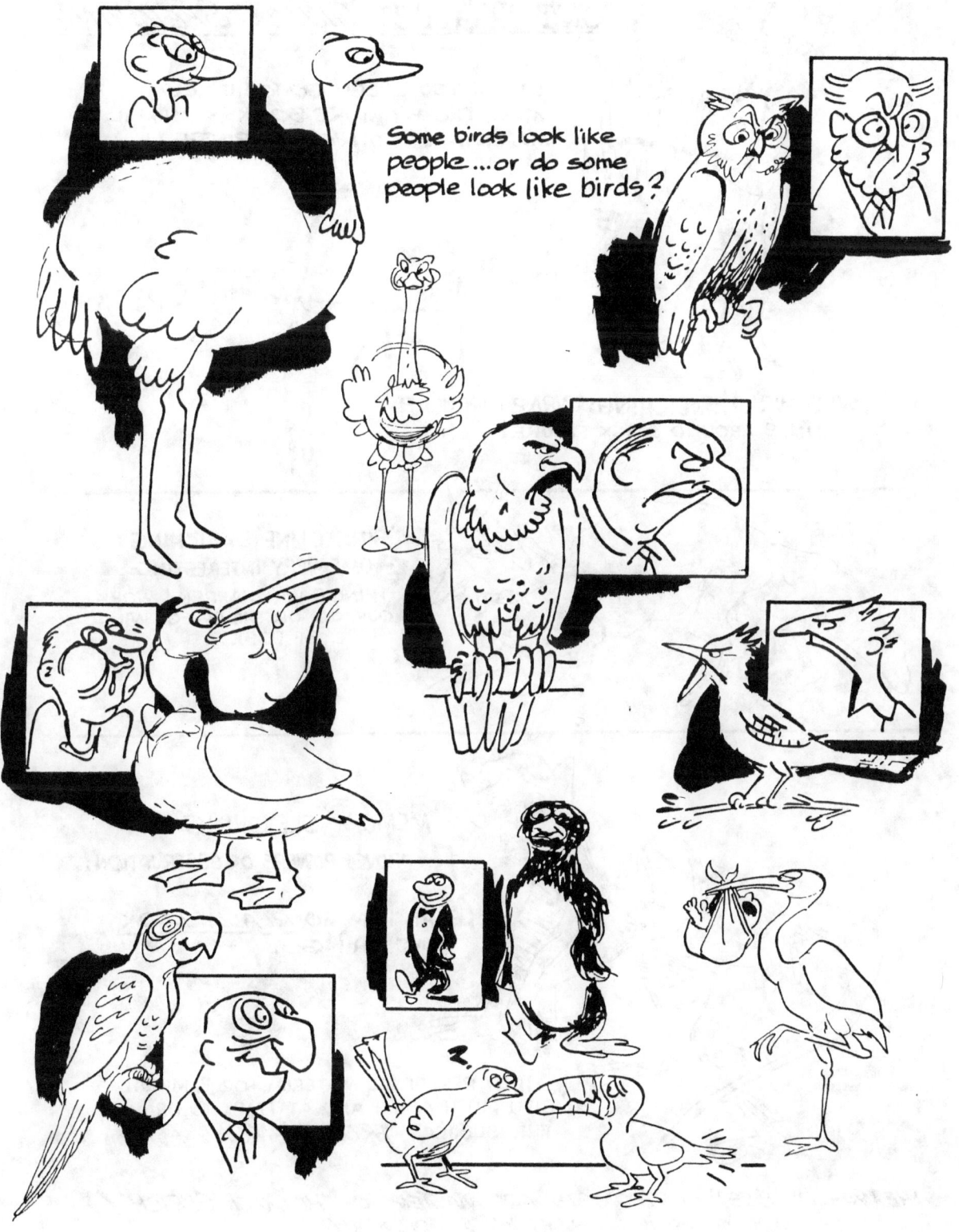

Some birds look like people...or do some people look like birds?

Be original!　Work only from live models, photos, or accurate, well-done illustrations.

DON'T NEGLECT *QUICK SKETCHING*!

SKETCH YOUR PETS! GO TO THE ZOO! WORK FROM NATURE BOOKS & ANIMAL MAGAZINES! COLLECT CLIPPINGS!

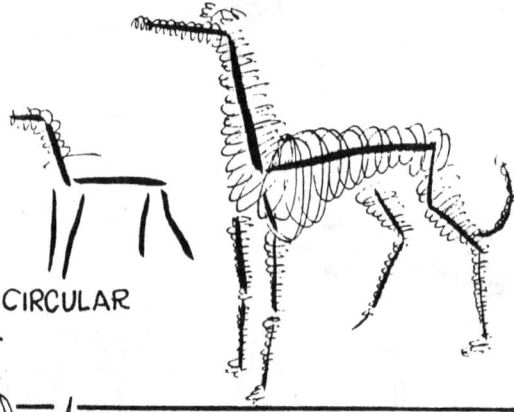

'WIRE-WRAP' SKETCHING: WRAP CIRCULAR LINES AROUND STICK FIGURE.

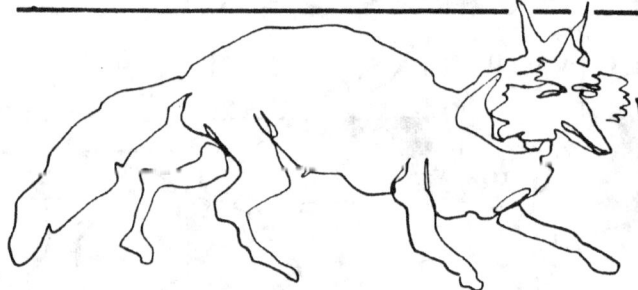

'SINGLE LINE' SKETCHING: **S**OME VERY INTERESTING THINGS WILL HAPPEN! WORK QUICKLY OR THE EFFECT WILL BE LOST.

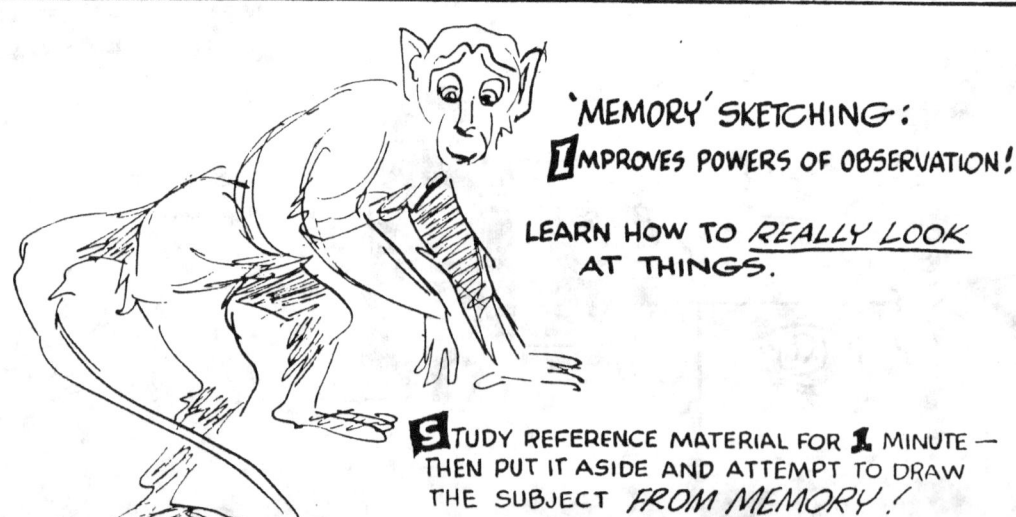

'MEMORY' SKETCHING: **I**MPROVES POWERS OF OBSERVATION!

LEARN HOW TO *REALLY LOOK* AT THINGS.

STUDY REFERENCE MATERIAL FOR **1** MINUTE — THEN PUT IT ASIDE AND ATTEMPT TO DRAW THE SUBJECT *FROM MEMORY!*

THE WORLD'S BEST CARTOONISTS ARE MASTERS OF THE 'QUICK SKETCH'! LET YOUR NATURAL TALENT *WORK FOR YOU!!*

Sketch these animals. <u>Experiment with line and shading techniques.</u> Interpret and exaggerate moods, personalities, and characters. Create simple little "tag lines," gags, and <u>humorous situations</u> to go along with your drawings. Combine two or more animals in a group. Imaging that they think and act just like humans. Attempt to draw them as they might appear from a variety of different vantage points.

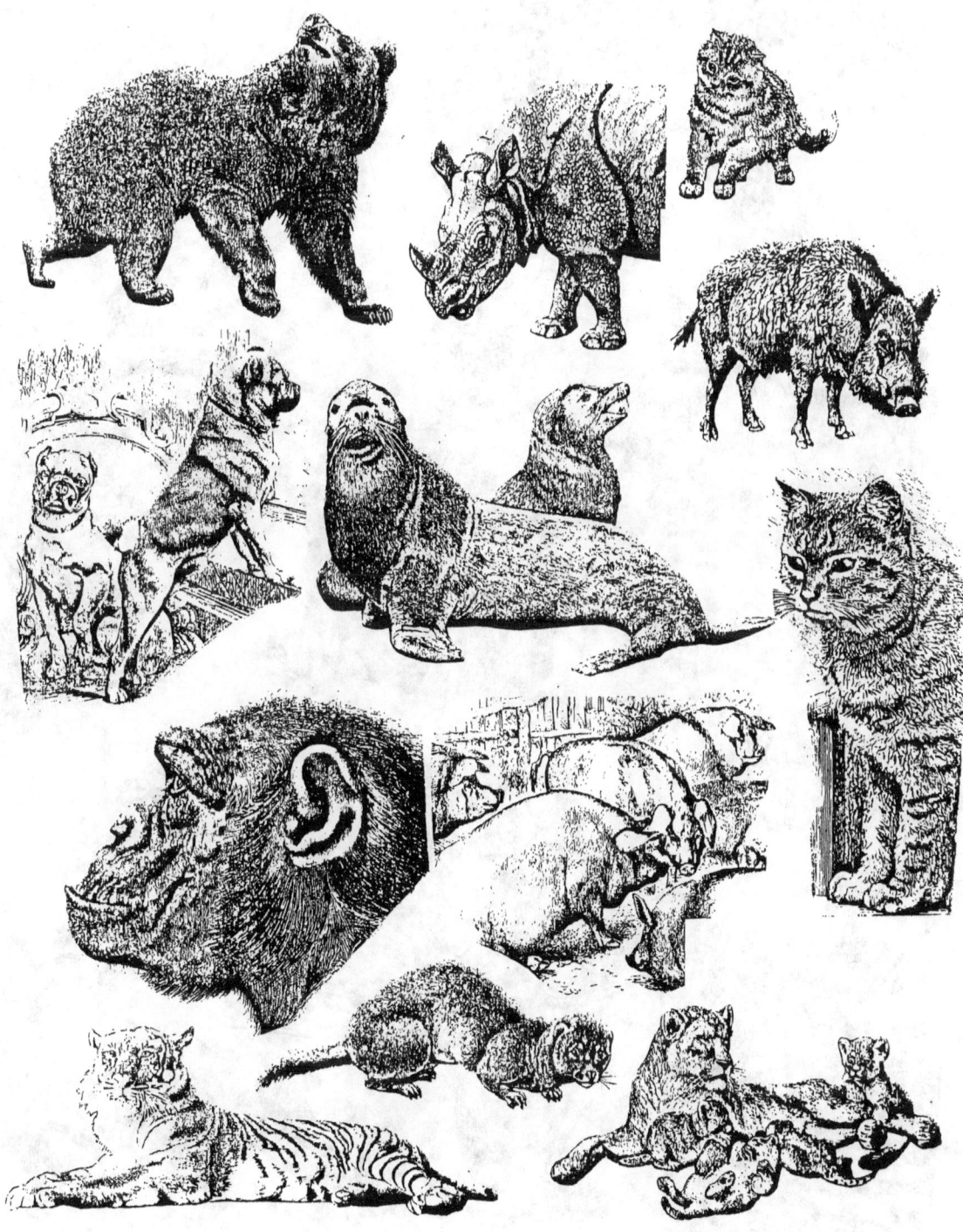

MORE WONDERFUL CREATURES TO WORK WITH. WATCH FOR GESTURE LINES AND GENERAL BODY CONSTRUCTION. **SIMPLIFY! EXAGGERATE!**

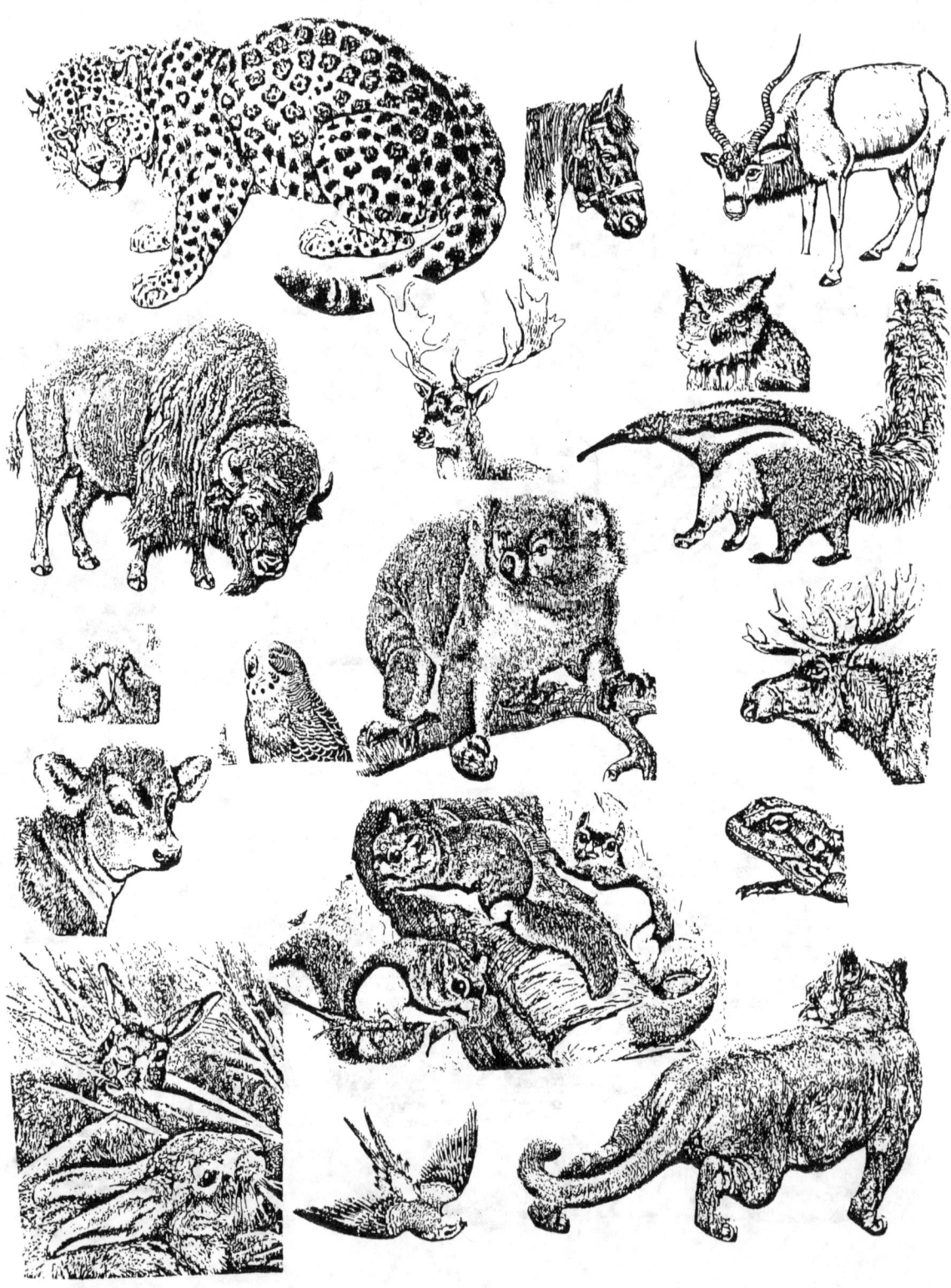

Quickie Review Chapters 3 & 4

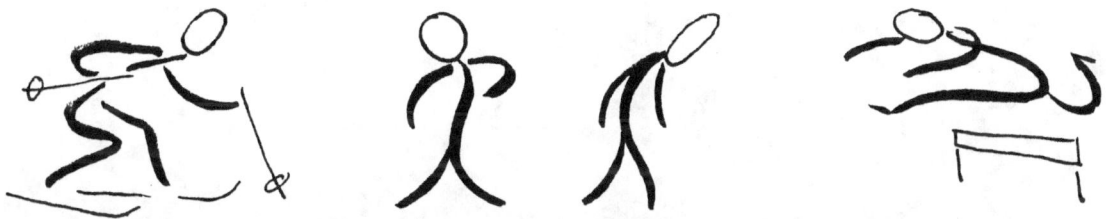

BODY LANGUAGE 'TALKS' MOOD, PERSONALITY, ACTION.

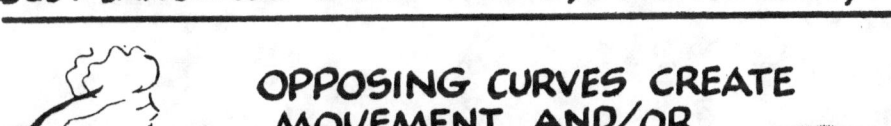

OPPOSING CURVES CREATE MOVEMENT AND/OR EMPHASIZES ACTION.

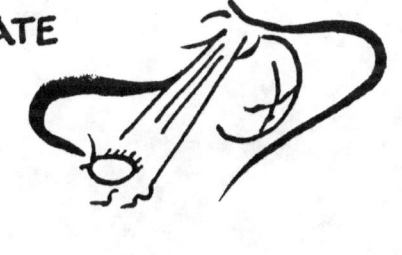

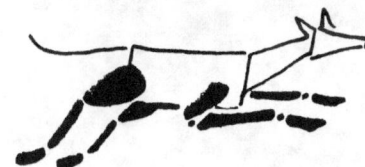

THREE PART LEG CONSTRUCTION. RIGHT ARM/LEFT LEG MOVEMENT.

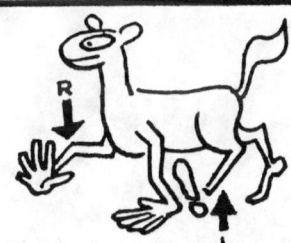

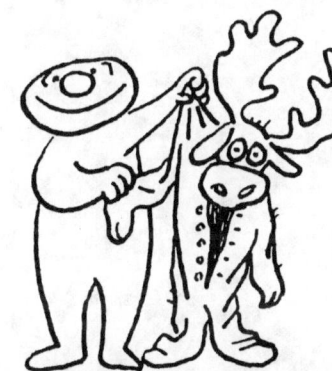

CARTOON ANIMALS ARE OFTEN JUST <u>PEOPLE</u> IN COSTUME!

RESEARCH & IMAGINATION IS ALL THAT IS NEEDED.

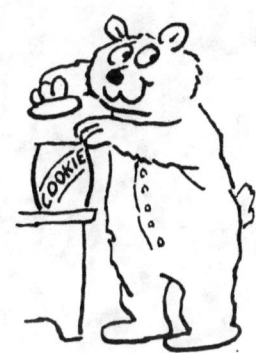

CARTOON WORK MUST SHOW SKILL, CREATIVITY, AND ORIGINALITY TO BE SALEABLE.

CHAPTER FIVE
Creating Humor

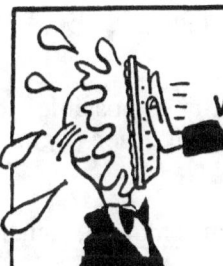

INTRODUCTION
WHAT IS HUMOR, ANYWAY?

- A PRATFALL?
- A SLY WINK AND A GRIN?

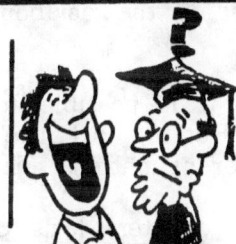

TYPES OF HUMOR
WHY DO WE LAUGH?

- RIDICULE?
- SURPRISE?
- TRUTH?

IDEAS

SUDDEN INSPIRATIONS?

SPECIAL FORMULAS?

JUST PLAIN HARD WORK?

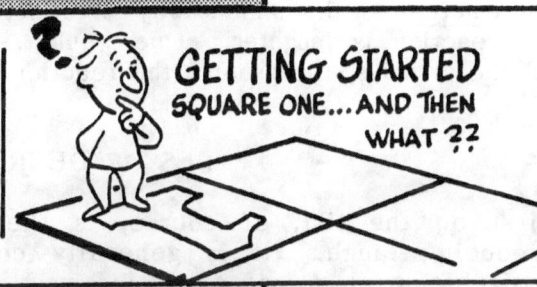

GETTING STARTED
SQUARE ONE... AND THEN WHAT??

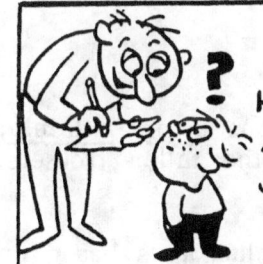

SOURCES
HUMOR IS EVERYWHERE!

"HA HA, THAT WAS FUNNY, JUNIOR! SAY IT AGAIN... SLOWLY."

BRAINSTORMING
PYRAMIDING IDEAS

ONE GOOD IDEA CAN LEAD TO 100 OTHERS. GET THEM STARTED... KEEP THEM GOING!!

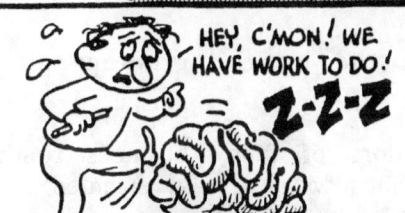

HEY, C'MON! WE HAVE WORK TO DO!

Z-Z-Z

WRITER'S BLOCK!
THE IMAGINATION PLAYING HOOKY

THE MIND'S "BLAHS" CAUSES & CURES!

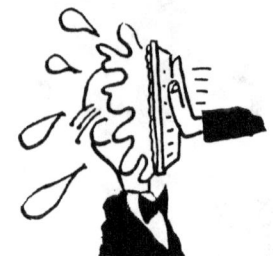

WHAT IS HUMOR?

Humor is the pie in the face, the purloined pie, the pratfall. Humor is the wink, the wart, the woe.

Humor is an intangible thing. It is all around us, if only we notice it -- like the air we breathe. It is the cartoonist's task to capture it, package it, and present it to mankind.

Someone once said that it is possible to analyze humor, just as it is possible to dissect a butterfly. Putting all the bits and pieces back together again, however, is a whole different matter. That's the problem.

For the purpose of this chapter, let's define humor as simply an emotion, much like anger, sadness, hate, and love.

An emotion is the mind's way of reacting to a stimulus. In the case of humor, the reaction is laughter. One would assume that the stronger or more meaningful the stimulus, the greater the reaction.

TYPES OR DEGREES OF LAUGHTER

First on the list, of course, is the explosive, hearty, knee slapping, tear-producing laugh. It is generally considered that this is the ultimate, most desirable goal. Unfortunately, most of us have to settle for something less, such as the GUFFAW, CHUCKLE, CHORTLE, GIGGLE, SNICKER, or TITTER.

WHAT MAKES US LAUGH?

Some authorities on humor maintain that all humor is based on ridicule, embarrassment, or discomfort. The slip on a banana peel, the fallen trousers, the black eye, and the hand stuck in the cookie jar.

Other experts will pontificate from the mountain top that all humor is based on surprise, the unexpected, or incongruity. Often, this brand of humor requires a bit of preliminary misdirection -- a "setup."

It is held by some that conflict is the basic ingredient of humor. Good triumphs over evil -- that sort of thing.

Ultimately, however, all successful vendors of funny business readily admit that TRUTH is the essence of humor. Perhaps Mark Twain summed it up best when he said, "Humor is the good natured side of truth."

Rich or poor, young or old, everyone has a sense of humor. Week-old infants have been known to laugh, usually when doing poo-poo.

The stimulus required to produce laughter, however, and the manner in which it is presented, can vary from one type of individual to another. Such things as background, education, and experiences affect one's general outlook on life and his or her concept of humor.

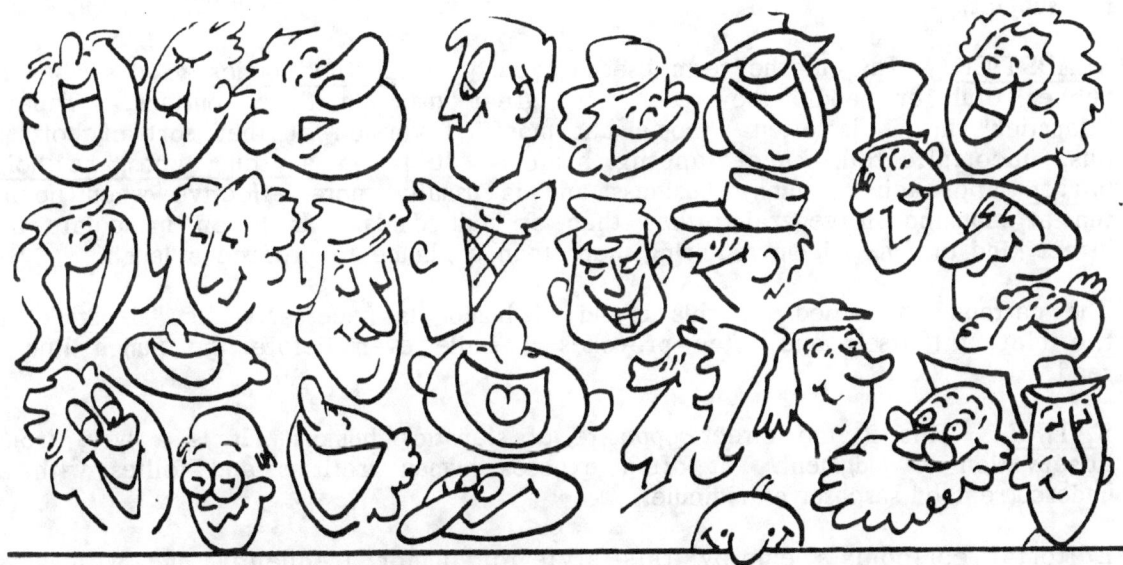

The person with a strong inner city background cannot easily create "down home" humor. A high school dropout cannot easily create the type of humor that would make a college professor laugh.

Therefore, the student is advised to limit his or her creative efforts to the type of humor they personally enjoy most, and to focus on the things with which they are most familiar.

GENERAL CATEGORIES OF HUMOR

HUMAN INTEREST. This is the most common and popular type of funny business because it is based on things to which we can all relate. Usually, one does not "create" it, but merely reports it or comments on it.

Friends, relatives, children, spouses, pets, co-workers, shopkeepers, EVERYONE, says or does things that could be considered amusing, if not downright funny. Even those little everyday annoyances, aggravations, frustrations, and disappointments can provide lots of humorous material. One needs only to be on the alert and learn to recognize humorous possibilities. Occasionally, a slight twist or exaggeration can transform even the smallest glimmer of humor into a bright, shiny gem. That gem, in turn, when examined from a number of different viewpoints, can lead to a whole string of great ideas.

SPECIAL INTEREST. This is the brand of humor that is "slanted" or aimed at a specialized segment of society or field of interest. It is commonly seen in trade publications, professional journals, hobby magazines, and the specialized sections of the newspaper.

Although it is based on the "human interest" element, it can be more difficult to produce since it often requires extensive research or in-depth knowledge of the subject.

SLAPSTICK. This is the term used by early vaudeville comics to describe the rubber club or paddle they used with great gusto in their routines. Today's "slapstick" humor is often a somewhat modified version of that sort of boisterous, uncomplicated, knee-slapping humor. It is an anything goes, no holds barred approach to funny business and is usually more effective when poking fun at mankind in general rather than at individuals. It is an immediate and direct kind of fun, seldom requiring more than a glance to produce a laugh.

The cartoon style used for this brand of humor is necessarily as "slapstick" as the material itself and often provokes a smile even before the punch line is read.

SATIRE. This is the direct opposite of slapstick humor. It is a wry, ironic observation or judgment. It often exposes human frailties and follies with an undercurrent of sarcasm or ridicule.

Editorial cartoonists employ this style of humor frequently and with great effectiveness, although it is not limited to that use by any means. It is probably the most difficult type of humor to create successfully and consistently. It requires an almost philosophical outlook and a keen insight into the human element. It can be a sharp stick wielded in a tongue-in-cheek, wink-of-the-eye manner, and is often sophisticated and/or intellectual.

SEX HUMOR. Recent surveys of this brand of humor, although somewhat limited and informal, indicate that the "hard core" stuff is losing whatever acceptance or appeal it might once have enjoyed. This may be due to the fact that the markets for this style of humor are modifying their formats or have closed up shop completely. Milder and more subtle versions of the subject, however, are popping up all over the place and often provide an interesting and entertaining diversion from the standard cartoon fare.

It will always be a touchy subject and should be handled in a manner that is not offensive or degrading.

STRANGE HUMOR. This is the brand of humor that is often a puzzlement to the casual reader, who frequently reacts in a head scratching, "I don't get it" manner, and therefore becomes, unwittingly perhaps, a participant in the joke. To a degree, it is "cult" humor, where those who "get it" somehow feel a bit superior to those who don't. Its cleverness is usually well hidden and those who take the time to analyze it are rewarded with a chuckle, at least.

"Strange" humor is not necessarily new to the scene.   George Herriman's comic strip, "Krazy Kat," published from about 1913 to the mid 1940s, was considered to be a bit strange by many readers of the era, and was often published in the more obscure sections of the newspaper, It lasted for more than 30 years, however, and is now considered by many to be a true classic.

Some cartoonists, editors, humorists, and even readers think of "strange" humor as a sort of "put on" and in some instances, perhaps it is, which makes it even funnier and more appealing that ever.   Unfortunately, the market for true "off the wall" humor is somewhat limited and should be approached with caution.

Admittedly, all of the foregoing categories of humor are quite general in nature. Successful funny business can be a combination of any or all of them.   More importantly, there might be an entirely new and unique style of humor out there somewhere, waiting to be discovered.

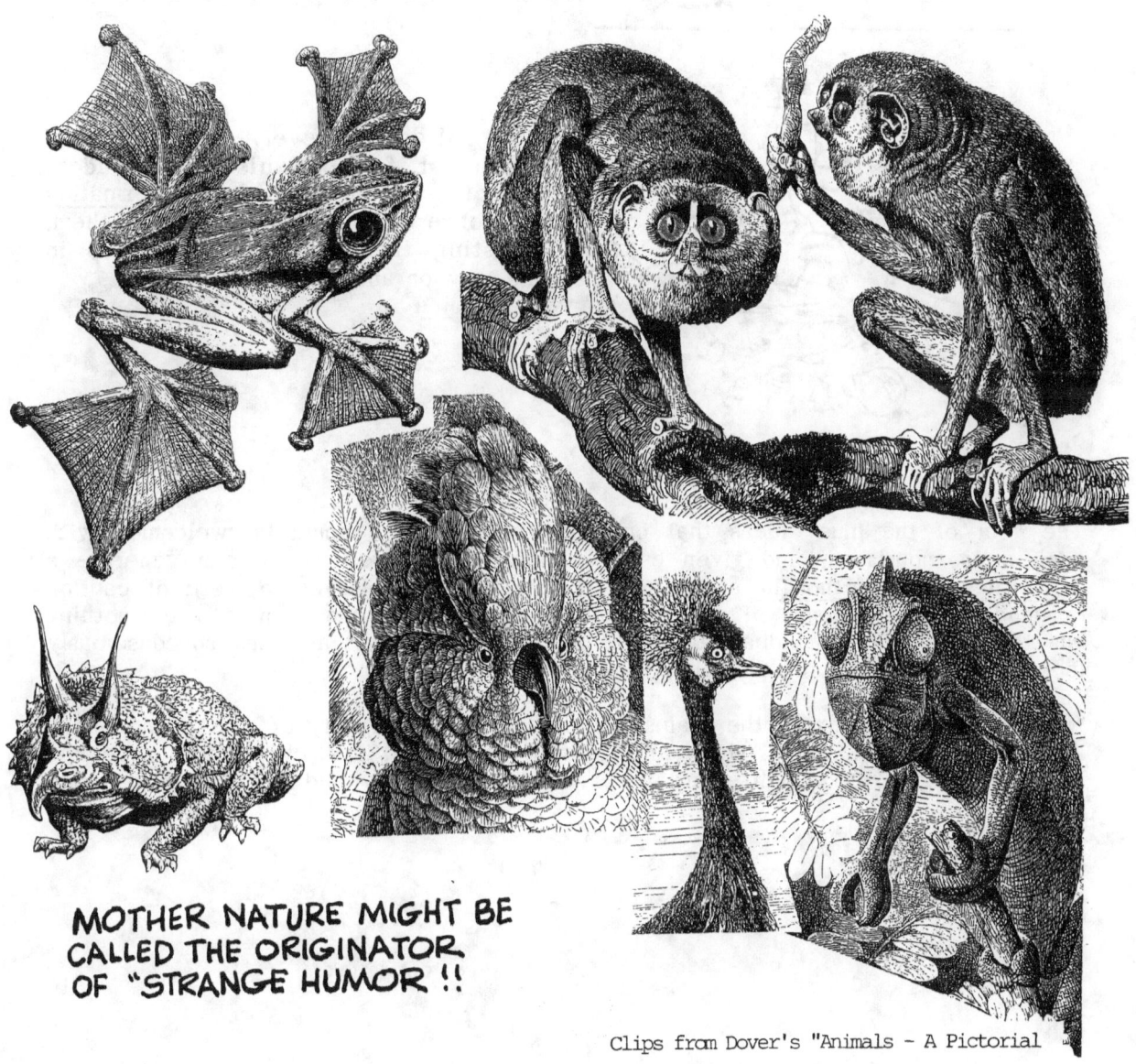

MOTHER NATURE MIGHT BE CALLED THE ORIGINATOR OF "STRANGE HUMOR!!

Clips from Dover's "Animals - A Pictorial

"WHERE D'YA GETCHER IDEAS?"

That is the question cartoonists probably hear more often than any other. Fortunately, it is usually asked in much the same way as one might ask, "Nice day, isn't it?" where the asker isn't really expecting too much of an answer.

"Oh, they just seem to pop into my head," is a popular response to the question, and in a way it isn't too far from the truth, although the complete and accurate answer is a bit more complicated than that.

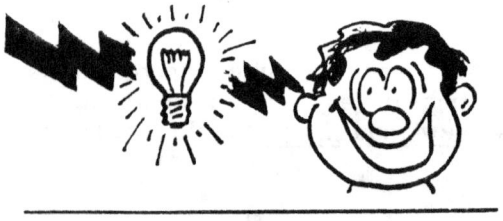

Occasionally, a great, new, bright, and shining idea can strike the creative mind like a bolt from the blue.

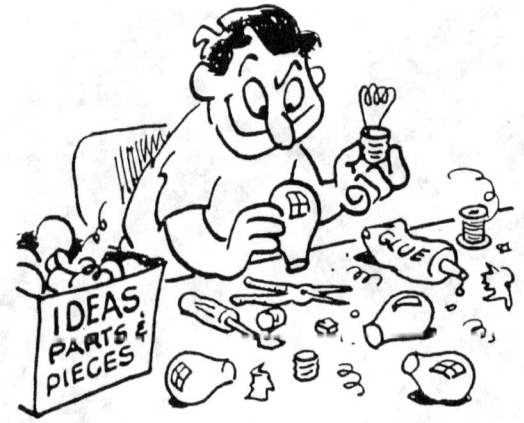

More often, however, the workaday cartoonist fashions his or her ideas out of bits and pieces of information and observations, tinkering with them, adjusting them, polishing them up in one way or another.

The "out of the blue" ideas that one gets occasionally should be welcomed with open arms, nourished, and given every chance to survive. They can generate a whole new line of thought and a ton of new ideas. However, a word of caution is needed here. Some of these "sudden inspirations" can prove to be nothing but the residue of an idea that one has seen somewhere and has subconsciously locked up in the back of the mind.

"Hand crafted" humor is the mainstay, the real breadwinner, of most cartoonists. At times, it can be a slow and painful procedure, but eventually, once the imagination gets into high gear, ideas start popping up and bounce around like crazy.

SQUARE NUMBER ONE ... AND PERSISTENCE!

Clearly, all ideas have a starting point. In the case of the cartoonist, the starting point can be a sort of "person, place, or thing" game. A subject or topic is required. Current fads or events, unusual situations, and impossible or improbable occurrences can produce some great funny business. So can common everyday trials and tribulations which, all too often, we consider uniquely our own but are actually universal in nature.

We should now add the human element to our chosen topic. Nobody is perfect, as the saying goes, and the cartoonist can be grateful for that state of affairs. We all have similar faults and flaws, shortcomings, likes and dislikes. Human frailties and follies must be carefully considered and observed by the cartoonist, not with a critical eye, but with a humorous viewpoint.

A popular and successful cartoonist once said, "I try to find something funny in everything I see or hear, even a G.D. funeral!" With certain limitations, that can be a very good attitude to develop. Unlike many other fields of endeavor which may require lots of expensive tools and equipment, the cartoonist's most valuable tool is humor, which happens to be free and in plentiful supply, if only we watch for it.

Now, your imagination has three key elements with which to work; that is, you have a subject, a person, and a humorous mental attitude. See there? Things are beginning to get funny already! The creative part of your brain is beginning to percolate.

Do you have an ordinary subject with an unusual person? Could be. Do you have an unusual subject with an ordinary person? Possible. Do you have a ridiculous subject with a ridiculous person? Why Not!

One must remember that all these thoughts are flashing through your mind faster than it takes to describe them. It's entirely possible that, at this point, your imagination has presented you with the best and purest form of humor there is -- the CAPTIONLESS GAG. Wham, bang! One brief glance and the reader is thrown into a fit of hysterical laughter. Terrific! Go for it!!

At the very least, the imagination is beginning to form a sort of scene which includes the subject/topic and an individual. For example, we have selected, for whatever reason, typing as our topic. The mind will likely create a typical office scene ... a desk, chair, filing cabinet, and typist. Nothing very funny in all that. How about the desk? It is plain, fancy, or unusual in some way? If so, why? What about the typist? Male, female, young, old, good looking, ugly, rich, or poor? Why?

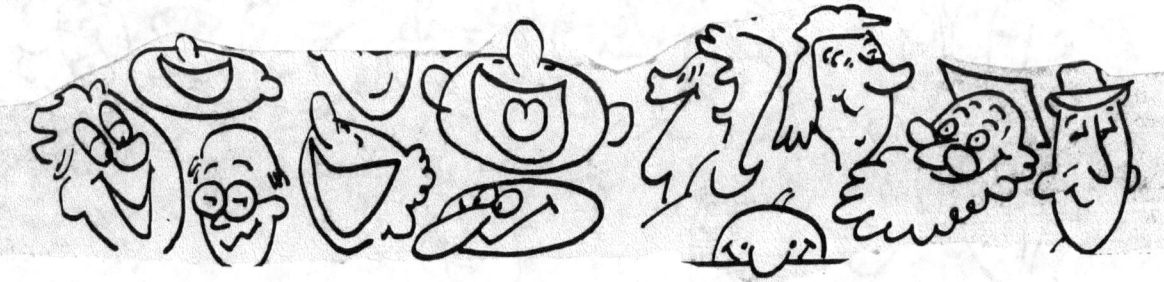

Our mental picture should include a typewriter, of course. Is it a brand new model or an antique? These days, typewriters can do all sorts of things. Is the one in your scene doing something unusual? Broken? Being repaired or overly complicated?

At this point, you very likely have concocted a dozen or so amusing though perhaps not hilarious possibilities. You might choose to concentrate on those for a while, or at least make a few notes. You can then proceed with the brainstorming in your little scene. What else do you have to work with? The filing cabinet, chair, pictures on the wall, or perhaps plants, flowers, other office equipment, anything and everything that might, even in a far-fetched way, relate to an office.

Now you have a zillion possibilities to work with. Perhaps you will want to play a "mix and match" game. A shabby typist in a ritzy office, a ritzy typist in a shabby office. Big pictures on a small wall or small pictures on a large wall. Why? A beautiful bouquet or wilted posies? What happened?

As you can see, the brainstorming possibilities on any given topic are endless and can be extremely productive. You now have two zillion amusing situations. With any luck at all, some of them might even be very funny, outrageous, or hilarious, not requiring any further work or caption.

As for the rest of your ideas, amusing as they might be, they will need to be zapped a bit, shaken loose, wrung out. We don't want "amuse," we want FUNNY! And we know what funny is, or at least, from preceding pages, we have some clues. Ridicule, embarrassment, and discomfort are funny. Surprise, incongruity, and the unexpected are funny. Truth is funny -- modified, exaggerated, subtle, or pointed.

Okay, so now you have three zillion possibilities, but you can't stop there. (Nobody ever said creating humor was easy.)

How much attention have you given to the punch line (gag line, story line, caption, or whatever)? There are at least half a zillion of those!

THE WORLD'S FUNNIEST CARTOON HAS NOT YET BEEN CREATED!

WHY NOT GO FOR IT!!

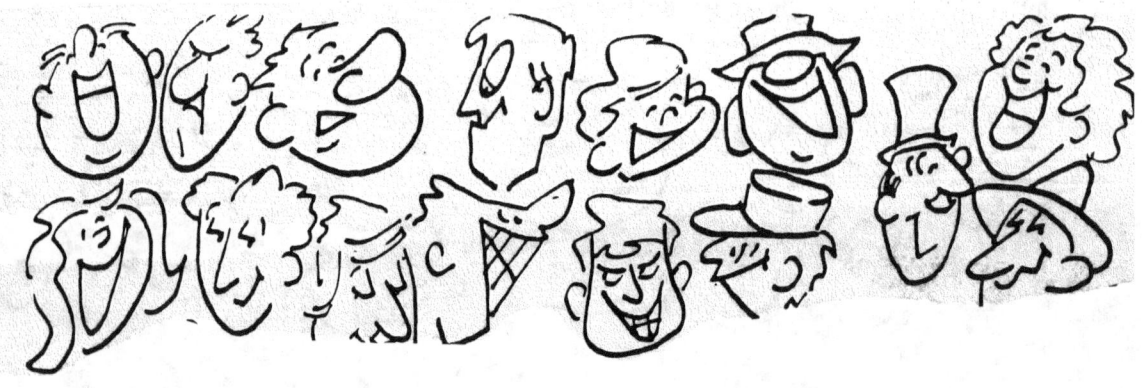

TYPES OF GAG LINES

The most frequently used punch line is the one that <u>explains</u> a common, unusual, strange, or weird situation ... the dented fender, the burnt roast, the mischievous child, or the bull in the china shop. You might create a totally <u>improbable</u> situation and then think up a <u>logical</u> explanation for it. In the case of the typist, perhaps the boss or a co-worker is shown hanging up a huge picture on the wall. What kind of picture is it? Why is it being hung? Who offers the <u>explanation</u>? The boss? The typist? An onlooker? Remember: <u>RIDICULE, EMBARRASSMENT, DISCOMFORT, SURPRISE, INCONGRUITY, AND TRUTH</u>.

Quite often, a <u>question</u> can be used as a punch line. It might be a very <u>dumb</u> question where the answer is perfectly obvious. Perhaps it's a completely <u>normal</u> question asked in a very <u>unusual situation</u>. It could be a <u>sarcastic</u> question based on an element of truth. Questions that relate to popular topics of the day, current events and trends, strange happenings, and newsworthy events can provide the "clincher" to a humorous situation.

COMMON SENSE STRATEGY

Every successful cartoonist studies his target market carefully before submitting material. <u>Every publication has certain standards and taboos that must be taken into consideration.</u> A little time spent researching a possible market can pay tremendous dividends.

Publications aimed at "general" readership, for instance, would not likely be interested in material of a highly technical nature, or that is offensive or degrading in some way.

Readership consideration is especially important when "slanting" humor in a specific direction, such as professional journals, trade publications, or specialty magazines.

A physician's magazine certainly would not look favorably at material that portrays doctors as bungling nincompoops. A journal published specifically for the legal profession would not print material that puts attorneys in an unfavorable light. A beautician's magazine would not be expected to publish work that degrades the profession in any way.

<u>Fun is fun, humor is humor.</u> A pie in the face is one thing; a kick in the face is something else again.

NEVER SUBMIT MATERIAL TO A PUBLICATION WITHOUT FIRST BECOMING THOROUGHLY FAMILIAR WITH THE TYPE OF MATERIAL THEY USE.

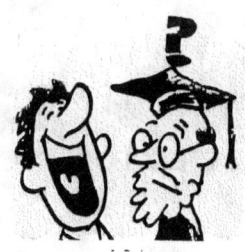

THE IDEA MACHINE

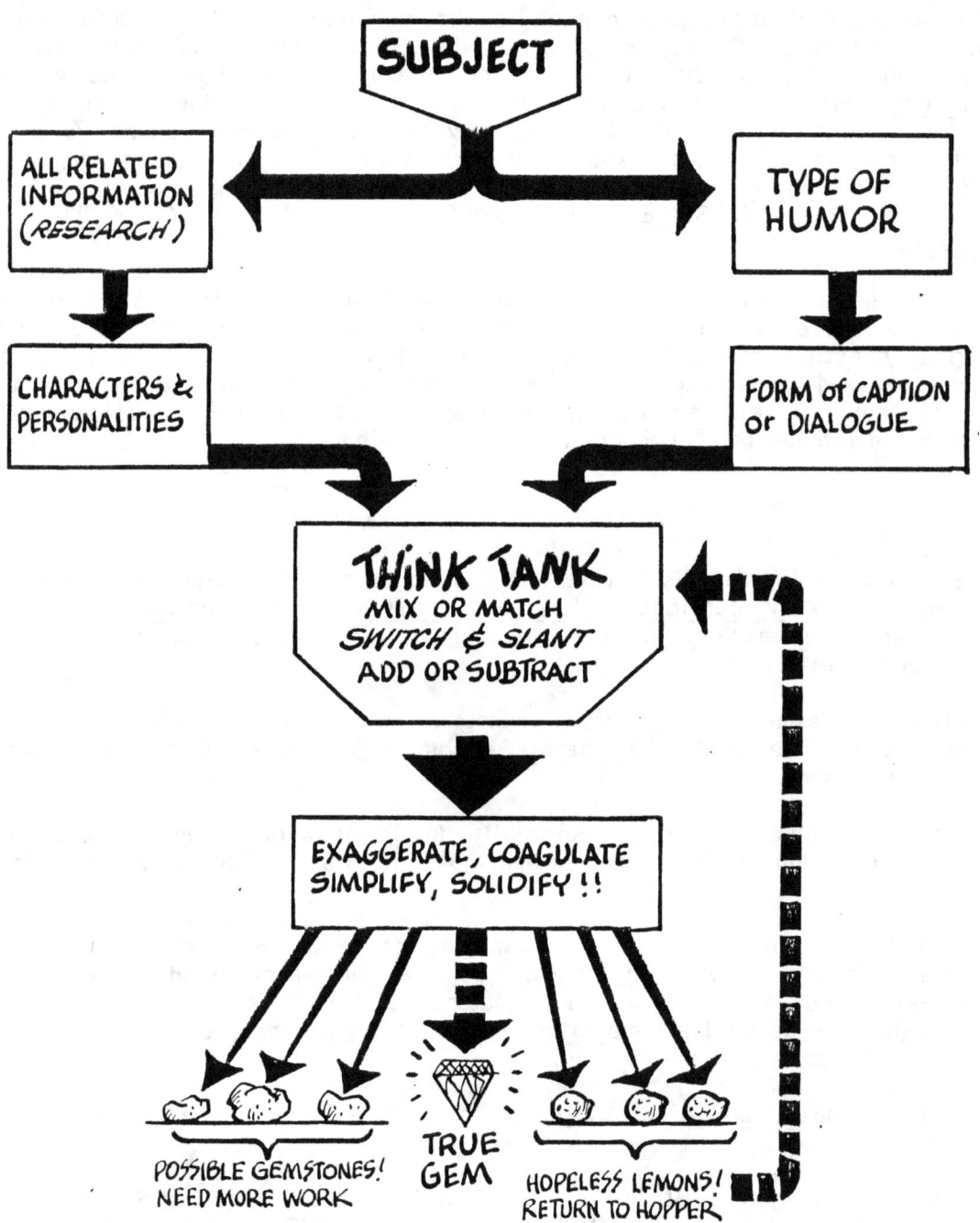

THE WORLD'S FUNNIEST CARTOON HAS NOT YET BEEN CREATED!

WHY NOT GO FOR IT!!

BEGINNING WITH A SPECIFIC TOPIC

This is the most controllable, and perhaps most efficient, method of creating humor because it allows us, in a general way, to establish a definite goal. The method will work for all types of humor and is especially helpful with "slanting" gags toward a particular audience.

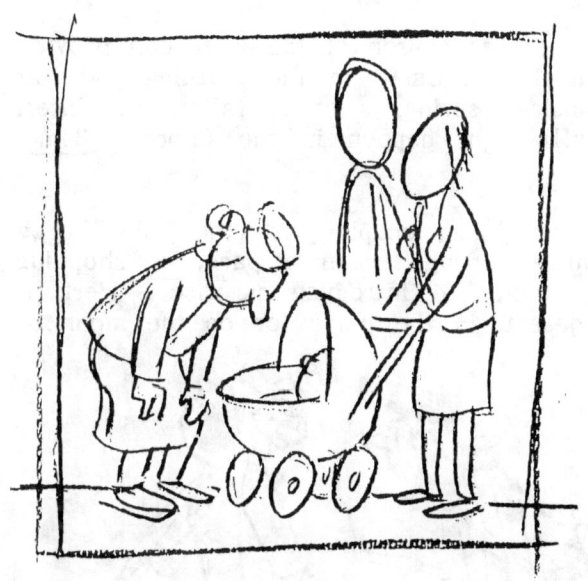

EXAMPLE: We decided on "young marrieds" as a topic. We doodle out the first little scene that comes to mind. It might indicate a living room, super-market, backyard, housework, or anything of that sort. Shown here is a typical "young marrieds" scene.

THE FIVE W's

The Five W's (WHO, WHAT, WHY, WHEN, and WHERE) are used by journalists as a "lead" to a story and can be very helpful in creating humor. In our little "situation doodle" above, we may ask, "Who is involved, What is happening, Why is it happening, When and Where is it happening?"

We'll take the W's one at a time.

WHO is involved? The LOGICAL part of our minds likely presents a vision of ordinary people in a normal setting. But LOGIC isn't necessarily an element of humor, so let's put it aside for a moment. Perhaps the people are unusual or interesting in some way. They might be Eskimos, Indians, stone-age people, circus clowns, farmers, cowboys, or even ducks!

WHAT is happening? Two people, parents perhaps, out for a stroll with baby. Someone is peering into the baby carriage. What emotions are being shown? Happiness, pride, annoyance, embarrassment, boredom?

<u>WHY</u> is it happening? This is where the punch line starts to develop. Perhaps someone is asking a question or offering an explanation or excuse. Maybe it is in the form of a "fad" expression, an old cliche, or a well-known quote.

It is at this point in your "brainstorming" that you might need the added <u>element of surprise.</u> Our attention is focused on the baby buggy. Perhaps the infant will do something totally unexpected, improbably, unusual, or even weird. Perhaps there is no baby at all. Put something else in the buggy -- a huge potted plant of some sort, or office equipment. Put something in the carriage -- anything EXCEPT the baby.

<u>WHEN</u> is it happening? The time of day or the season of the year can provide additional possibilities for humor. It might be early in the morning, late at night, or somewhere in between. Consider spring, summer, fall, and winter. Perhaps it happened years ago, or will/might happen in the future. <u>Time, science, and history</u> can be useful tools.

<u>WHERE</u> is it happening? Ordinarily, our young couple with the baby buggy would be seen in some sort of residential setting, or in a park, or shopping somewhere. This presents another opportunity to introduce surprise. Perhaps they are on a mountain top or in the desert, in the jungle or on the moon as robots.

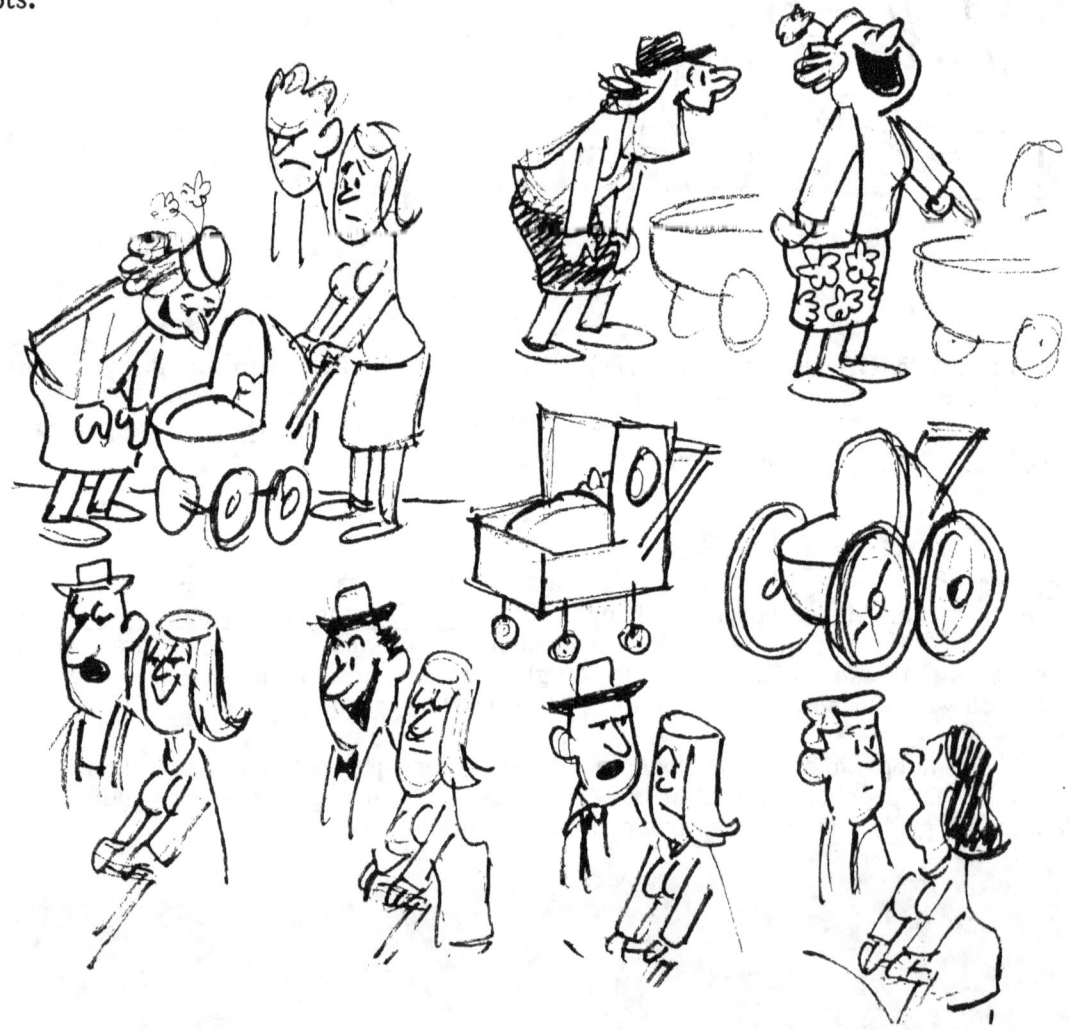

FOCUSING ATTENTION

By now, the imagination has more than enough input of possibilities and is ready for the front burner. Hopefully, you have been making notes, doodles, and rough sketches as we went along on this brainstorming trip. Chances are, you have a dozen or so excellent possibilities on which to concentrate. Review those, keeping in mind the basic "types" of humor (human interest, special interest, slapstick, satire, sex, and weird) and the elements of humor (ridicule, surprise, truth).

Eliminate captions or punch lines wherever possible. Captionless gags are usually the best and funniest. Captions that cannot be eliminated should be edited, revised, shortened, or switched around. Keep in mind that there are hundreds of ways to say the same thing.

Another point to consider, in the case of single panel gag cartoons, is the use of multipanels to "set up" a punch line.

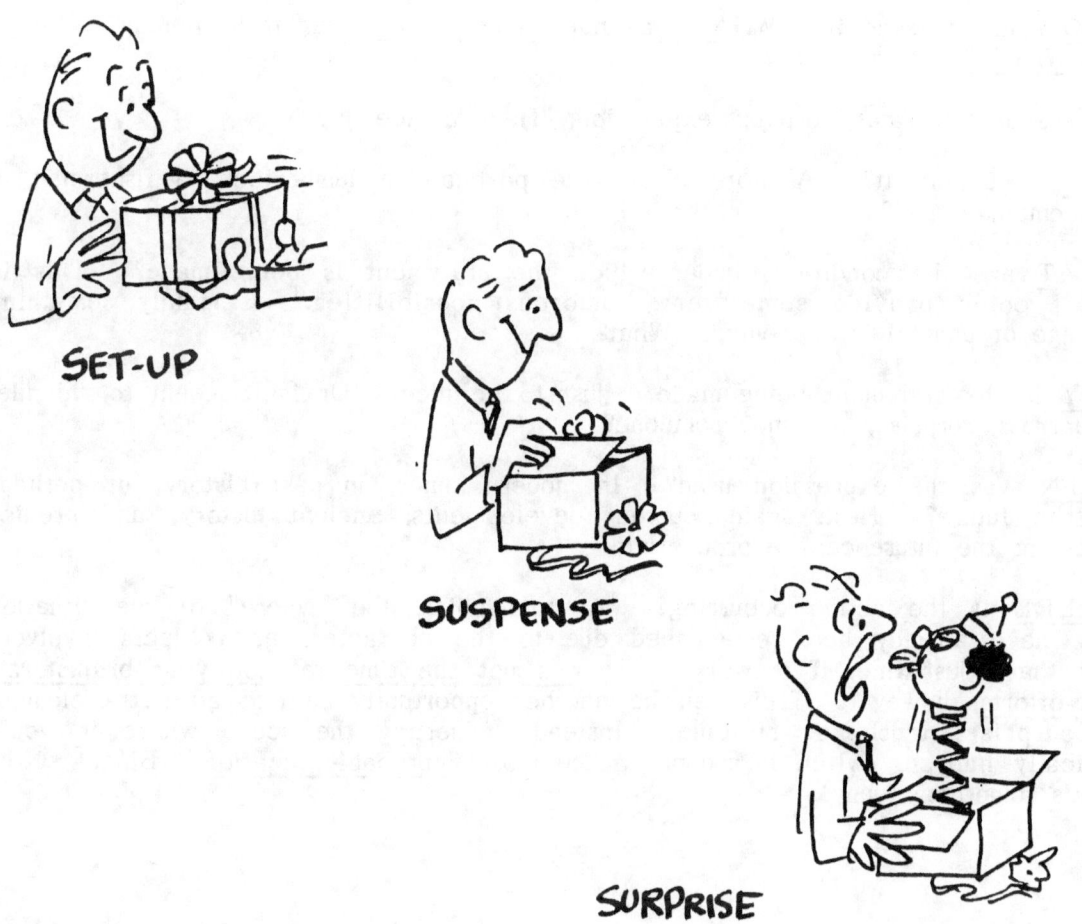

SET-UP

SUSPENSE

SURPRISE

THE WORLD'S FUNNIEST CARTOON HAS NOT YET BEEN CREATED!

WHY NOT GO FOR IT!!

REVERSING THE PROCEDURE

Using a specific topic as the starting point to create humor is the most "controllable" method because you begin with a situation and work your way to a punch line. However, reversing the procedure can frequently be more productive. With this system, you start with a caption, then illustrate or explain it with the drawing. Oddly enough, this method works every time because the imagination can form pictures just as easily as it can words.

We start with a sentence, an expression, a phrase, or even a single word. Anything will do, so don't struggle with it. Make up a sentence, a question, or a silly expression of some kind. Randomly choose a sentence or even group of words unrelated to each other from a newspaper or magazine, or even a dictionary. It doesn't have to be funny or make any sense at all.

Then proceed to illustrate the sentence or phrase as humorously as possible. If necessary, use the Five W's method for help.

WHO said or asked it? WHAT was happening? WHY was it happening? WHEN and WHERE did it happen?

Let's start with that worn out expression, "Have a nice day."

WHO is saying it? A store clerk, the postman, a lumberjack, a fisherman, a policeman, a boss?

WHAT are the conditions under which the statement is being made? This in itself could provide some very humorous possibilities. Certainly something strange or unusual is happening. What?

WHY is the statement being made? Just to be nice? Or is it meant to ridicule, embarrass, surprise, or annoy someone?

WHEN was the expression used? In modern times, in past history, or perhaps in the future? Here again, current developments, ancient history, and predictions for the future can be productive.

WHERE is the action occurring? At this point, the "where" of the situation may have already been established due to the characters and objects involved, and that's just fine, if it works. This is not the time to stop your brainstorming efforts, however. This can be another opportunity to add an extra element of surprise, truth, or ridicule. Instead of setting the scene where it would logically happen, switch it around to the most improbable location. Bingo! Now that's something funny!

THE WORLD'S FUNNIEST CARTOON HAS NOT YET BEEN CREATED!

WHY NOT GO FOR IT!!

CLICHES PROVE A POINT

The cartoon situations shown below are familiar to us all. It is but a mere sample of the many "gag cliches" that have been around for many years. Yet they continue to pop up from time to time, <u>each one funnier than the ones that preceded it</u>. Although based on almost identical situations, each has been given a new, unique twist, with excellent results. One wonders if there will ever be an end to them, and that's exactly the point:

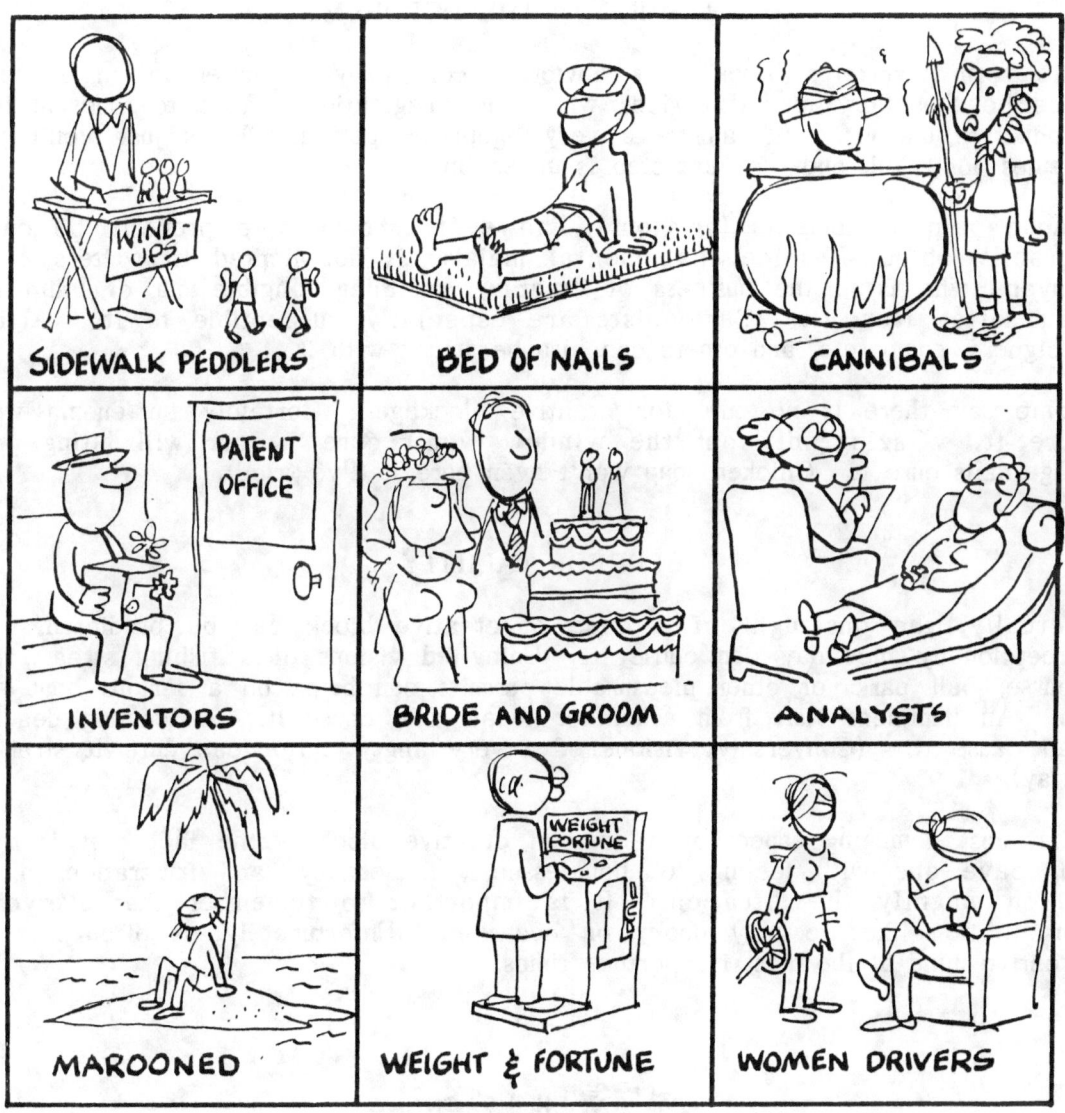

THE WORLD'S FUNNIEST CARTOON HAS NOT YET BEEN CREATED!

WHY NOT GO FOR IT!!

ONE GOOD GAG IDEA CAN LEAN TO A HUNDRED OTHERS!

All too often, a student will create a humorous cartoon and then move on to a different subject. <u>That's like walking away from a newly discovered pot of gold!</u>

When a good idea develops, stick to it. Give it additional little twists and slants. Extend it. Carry it as far as you can, and then carry it even farther. Bingo! Instead of one funny idea, you might end up with a dozen!

WRITER'S BLOCK:
THE MIND IN THE DOLDRUMS

The term "writer's block" was obviously coined by a writer in an effort to describe those dry mental periods when the imagination refuses to function in a productive manner. It can be a very agonizing period. Ideas just won't pop, themes don't jell, and the next step is uncertain.

Those painful moments (or hours), however, should more properly be called "creative blocks" since that mental malaise is not limited to writers alone. Anyone who is in the business of creating something tangible out of "thin air" can suffer from it. Cartoonists are especially susceptible to it. Artists, designers, composers, and others can also be struck with it.

Some say there is no cure for creative blockage. Certainly an enema won't cure it. Gazing idly out the window won't cure it, nor will biting one's fingernails cure it. Chicken soup won't even cure it (I've tried).

PREDICTABILITY

Actually, the onslaught of a case of creative block can be predicted. An exceptionally nice day can cause it. Uninvited visions of a fishing stream, golf course, ball park, or other pleasurable pursuits can bring on a serious bout with it. An imminent visit from a mother-in-law can cause it. A looming deadline can cause it. (Conversely, visions of a very angry editor can cure it straight-away).

The most damaging aspect of a dose of creative block is the fact that it tends to leave one with feelings of hopelessness, inadequacy, and frustration, all of which magnify the situation. It is important to remember that everyone's imagination likes to play hooky on occasion. Unfortunately, it often hits the creative mind at the most inopportune times.

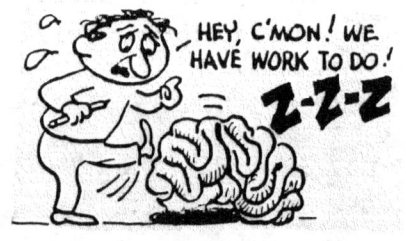

THE CREATIVE BLOCK:
CURE IT ... COPE WITH IT ... SUCCUMB TO IT

THE CURE. Oddly enough, an <u>overabundance</u> of ideas can cause creative block just as quickly as the <u>lack</u> of ideas. It's like a log jam in a fast-moving river. One has lots of ideas, but they just aren't moving along. The solution, therefore, is to concentrate on one key log (idea) and forget about the others for the moment. Work on that <u>one single idea</u> until it begins to show some possibilities, then work on it some more. Gradually, the <u>mental log jam</u> will loosen up and will soon begin to move along at a very rewarding pace.

COPING WITH IT. Let's say that your creative imagination refuses to move in its assigned direction. In spite of your efforts, it has decided to go trotting off on its own little adventures (daydreaming, so to speak). <u>Go along with it!</u> If it wants to settle down on some deserted tropic isle, relax and enjoy it! There's lots of humor to be found there ... coconuts, palm trees, seashells, a distant steam ship, all kinds of good stuff.

Or perhaps our imagination would prefer to worry about some nagging little problem we have. Fine! There's plenty of funny business even in our everyday problems and concerns. In fact, some of the best humor is based on some sort of trouble, annoyance, or aggravation. These are universal in nature. <u>Everyone can relate to them.</u> Presented in a humorous fashion, everyone laughs at them.

SUCCUMB TO IT. Get away from the problem for a while. Take a walk, cut the grass, do some pushups. <u>Exercise can clear the mind and stimulate the brain cells.</u>

Tension or boredom can cause a serious case of creative block. I know of one very successful cartoonist (who warns that he will perform the kind of surgery that would turn me into a soprano if I reveal his name) who has a six-foot stepladder set up in one corner of his studio. On it, he carefully places an assortment of old pots, pans, pie tins, cymbals, and cowbells. On those rare occasions when he is at a total loss for an idea, or when he starts to feel bored with his work, he walks over to the ladder and gives it a good kick. He swears that the resulting crash and clatter, plus the exercise he gets from picking up and replacing all that stuff, relieves his tension and clears his mind. On one particularly bad morning, he went through this routine three times in succession and then went back to his drawing board. Before the day was over, he had completed, from start to finish, <u>five of the best comic strips he ever turned out.</u>

We do not, by any means, recommend his cure for the blahs. We cite it here merely to illustrate that a slight change of pace can often cure a stagnant mind.

THE WORLD'S FUNNIEST CARTOON HAS NOT YET BEEN CREATED!

WHY NOT GO FOR IT!!

QUICKIE REVIEW
CHAPTER FIVE – CREATING (REPORTING) HUMOR

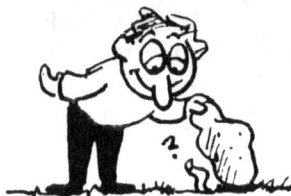

HUMOR IS *EVERYWHERE!* ONE SHOULD DEVELOP THE ABILITY TO FIND SOMETHING FUNNY IN EVERYTHING THAT IS SAID OR DONE.

THE BASIC FORMS OF HUMOR ARE: HUMAN INTEREST, SPECIAL INTEREST, SLAPSTICK, SATIRE, SEX, AND STRANGE.

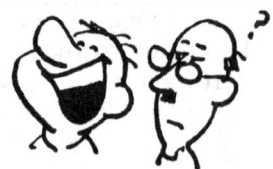

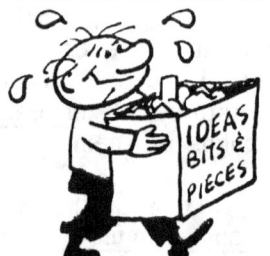

'HAND-CRAFTED' HUMOR IS MADE OF BITS AND PIECES OF INFORMATION, OBSERVATIONS, HARD WORK, AND A TOUCH OF INSPIRATION!

THERE IS NO LIMIT TO THE HUMOR THAT CAN BE FOUND IN A SINGLE SITUATION. HOW MANY CARTOONS HAVE YOU SEEN ABOUT NOAH'S ARK, FOR INSTANCE! EACH IS DIFFERENT – ALL ARE FUNNY!

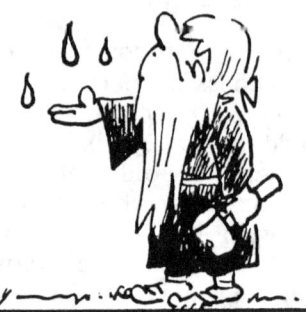

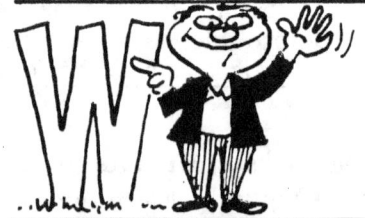

THE 'FIVE W'S' CAN BE VERY HELPFUL IN CREATING HUMOR! SIMPLY ADD *R.S.T.!* (RIDICULE *OR* SURPRISE AND/OR TRUTH)

WRITER'S (CREATIVE) BLOCK! THE IMAGINATION PLAYS HOOKY... OR MAYBE IT'S JUST A MENTAL LOG JAM!

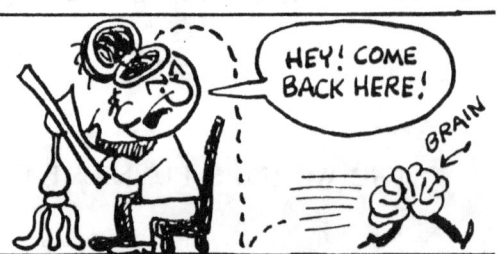

CHAPTER SIX
Gag Cartoons

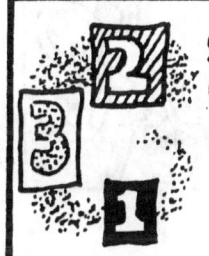

SECTION ONE
COMPOSITION
LEADING THE EYE THROUGH THE DRAWING.

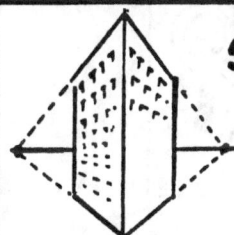

SECTION TWO
PERSPECTIVE
REVIEW THEORY

ADVANTAGES OF "EYEBALLING"

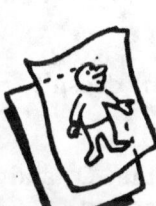

SECTION THREE
TRANSFERRING
- ROUGH TO FINISH
- THE LIGHTBOX
- REVERSING

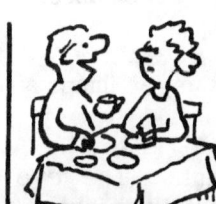

SECTION FOUR
THE SCENE
- KEY ELEMENTS
- VARIATIONS
- EXTREMES

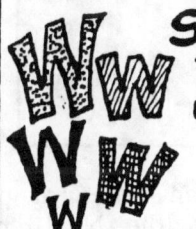

SECTION FIVE
THE CAPTION
NOTHING IS SO FUNNY THAT IT CAN'T BE FUNNIER!

WHO DID WOT?

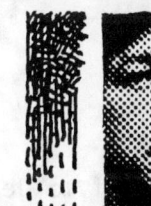

SECTION SIX
SHADING
- TECHNIQUES
- REPRODUCTION

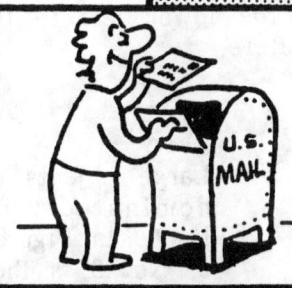

SECTION SEVEN
SELLING
- THE MARKETS. WHO IS BUYING WHAT?
- THE CARTOON "EDITOR"...NICE PERSON?
- COVER LETTER AND PRESENTATION.
- BOOKKEEPING AND RECORDS.

THE PLACEMENT OF ESSENTIAL ELEMENTS

Pictorial composition is nothing more than arranging, in a pleasing manner, a variety of objects within a given area so as to form a whole. Ordinarily, there is no great need to place those objects so they will be viewed in a particular sequence.

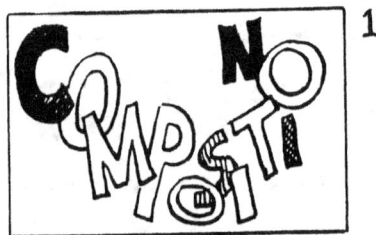
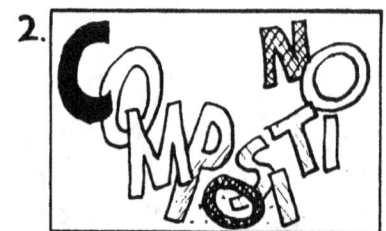

DIRECTING THE VIEWER'S EYE

The manner in which objects are arranged within a <u>cartoon</u> composition, however, is very critical. The observer's eye must be directed to certain key elements within the drawing.

In Figure 1, the viewer's eye jumps from C to the N and then doesn't really know where to look.

Figure 2 is an improvement. The eye is lead from the C to the O and then back up toward the N, hopefully picking up the entire word in one sweep.

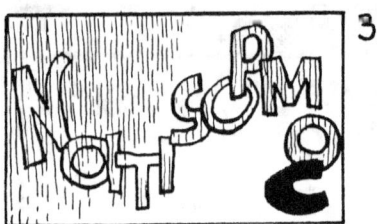
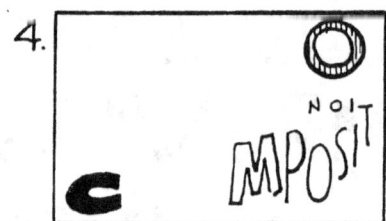

In Figure 3, we have managed to lead the viewer's eye in an unnatural path, starting at the lower right and working counterclockwise to the N, literally forcing the observer to read backwards.

Figure 4 forces the eye to make a big jump from the lower left to the upper right, then back down to the M and the rest of the letters.

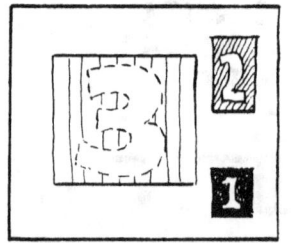
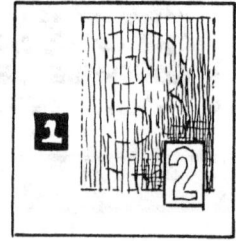

Large objects need not dominate a composition! In Figures 5 and 6, No. 3 is the largest element, but No. 1 is the attention getter and No. 2 is secondary.

USING ACCENTED AREAS TO CREATE A VISUAL "PATHWAY".

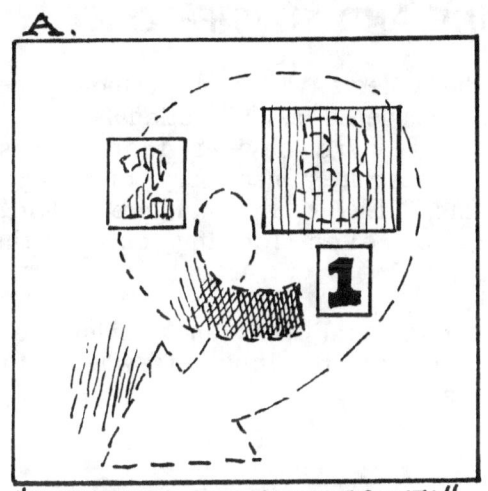

A.

"CAPTION LINE - SNAPPY & TO THE POINT!"

Drawing a cartoon is a lot like telling a joke -- the basic ingredients must follow a certain sequence.

Just as needless details and misplaced key elements ruin a good joke, so too will a good cartoon idea be spoiled.

A successful gag cartoon seldom has more than three key elements (expressions, reactions, and objects).

In Figure A, the viewer's eye is lead quickly around the important details of the gag and then down towards the caption.

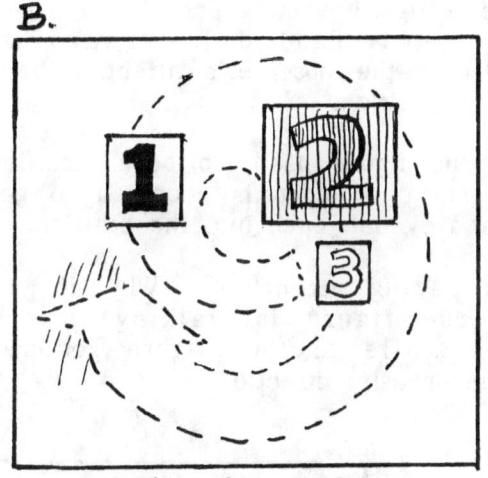

B.

CAPTIONLESS GAG

Figure B illustrates an ideal composition for a captionless cartoon. The main units are placed left to right, down and around.

There are no unnecessary accessories to direct the reader's attention away from the main points.

Careful arrangement of one or two minor details of the drawing can lead the viewer's eye around and back into the composition.

A successful composition will accomplish two things. First, it will capture the attention of even the most casual of readers. Second, it will then tell the story as briefly as possible.

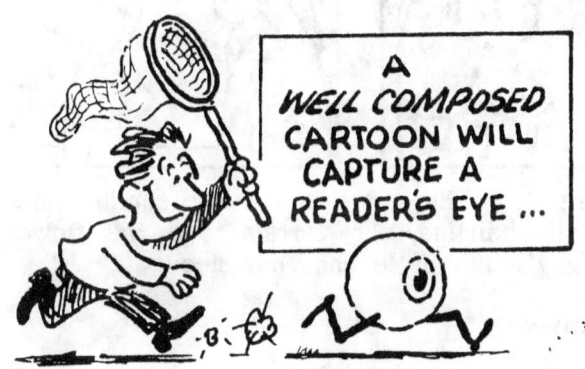

A WELL COMPOSED CARTOON WILL CAPTURE A READER'S EYE ...

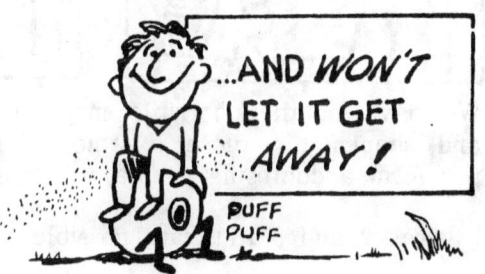

...AND WON'T LET IT GET AWAY!

PUFF PUFF

MOST READERS ARE BUSY PEOPLE !
DON'T CONFUSE THEM. BE BRIEF AND TO-THE-POINT.

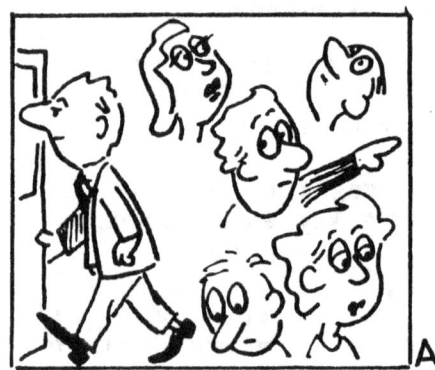

ALL of the objects within a cartoon panel should be considered as "directionals," some of which are more obvious than others. Unless it is absolutely necessary to the gag or story line, NEVER have a figure walking, gesturing, or even looking out of the composition.

Figure A is a total mess and would likely cause a viewer to look elsewhere for entertainment.

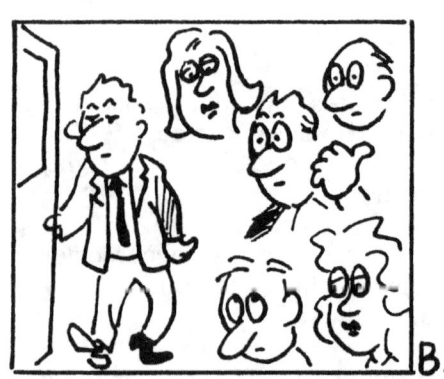

Figure B is a little better. Although we still have a figure walking out of the panel, his left arm is handled in a way that should direct the observer's attention back into the composition.

The pointing figure has also been modified and the right shoulder is accented to get the reader's eyeball back into the drawing.

Are you paying attention? Why do you suppose the figure is walking in one direction while another figure gestures toward the opposite direction?

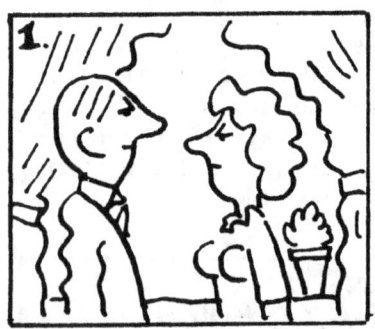
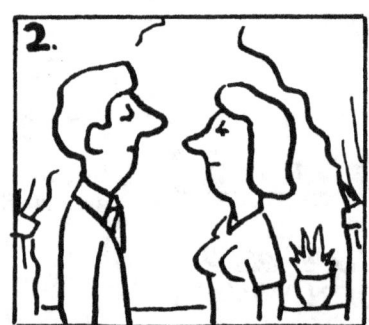
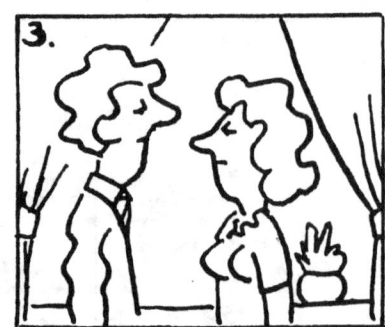

We have another horrible mess in Figure 1. There are too many similar lines and shapes too close together. The gal's hairline, the curtain, and the flower pot form a confusing jumble, as does the guy's hair style and coat sleeve.

Figures 2 and 3 illustrate possible alternatives.

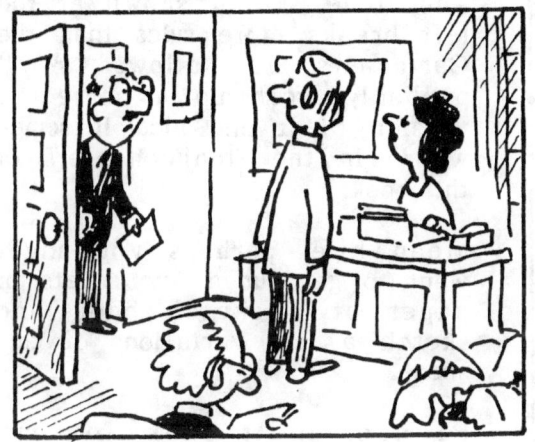

THE "FULL PANEL" COMPOSITION:

This is where the entire panel is pretty well filled up with the drawing, and all the elements actually touch the borders.

Accents should be used sparingly. A little shading and overlapping of figures can help hold the entire composition together.

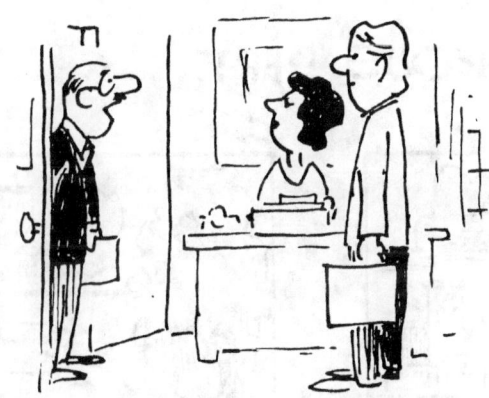

THE "VIGNETTED" COMPOSITION:

This arrangement sort of "floats" in the air. There is a lot of white area around it, with the lines fading away around the outer border areas. This type of composition strictly adheres to the rule of "don't put anything in the cartoon that isn't absolutely essential to the gag." A border is only rarely put around the vignette composition.

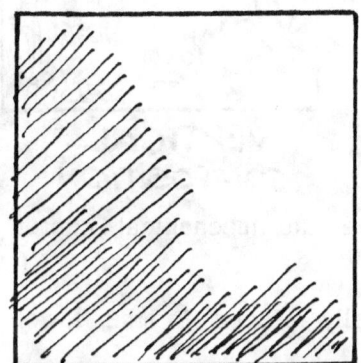 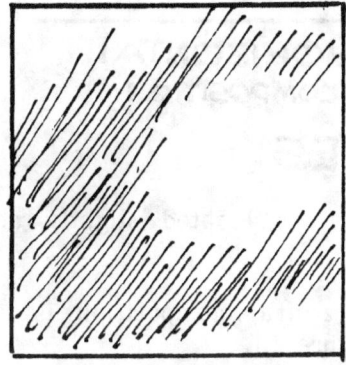 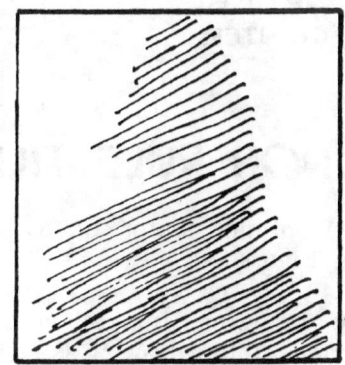

It should be remembered that every square inch of a composition need not be filled up. "Open" areas can add interest to the arrangement.

NEEDED: One Cartoon Repair Person.

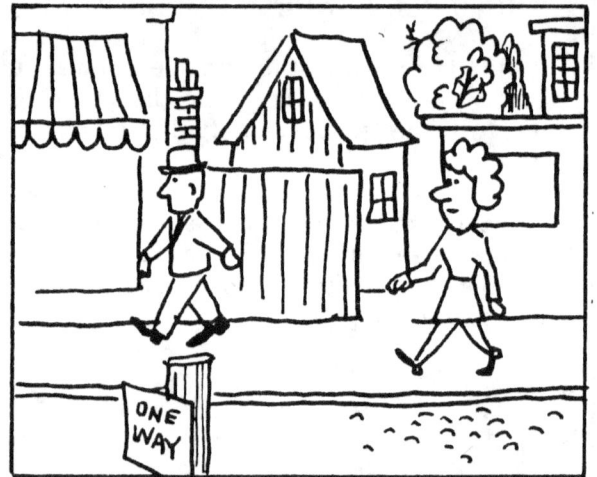

The little sketch shown at the left breaks more rules than the Cartooners' Law allows. We'll probably work up a corrected version of it and hide it somewhere in the final chapters of this book.

Meanwhile, perhaps you might want to get out a few sheets of paper or a sketch book and sketch a few variations of this scene.

Please don't look for my corrected version until you've done several of your own.

FROM THE MISCELLANEOUS DEPT.

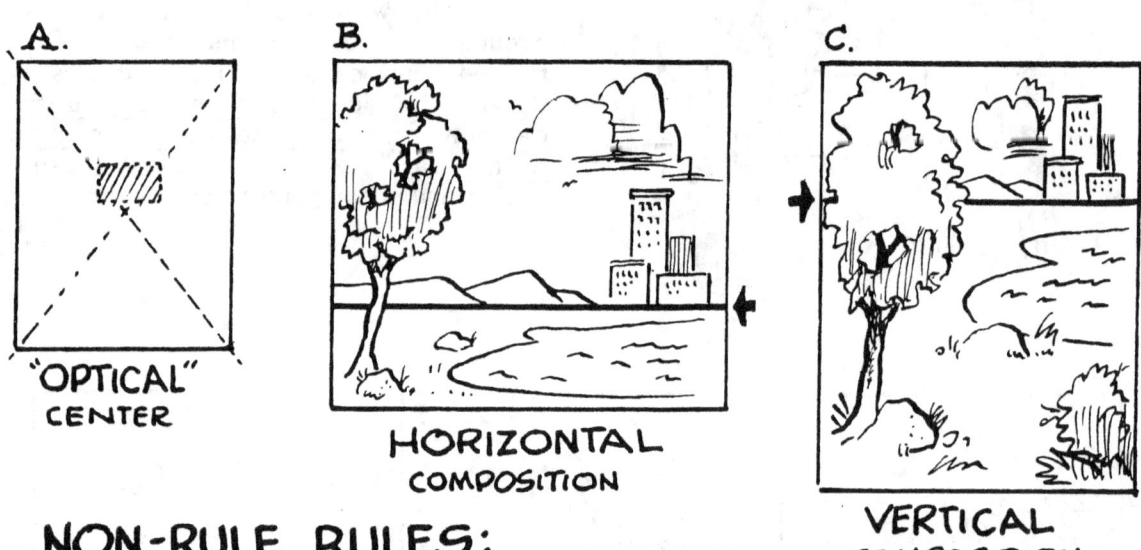

A. "OPTICAL" CENTER

B. HORIZONTAL COMPOSITION

C. VERTICAL COMPOSITION

NON-RULE RULES:

The optical center of a panel is located slightly above the mechanical center (see Figure A).

The horizon line in a horizontal composition is usually placed in the lower portion of the drawing (see Figure B).

The horizon line in a vertical composition is generally placed in the upper portion of the drawing (see Figure C).

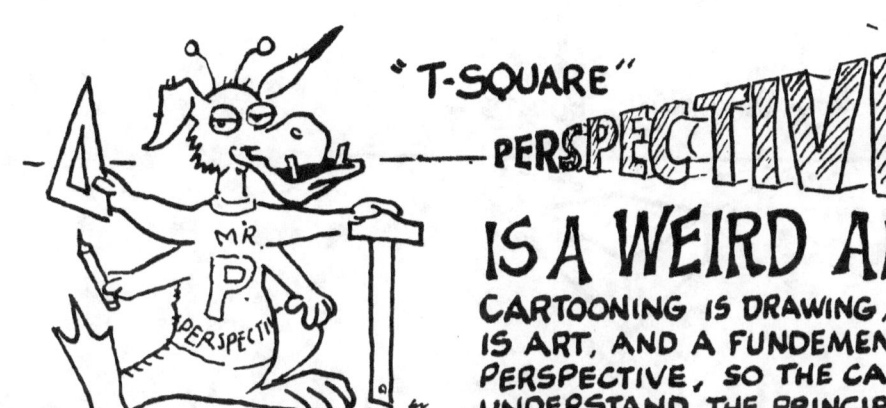

"T-SQUARE" PERSPECTIVE IS A WEIRD ANIMAL!

CARTOONING IS DRAWING, AND DRAWING IS ART, AND A FUNDEMENTAL OF ART IS PERSPECTIVE, SO THE CARTOONIST MUST UNDERSTAND THE PRINCIPLES OF IT ... EVEN THO HE RARELY USES IT!

IN PERSPECTIVE, THE HORIZON LINE (ALSO CALLED *EYE LEVEL*) ESTABLISHES THE POINT FROM WHICH THE OBSERVER VIEWS THE PICTURE. IT PUTS HIM "INTO" THE SCENE.

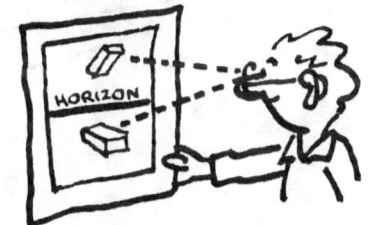

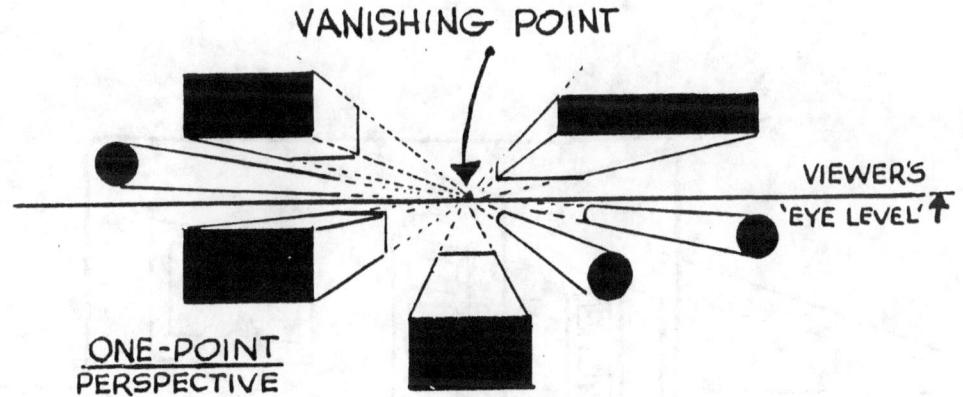

VANISHING POINT

VIEWER'S 'EYE LEVEL'

ONE-POINT PERSPECTIVE

TWO-POINT PERSPECTIVE

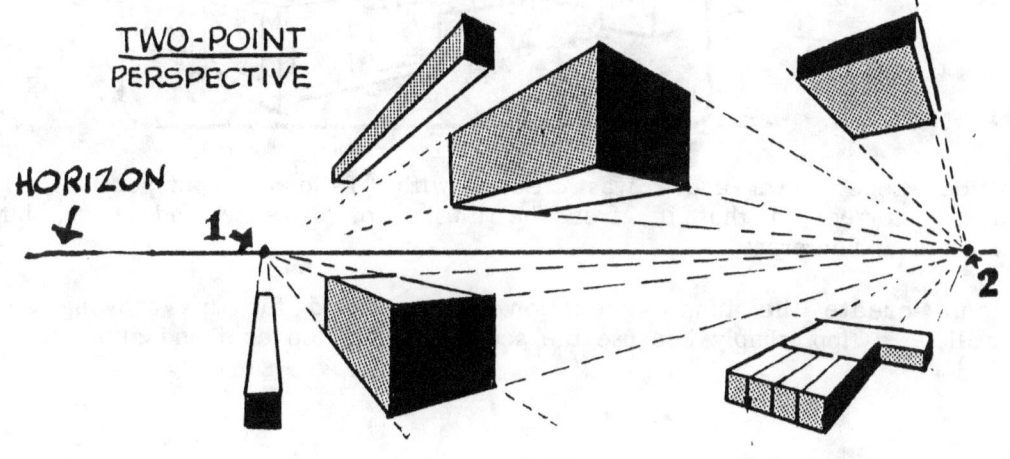

HORIZON

1

2

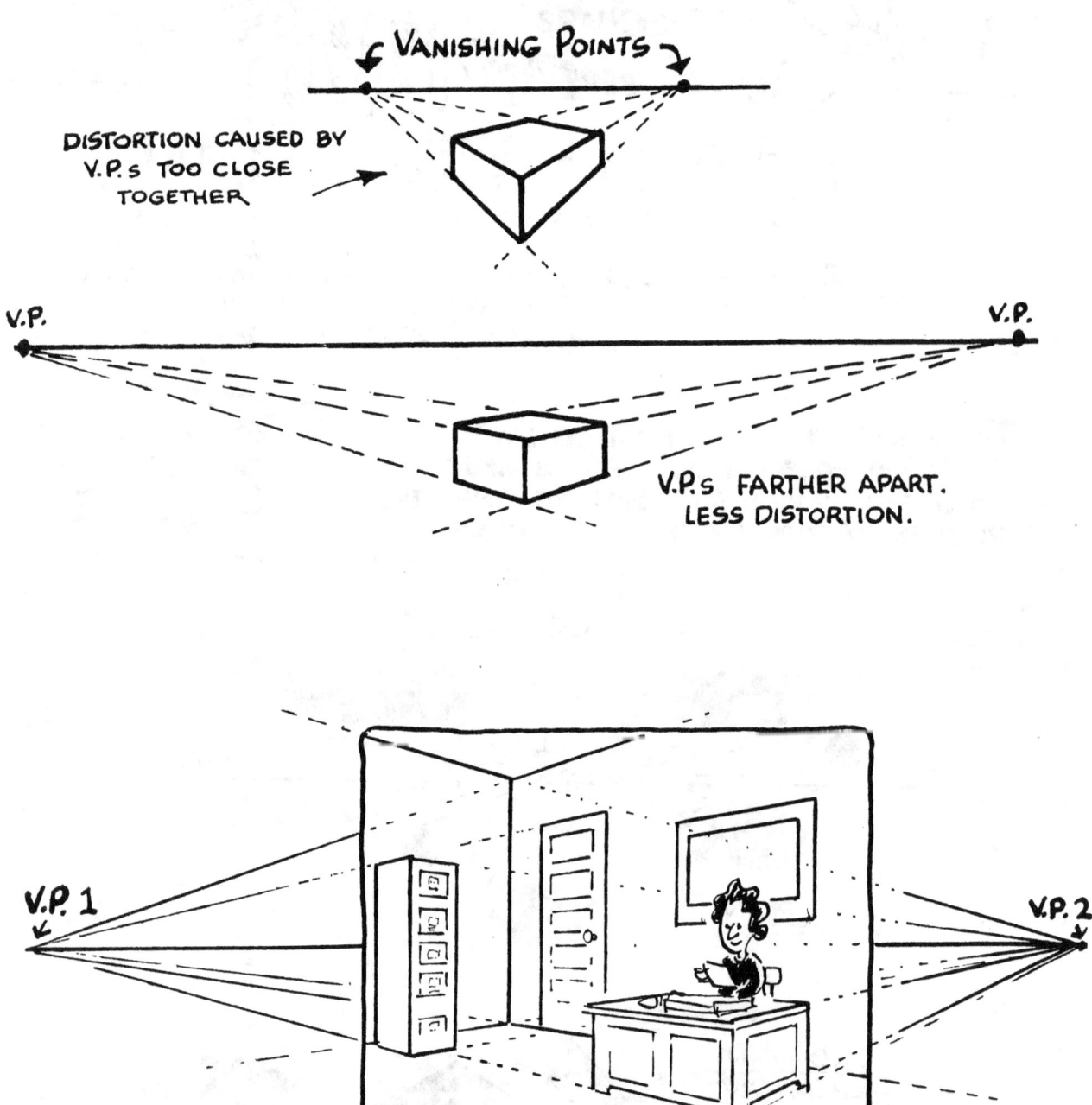

The office scene shown above was created with "T-Square" perspective. It is technically correct in that it gives the illusion of distance and space, but it lacks warmth and interest.

One could create the funniest caption in the world for this drawing and it would still be a flop, simply because the scene itself is too cold and clinical.

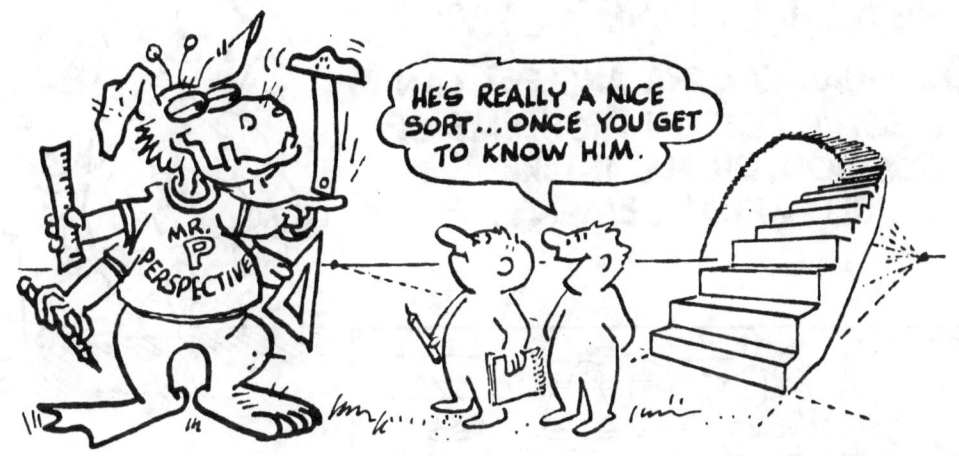

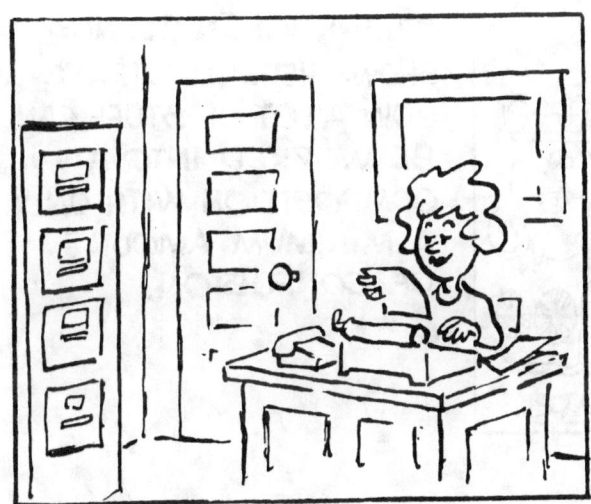

EYEBALL PERSPECTIVE

PERMITS CONSTRUCTION OF A MORE INTERESTING COMPOSITION AND BETTER USE OF SPACE. COMPARE THE SKETCH AT LEFT WITH THE OFFICE SCENE ON THE PRECEEDING PAGE.

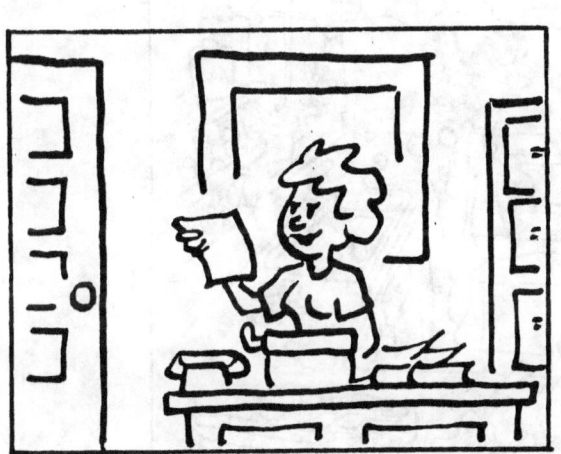

NO PERSPECTIVE

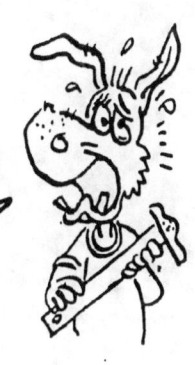

YOU MEAN...WITHOUT ME?

THIS "FLAT-ON" STYLE ELIMINATES PERSPECTIVE, SIMPLIFIES COMPOSITION AND PERMITS A BOLDER LINE TECHNIQUE.

DISTORTED PERSPECTIVE

UNUSUAL "CAMERA ANGLES" CAN HELP SOLVE CERTAIN PROBLEMS OF COMPOSITION, OR ADD INTEREST TO A DULL ARRANGEMENT.

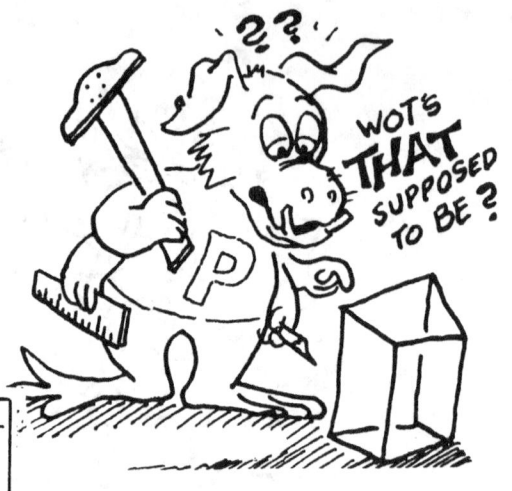

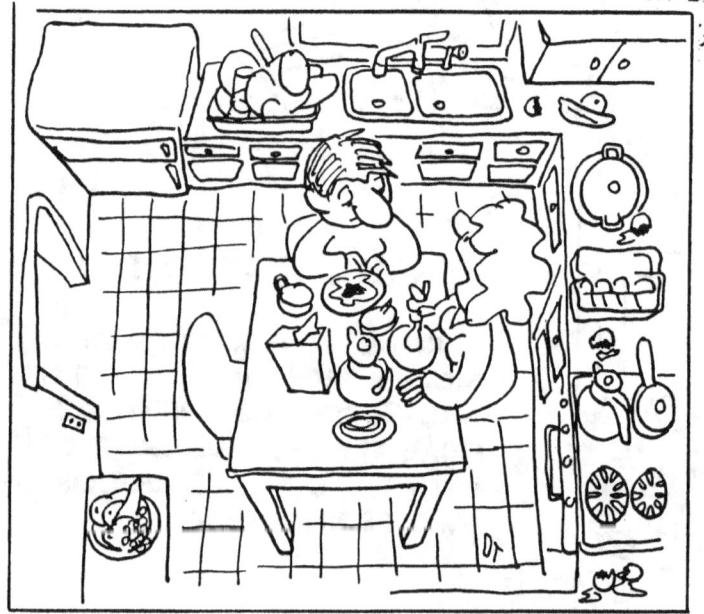

THE KITCHEN SCENES SHOWN HERE ILLUSTRATE HOW A LOT OF STUFF CAN BE WORKED INTO A COMPOSITION WITH ONLY A MINIMUM AMOUNT OF CONFUSION.

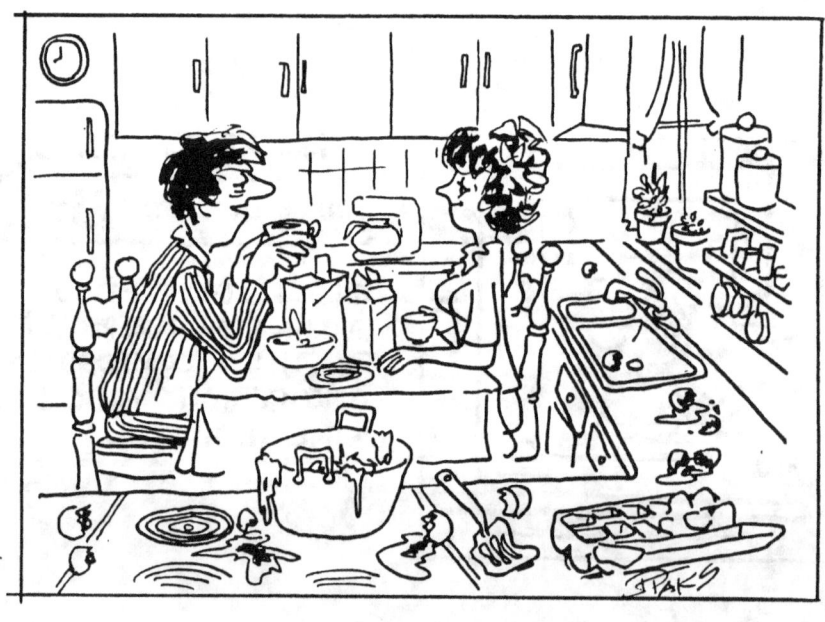

TRANSFERRING DRAWINGS

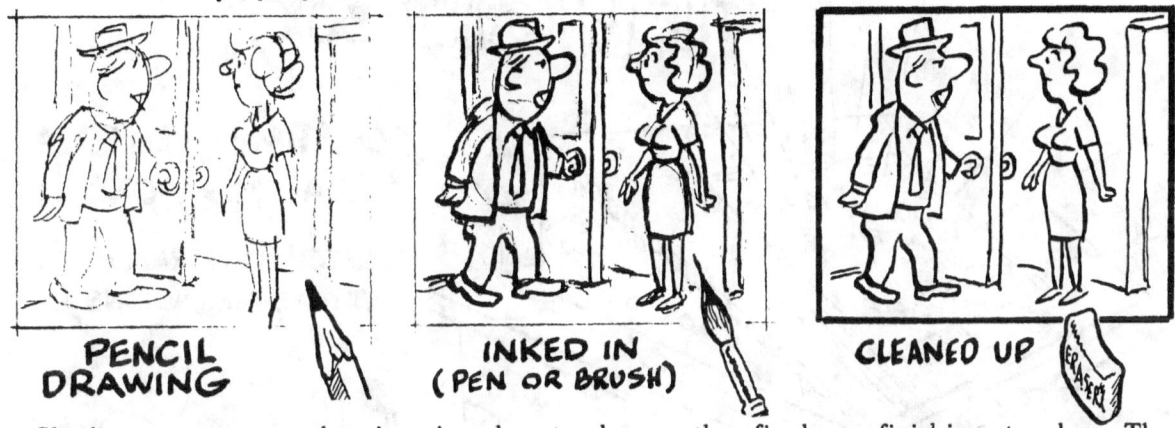

PENCIL DRAWING

INKED IN (PEN OR BRUSH)

CLEANED UP

Shading a cartoon drawing is almost always the final or finishing touch. The "basic" drawing is usually inked in and cleaned up thoroughly, removing all pencil lines and smudges.

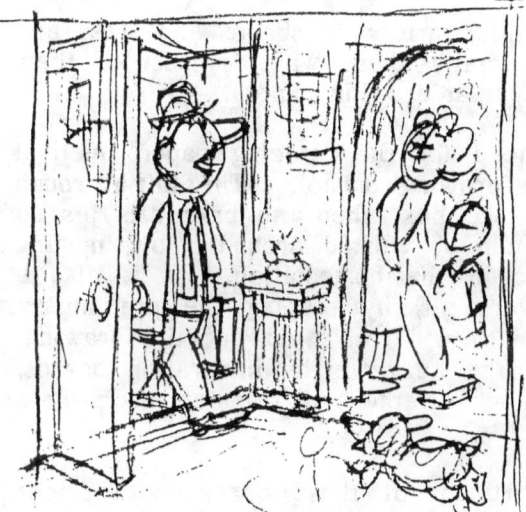

WATTA MESS!

Many cartoonists do their preliminary sketching directly on drawing bristol, ink it in, clean it up, add a dab of pen and ink shading here and there, and that's it.

In other cases, especially when the composition is a difficult one, the preliminary sketch is such a mess that it would be impossible to ink in or clean up properly (see the sketch at left).

There are two ways to transfer this mess onto a clean sheet of drawing bristol or illustration board:

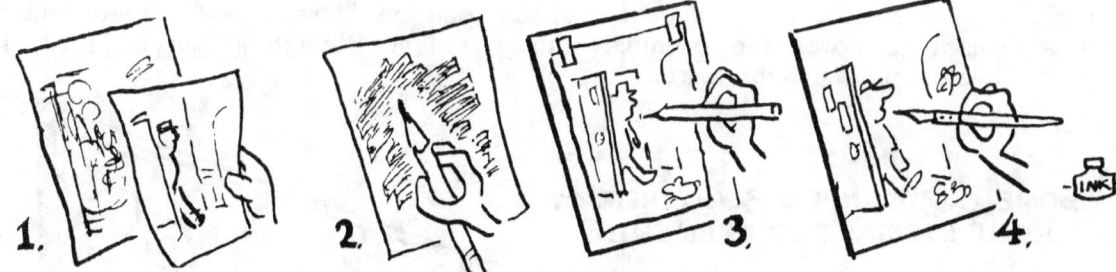

1.   2.   3.   4.

1. Tracing paper is placed over the preliminary sketch and a clean drawing is made. This is a good time to add improvements or minor changes to the composition.

2. The flat side of a pencil is rubbed on the back of the tracing where needed, forming a "carbon."

3-4. The tracing is transferred to a clean drawing bristol and inked in.

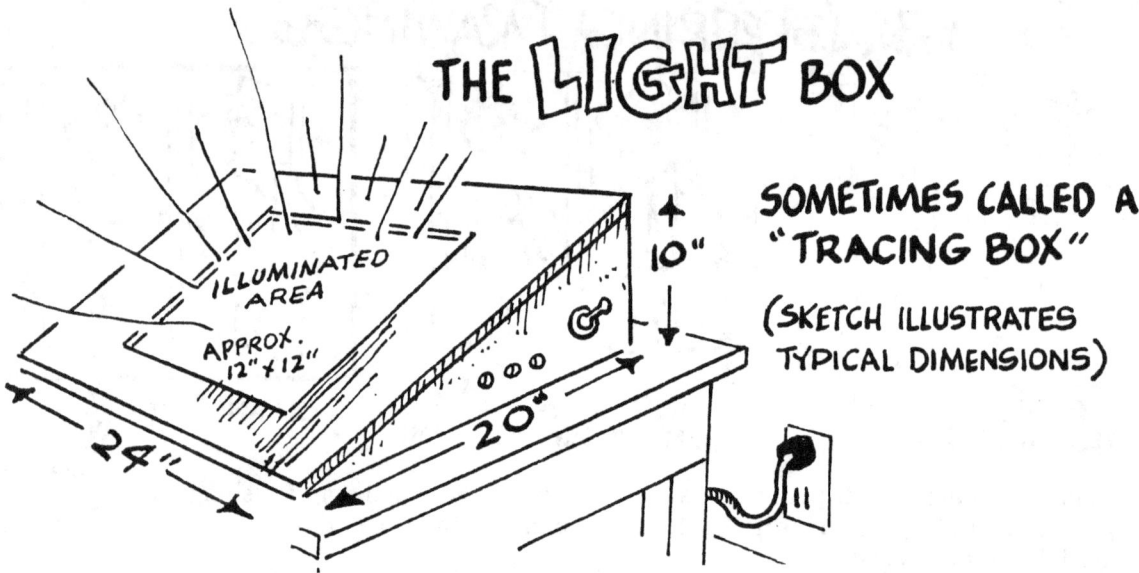

THE LIGHT BOX

SOMETIMES CALLED A "TRACING BOX"

(SKETCH ILLUSTRATES TYPICAL DIMENSIONS)

This handy piece of equipment comes in a wide variety of shapes and sizes and is used by many professional cartoonists, especially those who do most of their final drawings on lightweight bristol or other special drawing papers.

In most cases, the lightbox eliminates the need for the "tracing paper" method of transferring the preliminary sketch to the drawing bristol. The initial rough drawing is placed on the illuminated area of the box, then the bristol is placed over it and inked in directly. The bristol can be shifted around a bit, making necessary changes in the location of objects in the composition. It is also a quick way to check a composition (or reverse it) by placing the preliminary sketch face down, providing the cartoonist with a "fresh" look at the drawing. Obviously, the lightbox cannot be used with the heavyweight illustration boards, but it can be used to make the "tracing paper" method of transfer much more accurate.

Most major art supply stores carry an assortment of these boxes, with prices ranging from about $40 and up. Or, if one is handy with tools and has the proper equipment, a fairly decent lightbox can be "homemade." Plate glass is usually used to cover the opening, although clear Plexiglass can be used if it isn't too close to the light source.

SOME CARTOONERS BUILD THEIR OWN TO SUIT SPECIAL REQUIREMENTS.

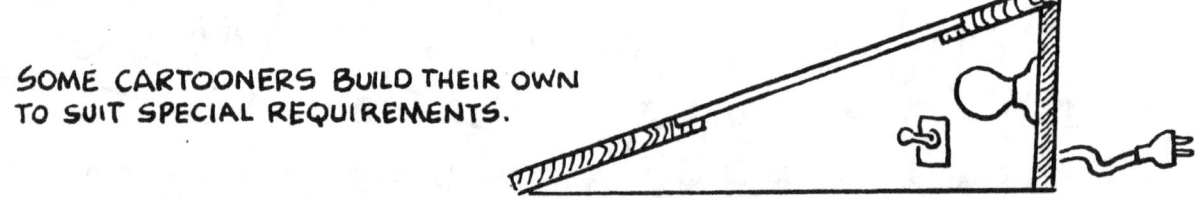

BASIC CONSTRUCTION

THE LIGHT SOURCE CAN BE A 60 WATT BULB OR A 20" FLUORESCENT LIGHT FIXTURE. USE APPROVED WIRING METHODS ONLY. PAINT INSIDE OF BOX WHITE FOR MAXIMUM ILLUMINATION. DRILL VENT HOLES ALONG SIDES & BACK TO PREVENT HEAT BUILD-UP.

LIGHTS!   CAMERA!   ACTION!

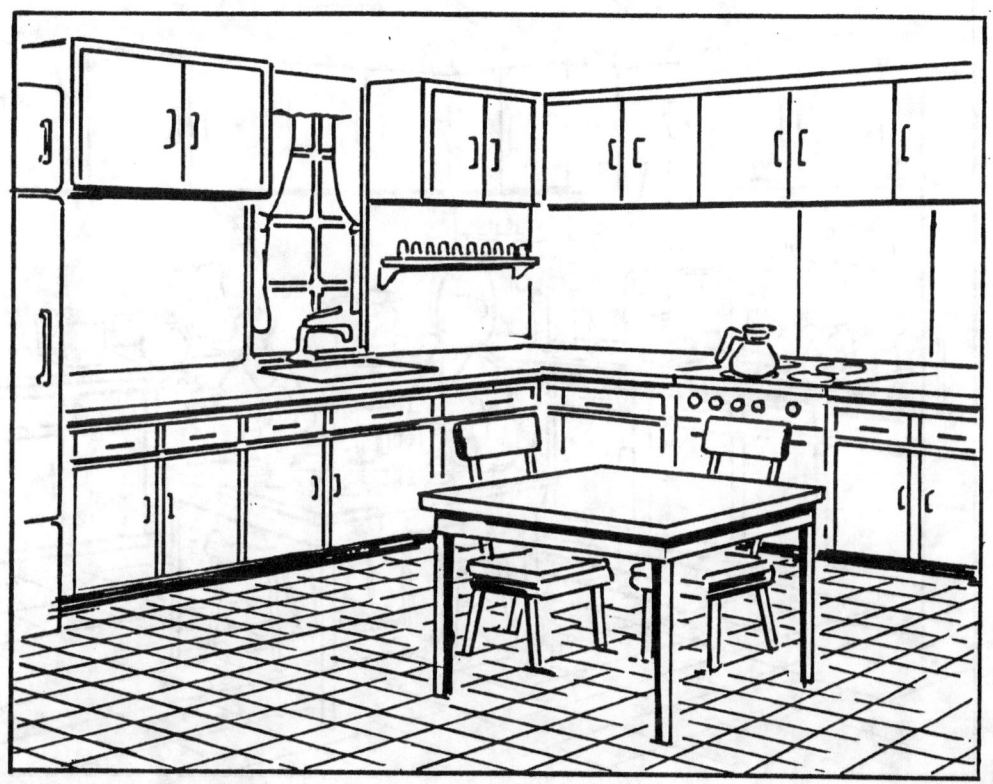

Once again, we have the opportunity (as we did in Chapter 1) to compare the tasks of the cartoonist with those of a film director. Both are in charge of locations, set designs, casting, scripts, lighting, special effects, and editing (not to mention promotion and marketing).

In the successful gag cartoon, as in films, the major elements are all interrelated. The location, props, cast of characters, and presentation must all be compatible with the type of humor being used.

Human interest gags are usually done with a nice "homey" touch, with a pleasant looking cast of characters. In slapstick humor, all of the elements are done in a comical, if not outrageously funny, manner. The "stage" is completely bare except for the props that are absolutely necessary to the "script." Satire is most often handled in an arty, somewhat decorative style.

The following pages of this section will illustrate how a scene can be composed and will depict the various styles and techniques that might be used.

For purposes of comparison, the same basic scene (kitchen) has been used. The methods shown, however, could be applied to any scene or location.

THE OVERLY AMBITIOUS SET DESIGNER

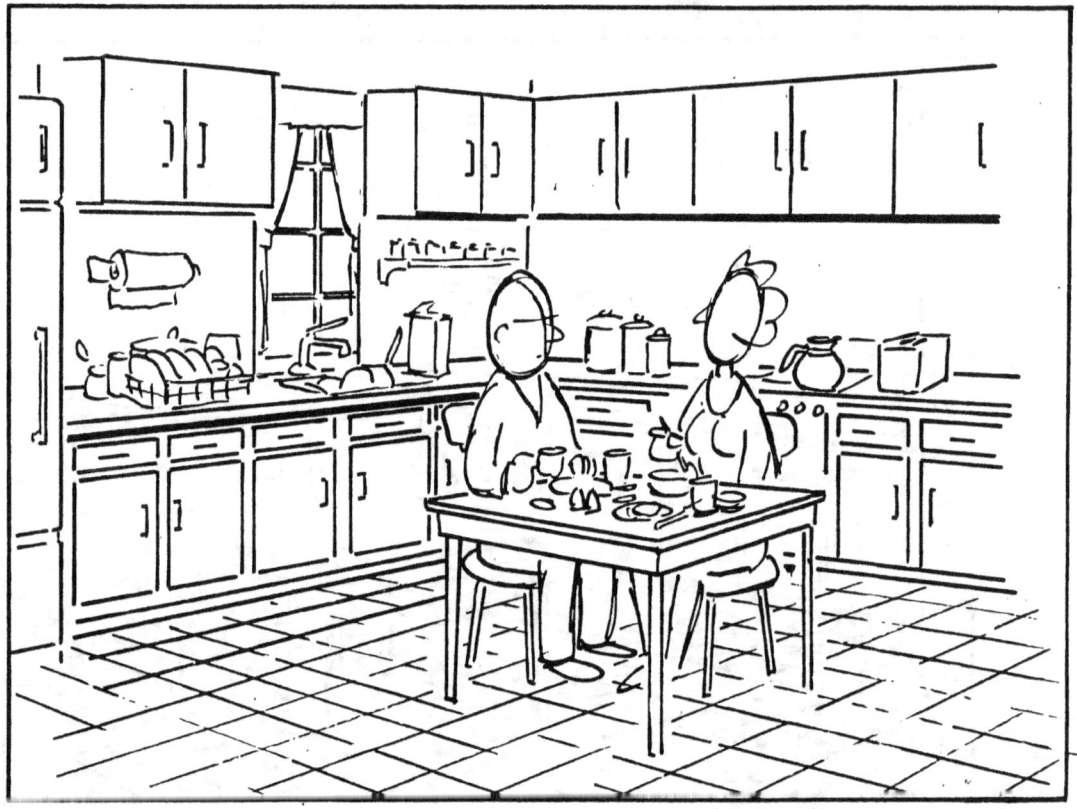

Occasionally, the student will spend too much time and effort to establish a scene (see Figure A). Generally, one need not put more into the setting than is absolutely necessary to briefly describe the location.

Figure B is a slight improvement, although far from successful.

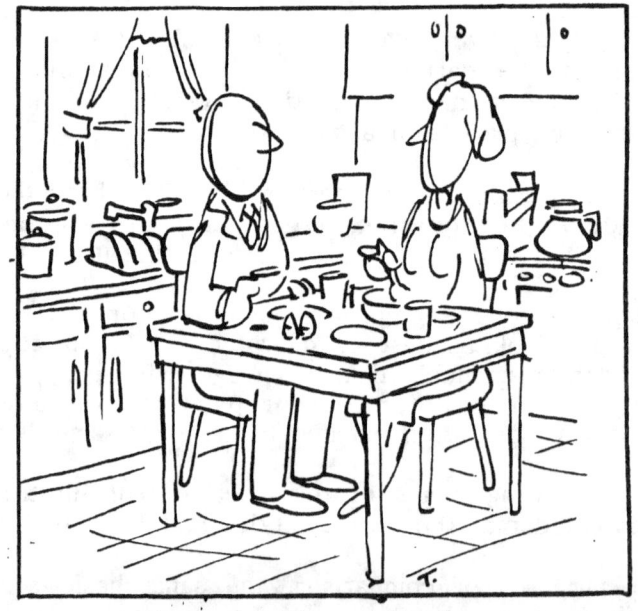

ARE THEY PLAYING FOOTSIE, OR WHAT?

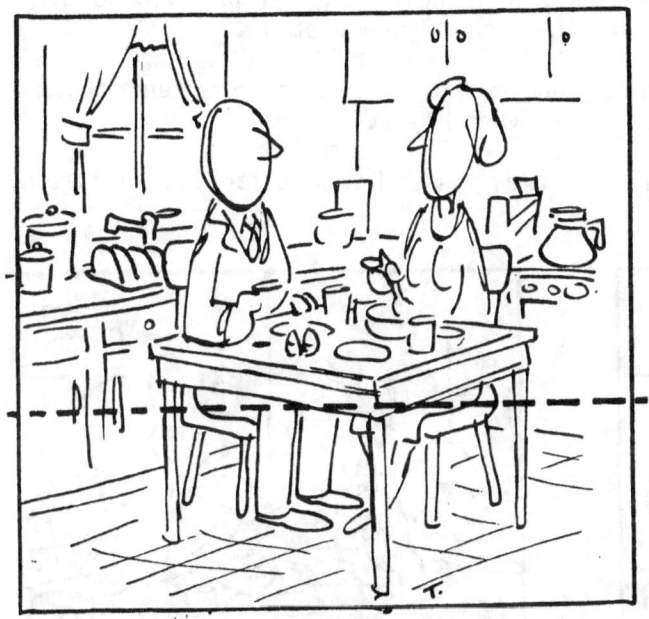

A major flaw in our kitchen scene (left) is that everything below the tabletop is unnecessary (unless there is something there that relates to the situation).

The composition could be chopped off at the dotted line without any great loss.

Ordinarily, it's a good idea to keep the composition as simple and direct as possible. One or two minor elements in the background will usually serve to indicate the location.

Gag cartoons are best when presented with a quick "one-two" punch.

THE TABLECLOTH TRICK ... AND ZOOMING IN

Under ordinary circumstances, one would not expect to see a tablecloth used on a kitchen table, especially at breakfast.

Logic, however, is not necessarily a part of the composition. In this case, the need for simplicity outweighs the need for accuracy.

The sketch at the right takes up the same amount of space as the one above, but it does so in a more effective way.

Had we approached the situation properly, we would have worked up several small sketches first, getting the composition arranged properly before working on the full-sized drawing.

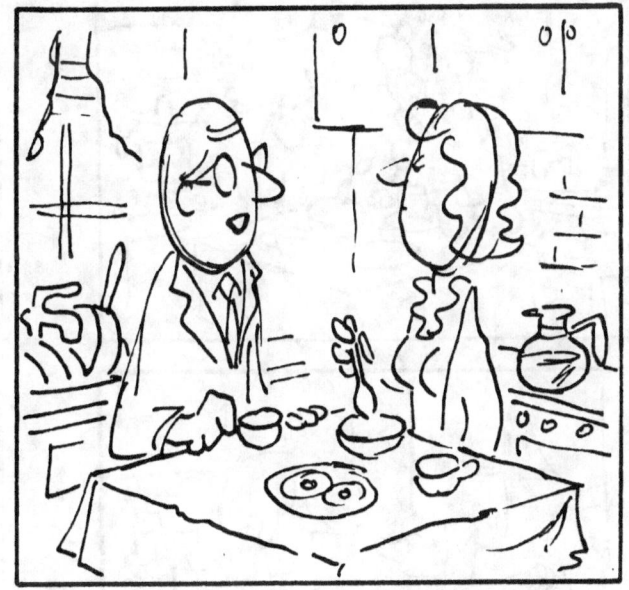

The captioned gag will usually have better "readability" if the speaker is placed in the left portion of the composition. This is not a firm rule, however, since expressions and reactions of secondary characters may be more important than the main, or speaking, character.

KEEP THE SCENE GOING!

When working on a particular cartoon idea, it is never a good practice to stop with just one version. Doodle around with a dozen or so variations.

Work on the Pyramid Theory of creating humor, add new characters, and change background details. Play the "what if this or what if that" game.

Remember that there is NO LIMIT to the possibilities offered in a given situation or idea.

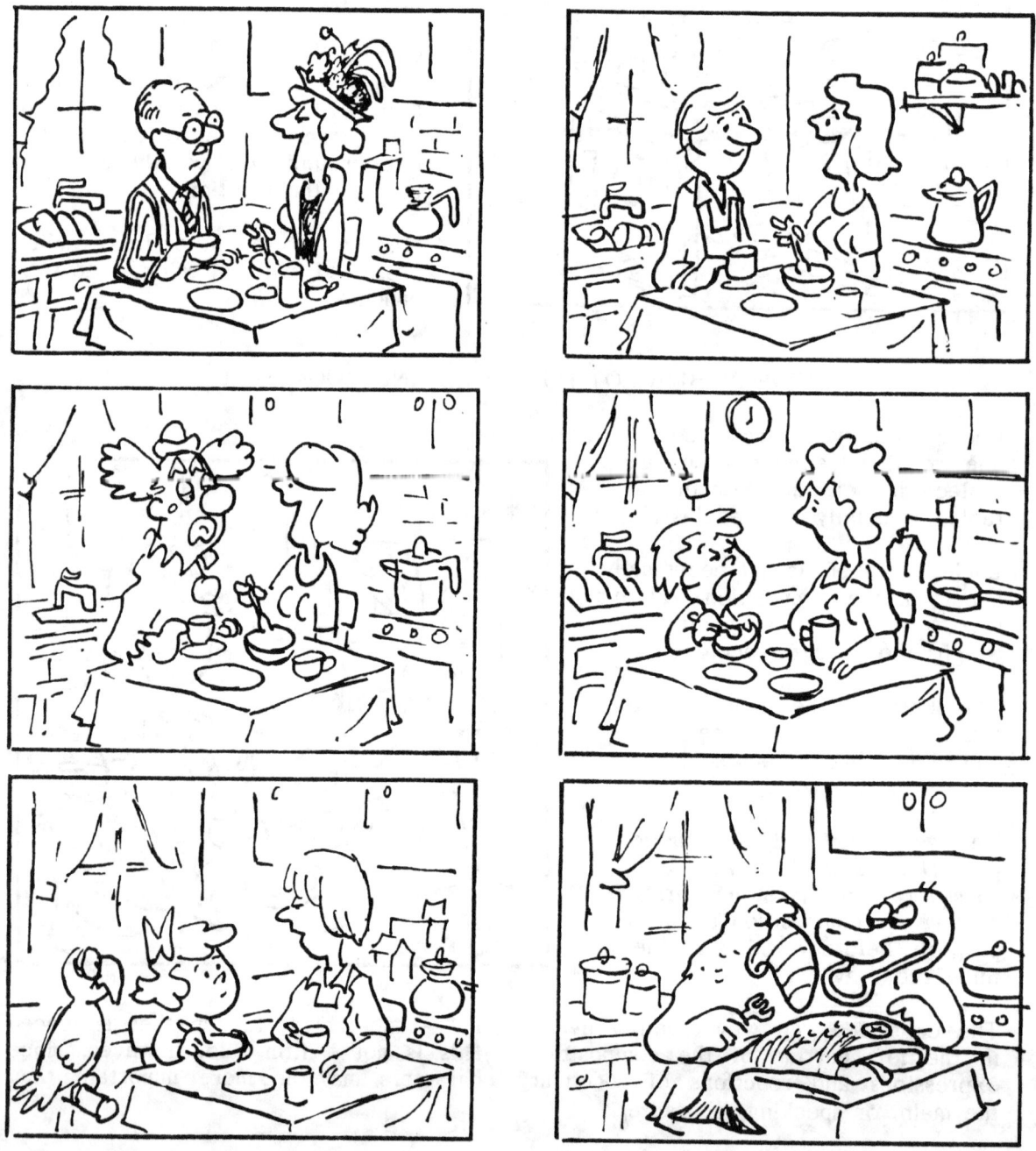

EXPERIMENTING WITH STYLES AND TECHNIQUES

Generally, it is not a good idea for the student to attempt to develop an individual style or technique too early in his or her studies. This is something that develops and improves over a long period of time. Experiment with lots of styles and techniques. Be creative. Give your own natural talents a chance to grow and develop. Shown below is only a small sample of the hundreds of ways our cartoon might have been drawn.

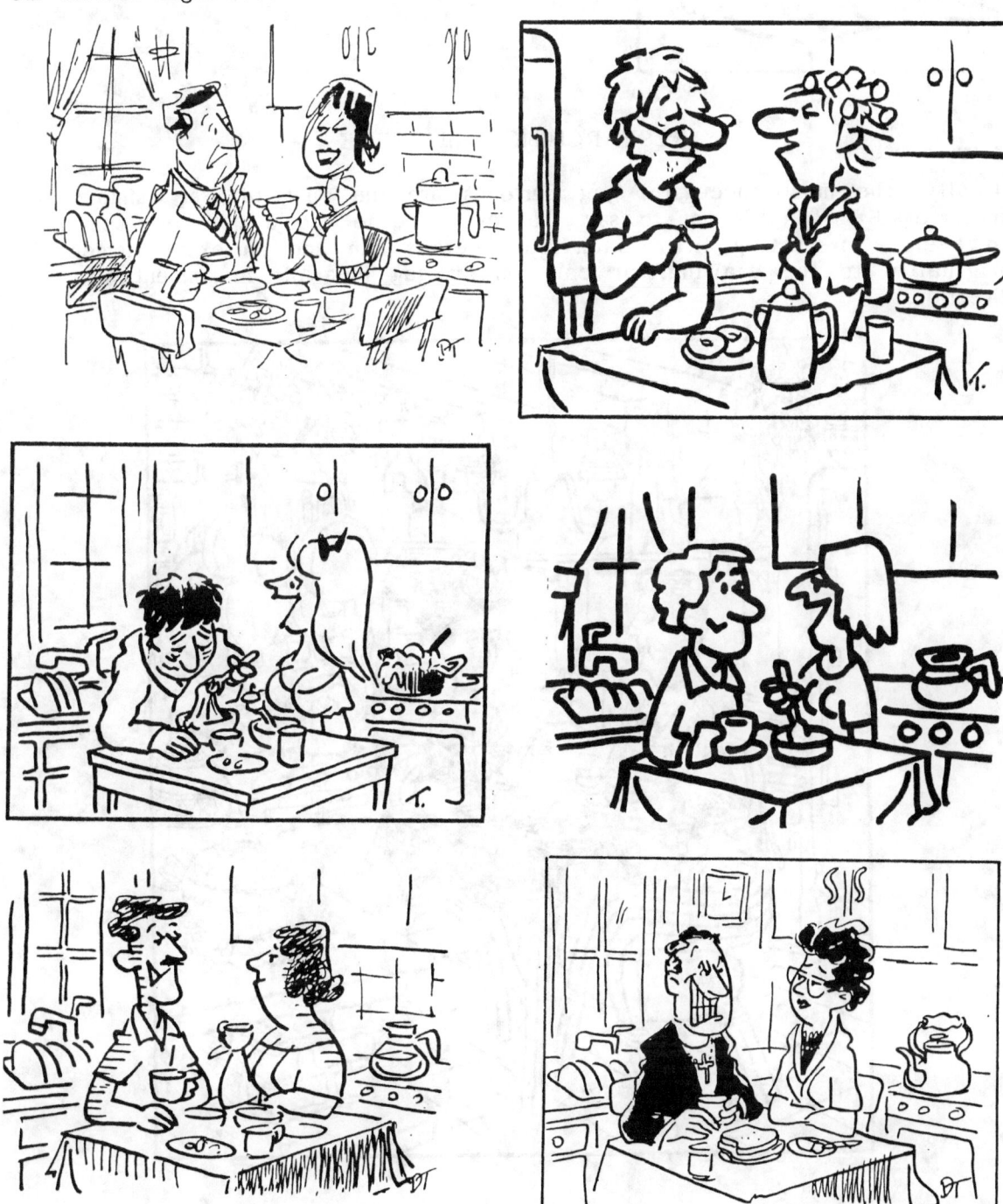

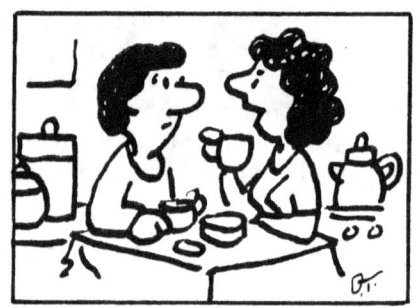

INVESTIGATE THE EXTREMES!

The student who experiments with composition, style, and technique will have a tremendous advantage over the competitor who doesn't!

RESEARCHING THE SCENE

Usually, the most successful gag cartoons are the ones that are simple and uncluttered. That is not to say that every scene should not be researched, however. Interesting little background details can add an extra element of originality to the drawing, or can send a gag idea off in an entirely new direction.

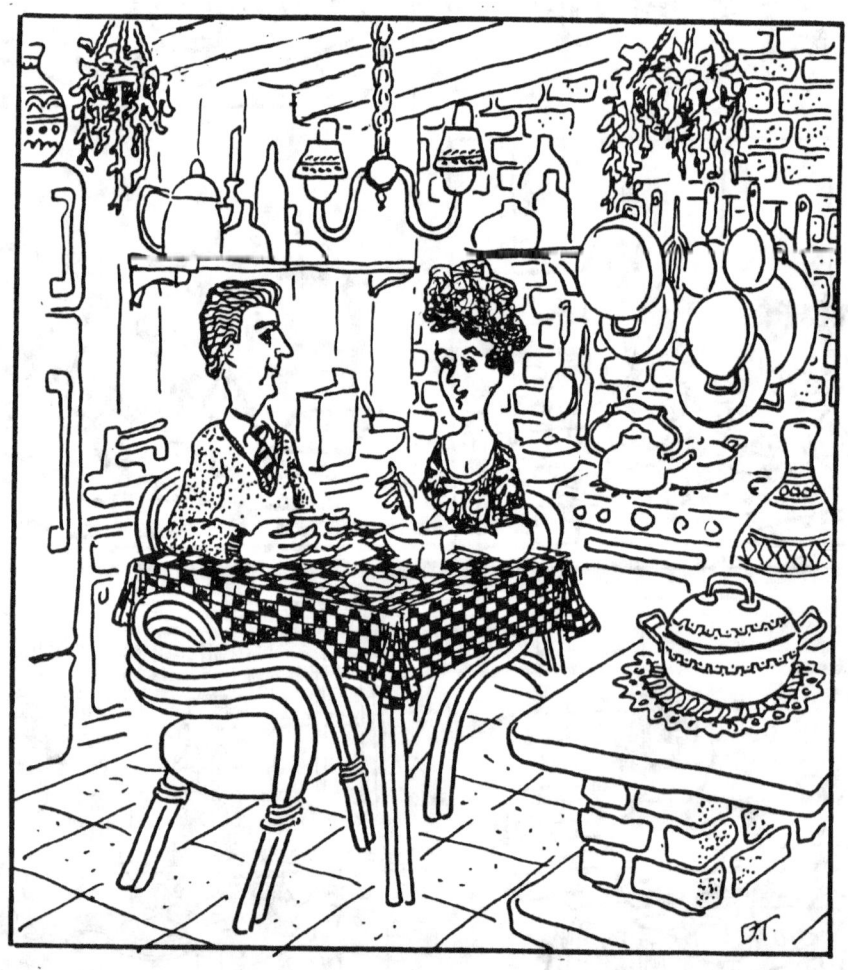

REVERSING / ƎNISЯƎVƎЯ
the drawing...
CAN IMPROVE COMPOSITION AND "READABILITY", CHANGES EMPHASIS AND OFTEN PROVIDES ADDITIONAL GAG IDEAS!

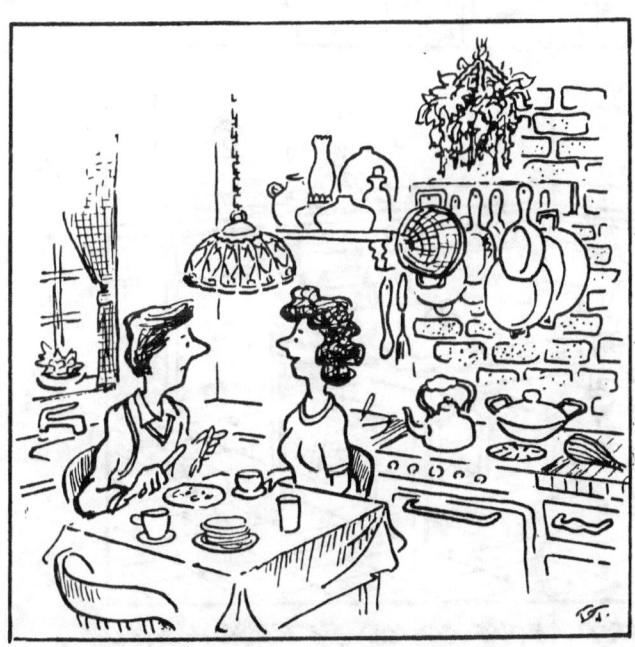

The drawing at the left -- a simplified version of the kitchen scene on the preceding page-- opens up a whole new area of gag possibilities. The empty space in the upper left corner forces the attention to the couple seated at the table. The stove and wall arrangement seem incidental to the situation and play only a secondary role in the composition.

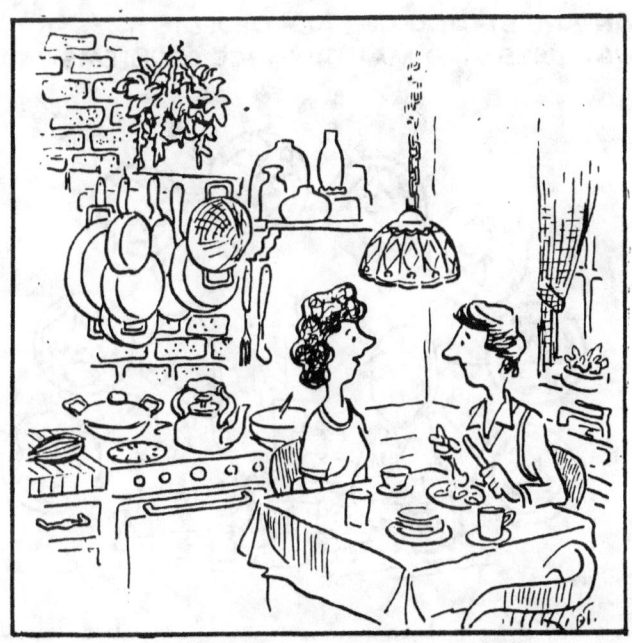

By reversing the drawing -- by means of tracing paper or the lightbox -- we get a fresh, new look at the scene and perhaps a better composition. The eye travels smoothly down from the upper left to the table scene, and then back up and around.

In this case, the wall arrangement takes on a major role in the composition, with everything else secondary.

Typical Research Project...

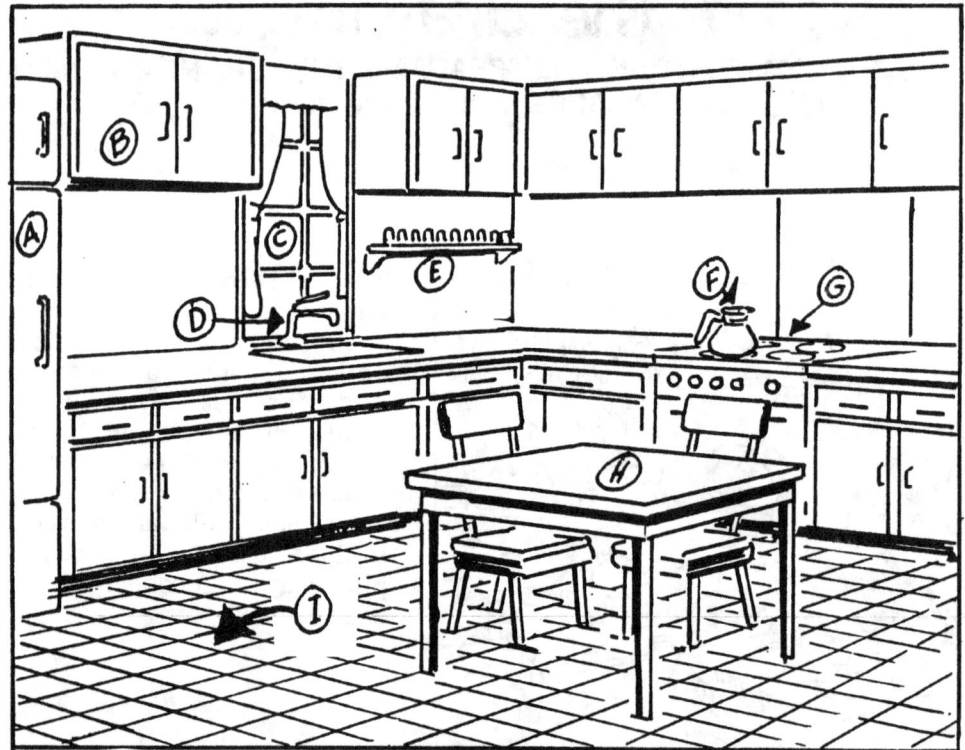

ALL OF THE OBJECTS INDICATED ABOVE COULD BE RESEARCHED
THOROUGHLY FOR HUMAN INTEREST / HUMOR POTENTIAL.

CONSIDER THE HISTORY, FUNCTION AND STYLING OF EACH OBJECT,
POSSIBLE ALTERNATE OR UNUSUAL USES AND MAINTENANCE PROBLEMS.

ATTEMPT TO VISUALIZE WHAT
TYPE OF PERSONS AND EMOTIONS
MIGHT BE INVOLVED IN THE
SCENE AND HOW THEY RELATE OR
REACT TO THE OBJECTS.

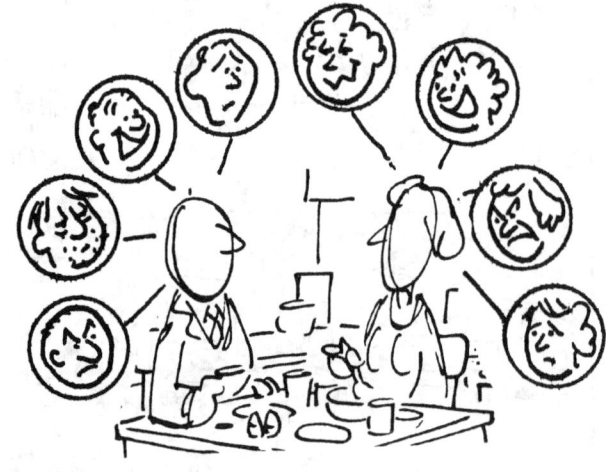

PLEASE REMEMBER... THE METHODS & TECHNIQUES OUTLINED THROUGHOUT
THIS CHAPTER CAN BE APPLIED TO ANY SCENE OR LOCATION !

SKETCHING MAKES THE SCENE GO BETTER

Once again, we bring out the soapbox and harp about the importance of the Quick Sketch Habit. The kitchen scenes shown throughout this chapter represent only a small fraction of the situations that you should become familiar with and be able to sketch up with a minimum amount of difficulty.

Collect clippings of photos of all sorts of scenes and locations. Save them. Quick sketch them. Load up your mental inventory. Doing so will improve your drawing skills and provide tons of potential gag ideas.

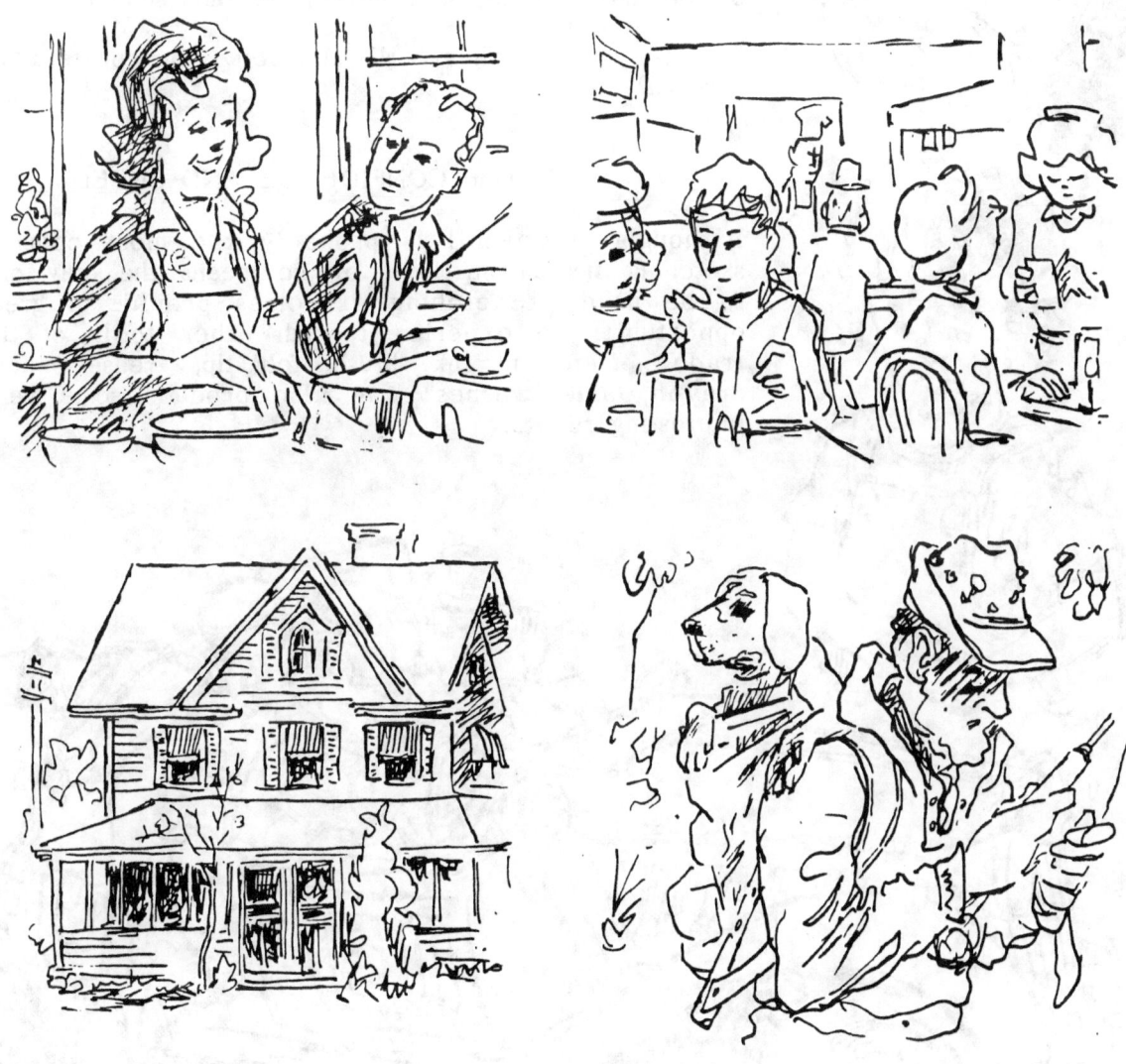

CARTOONING IS ART — ART IS DRAWING - DRAWING IS SKETCHING! SKETCH ANYTHING & EVERYTHING!

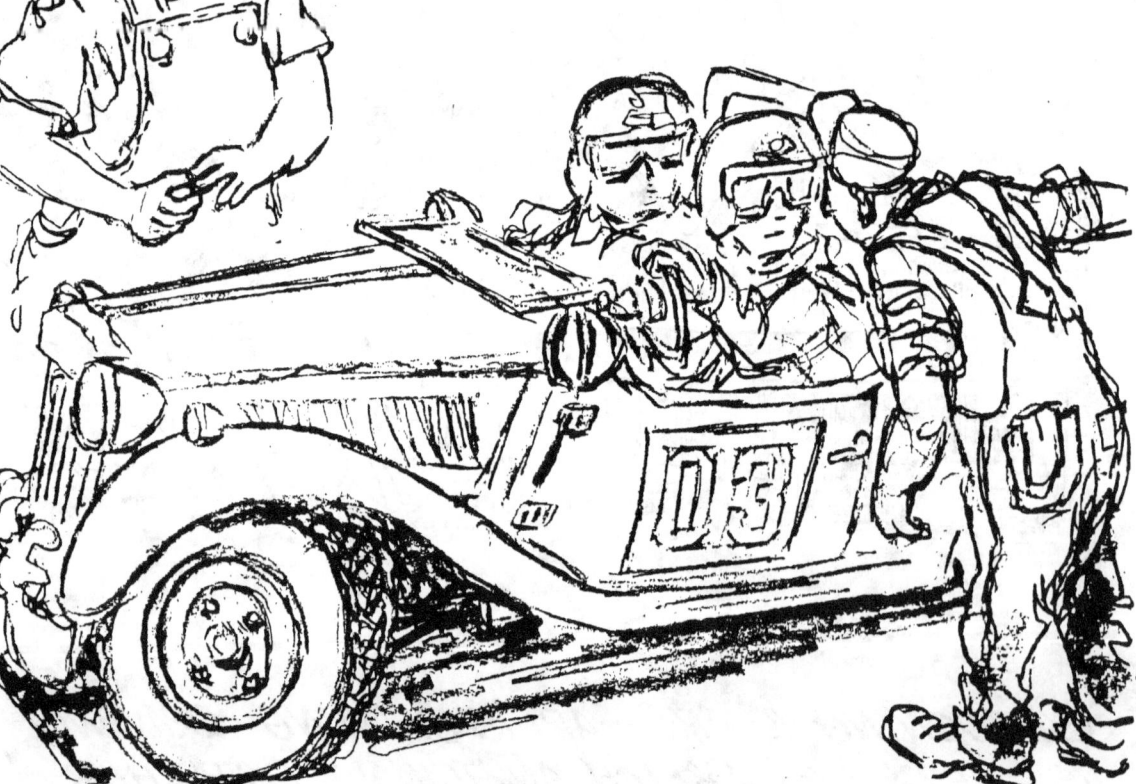

QUICK SKETCHES ARE NOT MEANT TO BE MASTERPIECES

There is no need to labor over the sketching exercises outlined throughout this book.   Exactness of detail is not as important as capturing the mood and spirit of the subjects involved.

The "Single Line" sketching exercise will help you develop a basic technique.

"Tornado" sketching methods will help you develop a better understanding of forms, shapes, and shading.

"Memory" sketches will sharpen your powers of observation.

DEVELOP CONFIDENCE AND SPEED

Although the pencil is probably the most common sketching instrument, it is by no means the only one to be used.   Sketching exercises provide a great opportunity to experiment with other tools of the trade.   Pen and ink, brush, felt tip, grease pencil, crayon, and "washes" can also produce some very interesting results.

CREATING CAPTIONS

The kitchen scenes shown throughout this chapter were not drawn with any particular gag ideas in mind, since we were more concerned with illustrating certain principles of perspective and composition and the unlimited number of possibilities that are provided in a given situation.

However, the scenes present an excellent opportunity for you to exercise your creative powers since all of the drawings contain three of the five W's (see Chapter 5).

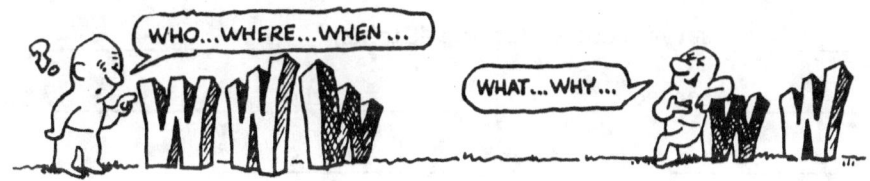

Obviously, the scenes indicate the Who, Where, and When. Only the WHAT and WHY remain unanswered. WHAT is being said, and WHY is it being said?

TRUTH ... RIDICULE ... SURPRISE

As outlined in Chapter 5, the element of TRUTH in everyday life is perhaps the most popular form of humor -- a sort of reflection of human frailties and follies. This is the type of humor that is all around us every day. One need only be on the alert for it and, with a little twist or two, report it. WHAT was said or done at your breakfast table this morning, and WHY?

Ridicule is probably the second most widely used form of humor. The dumb question when the answer is obvious. The dumb answer when the question is obvious. The lame excuse, the big mistake, the coverup.

Surprise and misdirection can be a useful tool in creating humor. This is where we lead the reader to expect one thing and then zap him with a totally unexpected punch line. It is most effective when used with a multipanel, captionless cartoon, although it can be successful when used with a slapstick approach. Our kitchen scene, for instance, seems normal enough, but it contains lots of possibilities for surprise. The window, sink, stove, table, and food all provide clues to the unexpected. A horse at the window? A duck in the sink? A huge kettle or block of ice on the stove? A very small table, or a very large one?

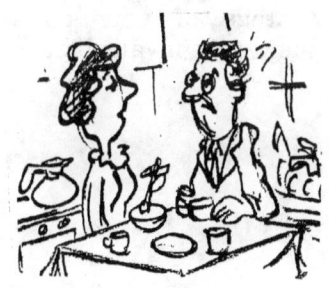

WHO ... WHAT ... WHERE ... WHEN ... WHY?

The five W's can provide a good starting point for a lot of high-powered creative thinking, and it will work with any gag idea or situation.

Let's begin by reducing our kitchen scene to a single sentence: "The lady served coffee at the kitchen table."

By using a few blank lines in place of the words, our basic situation changes:

"The lady served _____ at the kitchen table.

"The _____ served coffee at the kitchen _____.

"The _____ served _____ at the _____.

"The lady _____ coffee at the _____.

The Whats, Wheres, Whens, Whos, and Whys can go on and on throughout the entire scene, or we can change our line of thinking by simply changing our lead line:

"The man ate cereal for breakfast."

The man did WHAT with cereal, and WHEN, and for gosh sakes, WHY?

THE CAPTION SAGA CONTINUES ... EXPANDING OUR HORIZONS

So far, our attempts to introduce humor into a given situation have been directed toward a general market -- common, everyday stuff to which we can all relate.

However, there is a vast market for cartoons of a specialized (slanted) nature. Every trade, profession, hobby, or special interest group has a publication devoted to that particular field of endeavor. The butcher, the baker, the candlestick maker. Doctors, lawyers, veterinarians, zoologists, archaeologists, contractors, stamp collectors, and hobbyists of every description. You name it and it's a good bet there is a publication for it. Most if not all professional cartoonists -- be they editorial, gag, comic strip, or special features -- used the trade journals to develop their skills and as stepping stones to their ultimate goals.

Admittedly, the pay is not great in many cases, and is frequently on an "on publication" basis. Even so, you should be more concerned with getting published, at least in the early stage of your career. The experience to be gained through the trade journal market is invaluable.

WHERE ARE THE MARKETS?

If you are not yet familiar with the Writer's Digest publication, and especially their annual Artist's Markets report, we urge you to do so at the earliest opportunity. The book is constantly updated and lists hundreds of publications that use freelance cartoons, what their requirements are, their payment method, who to contact (very important), the length of time required for a response, and much more. For further information, write to:

Artist's Market
1507 Dana Avenue
Cincinnati, OH 45207

In the meantime, check out your local veterinarian, barber/beauty shop, auto body shop, doctor, dentist, contractor, hobby shop, etc. These places often have several old copies of their trade journals lying around that they can give away or lend out. Make sure you introduce yourself and present your business card. One never knows where such contacts will lead.

EXPERIENCE AND/OR RESEARCH

Students should aim their work at a trade or profession with which they have had some experience. A shoe clerk might do cartoons about retail sales. A plumber should have some funny ideas for a builder's journal. And so on. This is not to say, however, that each and every possible market should not be researched and studied thoroughly before submitting work. And, as pointed out in Chapter 5, never, but never, insult or degrade the particular trade or profession (although something funny about their competition might work).

Above all, when submitting to specialized markets, make certain that all details, technicalities, and terminology are correct. This will indicate that you have had experience with the subject, or at least have researched it thoroughly. This might be a big step toward a sale or possible assignment.

GETTING THE MOST MILEAGE FROM A GOOD GAG IDEA

Let's say that we have created a great cartoon about an auto mechanic. Fine. Now let's study every aspect of that idea, the elements involved, and the punch line. It's quite possible that the basic idea might work just as well or better with an airplane mechanic, or boat motors, or farm machinery, or any sort of motor driven equipment.

Switcheroo methods are common practice in the cartoon profession and are especially helpful when one is required to produce 30 or 40 (or more) cartoon ideas per week to make a buck.

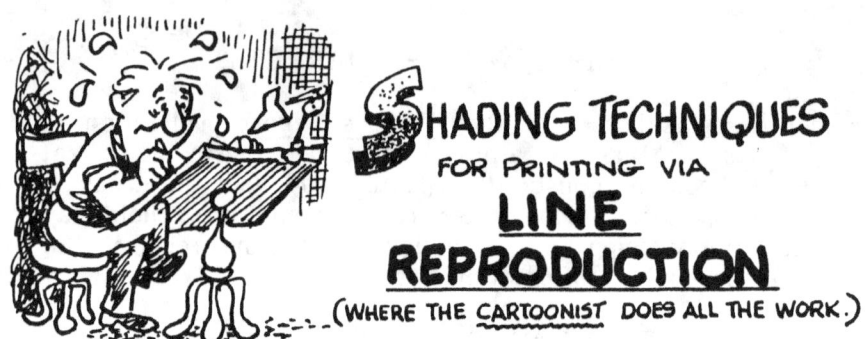

SHADING TECHNIQUES
FOR PRINTING VIA
LINE REPRODUCTION
(WHERE THE CARTOONIST DOES ALL THE WORK.)

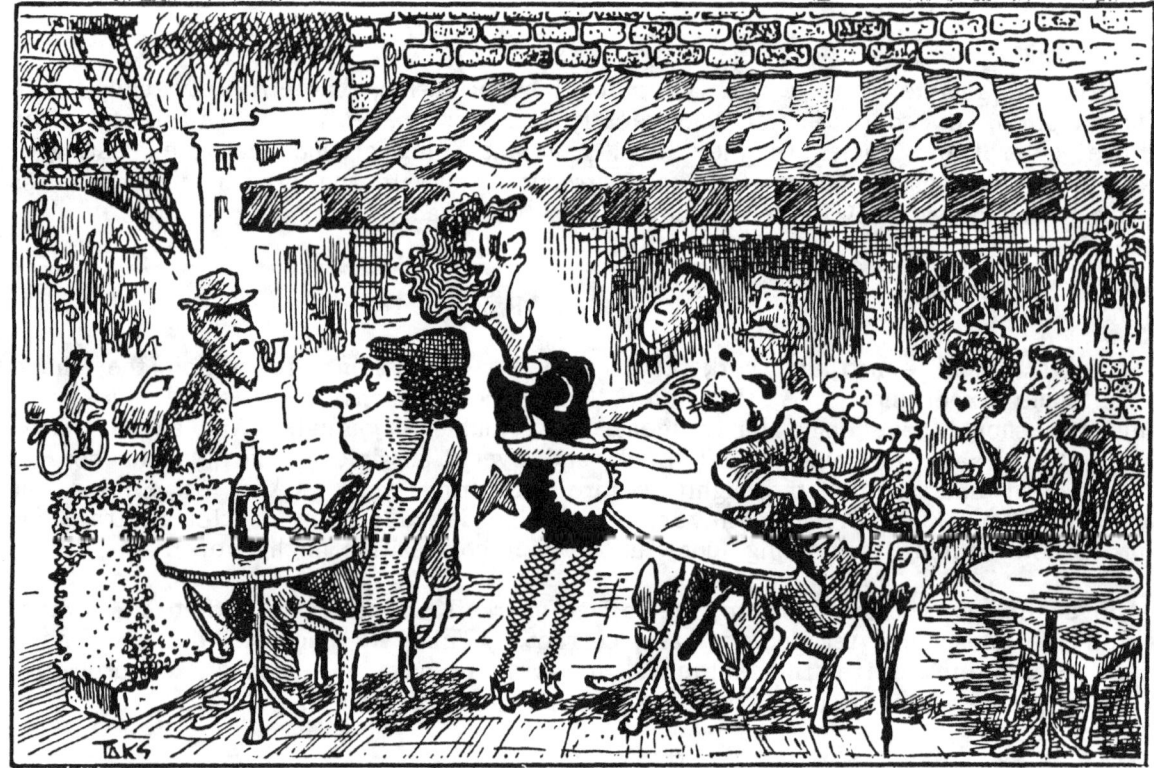

PEN AND INK DRAWING FOR *LINE REPRODUCTION*.
(SHOWN ACTUAL SIZE OF ORIGINAL.)

ADDITIONAL SHADING METHODS USED FOR "LINE REPRODUCTION."

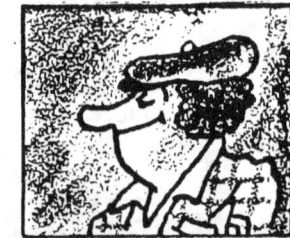

"GREASE" PENCIL
ON TEXTURED PAPERS
AND BOARDS.

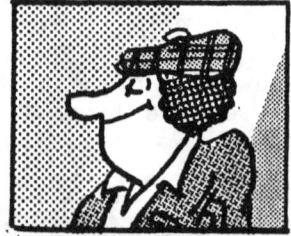

SHADING "FILMS"
ON SELF-ADHESIVE
ACETATE SHEETS.

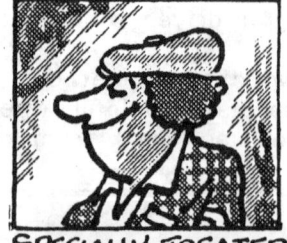

SPECIALLY TREATED
PAPERS & BOARDS.
"GRAFIX"

A TIME-HONORED TECHNIQUE: PEN (AND/OR BRUSH) SHADING

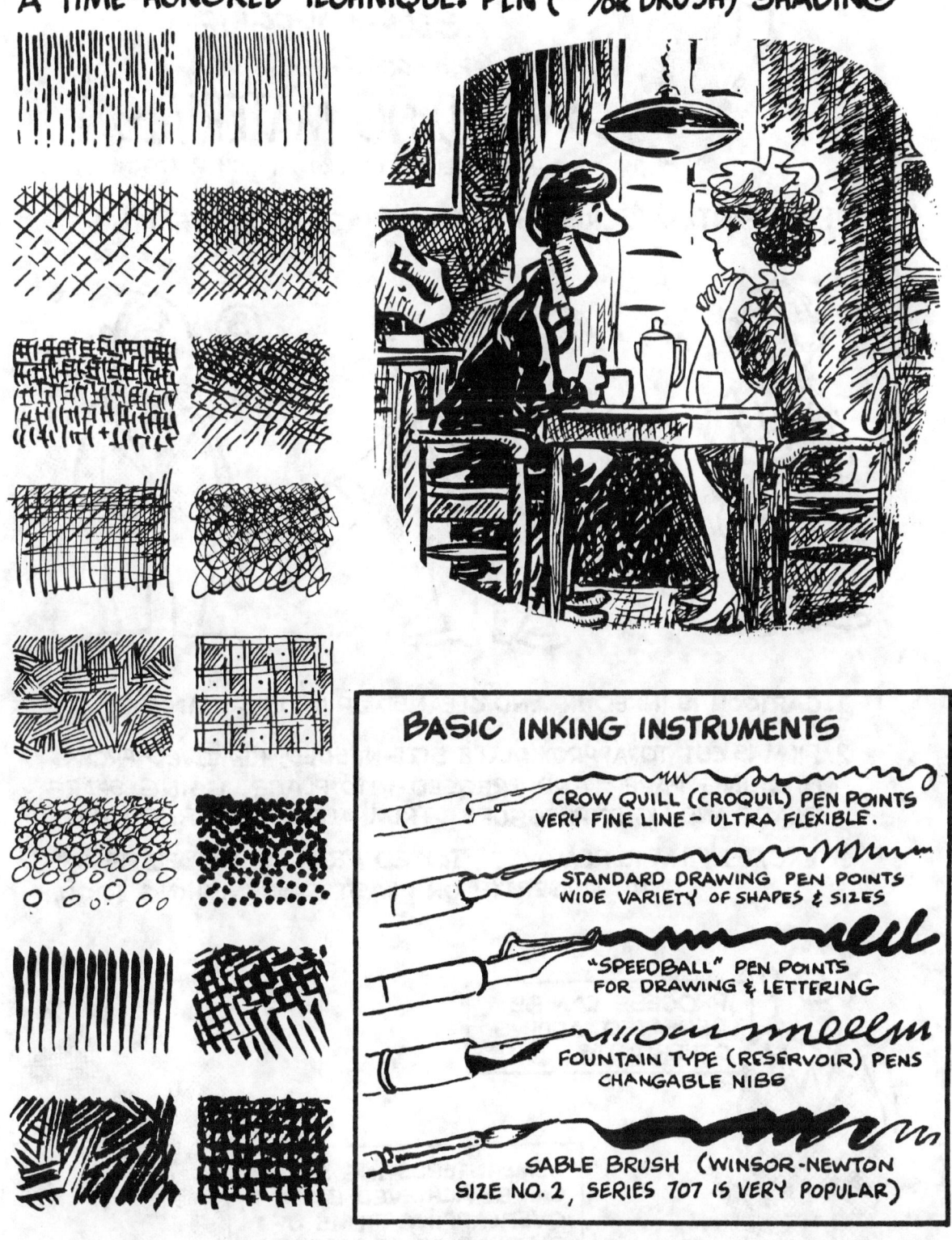

BASIC INKING INSTRUMENTS

CROW QUILL (CROQUIL) PEN POINTS
VERY FINE LINE - ULTRA FLEXIBLE.

STANDARD DRAWING PEN POINTS
WIDE VARIETY OF SHAPES & SIZES

"SPEEDBALL" PEN POINTS
FOR DRAWING & LETTERING

FOUNTAIN TYPE (RESERVOIR) PENS
CHANGABLE NIBS

SABLE BRUSH (WINSOR-NEWTON
SIZE NO. 2, SERIES 707 IS VERY POPULAR)

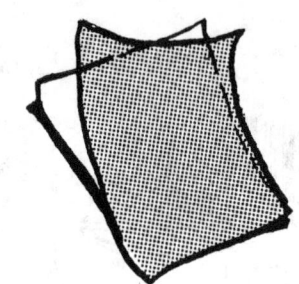

SELF-ADHESIVE
(PRESSURE-SENSITIVE)
SHADING MATERIALS
IN DOT, LINE, OR CROSS-HATCH PATTERNS

PREPRINTED "SCREENS" ON LOW-TACK ACETATE FILM

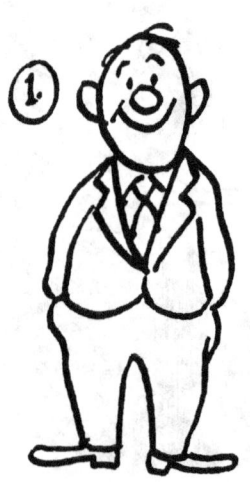

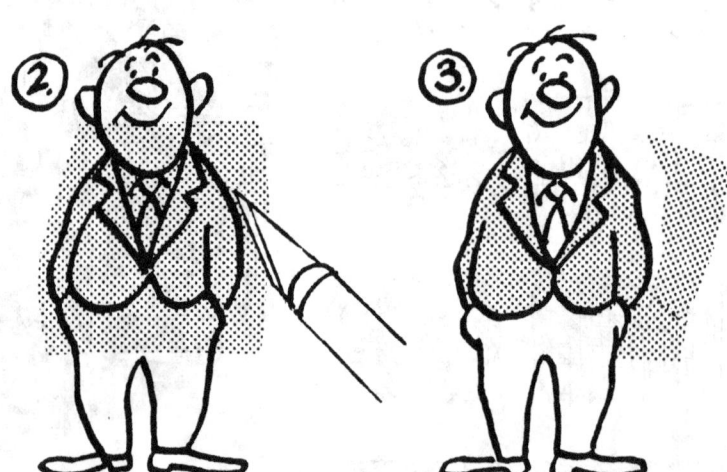

1. CARTOON IS INKED IN AND CLEANED UP IN USUAL MANNER.

2. FILM IS CUT TO APPROXIMATE SIZE NEEDED, REMOVED FROM BACKING PAPER AND PRESSED INTO PLACE. USING SHARP BLADE AND LIGHT PRESSURE, TRIM ALONG DESIRED LINES.

3. EXCESS FILM IS REMOVED. TINTED AREA IS RUBBED FIRMLY WITH FINGERTIP OR PLASTIC BURNISHING TOOL.

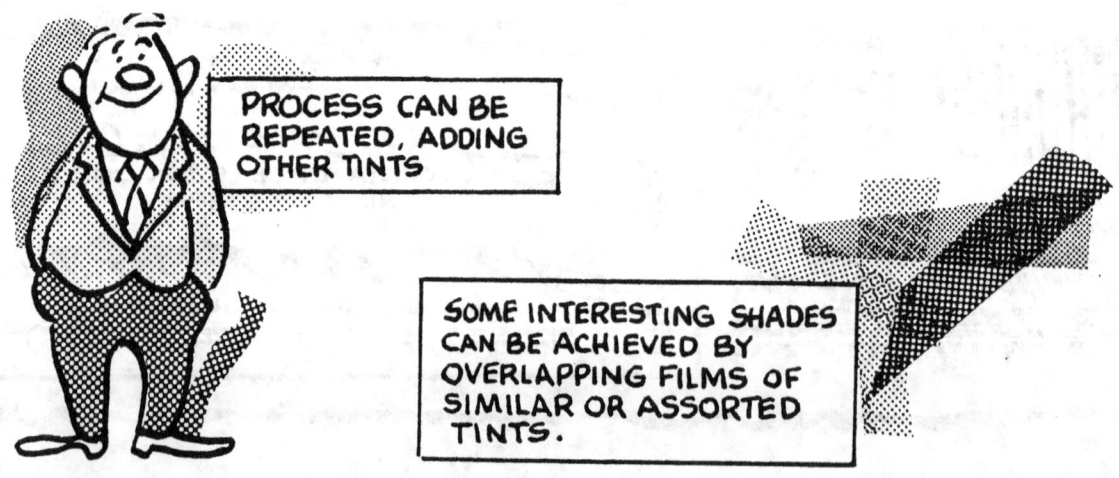

PROCESS CAN BE REPEATED, ADDING OTHER TINTS

SOME INTERESTING SHADES CAN BE ACHIEVED BY OVERLAPPING FILMS OF SIMILAR OR ASSORTED TINTS.

SELF-ADHESIVE SHADING FILMS

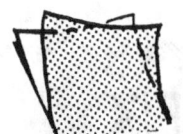

THIS HANDY STUFF COMES IN HUNDREDS OF SCREEN EFFECTS & PATTERNS. SMALL SAMPLING SHOWN HERE.

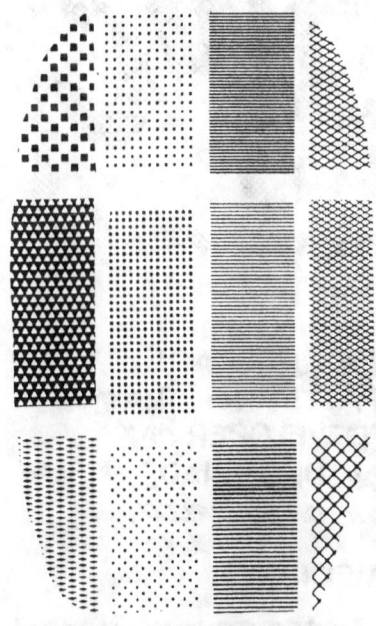

SHEET SIZES RANGE FROM 8½" × 11" TO 18" × 24".

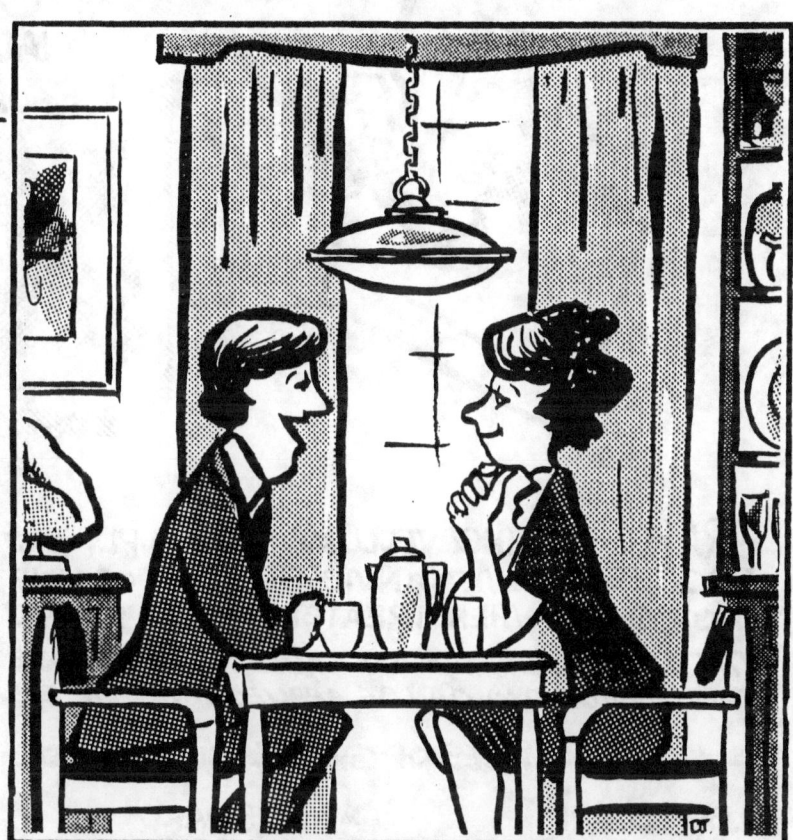

REDUCED 65% FROM ORIGINAL SIZE OF 7" × 7"

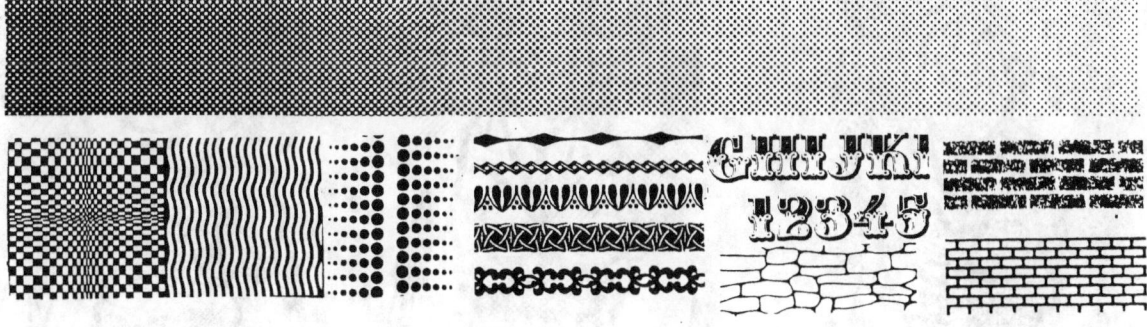

THE STUDENT'S RANGE OF CAPABILITIES WILL BE INCREASED CONSIDERABLY THROUGH A GOOD WORKING KNOWLEDGE OF TINTING FILMS AND OTHER MECHANICAL SHADING METHODS.

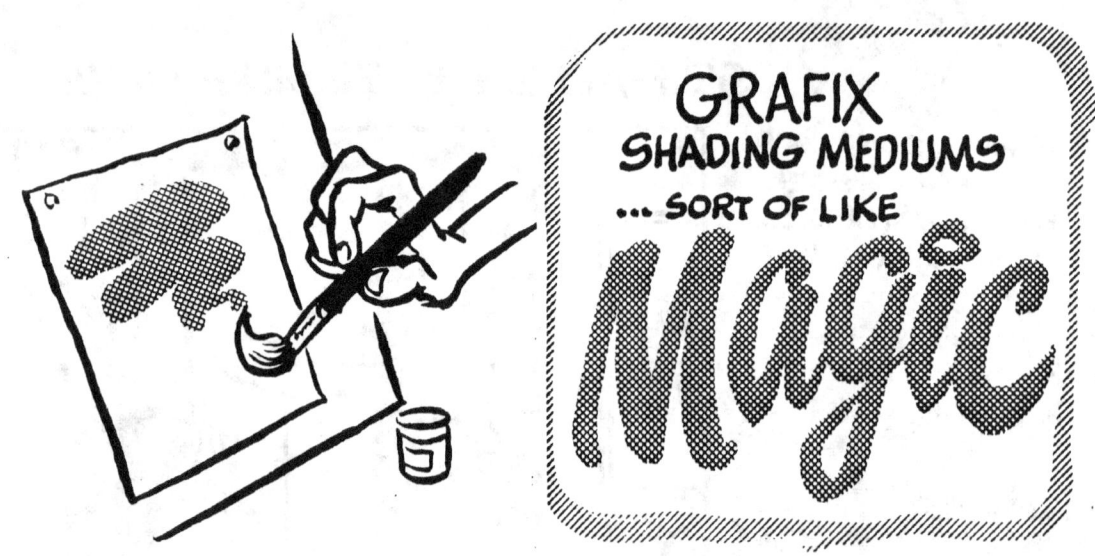

GRAFIX TRACING VELLUMS AND 3-PLY ART BOARDS ARE PROCESSED WITH INVISIBLE DOT OR LINE PATTERNS THAT "POP OUT" WHEN TREATED WITH A CLEAR "DEVELOPER (S)" THE MATERIALS ARE AVAILABLE IN UNI-SHADE OR DUO-SHADE. THE DEVELOPER (S) CAN BE APPLIED WITH PEN, BRUSH, OR STIPPLED.

EXAMPLES OF GRAFIX DUO-SHADE MEDIUMS.

＊269 BOARD   #232 BOARD   #253 TRACING VELLUM

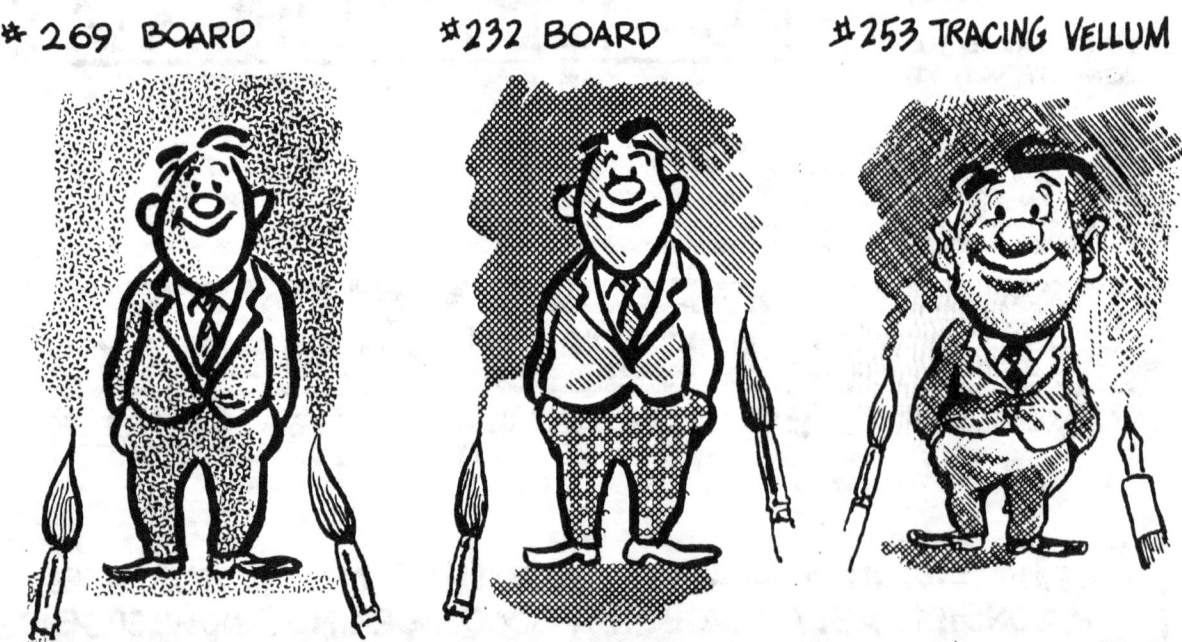

DRAWINGS ARE SHOWN "ACTUAL SIZE" OF ORIGINALS.

GRAFIX SHADING MEDIUMS

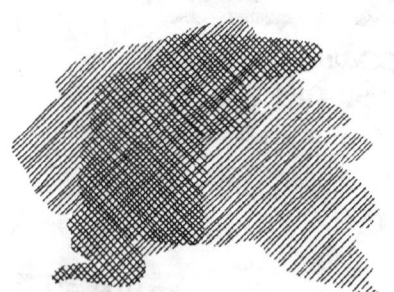

*253 TRACING VELLUM
SHOWN ACTUAL SIZE

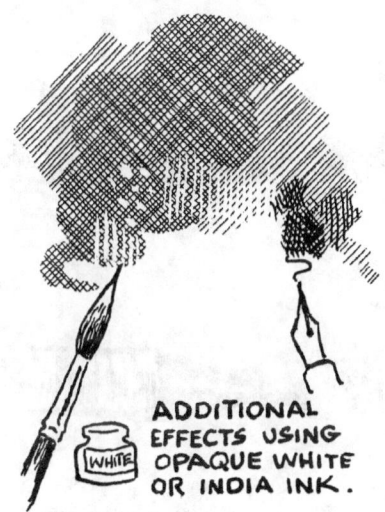

ADDITIONAL
EFFECTS USING
OPAQUE WHITE
OR INDIA INK.

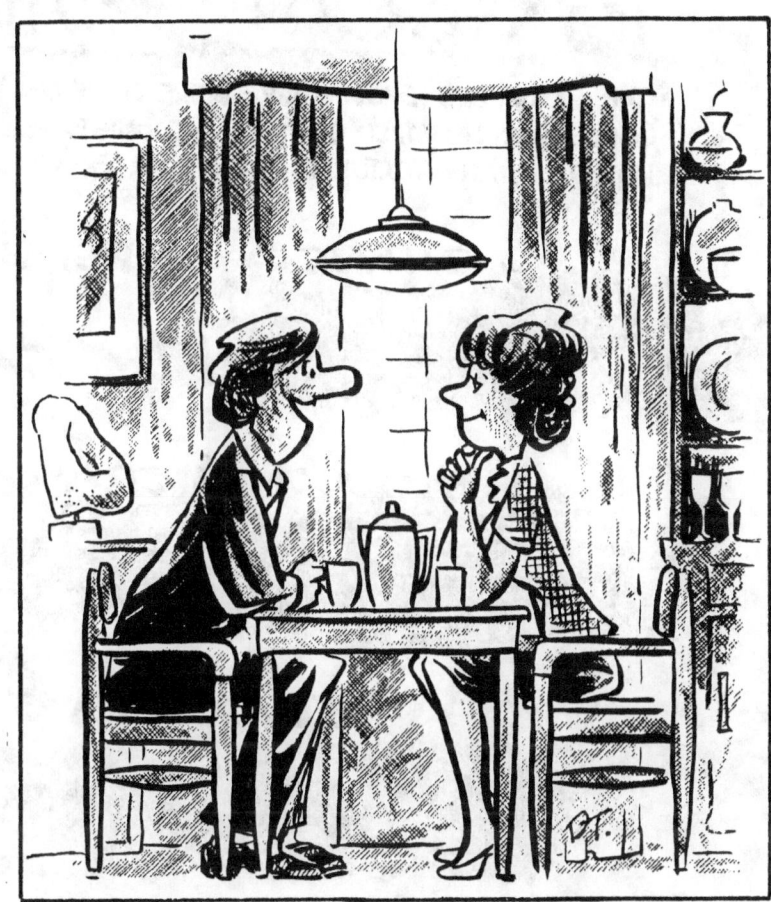

*253 VELLUM REDUCED 65% (ORIGINAL SIZE –6¼" × 7½")

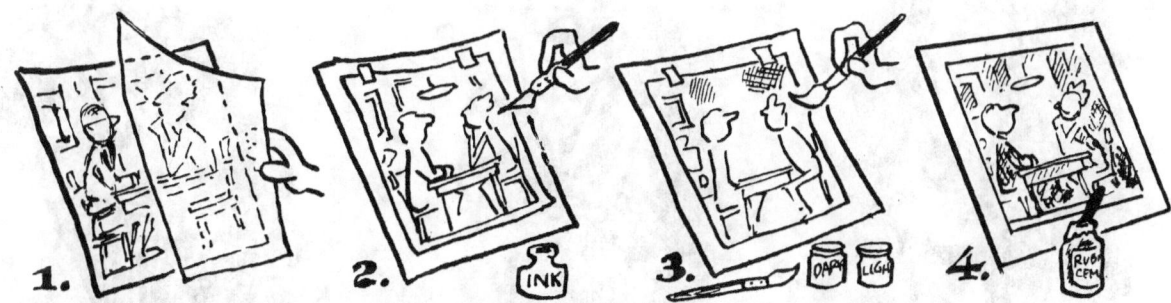

1.) GRAFIX VELLUM SHEET PLACED OVER PRELIMINARY SKETCH.
2.) CARTOON INKED-IN DIRECTLY ON VELLUM.
3.) GRAFIX DEVELOPERS APPLIED.
4.) FINISHED DRAWING RUBBER CEMENTED TO CLEAN WHITE BRISTOL.

"CRAYON" SHADING

THE EXAMPLES SHOWN HERE WERE DONE ON "COQUILLE" BOARD (GENERALLY FAVORED BY THE CARTOONISTS WHO USE THIS TECHNIQUE). HOWEVER, ANY TEXTURED PAPERS OR BOARDS CAN BE USED.

CHARCOAL PENCIL

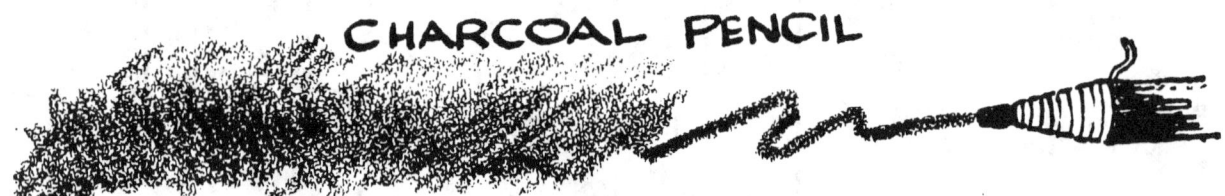

CONTÉ CRAYON

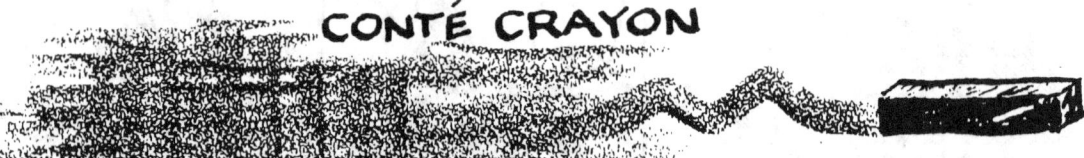

REGULAR CRAYOLA

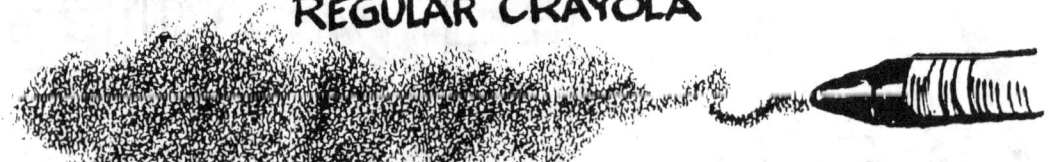

"CRAYON" SHADING WORKS WELL WITH A "SKETCHY" STYLE.

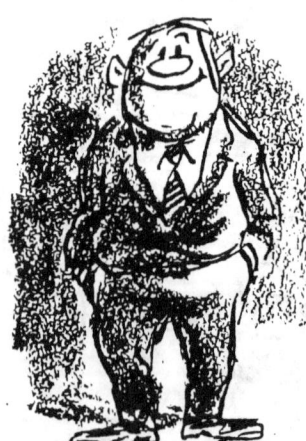

FINE POINT PEN OUTLINE, CHARCOAL PENCIL SHADING.

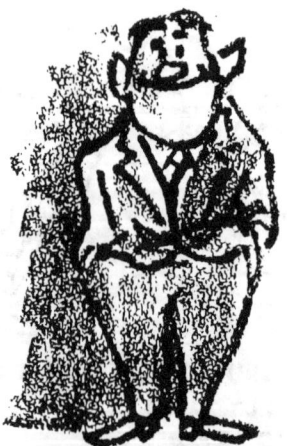

FELT-TIP PEN OUTLINE, CONTÉ CRAYON SHADING

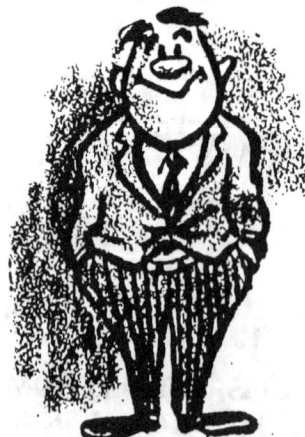

BRUSH OUTLINE CRAYOLA SHADING

CRAYON SHADING ON TEXTURED PAPERS AND BRISTOLS

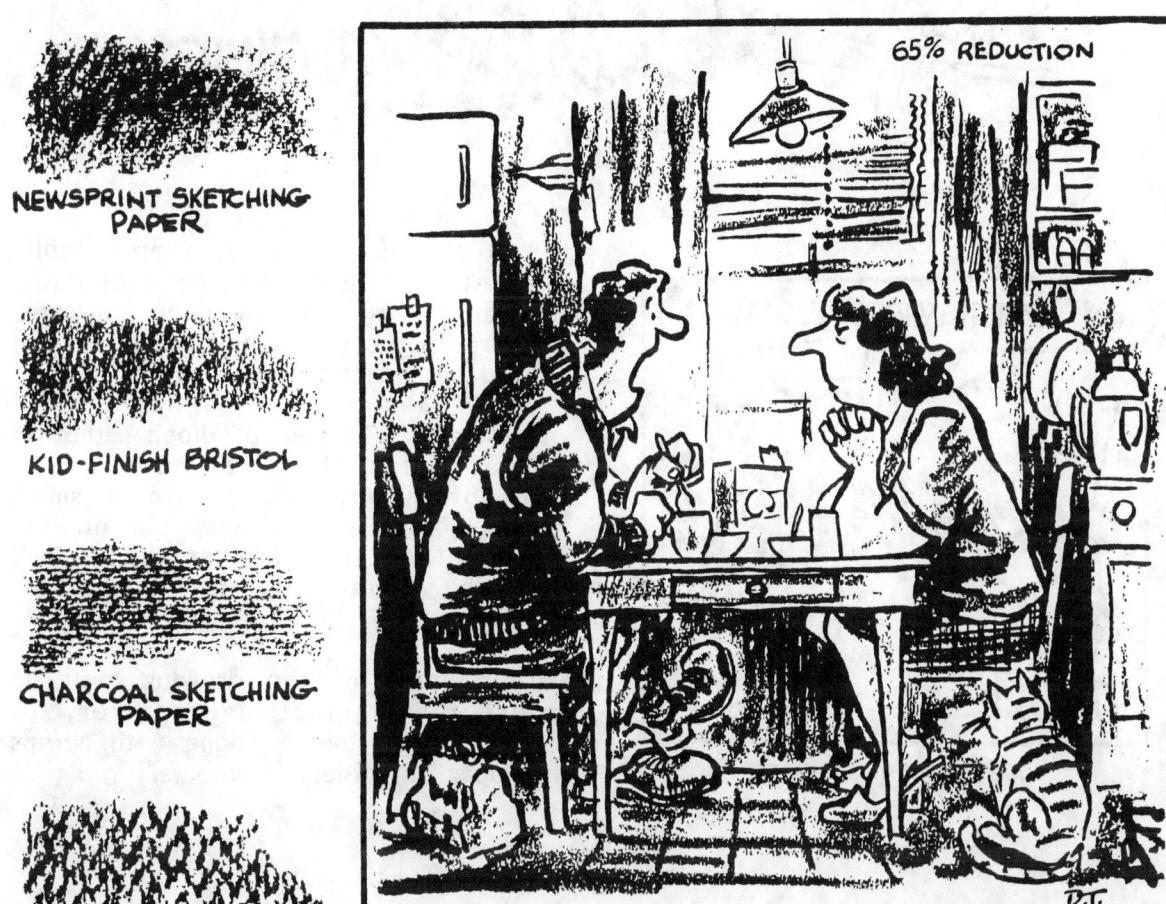

NEWSPRINT SKETCHING PAPER

KID-FINISH BRISTOL

CHARCOAL SKETCHING PAPER

COLD-PRESS WATERCOLOR PAPER

65% REDUCTION

INK & CRAYON DRAWING ON COQUILLE BOARD.

SOFT PENCIL (2B)
FELT-TIP MARKING PEN
CHARCOAL STICK
DRY BRUSH (INK)

2 PLY COQUILLÉ BOARD

DON'T FORGET TO "FIX-IT"

All pencil, charcoal, or crayon techniques smear and smudge easily when handled. It is therefore necessary to protect them with one or two light coats of a clear, spray-on material called "fixative," although almost any type of clear plastic spray (even hair spray) will work.

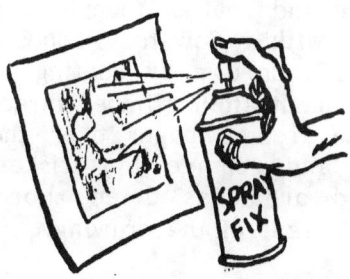

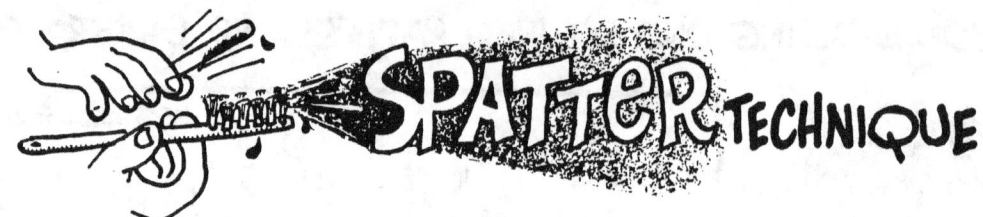

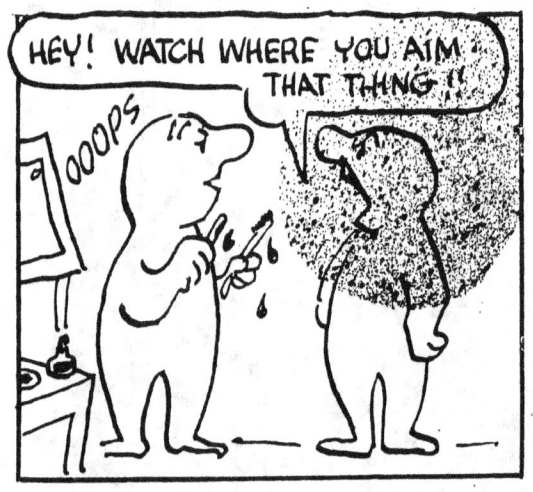

Spattering is a messy, unpredictable, and often time-consuming technique. It can be used occasionally, however, to create certain unusual effects and should not be dismissed entirely.

It's simply a matter of dipping the tip of a stiff-bristle brush (an old toothbrush will work) into a small puddle of waterproof ink, tap off the excess, and then spatter the desired area by rubbing a stick across the bristles.

Other areas of the drawing must be protected against overspatter, of course. This can be done with scraps of paper or cardboard cutouts.

Making a "FRISKET"

The frisket is a masking method commonly used by airbrush artists and can be used with the spatter technique. It is a transparent sheet of paper, coated on one side with a low-tack adhesive. Art stores usually carry the stuff, or you can make your own by coating one side of a sheet of tracing paper with diluted rubber cement (follow label directions). After the cement has completely dried, place the treated paper over the drawing, rub it down gently but firmly, and cut out and remove the frisket from the area(s) to be spattered. Once the spattered area has dried thoroughly, remove the remaining frisket from the protected areas of the drawing.

SPATTER

IT'S MESSY, OUTDATED AND SELDOM USED!
...YET, ALL OF ITS POSSIBILITIES HAVE
NEVER BEEN FULLY EXPLORED!

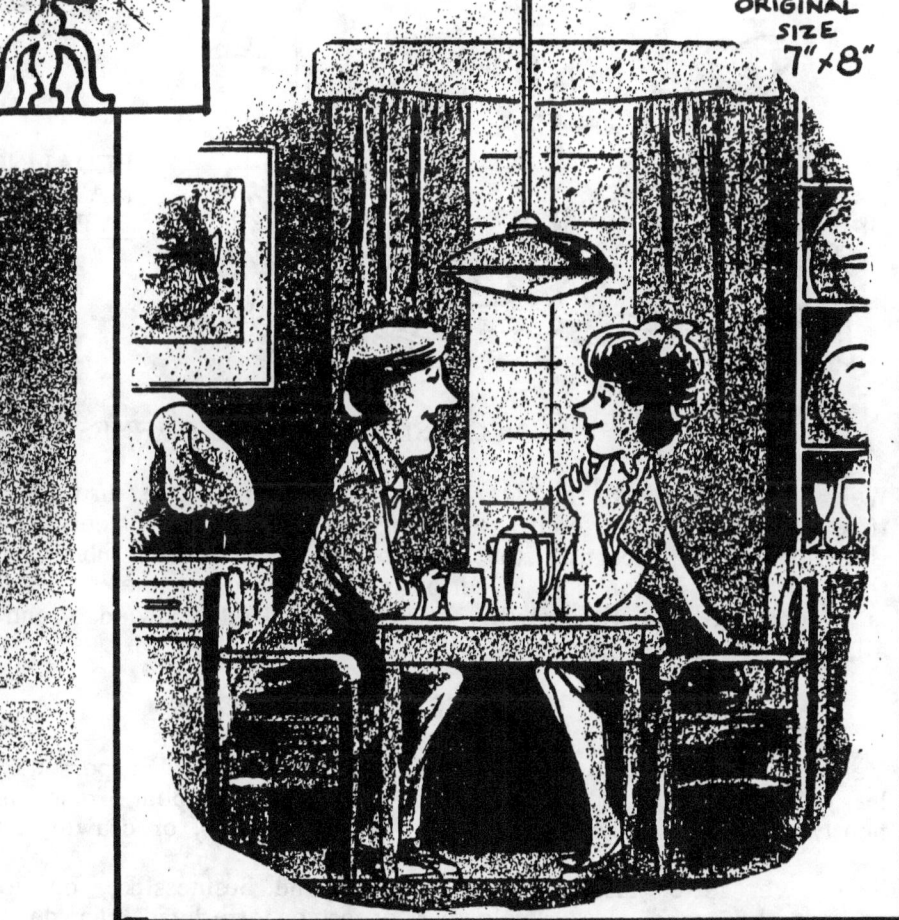

ORIGINAL SIZE 7"×8"

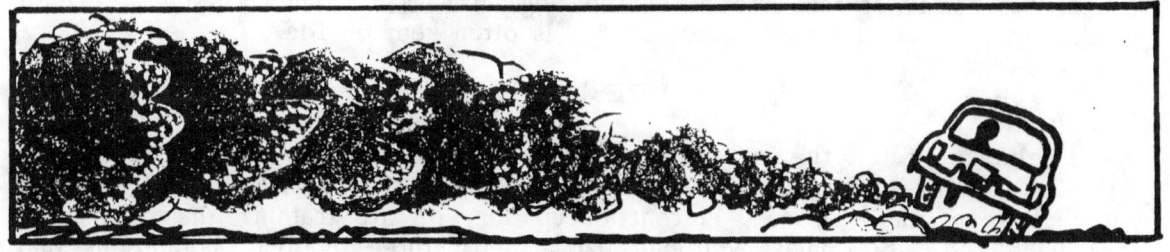

THE CARTOON EDITOR

This is an associate editor who, among his or her other duties, is responsible for the purchase of freelance cartoon material. The job of a cartoon editor is not an easy one. There are always space problems, budget restrictions, publication policies, pressures from co-workers (my cousin wants to become a cartoonist), and criticism from superiors (why did you buy this piece of junk?!)

Not the least of the problems faced by the cartoon editor is a constant underlying fear that he or she might unwittingly purchase and publish a piece of stolen material. It is therefore understandable that most major buyers of cartoon material are a bit wary, if not outright suspicious, of unknown or unproven cartoonists.

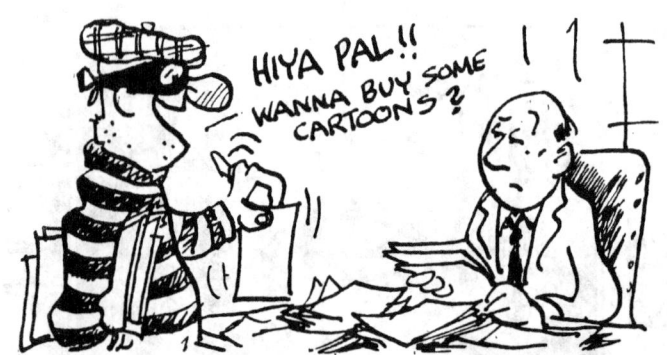

PEDALING PILFERED
MATERIAL CAN GET
<u>EVERYONE</u> INTO TROUBLE

THE NECESSITY OF BEING EARNEST

Well over 90% of all gag cartoon purchases are done through the mail. Rarely, if ever, will the cartoonist and cartoon editor ever meet face to face. It is therefore very important that the aspiring cartoonist submit work in a manner that indicates he or she is seriously committed to the profession of cartooning, is responsible and trustworthy, has the required knowledge and skill, and above all, is creative and original.

THE JUDGING BEGINS

Very likely, the cartoon editor will begin to judge a person's work the minute he or she picks up the envelope. It should appear fresh and clean, and be neatly addressed without any fancy swirls, curlicues, or drawings.

The cover letter inside should be brief and businesslike, on good quality paper, and neatly typed. A simple but creative letterhead can do wonders for one's image, but don't get too cute or overbearing with it! Attaching a business card to the cover letter is common practice and is often kept on file.

RESUMES

As a general rule, the cartoon editor is interested in only three things: Drawing Skill -- Originality -- Previously Published Material. They are not interested in the age, sex, current occupation, or art training the contributor may have had. So, unless you can list at least three or four publications that have purchased your work, it's best to let the cartoons speak for themselves.

TYPICAL COVER LETTER

Date

Mr. John W. Doe, Cartoon Editor
Anybody's Magazine
1000 West Commerce Plaza
Big City, U.S.A. 99999

Dear Mr. Doe:

The enclosed roughs are respectfully submitted for your consideration and are available "as is" or finished to your satisfaction, at your regular rate. Also enclosed is a photocopy of a recently finished cartoon (for your files) and a S.A.S.E.

I certify that this is original work of my own creation and is not being made available to other publications at this time.

Hoping for a favorable report, I am

Very truly yours,

Wilbur W. Whatsyername

The above cover letter is, of course, subject to varying situations. You may have to use Ms. Jane W. Doe, Cartoon Editor, or if the name of the cartoon editor is not known (perish the thought!), it would be addressed to Cartoon Editor and Dear Sir or Madam:

This letter looks well on a 5½" x 8½" sheet of paper with a simple, well designed letterhead. And remember, editors like the feel of nice, crisp paper, so always use high quality bond for your letterhead and sketches.

If you are able to include a copy of a recently published cartoon, and can list several publications that have purchased your work, you can do so in the lower half of an 8½" x 11" letter. In this case, you might offer a brief outline of yourself, art training, and a mention of other services you are able to provide, such as spot drawings, illustrations, and lettering.

USE PROPER POSTAGE!

A general rule of thumb is that a typical batch of cartoons, consisting of eight roughs, the cover letter, a business card, one sheet of photocopied examples of finished work, a paper clip, and a S.A.S.E. weighs approximately three ounces. This will vary, of course, so it is wise to invest in a small postal scale. These are relatively inexpensive and can prevent the use of excess postage and eliminate those tiresome waits in line at the Post Office.

THE COVER LETTER -- BRIEF AND SIMPLE . . . HOWEVER . . .

As mentioned previously, cartoon editors are busy people and usually have more important things to do than read through long-winded cover letters and insignificant resumes. This is especially true in the case of the major cartoon markets that receive hundreds of cartoons ideas every week.

The smaller trade journal marketplace, however, is usually a bit less hectic, and can often be downright friendly and helpful. This allows the "minor leaguer" to experiment with cover letters that are less formal, with perhaps a personal touch.

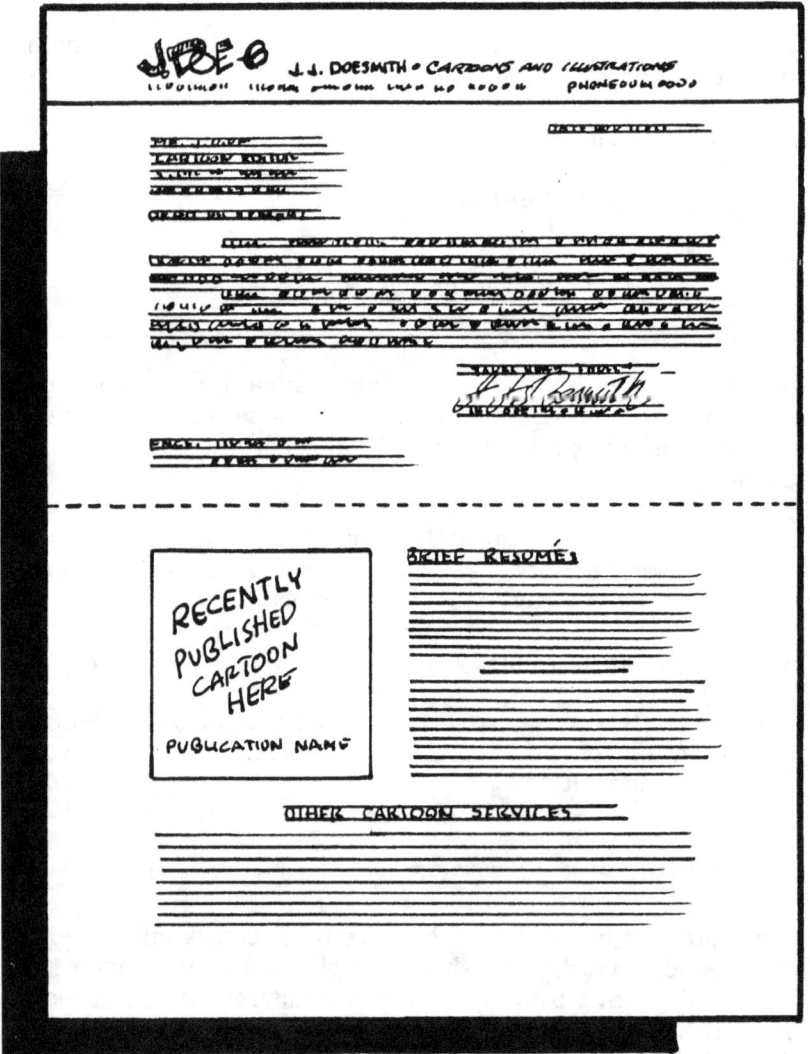

Instead of a brief resume in the lower half of the letter, one might use the space for a short questionnaire. Inquire about current needs, future stories and articles, spot drawings, illustrations, or the possibility of obtaining several recent issues of their publication.

Above all, don't hesitate to ask for suggestions, advice, or criticism. Occasionally, a friendly editor will offer a few words of encouragement, or perhaps even a "trial assignment to illustrate a particular feature!

CLEAN AND CRISP!

Nothing will "turn off" a cartoon editor quicker than to open an envelope and see a batch of shopworn roughs drawn on a cheap grade of paper. This sort of presentation will hardly put him in a receptive state of mind and the work will get a quick heave-ho right back to the contributor.

All work submitted should be neat and fresh looking, even if they have to be redrawn after the first few times around. Use a single sheet of high quality bond paper for each gag idea, leave lots of margin around it (as shown below), and neatly type, print, or rubber stamp your name and address in the lower left-hand corner. Leave lots of room in the lower right-hand portion of the page for the editor's possible approval, comments, or instructions.

HINT: Stick to one basic theme or subject in each batch. It tends to indicate originality and that the contributor is highly creative. Review all rejected material with a critical eye. Can the work be improved, simplified, or expanded?

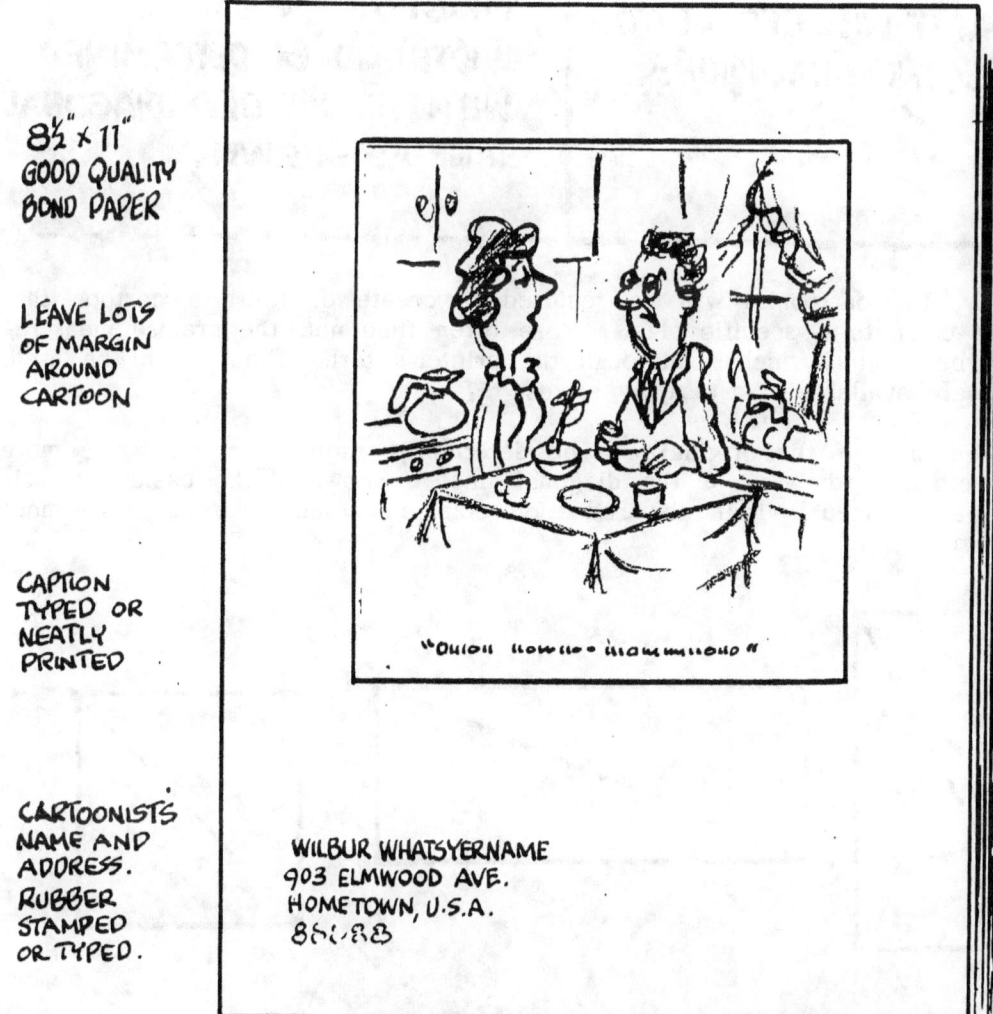

8½" x 11" GOOD QUALITY BOND PAPER

LEAVE LOTS OF MARGIN AROUND CARTOON

CAPTION TYPED OR NEATLY PRINTED

CARTOONISTS NAME AND ADDRESS. RUBBER STAMPED OR TYPED.

WILBUR WHATSYERNAME
903 ELMWOOD AVE.
HOMETOWN, U.S.A.

8 TO 10 "ROUGHS" MAKE UP A GOOD "BATCH"

FINDING CORRECT PROPORTIONS FOR REDUCTION

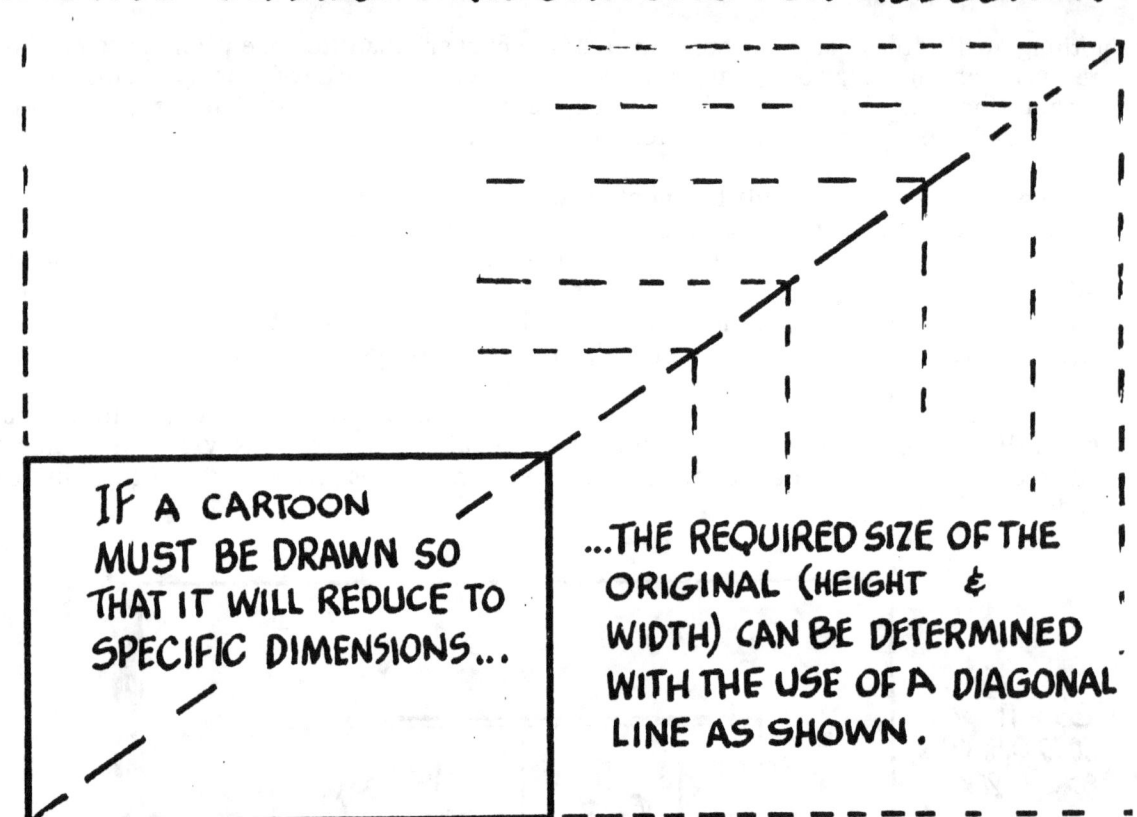

IF A CARTOON MUST BE DRAWN SO THAT IT WILL REDUCE TO SPECIFIC DIMENSIONS...

...THE REQUIRED SIZE OF THE ORIGINAL (HEIGHT & WIDTH) CAN BE DETERMINED WITH THE USE OF A DIAGONAL LINE AS SHOWN.

Occasionally, the cartoonist will be required to create or finish a cartoon that will reduce down to a specific size. More often than not, the precise measurements will be given in inches, although the printer's term "Pica" might be used. Pica rulers are available at art supply stores.

The required size of the original can be determined mathematically, but a more accurate method is the use of the diagonal line as shown. The basic composition can be "planned" within the reduction size and then enlarged to a more workable size.

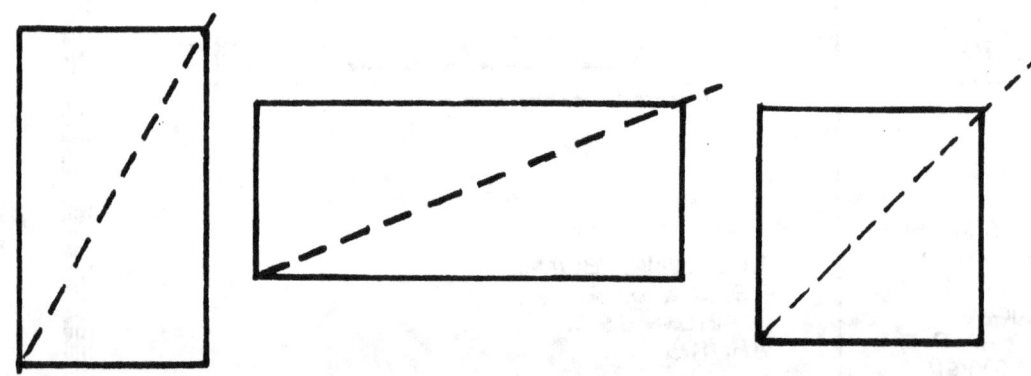

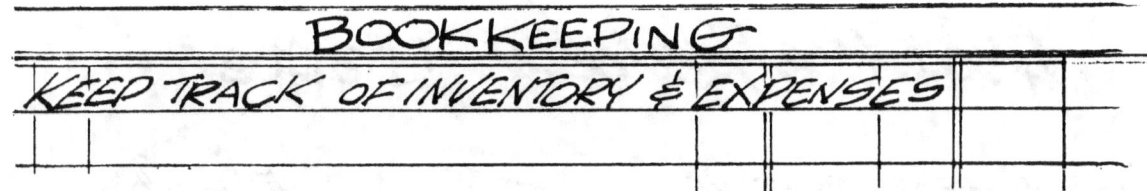

BOOKKEEPING

KEEP TRACK OF INVENTORY & EXPENSES

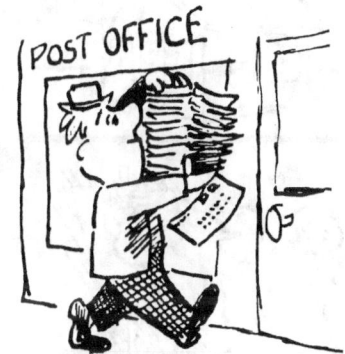

It is not unusual for the typical workaday gag cartoonist to have an inventory of several hundred gag cartoon roughs and/or finishes on hand, with 10 or 15 "batches" in the mails at all times. Needless to say, that requires some accurate recordkeeping. The efficient cartoonist knows what material has been sent, where it was sent and when, what sales have been made, the amount, method and time required for payment, and the name of the person who responded.

It is also a good idea to save all correspondence received from editors and publishers. Rejection slips, when read between the lines, can provide some important clues to the possibilities of future sales. Some are rather blunt and seem to discourage further submissions. Others can be very ambiguous, perhaps even encouraging. Personal letters or notes from editors should be responded to immediately with a brief thank you note and perhaps with additional submissions.

EXPENDITURES

Freelance cartooning is a business and should be operated accordingly. Complete records should be kept of all income and expenses. As outlined in the introduction of this book, the initial expenses can be significant, as can the daily operating costs. Postage, equipment, supplies, overhead, mileage (to art supply stores, post office, sales) should be well documented and recorded. Printing and advertising costs and miscellaneous expenses can add to the price of doing business and should be carefully recorded. The IRS code makes provisions for business expenses and every smart businessperson takes full advantage of them, beginning on day one.

HOBBY OR BUSINESS?

The recently revised IRS tax code sets forth new ground rules governing small businesses, self-employed persons, business use of home and car, hobbies, etc.

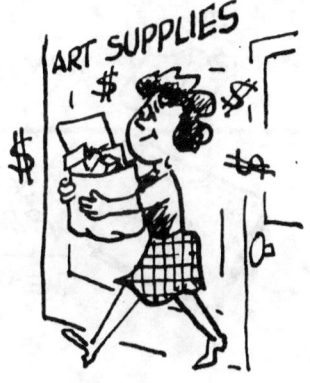

Your local library or IRS office has many booklets that can prove to be helpful in setting up a cartooning business. The serious student will do well to take full advantage of every deduction that the tax code allows.

Like my Grandpa used to say, "If you don't have time to do it right, when will you have time to do it over?"

Quickie Review Chapter 6

"T-SQUARE" PERSPECTIVE: SOMETIMES WE USE IT... SOMETIMES WE DON'T.

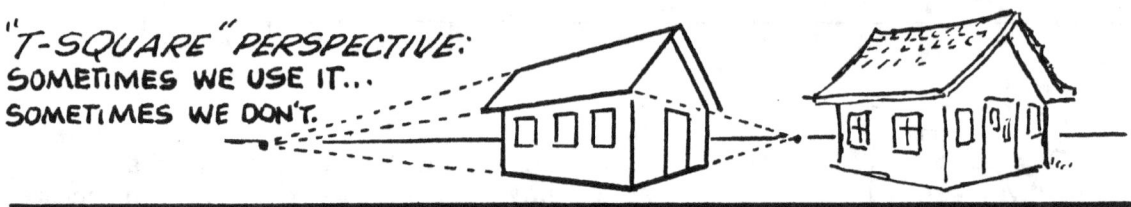

SIMPLIFY COMPOSITIONS: USE ACCENTS AND CONTRASTS TO DIRECT THE READER'S EYE.

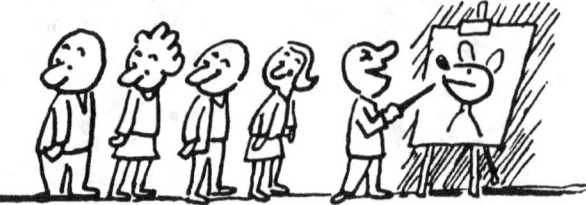

FIND THE BEST "CAMERA ANGLE" WHEN SETTING THE SCENE.

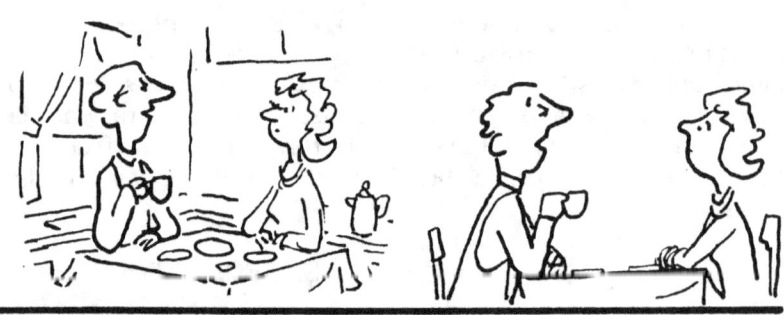

SHADING TECHNIQUES AND MATERIALS:

CRAYON	PENCIL	PEN	BRUSH	FILM	GRAFIX	HALFTON

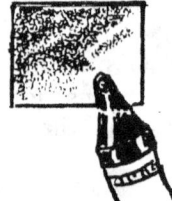 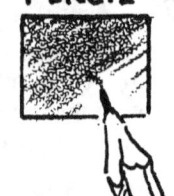 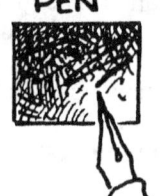 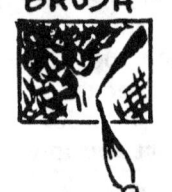 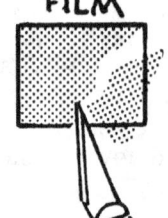 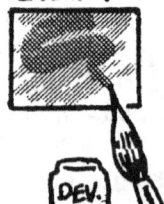 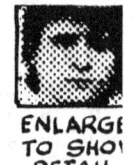

ENLARGE TO SHOW DETAIL

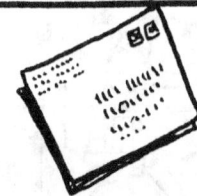

HUMOR CATEGORIES: HUMAN INTEREST • SPECIAL INTEREST • SLAPSTICK SATIRE • SEX • WEIRD

MAKE "POINTS" WITH THE CARTOON EDITOR. BE BRIEF, NEAT, ORIGINAL — AND FUNNY!

THE WORLD'S FUNNIEST CARTOON HAS NOT YET BEEN CREATED! ... WHY NOT GO FOR IT ?!?

CHAPTER SEVEN

Editorial Cartoons

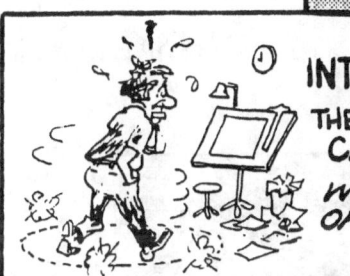

INTRODUCTION
THE POLITICAL CARTOONIST:

WHAT KIND OF PERSON ?

SECTION 1:
TECHNIQUES & COMPOSITIONS

BIG & BOLD OR LIGHT & AIRY ?

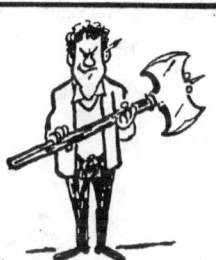

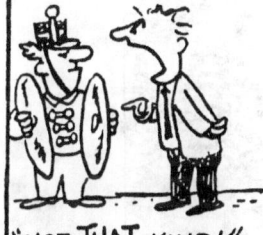

"NOT THAT KIND!"

SECTION 2:
THE IDEA

USING SYMBOLS TO CONVEY IDEAS !

SECTION 3:
CARICATURES

"3-STEP" METHOD

SCRATCHBOARD EFFECTS

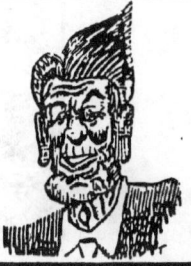

SECTION 4:
LETTERING

A VERY IMPORTANT ELEMENT OF THE POLITICAL CARTOON

SECTION 5:
A TYPICAL DAY IN THE LIFE OF *"CLYDE DIPPENSCRATCH"*

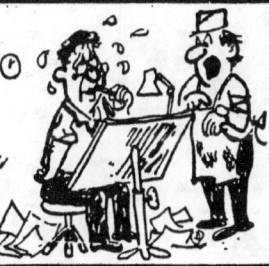

- *PAT CROWLEY*
- *GARY BROOKINS*
- *BOB GORRELL*
- *JEFF MacNELLY*
- *PAUL SZEP*
- *DON WRIGHT*

SECTION 6:
EXAMPLES OF THE WORK OF 6 AWARD WINNING POLITICAL CARTOONISTS!!

SECTION 7:
QUICK-SKETCHING FROM TELEVISED NEWS PROGRAMS & INTERVIEWS !

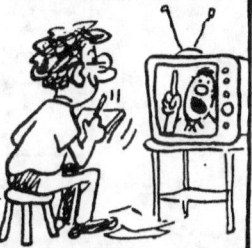

It seems fitting that this chapter begins with a brief look at the work of at least one political cartoonist of an earlier era.

The late Jay "Ding" Darling (1880-1962) produced tens of thousands of editorial cartoons and was awarded two Pulitzer Prizes during his fifty year career (mostly with the Des Moines Register and the New York Herald Tribune Syndicate, 1900 - 1950). His cartoon commentary was applauded by the common man everywhere, feared by crooked political leaders and foretold of many of the problems our nation, and the world, currently faces.

Many of "Ding's" editorial cartoons would have as much, if not more, impact today as they did decades ago.

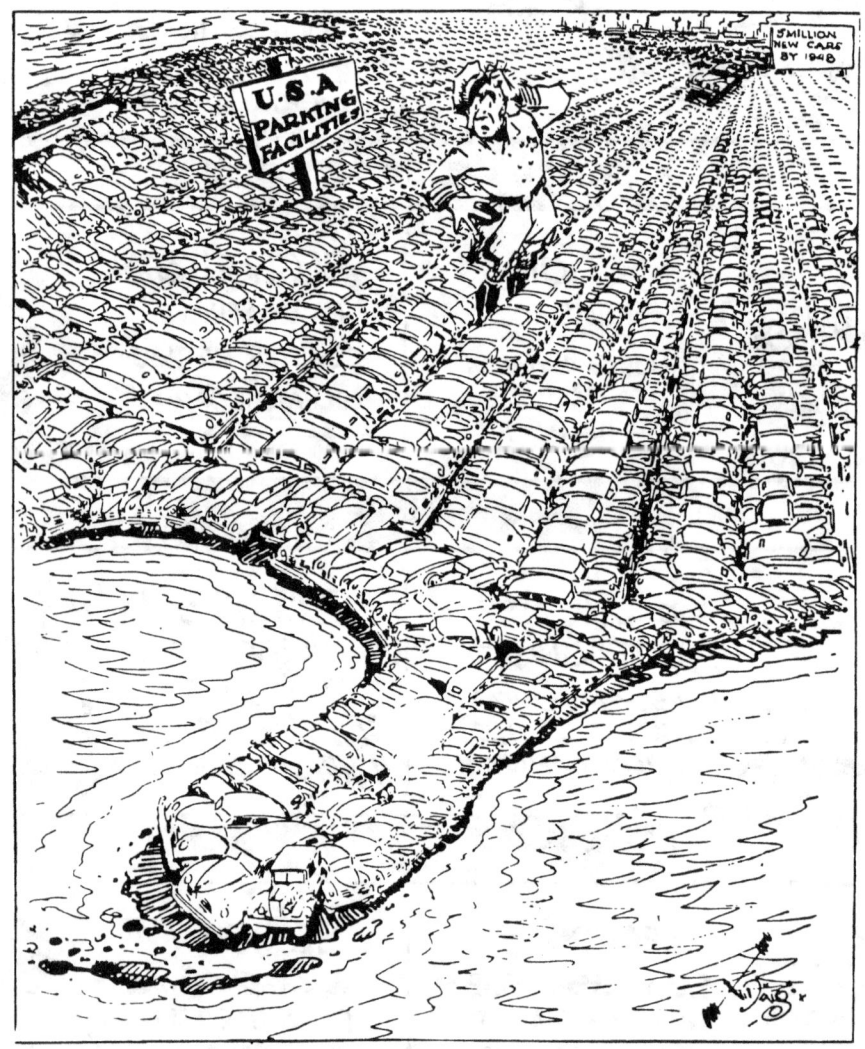

NO PLACE TO PARK

MEAT AND POTATOES STUFF

Most of our daily cartoon fare consists of the little treats and tidbits found on the comic pages of our newspapers. For the most part, these harmless little goodies are served up by some nearly anonymous person working in some distant place.

It is the highly profiled political cartoonist, working right there in our own River City, who serves the main course. Food for thought, so to speak. Often, it is served with the full knowledge that it will be unpalatable to some and will result in a serious case of indigestion to others.

The editorial cartoonist does not serve pablum to his or her readers. Properly seasoned meat and potatoes is his specialty.

Many people think of the editorial cartoonist as a knight in shining armor, in constant battle with the dragons of crime, corruption, injustice, and greed. Others are quick to call them rabble rousers.

Very often, the comments, observations, and assessments found in political cartoons are considered insensitive, and perhaps even bizarre. Just as often, however, those observations and assessments withstand the test of time ... the cartoonist is vindicated, his treatment of the subject justified.

Generally speaking, editorial cartoonists are a strong-headed bunch. Their ideas, opinions, and convictions are their own genuine feelings, offered with no apologies. Those opinions are not of the knee-jerk, shoot-from-the-hip variety, but are based on a thorough study of every aspect of the subject or situation. Occasionally, an editor might suggest a particular topic, but for the most part political cartoonists are given free rein to go charging up whatever hill they choose. Above all, they do not take kindly to any form of editorial restraints. Several well-known and highly-honored editorial cartoonists have walked off the job rather than compromise a thought or opinion.

No two editorial cartoonists work in exactly the same way. Some prefer to work amid the hustle and bustle of the newspaper's editorial department. Others do most of their work in their home studio. But, they all have one thing in common: a daily deadline ... a space to fill and only a short amount of time to fill it. Ultimately, we are all a bit wiser and perhaps more knowledgeable because of their efforts.

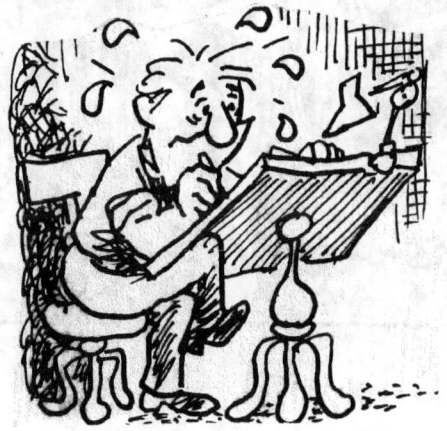

SETTING THE SCENE ... MAKING A POINT

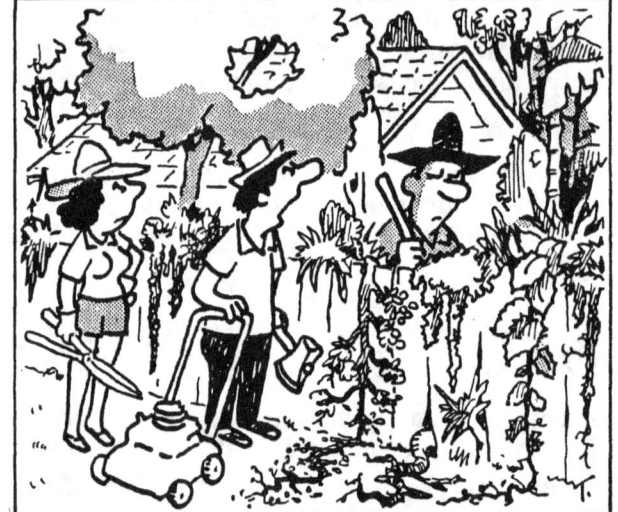

A gag cartoonist, whose work is usually confined to a relatively small area, might present a situation in a manner similar to that shown at the left.

An editorial cartoonist, with more space at his disposal, might visualize the same situation in a somewhat different manner, as shown below.

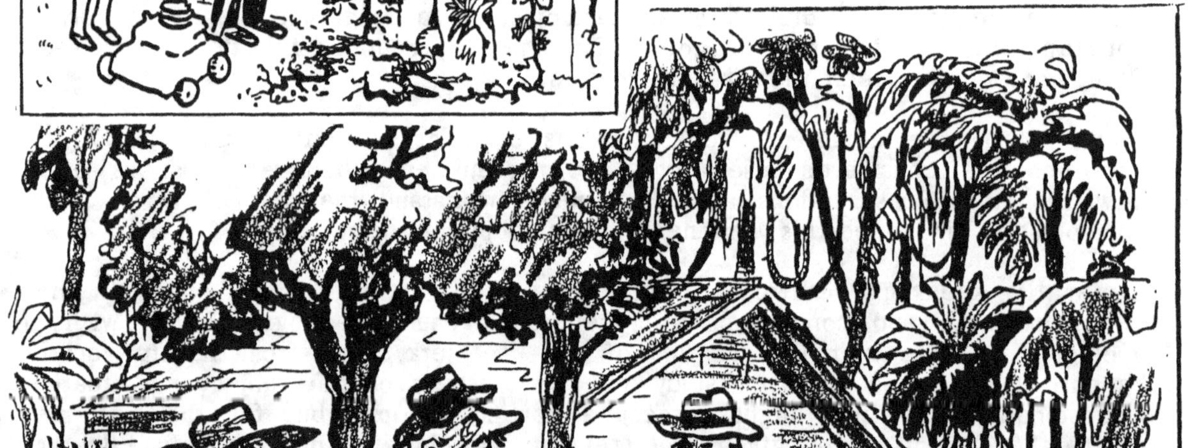

EXPERIMENTING WITH DRAWING STYLES, TECHNIQUES, AND MATERIALS

Eventually, every political cartoonist develops a particular style.   It is usually as unique and distinctive as his or her own handwriting.   It becomes their benchmark, so to speak, and one often needs not even look for the signature to ascertain the creator of a particular piece of work.

Most of them, however, are rarely, if ever, completely satisfied with their work and frequently make certain changes or adjustments in an effort to improve their product.   Occasionally, a particular topic will indicate the need for a special or unusual technique or presentation.

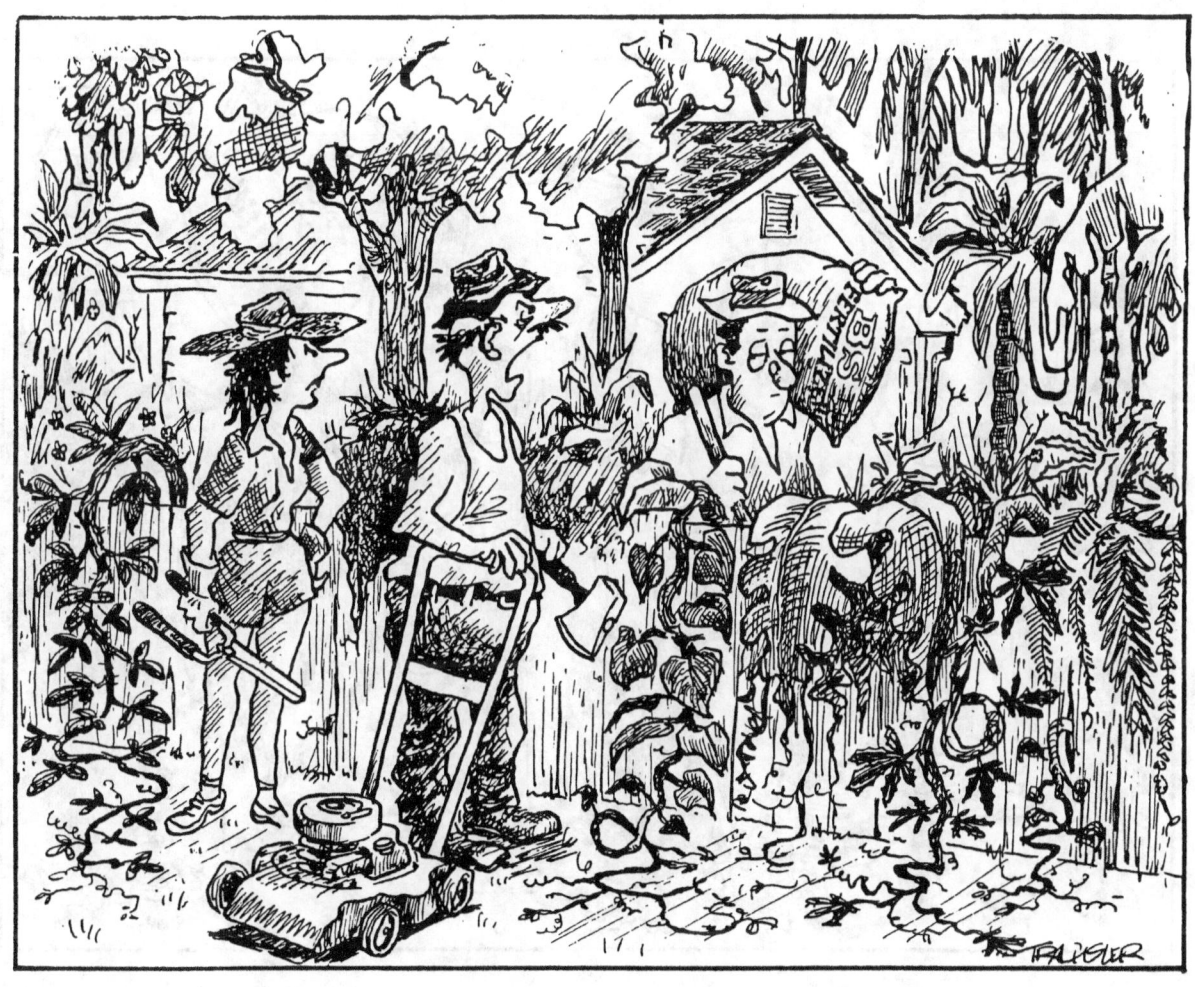

Pen and ink drawing.
Compare this with the brush and crayon drawing on the preceding page.

EXPERIMENTING WITH COMPOSITION

It is doubtful that anyone would disagree with the statement that there has never been a cartoon published that, to one degree or another, could not have been improved upon. Often, the principal flaw in a cartoon comes as a result of overstating the facts. One's main point can quickly become muddled by unnecessary details and accessories.

The drawing below occupies approximately the same amount of space as the two that preceded it. By eliminating background clutter, we have simplified the composition and enlarged the figures without any significant loss to the message.

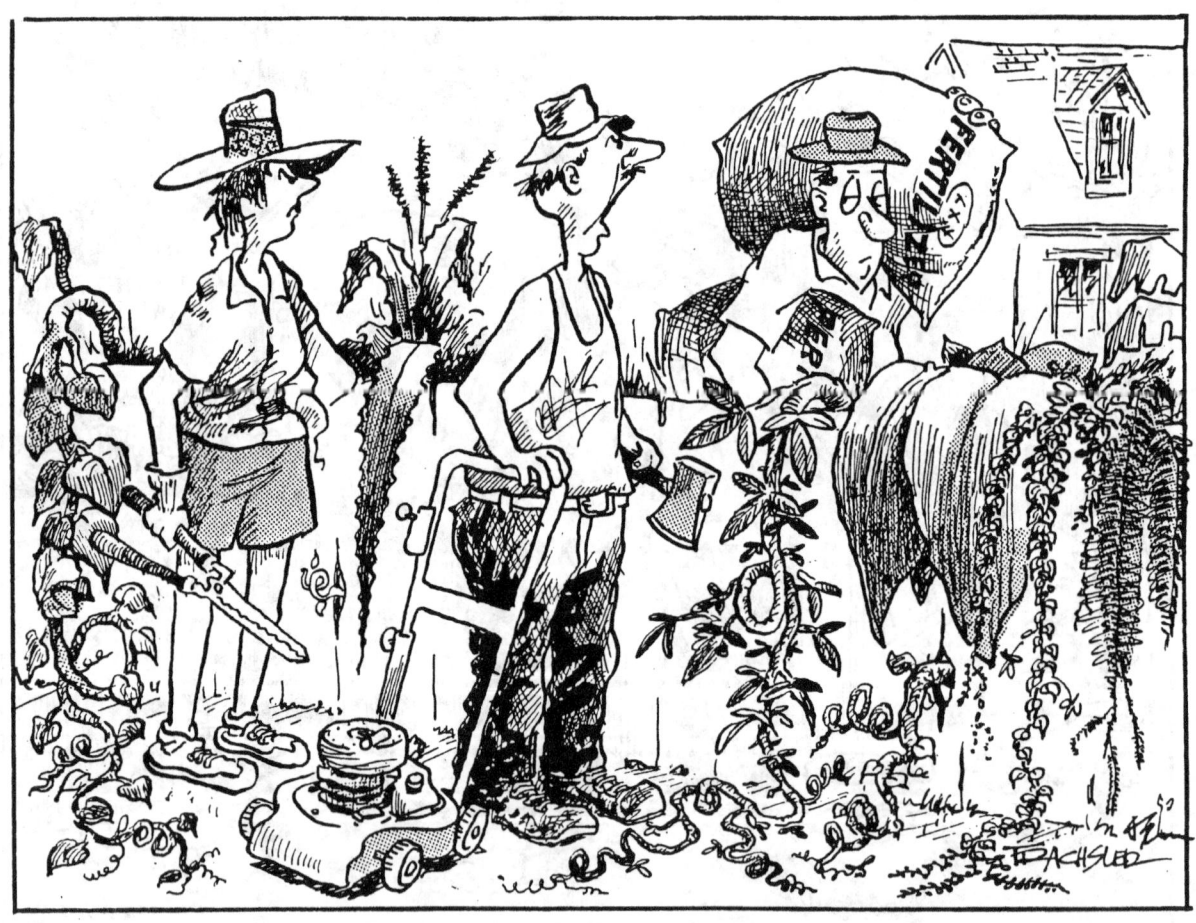

Pen and ink drawing with mechanical (film) shading.
Reduced approximately 65% from original size of 8½" x 11".

ANALYZING SUBJECT MATTER

The point that we have attempted to make in the previous three cartoons is that we have a person who cannot seem to keep his landscaping efforts within the boundaries of his own property. This can be an annoying situation, perhaps, but certainly not one that would stir up any anger, resentment, or sense of injustice with anyone except those directly involved.

By analyzing a particular state of affairs and studying every aspect of it, we can often arrive at, or even predict, the consequences of an event or situation.

In the cartoon below, we have attempted to demonstrate how "sympathy for a cause" might be achieved by expanding on an idea. Certainly, this presentation points out the fact that our central figure has every reason to be more than just mildly concerned or annoyed.

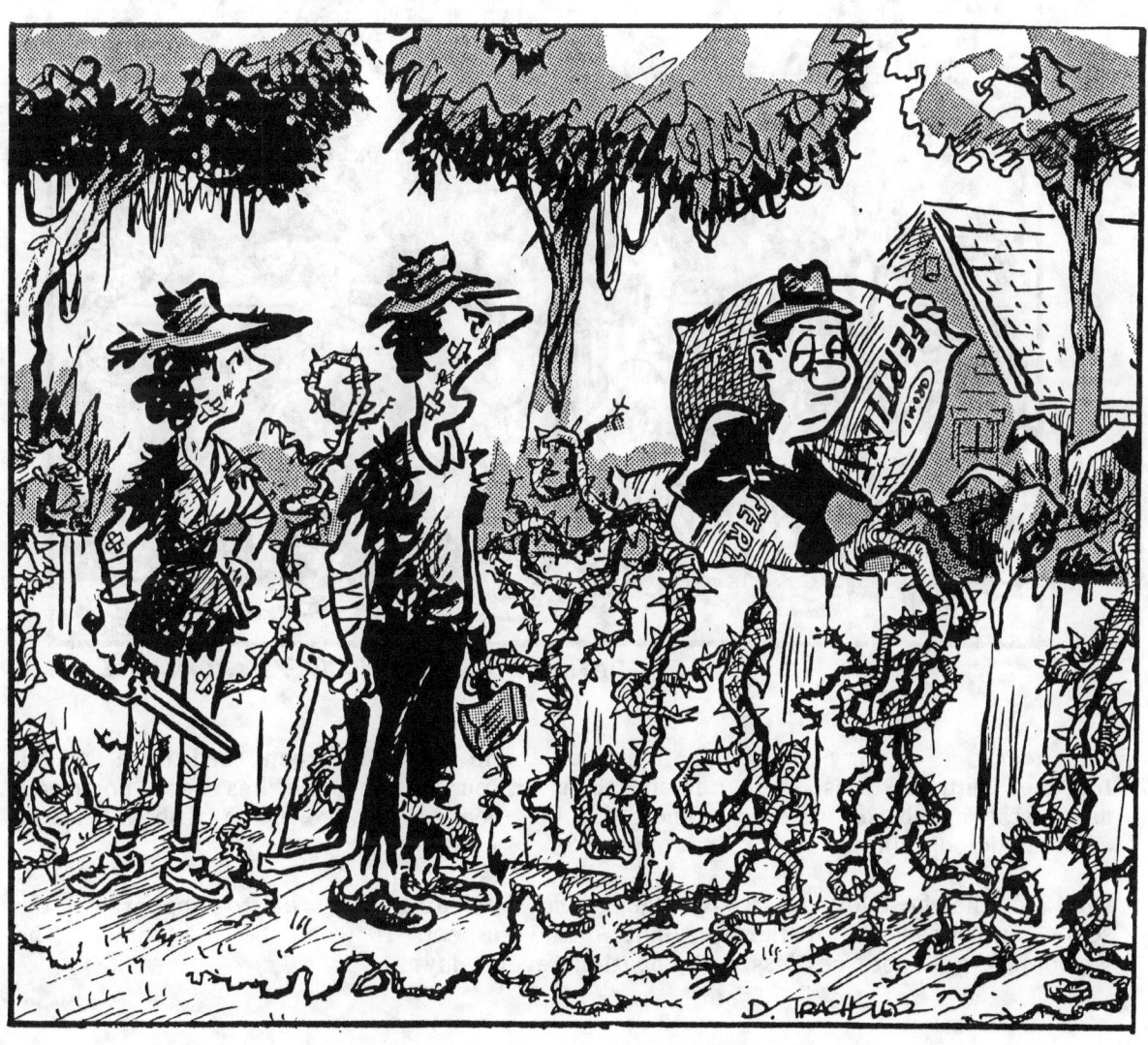

THE IDEA CONTINUES... INTRODUCING *AUNT SAMANTHA!*
WHY SHOULD POOR OLD UNCLE SAM KEEP GETTING ALL THE BLAME?

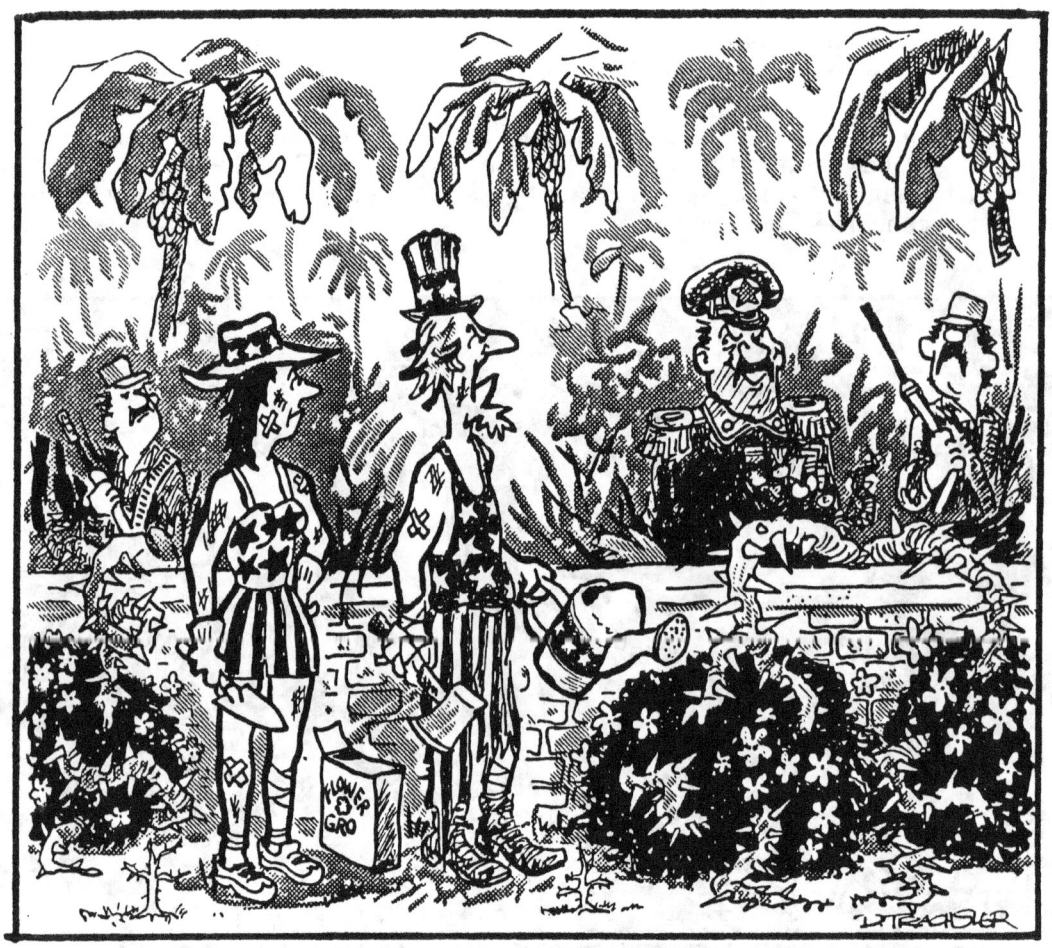

ON GRAFIX # 252 · REDUCED TO ⅔ ACTUAL SIZE

For nearly a century now, the figure of Uncle Sam has been used as a symbol for the United States. At certain times in our history, he has been portrayed as a stalwart hero; at other times, he has been shown to be a rather tattered and befuddled fellow.

But, to the best of our knowledge, Aunt Samantha has yet to appear on the scene for her share of the spotlight. One suspects it won't be long now. The womenfolk get more restless and impatient every day.

THE SEARCH FOR AN "HONEST" STYLE AND TECHNIQUE
SHOULD GO ON ... AND ON ... AND ON

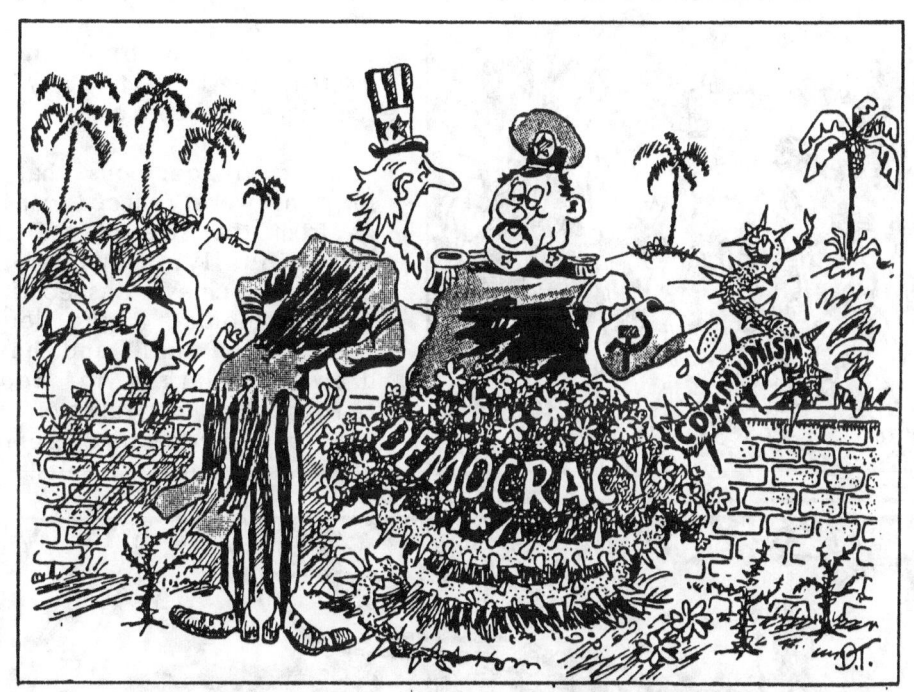

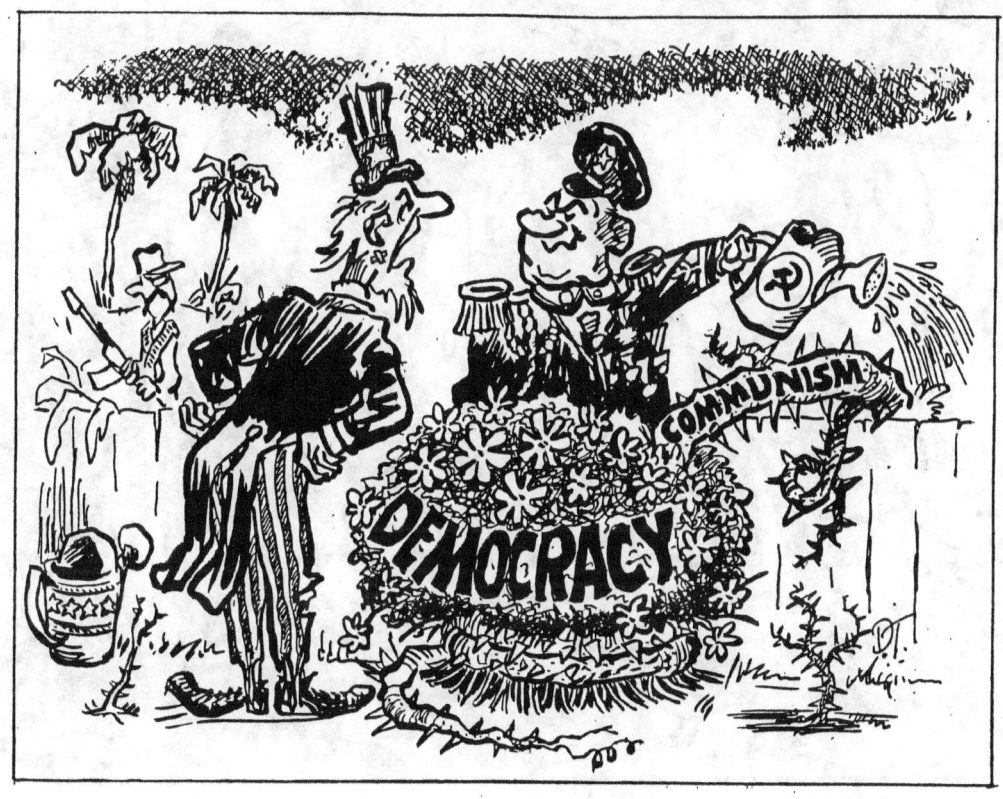

EXPERIMENTING WITH ENLARGED DRAWINGS

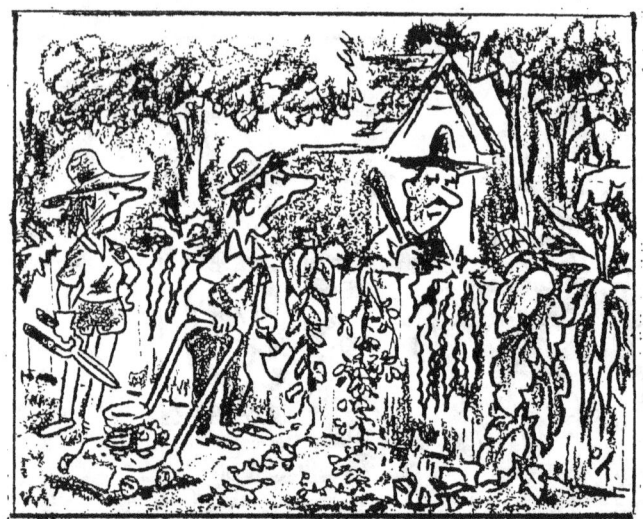

The development and availability of photocopy machines gives the cartoonist an opportunity to experiment with style and technique at little cost.

Almost all cartoons that appear in print were reduced considerably from the size of the original. Occasionally, however, in an effort to achieve a special effect, the cartoonist might decide to work very small and have the drawing enlarged for reproduction. While not always successful, the procedure sometimes produces surprising results!

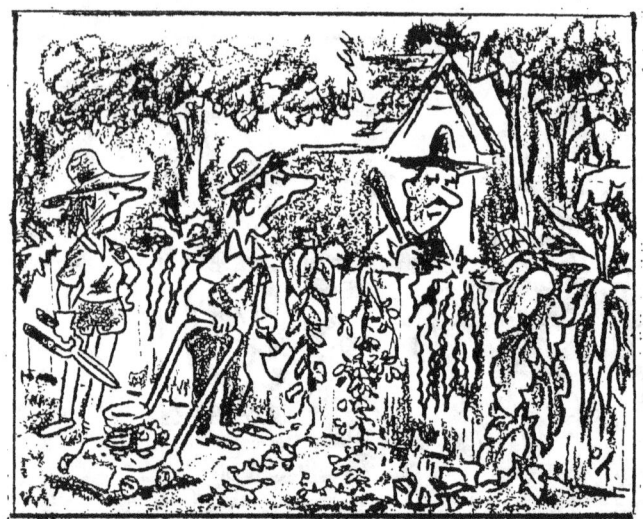

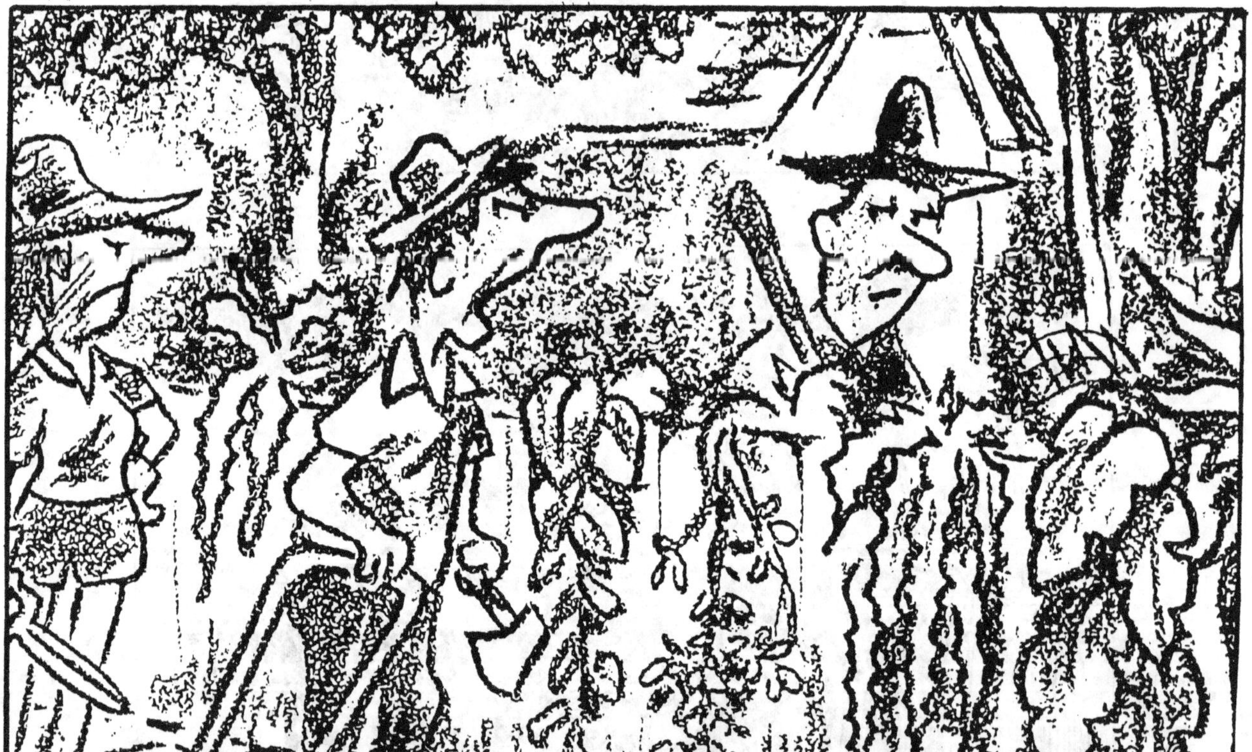

TAKING A SECOND LOOK

Be critical of your work.   Once the basic idea has been established and several possible compositions have been penciled in, pause and review the work. Frequently, a cartoon is not as successful as it might have been simply because the cartoonist was too anxious to "finish it up" ... a Hail Mary attitude (get it done and hope for the best).   That's bad thinking!

Reversing the drawing by means of tracing or the lightbox (or even holding it up to a mirror) gives the cartoonist a fresh look at his idea.   Certain flaws in the drawing will be made more obvious.   It might even suggest a newer and better way to present the intended message.

Editorial cartoonists are their own best (and harshest) critics.   That is why they are so darn good at what they do.

In the drawing below, we have retained the same basic idea but have reversed the composition and experimented with a more humorous possibility.

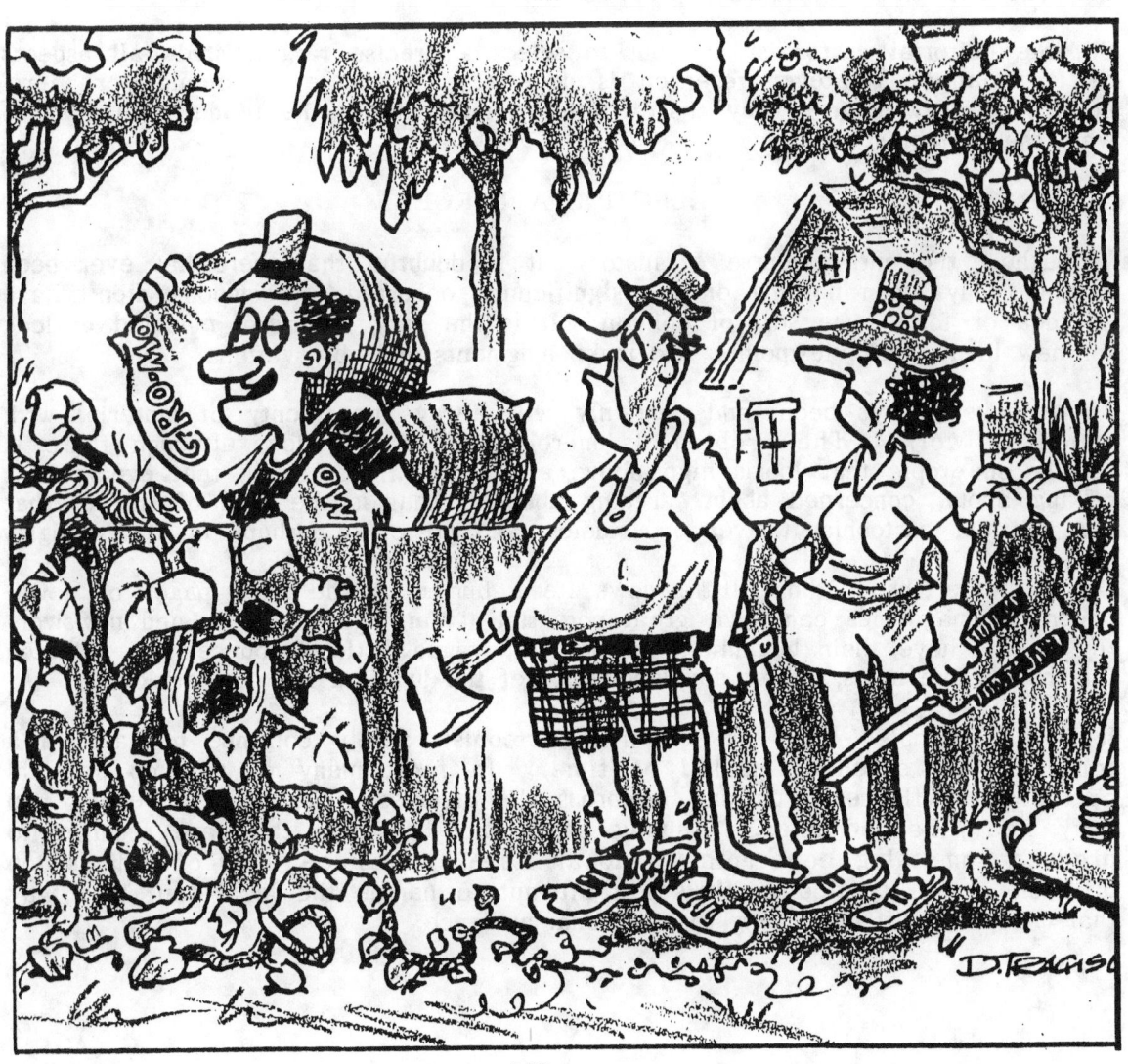

CREATIVE THINKING

In some respects, the editorial cartoonist has a bit of an advantage over his contemporaries in other fields of the profession, particularly gag cartoonists. The editorial cartoonist knows, at the beginning of each and every day, that his or her subject will concern a significant event. That event might have occurred that very morning, or the day before, or it might be a new development to an ongoing story locally, nationally, or in some far-off land.

Additionally, the editorial cartoonist is an authority on the subject of politics and world events and has an immense "mental inventory" with which to work. He has available for immediate use a vast amount of research material, either in his own personal files or those of his newspaper.

Of necessity, and to ensure survival in a demanding, often very competitive field, the editorial cartoonist has fine-tuned his daily work routine for maximum productivity. Every minute of his workday (often 12-14 hours) is geared toward the production of a high quality piece of work.

So, the editorial cartoonist has but to select a precise target, study all aspects of it, conduct whatever research is necessary, formulate an opinion or viewpoint, and draw it in a way that will leave no doubt in the reader's mind as to what the cartoonist is saying.

SELECTING A TARGET

Throughout the entire course of history, it is doubtful that there has ever been a single day when nothing of any significance occurred, or someone didn't have an idea or form some sort of opinion. It is the very nature of mankind to look for new ideas, seek viewpoints, and make judgments and observations.

There have always been, and certainly will always be, plenty of material with which to work. The problem is merely one of selection, although there is usually one topic that looms high above all others ... something that everyone is talking about, concerned about, arguing about. That is the kind of subject that the political cartoonist thrives on, studies, and presents, perhaps in a new light.

On the other hand, those little news items buried in the back pages of newspapers or magazines can have great potential. Many great stories and newsworthy events have their beginnings in obscure, vague little announcements. Watch for them, make notes, follow developments, get the jump on the competition.

It should be noted here that editorial cartoonists rarely continue to harp on a topic for an extended period of time. In fact, many of the top political cartoonists will serve up one humorous, lighthearted little dish for every two very heavy-handed ones. Usually about once a week, they are required to produce something concerning a local issue, but since most of today's top professional are syndicated, they will attempt to handle the local stuff in a way that might make it interesting to a national audience.

THE "START UP" IDEA

Often, a good editorial cartoon gets its start by merely illustrating a headline, story heading, subheading, or even a lead paragraph. Let's say we find a story heading that reads: "CONGRESSMAN PROPOSES NEW PLAN FOR THE NEEDY."

Our first reaction might be to visualize a Congressman handing a loaf of bread or a huge, fancy cake to an obviously needy person. The first thing the cartoonist might do is create a symbol to represent the "New Plan." The choice of a symbol would be based on the merits of the plan itself. If the program obviously offered only temporary, short-term relief, the symbol might be shown as a donut or a loaf of bread or a fancy piece of cake. If the plan promised some solid, long-range benefits, the symbol should reflect that. Perhaps a ladder to reach a higher income level. An armload of books labeled "Specialized Education." A key to unlock a treasure chest.

At this point, we might want to take a closer look at Mr. Congressman. What success has he had with other proposals? Should he be portrayed as a truly concerned political leader or as a crafty old fox with something up his sleeve?

The plan itself might offer some clues or ideas. What are the hazards involved, if any? How about pitfalls or hidden strings? Is it a bright new light in the wilderness or some rehashed old idea that never worked in the first place?

How best to portray the needs and what possible reactions there could be to the New Plan are other questions that might need to be resolved.

THE ZINGER

By now, the political cartoonist would probably review his notes, doodles, and penciled characterizations and arrive at a definite conclusion. But who or what will his target be? The Congressman who proposed the plan? The plan itself? The needy, in an effort to point out the possible disadvantages of the idea? Perhaps someone on the sidelines who strongly opposes the proposal?

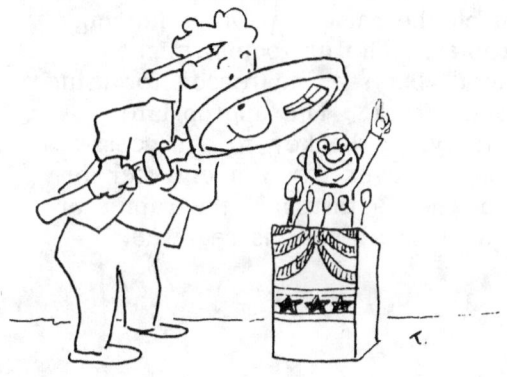

THE IMPORTANCE OF SYMBOLS

One of the most creative and enjoyable tasks the political cartoonist faces, almost on a daily basis, is transforming vague, shadowed, intangible thoughts and ideas into something solid and easily understood. A group of lobbyists might be represented as a huge steamroller charging down at the capitol building. Taxes could be indicated by a huge, ever-tightening vise. Crime, dope peddlers, greed, and corruption might be appropriately represented by a large, mangy rat or something equally as offensive.

Occasionally, the editorial cartoonist will employ more traditional symbols, ones that were created nearly a century ago by the early masters of the art. Uncle Sam is immediately recognized by millions of people throughout the world. The donkey (Democrats) and the elephant (Republicans) represent our two major political parties. Other familiar symbols have been created for peace, war, justice, famine, and hundreds of other intangibles.

Anyone who has ever looked at and studied a political cartoon can readily appreciate the importance of symbols and the impact they have.

THE BROAD-AXE ... OR THE RAPIER

The editorial cartoonist can make a point in many different ways. On extremely important issues, he may create a "big rock" cartoon, thrown skillfully and accurately. It is a bold, straightforward attack. Its message is clear and direct.

But situations vary in importance. A devastating attack is not always needed. Under certain circumstances, the cartoon's message might amount to nothing more than a tweak on the cheek of a political leader.

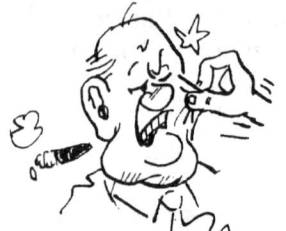 It is the cartoonist's way of saying, "You rascal, we know what you're up to, and you'd better straighten up your act or you'll get a swift kick in the pants." Oddly enough, a mild, even humorous attack can sometimes be as effective as a punch-in-the-nose approach.

In other cases, the political cartoonist might use his skill in much the same way as a fencing master uses his rapier. The cartoonist might want to "draw blood" but sees no reason for using a vicious broad-axe attack. The appropriate weapon, used skillfully, is the key to a successful editorial cartoon. Never throw a big rock or swing a broad-axe when a thrust of the rapier or a tweak on the cheek is all that is required.

THE SEASONAL STUFF

The major holidays provide the political cartoonist with lots of timely ideas and gives him or her a whole raft of ready-made symbols. You can be sure Old Father Time, complete with scythe and hourglass, will make his appearance in editorial cartoons all over the place during the final week of December, as will merry old Saint Nick. Cupids and leprechauns and Easter Bunnies and firecrackers and ghosts and goblins and the fattened turkey will all dutifully play their parts under the direction of the editorial cartoonist's pen at the appropriate times.

Since each of the holiday symbols have a "built-in" reputation and characterization, the cartoonist has but to tie in with a timely event or topic in a unique, surprising, or humorous manner.

The major holidays are, indeed, a sort of fun time for the political cartoonist. On those occasions, he will often show the more tender side of his nature.

THE OBIT

Drawing a cartoon that signifies the death of an extremely popular political figure or well known celebrity can be a difficult task for the political cartoonist, who is more comfortable with his job of prodding and poking at the living, not burying the dead. But, in the end, the cartoon will likely be an eloquent eulogy, a giant monument that expresses sadness with few, if any, words.

POLITICAL CARICATURES ... AN ART IN ITSELF

The editorial cartoonist is faced with a number of problems when he or she first sets out to create a caricature of a political leader. Not the least of those problems is size. In many cases, the caricature he produces will be reduced to a size not much larger than one's thumbnail. It is therefore necessary to create a likeness with a few strokes of the pen or brush.

The lack of adequate research material can frequently be a problem, especially when his or her subject is a newcomer to the political arena. Photographs or the individual will be scarce and difficult to locate. That is when televised interviews can be immensely helpful. In fact, many political cartoonists, in developing or revising caricatures, prefer to work from TV interviews. They offer a variety of views of their subjects and, due to the constantly changing camera angles, are forced to keep their drawings simple and uncluttered.

Character and personality can present some problems, too. Since the editorial cartoonist's opinion of his subject can vary from time to time (as do those of the public at large), so must his portrayal or characterization of his subject vary. In one cartoon, the artist might show his subject to be a clown or an idiot, while a later cartoon might portray the individual as a very astute statesman.

CARICATURES SOON BECOME SYMBOLS

The first few caricatures that appear portraying an emerging politician are often nothing more than a bland likeness. Gradually, as the individuals character and personality become more apparent, the caricatures begin to homogenize. Political cartoonists everywhere soon standardize the likeness, simplify it, until they all look just about the same. It's almost as though cartoonists have all arrived at the same conclusion concerning their subject.

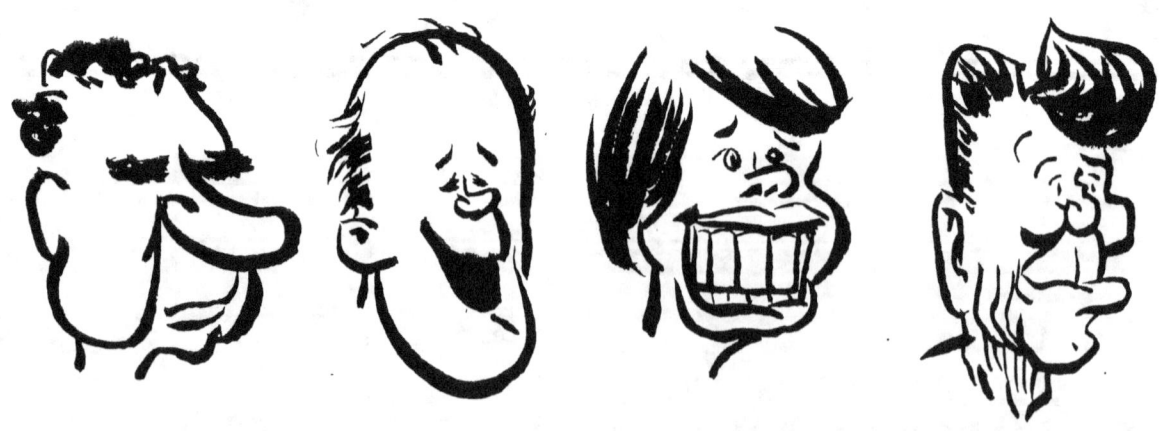

CARICATURING THE CARICATURISTS

As outlined on the previous page, political caricatures quickly become symbols more than caricatures. There is an advantage to this since it provides almost instantaneous recognition.

That, however, presents a problem when one attempts to demonstrate a procedure typically used by editorial cartoonists when creating a caricature. The end result would likely not be much different than the caricatures that have already been developed and well established. Any effort to rehash work that has previously been done, and done well, would not be of any great benefit.

So, we'll start from scratch. New faces, new people. And what better subjects could we have than the editorial cartoonists themselves?

A LOW BOW AND A TIP OF THE HAT TO THREE BRAVE AND TRUSTING SOULS!

A am grateful to three of the nation's top political cartoonists for granting me permission to use them as subjects. They are PAUL CONRAD of the Los Angeles Times, MIKE PETERS of the Dayton Daily News, and PAUL SZEP of The Boston Globe.

The photographs I used are those that appear in a great book, The Gang of Eight, featuring examples of the work of eight Pulitzer Prize winning editorial cartoonists: Tony Auth, Paul Conrad, Jules Feiffer, Jeff MacNelly, Doug Marlette, Mike Peters, Paul Szep, and Don Wright. Introduction written by Tom Brokaw. Published by Faber & Faber, Inc., Winchester, MA 01890. 192 pages.

We recommend the book without qualification. It presents many examples of contemporary political cartoons and brief biographies of the cartoonist, how they got where they are, and how they feel now that they're there.

TRIAL AND ERROR

It is a rare cartoonist who can come up with a new political caricature on the first attempt. More often than not, a dozen or more trial sketches are required to get just the right look and expression with just a few strokes of the pen or brush.

The successful caricature will not only exaggerate the subject's outstanding facial features, but should also indicate the person's basic character and personality.

CARICATURING: THREE-STEP METHOD

Subject: PAUL CONRAD
Editorial Cartoonist,
Los Angeles Times

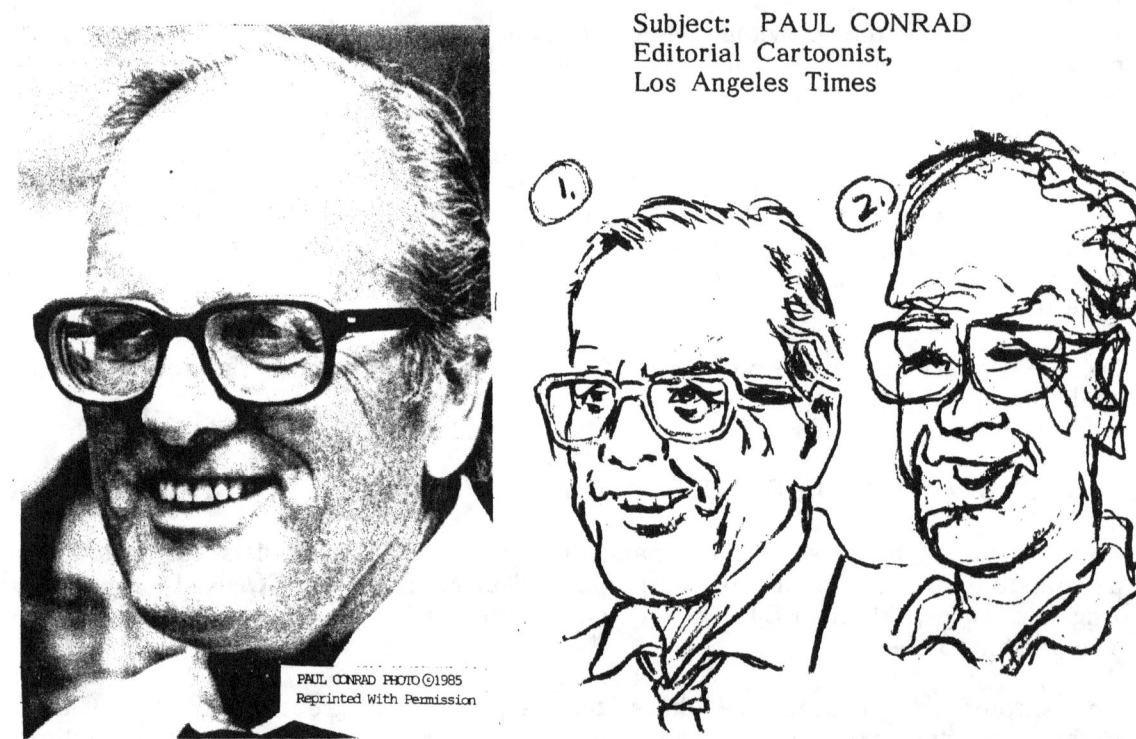

PAUL CONRAD PHOTO ©1985
Reprinted With Permission

Step 1:   The subject is studied closely in an effort to determine what facial features and characteristics, through exaggeration, would help identify the individual. A sort of "pencil portrait" can be helpful (Figure 1).

Step 2:   A single-line sketch (from memory) is drawn to loosen up the drawing style.

Step 3:   Numerous "quickie caricatures" are drawn until one is found that successfully represents the subject's features, character, and personality.

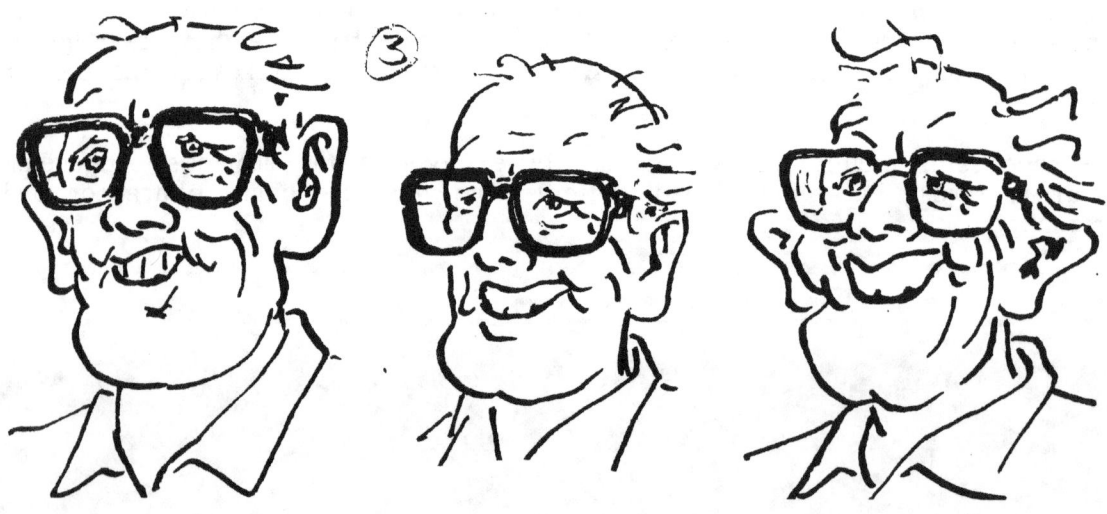

THREE-STEP CARICATURING

Subject: MIKE PETERS,
Editorial Cartoonist,
Dayton Daily News

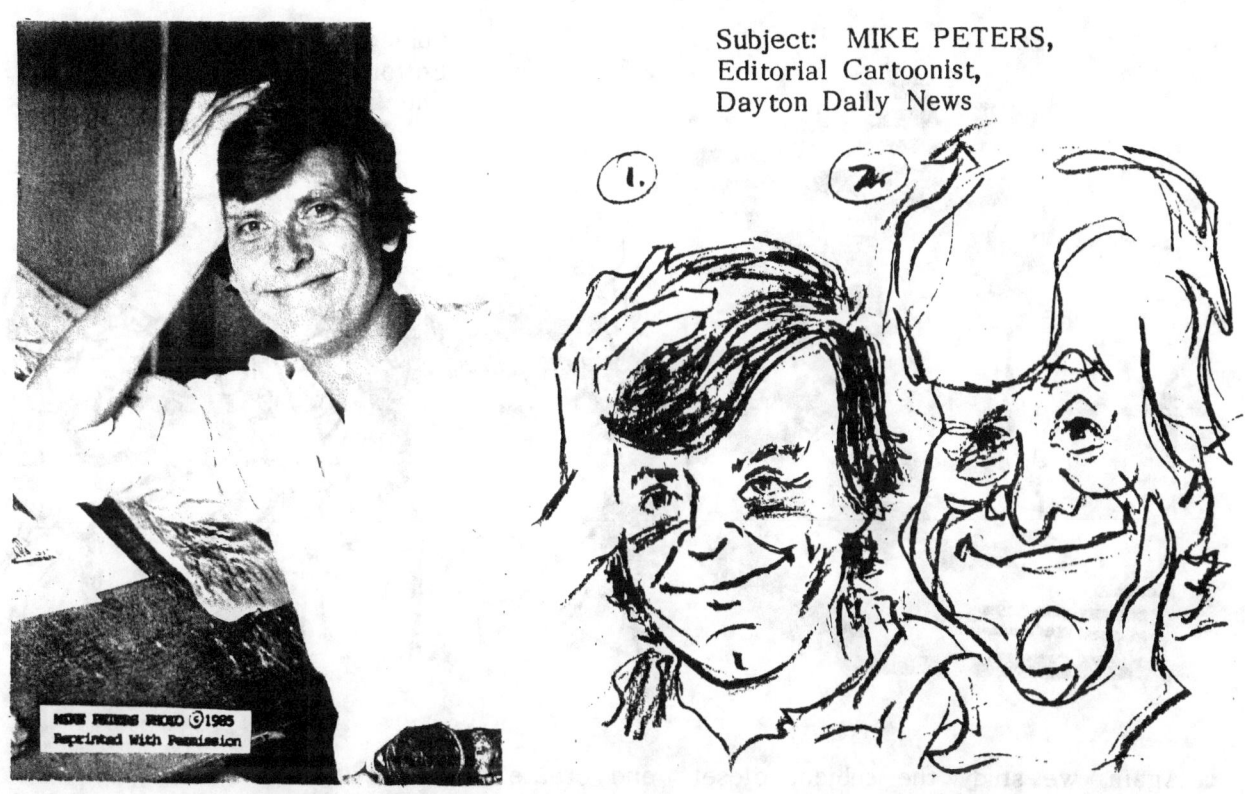

Step 1: Pencil portrait, or "discovery sketch," is made of the subject.

Step 2: A quick, single-line sketch of the subject is drawn to loosen up.

Step 3: Numerous trial and error caricatures are drawn in an effort to develop an accurate, and perhaps humorous, characterization of the subject.

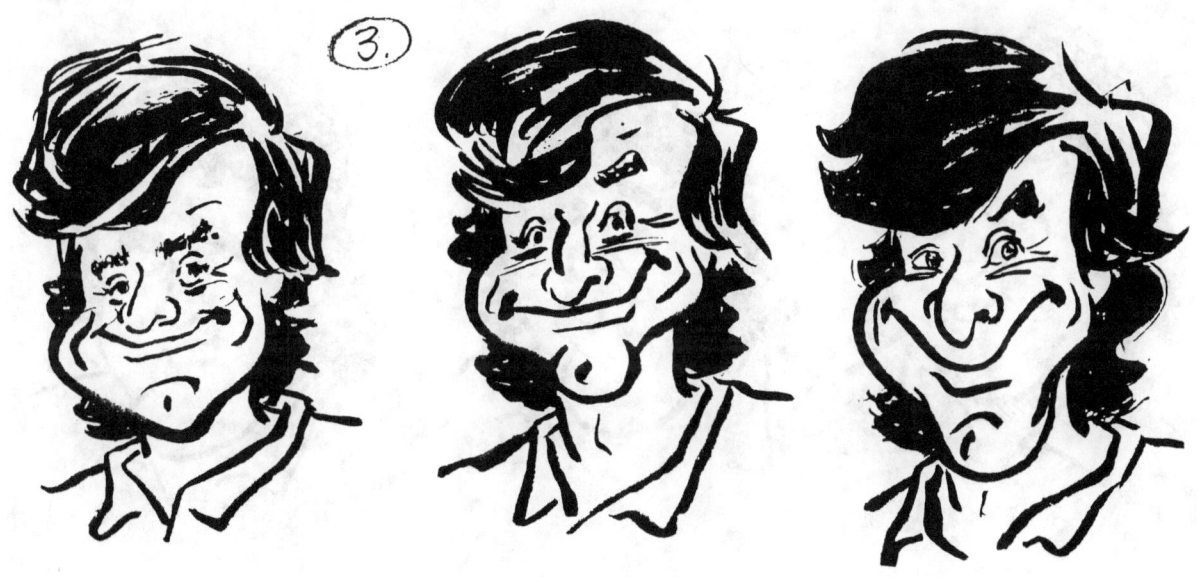

THREE-STEP CARICATURING

Subject: PAUL SZEP
Editorial Cartoonist,
The Boston Globe

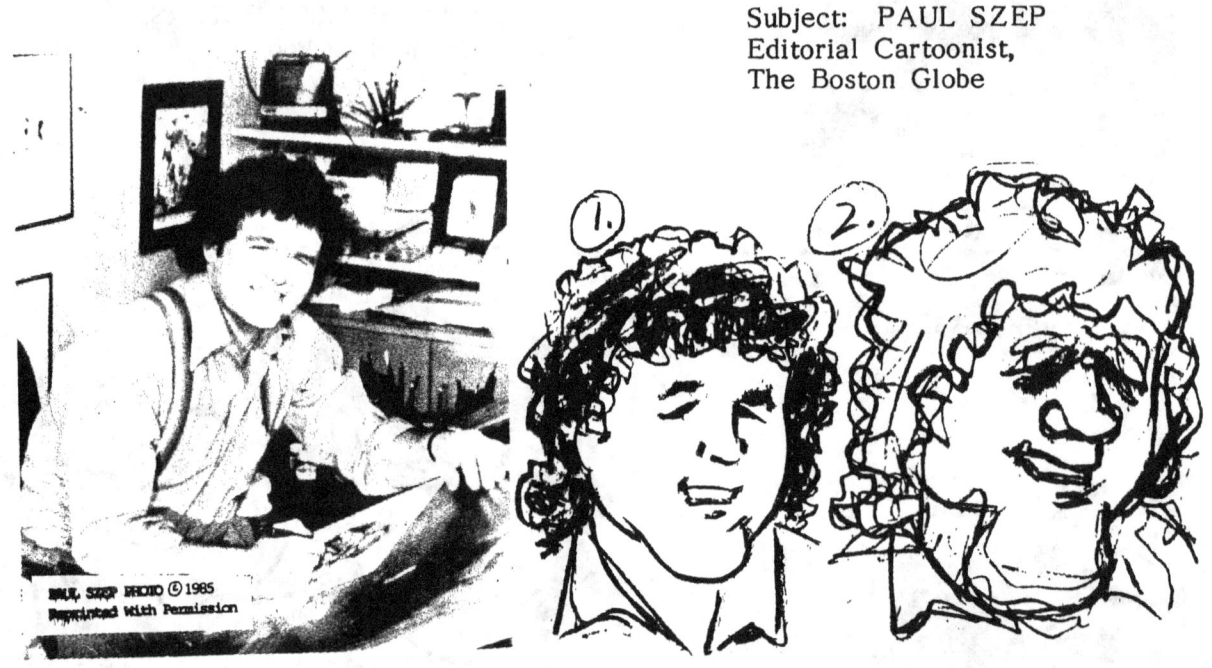

Again, we study the subject closely and create a "discovery sketch" (Figure 1) in an effort to find features and characteristics that might otherwise be overlooked.   We then do a quick single-line sketch of the subject (from memory) to loosen up our thinking.   Trying too hard can often do more harm than good.

More than a dozen trial caricatures were drawn for this caricature, experimenting with various possibilities.   Three are shown below.

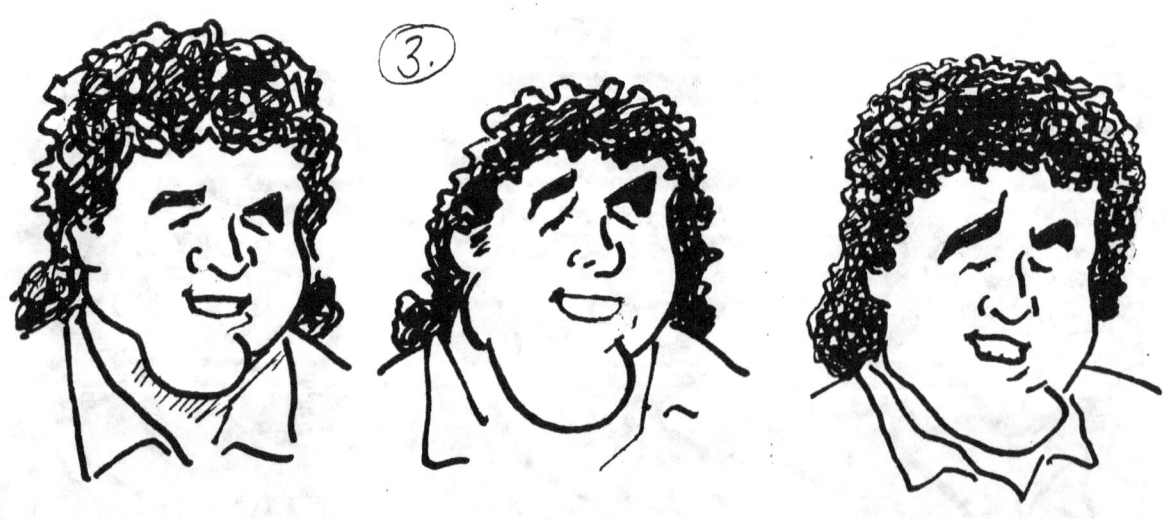

SPECIAL EFFECTS

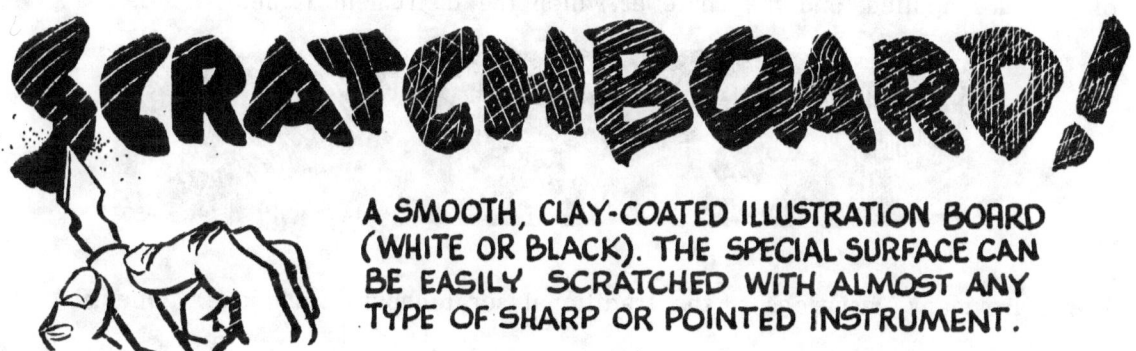

A SMOOTH, CLAY-COATED ILLUSTRATION BOARD (WHITE OR BLACK). THE SPECIAL SURFACE CAN BE EASILY SCRATCHED WITH ALMOST ANY TYPE OF SHARP OR POINTED INSTRUMENT.

Traditionally, the scratchboard technique begins with a solid black background. All details, highlights, and shadings are then "scratched in" with special little tools, most of which resemble pen points and fit into any standard pen holder. The technique is often slow and laborious, and the editorial cartoonist uses it only rarely to create a very unusual or dramatic effect.

Perhaps the main problem with the traditional technique is that the background is black and the surface of the board is comparatively soft, making it difficult to do any accurate preliminary sketching directly on the surface. A solution to that problem -- one used by most practitioners of the art -- is shown below.

TRANSFERRING DRAWING TO BLACK BACKROUND :

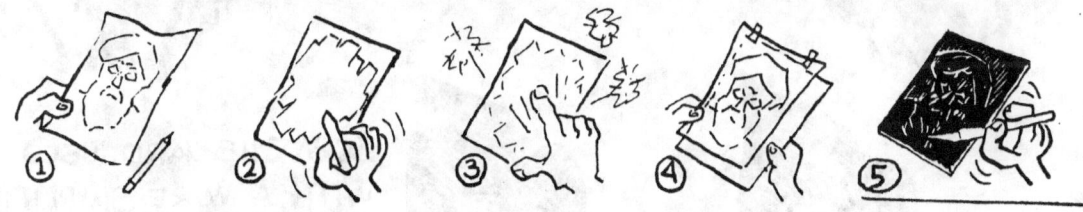

1. ACCURATE DRAWING ON TRACING PAPER.
2. CHALK RUBBED ON BACK OF DRAWING.
3. CHALK LIGHTLY SMUDGED WITH FINGER TO REMOVE EXCESS.
4. DRAWING TRACED ONTO SCRATCHBOARD.
5. DETAILS, HIGHLIGHTS & SHADING SCRATCHED IN.

NOTE: Many art supply stores carry a material called "white transfer paper." It can be used instead of the method shown above.

SCRATCHBOARD TECHNIQUES

The width of the line will depend upon the type of scratcher used, the amount of pressure applied, and the angle at which the instrument is held.

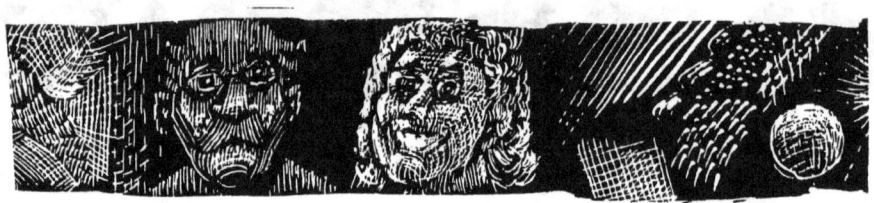

There are many variations to the traditional scratchboard technique.   One is:

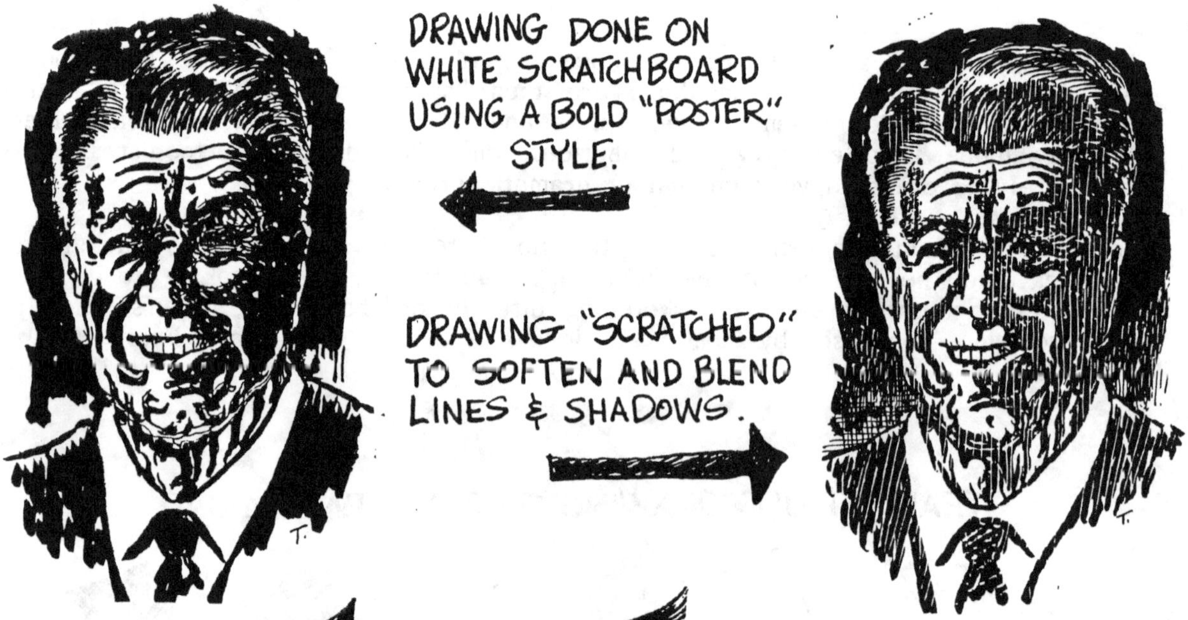

DRAWING DONE ON WHITE SCRATCHBOARD USING A BOLD "POSTER" STYLE.

DRAWING "SCRATCHED" TO SOFTEN AND BLEND LINES & SHADOWS.

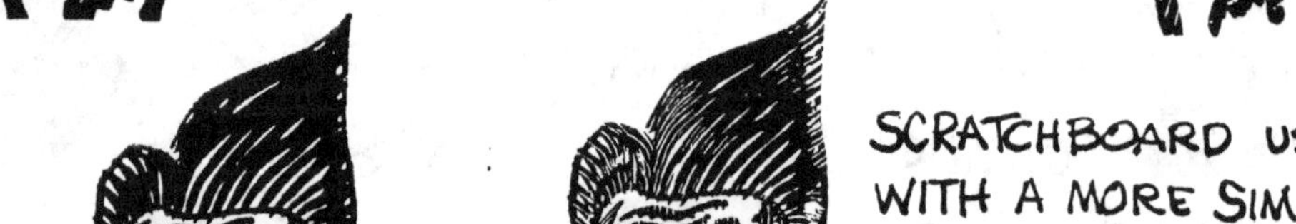

SCRATCHBOARD USED WITH A MORE SIMPLIFIED CARTOON STYLE.

SCRATCHBOARD TECHNIQUE -- BOLD LINE AND DRY BRUSH

This method often produces surprising and unique results.   It's a quick way to create an interesting look to a drawing.

1.   Drawing is inked in with a brush or pen using bold lines.

2.   Overall tone is dry-brushed in.   A cheap bristle brush works fine.

3.   Scratch in highlights with a light touch.

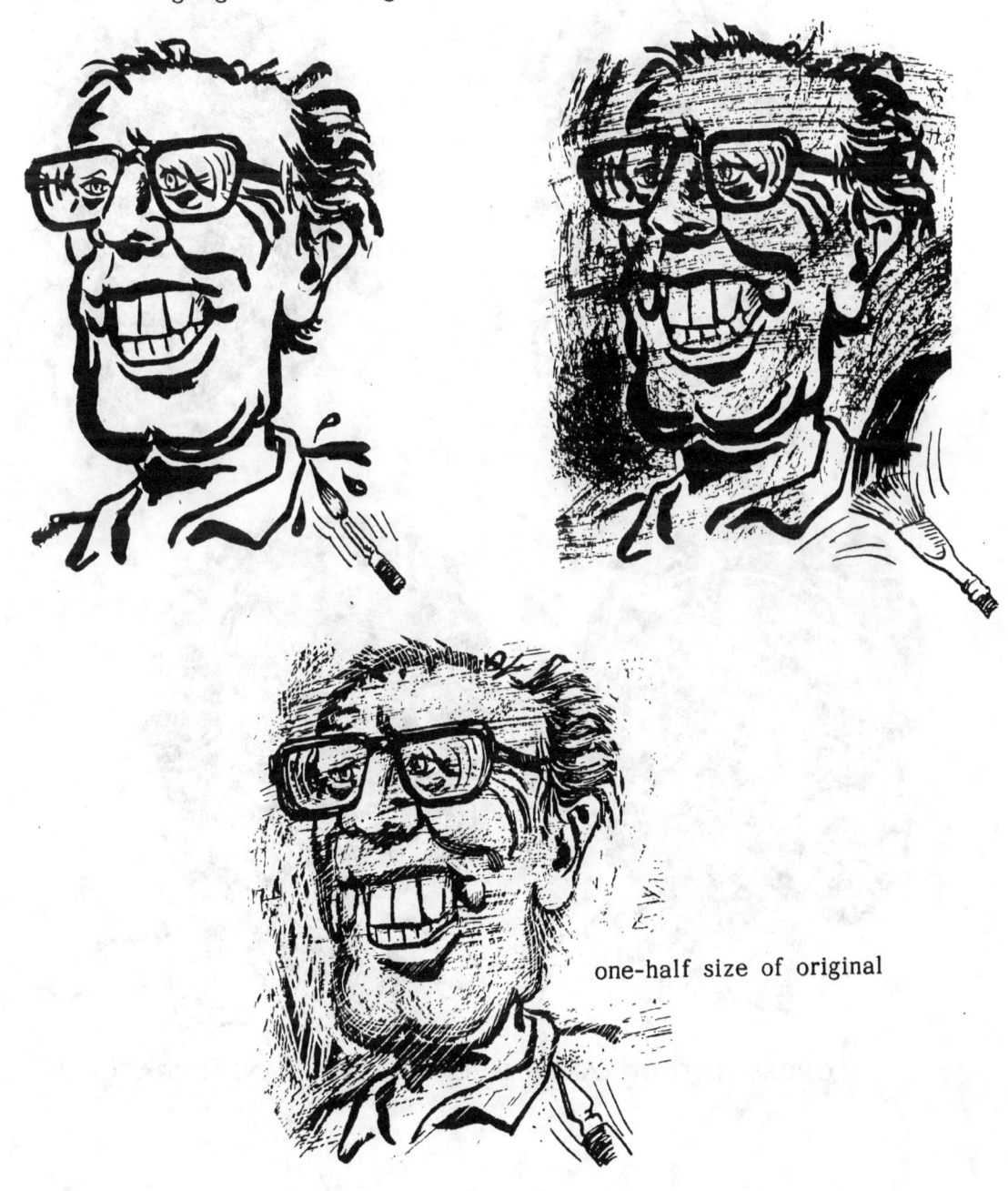

one-half size of original

SCRATCHBOARD TECHNIQUES

The key to developing an interesting and unique style is experimentation. The main element, perhaps, is the creation of middle tones.

SPATTER AND SCRATCH

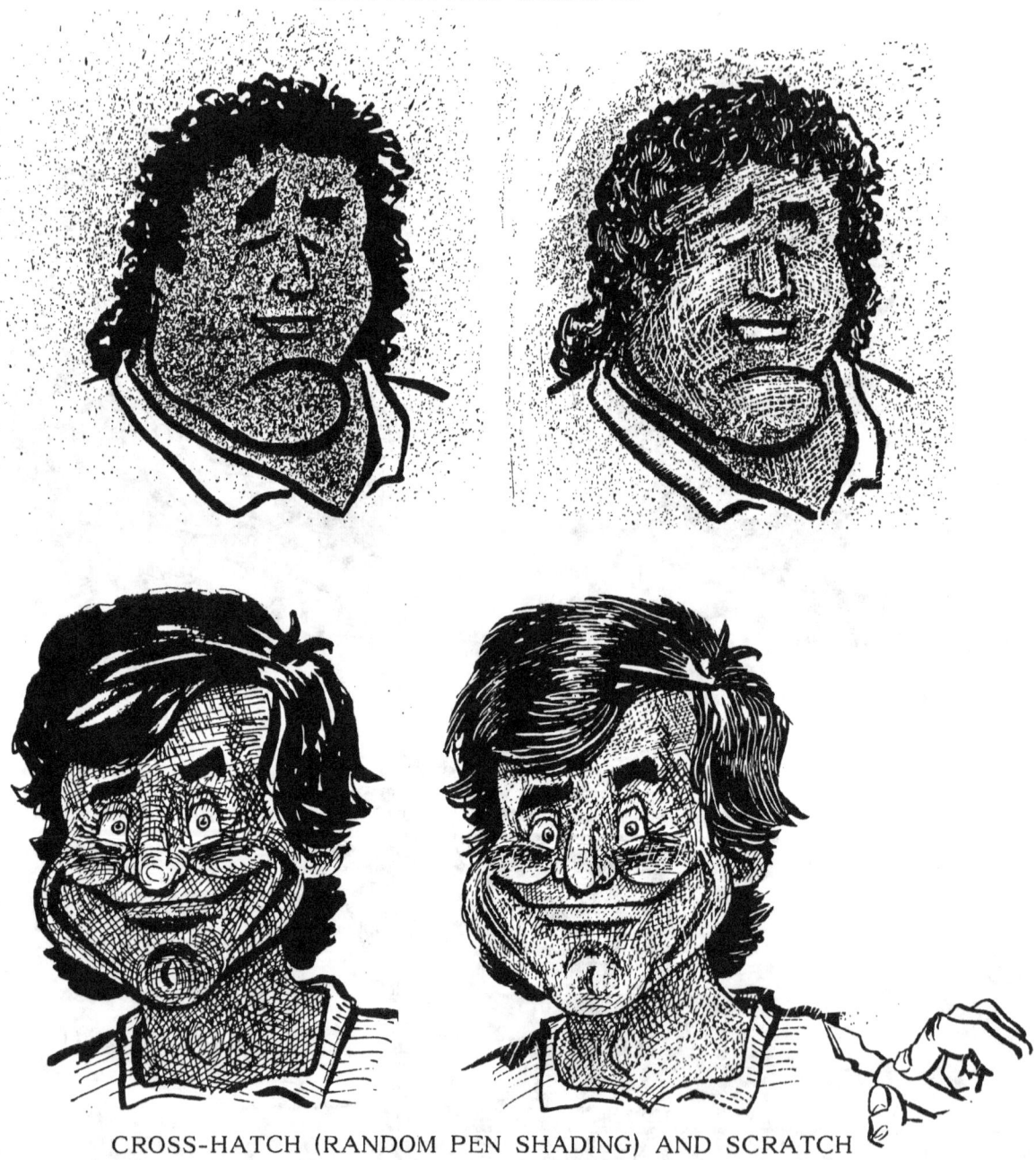

CROSS-HATCH (RANDOM PEN SHADING) AND SCRATCH

SCRATCHBOARD TECHNIQUES

Here is yet another way to develop an interesting and workable middle tone. It is not recommended for people who don't like to get their fingers dirty, however.

In the example below, the drawing was first inked in. The area was then filled in with finger and thumb prints. A blank ink pad (the type used for rubber stamps) works great. It will require a bit of practice, though, to learn to get just the right amount of ink on your fingertips.

Caution! The ink may be a bit difficult to remove from your fingers. Be prepared to do some scrubbing with soap and water.

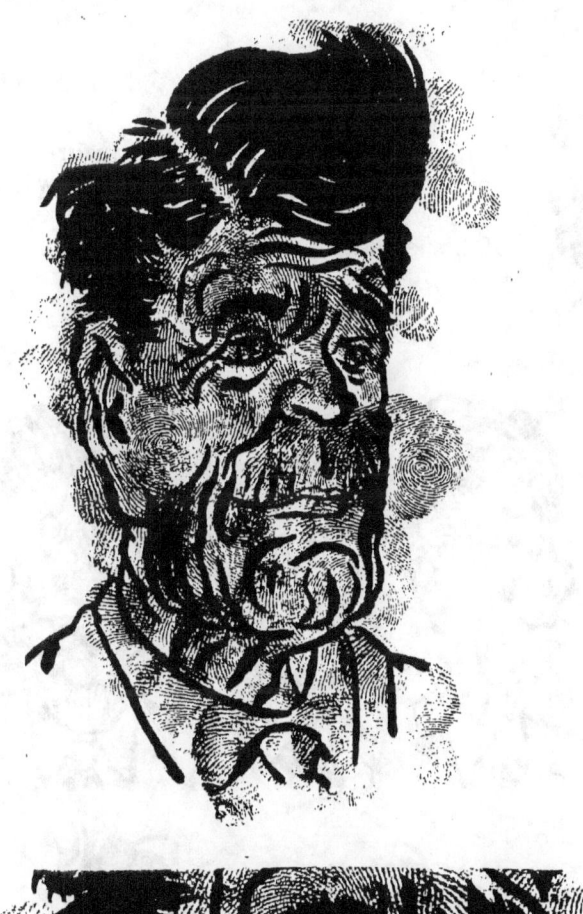
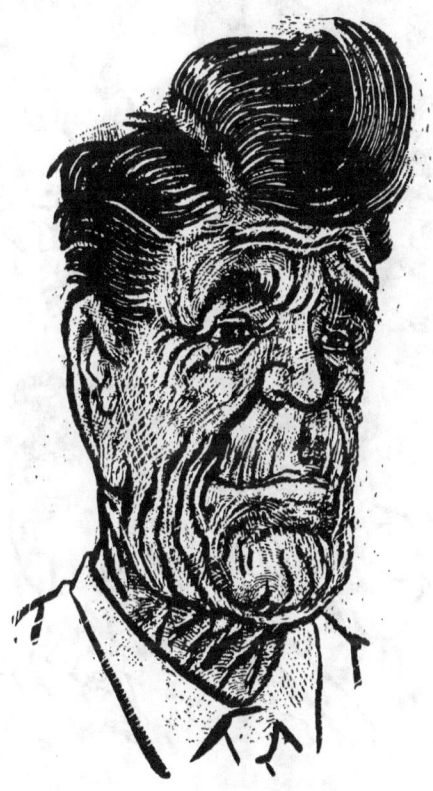

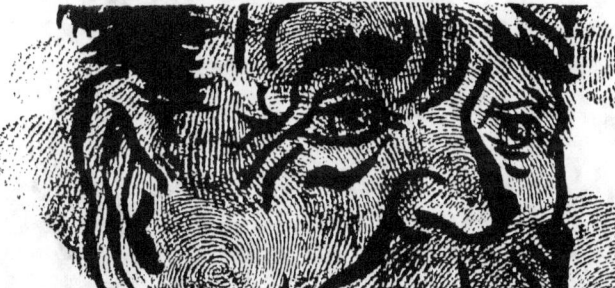

The drawings above were reduced approximately 65% of original size. At the left is a portion from the original drawing.

CARICATURING "IN THE ROUND"

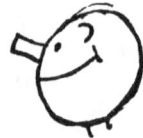 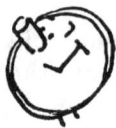 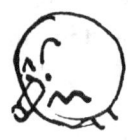 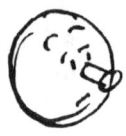 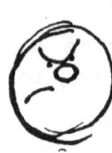 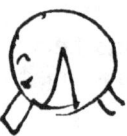 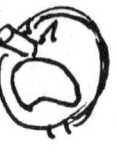

In public appearances, political leaders prefer to show their good side, both physically and spiritually. As a result, most published photographs of leaders present a cheerful face and pleasant attitude. The political cartoonist rarely has reference material available that depicts his subject facing in exactly the required direction with exactly the right expression.

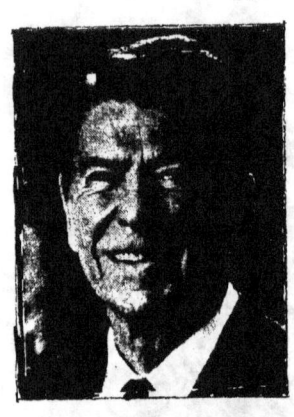 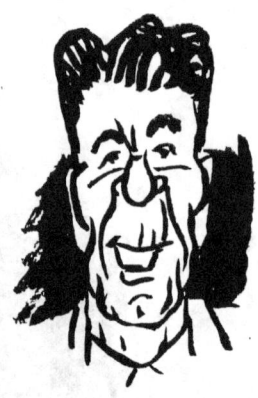

When developing a caricature, the cartoonist should experiment with a wide variety of views and expressions of his subject.

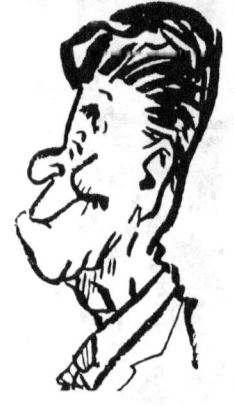 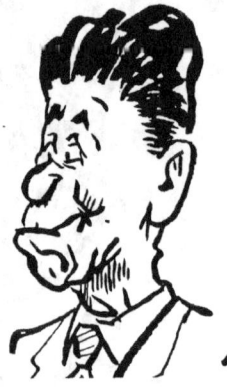 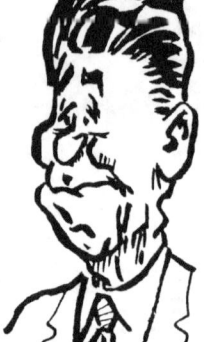 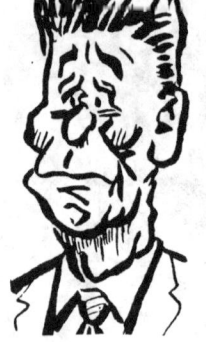 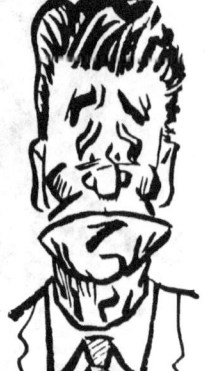

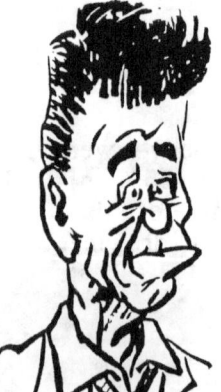 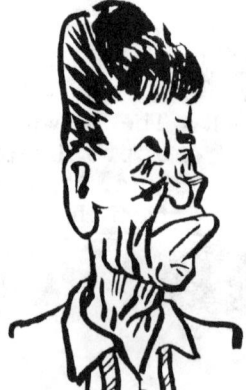 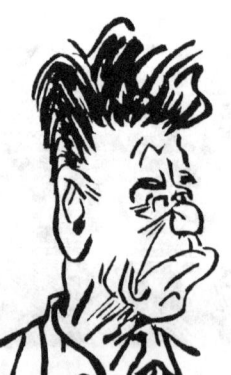 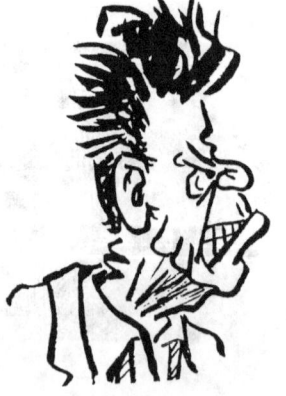

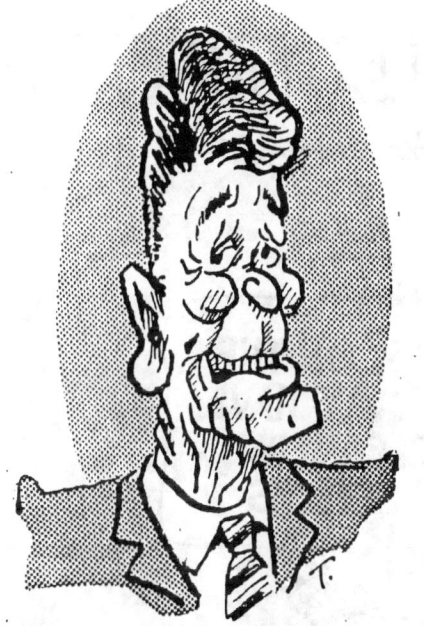

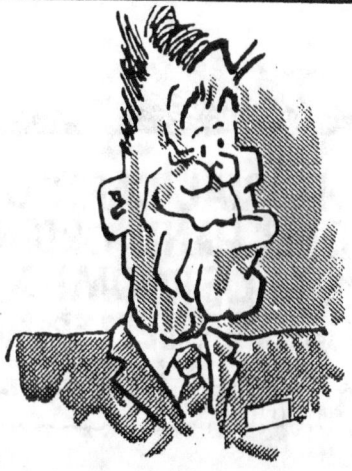

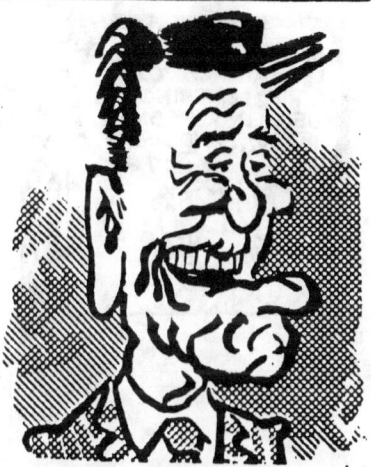

MECHANICAL SHADING
SHOWN ACTUAL SIZE, AND RESULTS OF REDUCTION.

SHADING FILMS   GRAFIX # 250 S   GRAFIX # 232 S

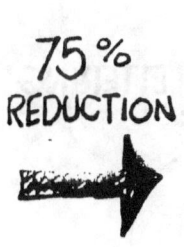

75% REDUCTION

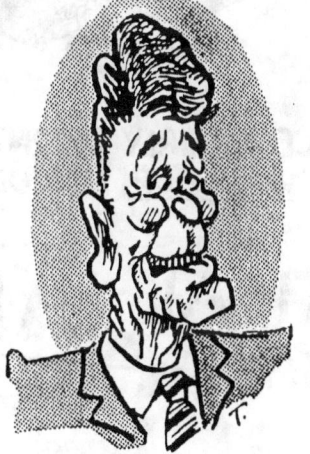

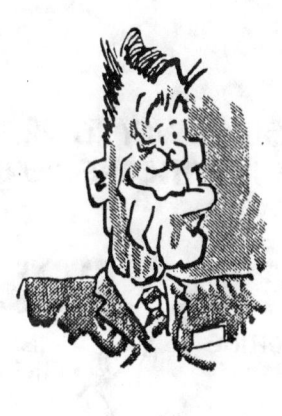

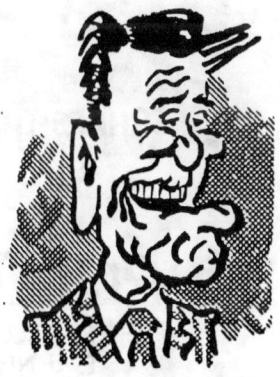

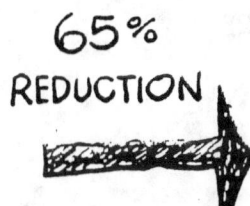

65% REDUCTION

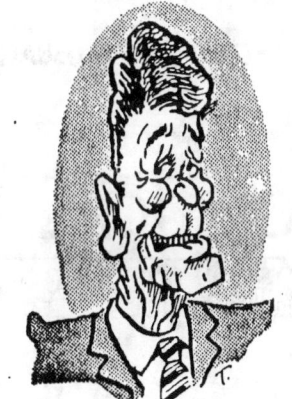

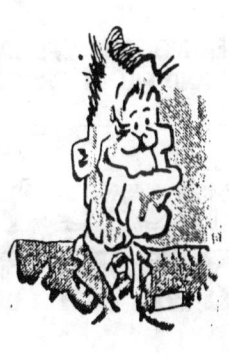

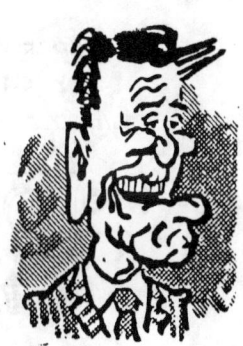

EDITORIAL CARTOON LETTERING
A VERY IMPORTANT ELEMENT OF THE COMPOSITION!

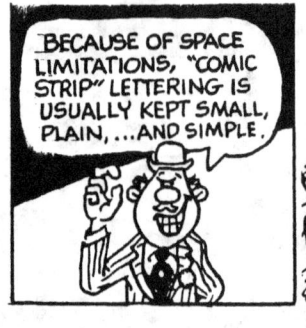

BECAUSE OF SPACE LIMITATIONS, "COMIC STRIP" LETTERING IS USUALLY KEPT SMALL, PLAIN, ...AND SIMPLE.

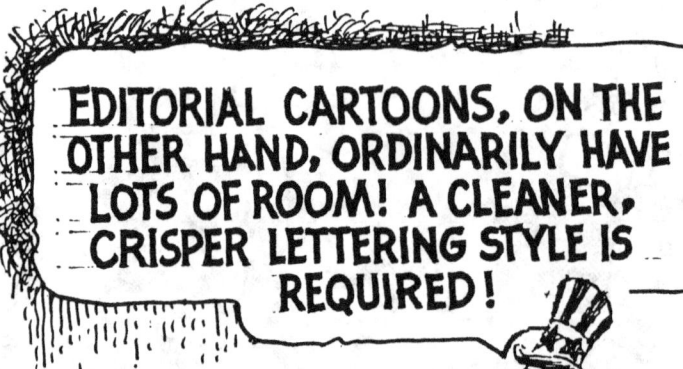

EDITORIAL CARTOONS, ON THE OTHER HAND, ORDINARILY HAVE LOTS OF ROOM! A CLEANER, CRISPER LETTERING STYLE IS REQUIRED!

PERHAPS THE EASIEST WAY TO PRODUCE A FAIRLY DECENT LETTERING JOB IS WITH THE "SHARPENING-UP" METHOD:

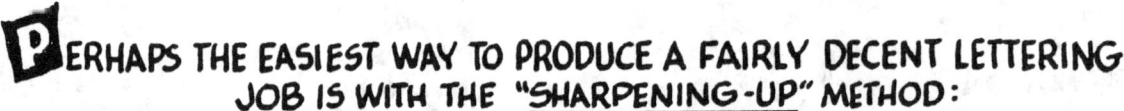

POLITICAL
SPEEDBALL LETTERING
B-5 NIB

POLITICAL
FINISH UP WITH FINE POINT PEN

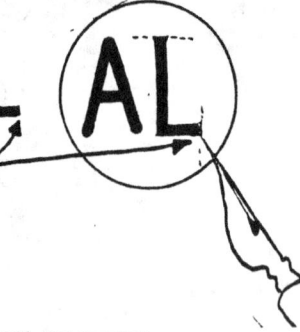
AL

LARGE LETTERING AND SPECIAL LETTER STYLES USUALLY REQUIRE AN OUTLINE AND FILL-IN PROCEDURE:

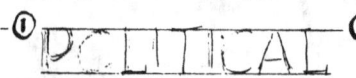
① POLITICAL

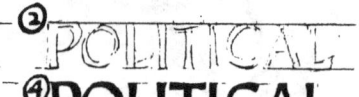
② POLITICAL

③ POLITICAL

④ POLITICAL

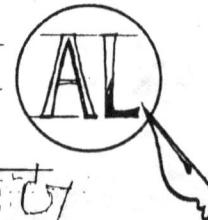
AL

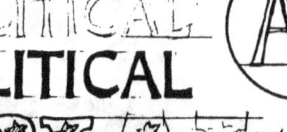
EDITORIAL

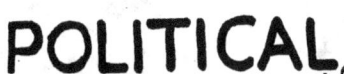

EDITORIAL CARTOON LETTERING

VERY OFTEN, THE CARTOONIST'S INDIVIDUAL *DRAWING* STYLE -OR the EDITORIAL CONTENT OF THE CARTOON- DICTATES A *LETTERING* STYLE:

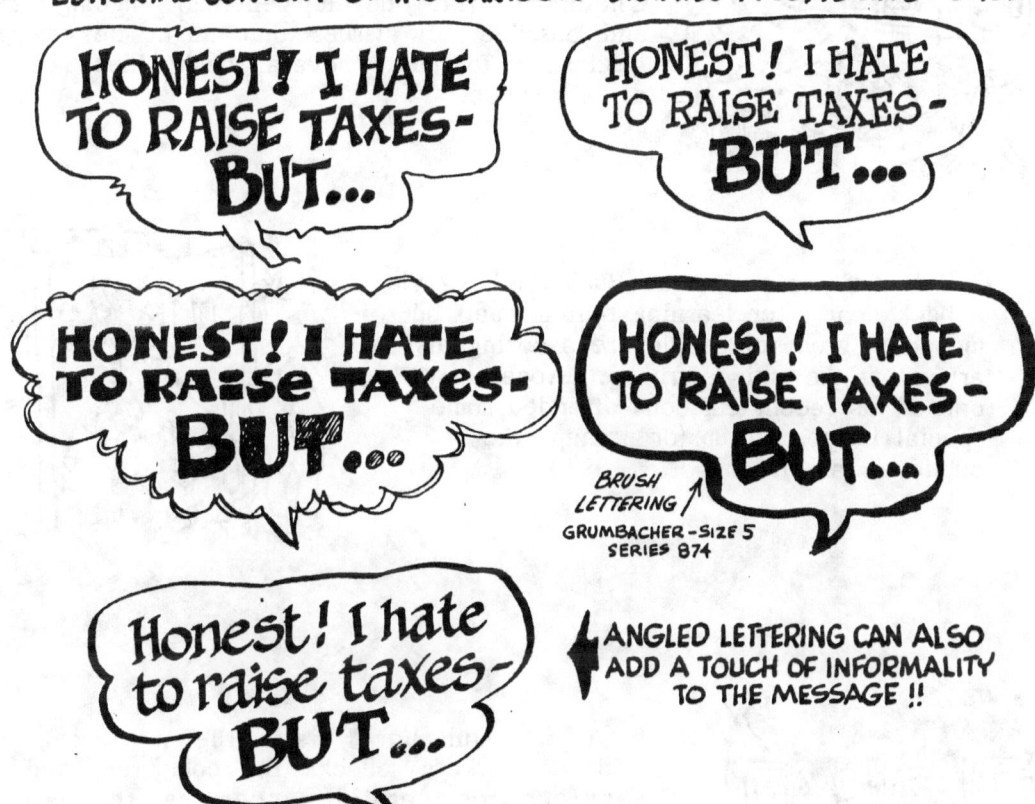

CREATIVE LETTERING CAN SOMETIMES ADD AN EXTRA ELEMENT OF INTEREST TO A COMPOSITION!

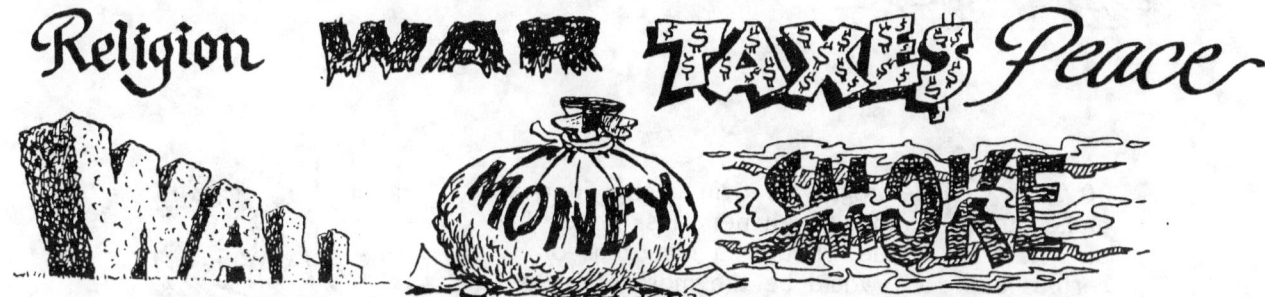

CAUTION: "CREATIVE" LETTERING (ALSO LABELS AND SYMBOLS) BECOME CORNEY AND INEFFECTIVE WHEN USED TOO OFTEN!! USE SPARINGLY!

A DAY IN THE LIFE OF CLYDE DIPPENSCRATCH
Editorial Cartoonist for the Yellville Daily Bugle

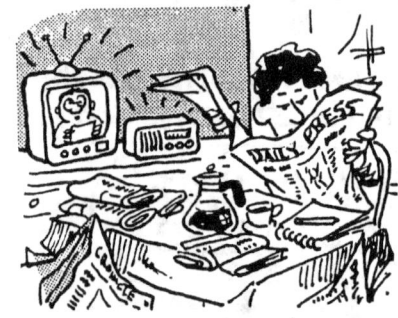

6 A.M.   Clyde reviews the early morning news. Checks for late developments to ongoing stories and possible new issues that might be emerging. Begins to formulate several basic ideas for that day's cartoon.

8 A.M.   Clyde enters the Bugle building via a back door after learning that a small but menacing group of people are awaiting his arrival at the main entrance. Apparently, one of his recent cartoons offended some special interest group (or perhaps the public at large).

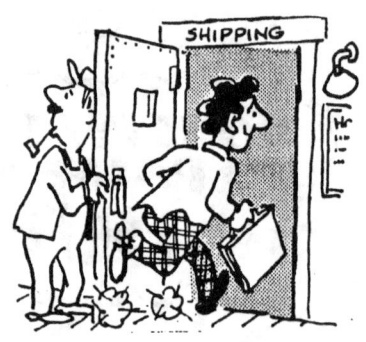

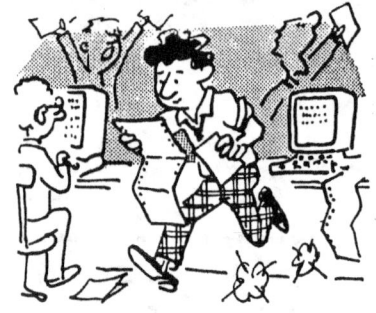

9 A.M.   Our hero visits the newsroom, chats with co-workers, checks the computers and wire services for details concerning the issue or political leader that will be his target for the day. He might even join a small group gathered around a nearby coffee pot.

10 A.M.   Clyde begins to firm up his idea and makes three or four rough pencil sketches in an effort to decide whether a humorous or serious approach would be the most effective. While working on his preliminary sketches, he discovers that the idea could also be presented as a multi-panel cartoon.

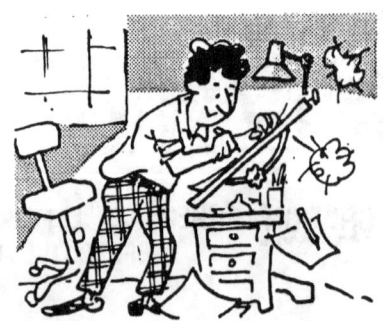

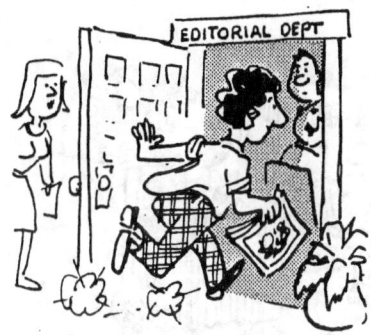

11 A.M.   Clyde feels the need to get away from the drawing board for awhile.   He takes his sketches to the daily 11 A.M. editorial meeting, only to learn that unexpected, last-minute turn of events renders his idea totally inappropriate. New topics are suggested and discussed.

Noon.   Lunchtime finds our hero in the newspaper's morgue (reference files) frantically doing some research on a new topic.   Returning to his drawing board, he makes a comprehensive pencil sketch of the hastily formed new idea.   Someone thoughtfully brings him a sandwich from a nearby fast-food restaurant.

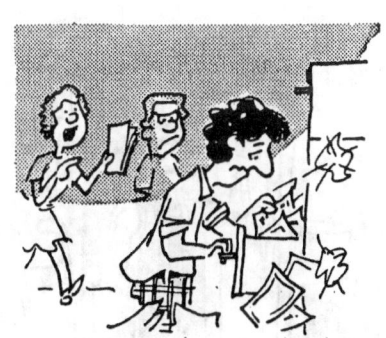

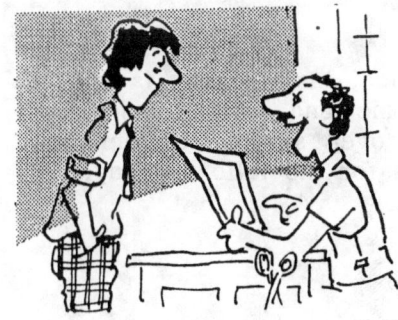

1 P.M.   Smelling of onion, pickle, and mustard, Clyde shows his new sketch to the editorial page editor, who might say, "Better check it out with legal," or "It's a bit strong, but we'll go with it."   The editor can usually be counted on to offer a few constructive suggestions, but says noting, realizing that Clyde is running short of time.

1:15 P.M.   Our cartoonist is back at his board. Confident that his new idea is both timely and appropriate, he inks in the pencil sketch.   He is tempted to add a few extra little details, but his deadline is now less than three hours away.   Playing it safe, he decides not to tinker with the idea or the composition.

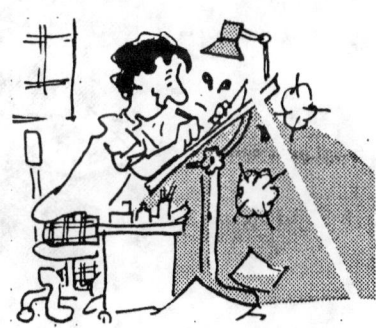

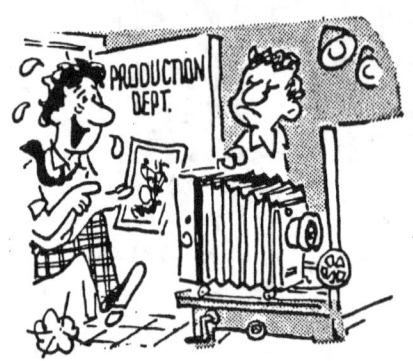

4 P.M. Clyde meets his deadline without a minute to spare. The production department will quickly reduce his drawing to the proper size. Printing plates made of the entire op-ed page and the presses will be rolling within one hour, and subscribers will be reading that issue early the next morning.

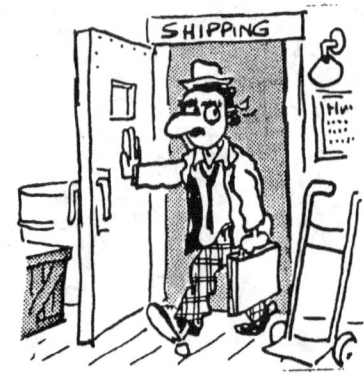

4:30 P.M. Several disgruntled readers are still milling about at the main entrance, so Clyde exits via the back way. He dons a mask, just to be on the safe side. By now, his mood is such that he would like nothing better than to confront the small but angry group. However, the onion, pickle, and mustard stains on his shirt would put him at a slight disadvantage.

Although Clyde has left his Yellsville Daily Bugle office, his workday is not yet finished. He has a well-equipped studio in his home and, after dinner, will likely catch the evening TV news programs, read over several current news magazines, and perhaps doodle around with several ideas for the following day.

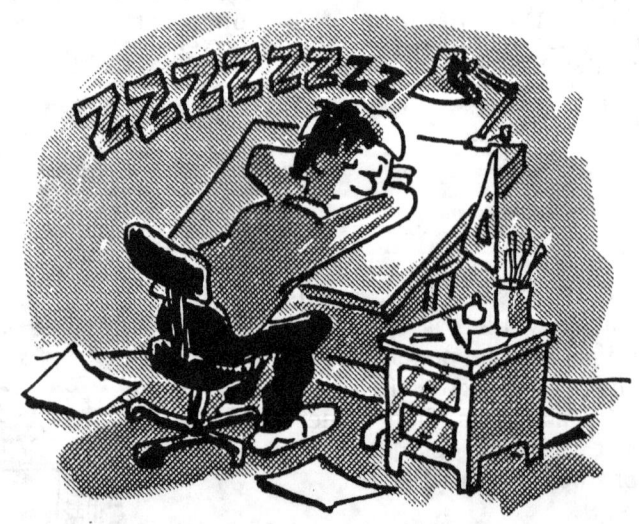

Award Winning Political Cartoonists

GARY BROOKINS, Richmond Times Dispatch

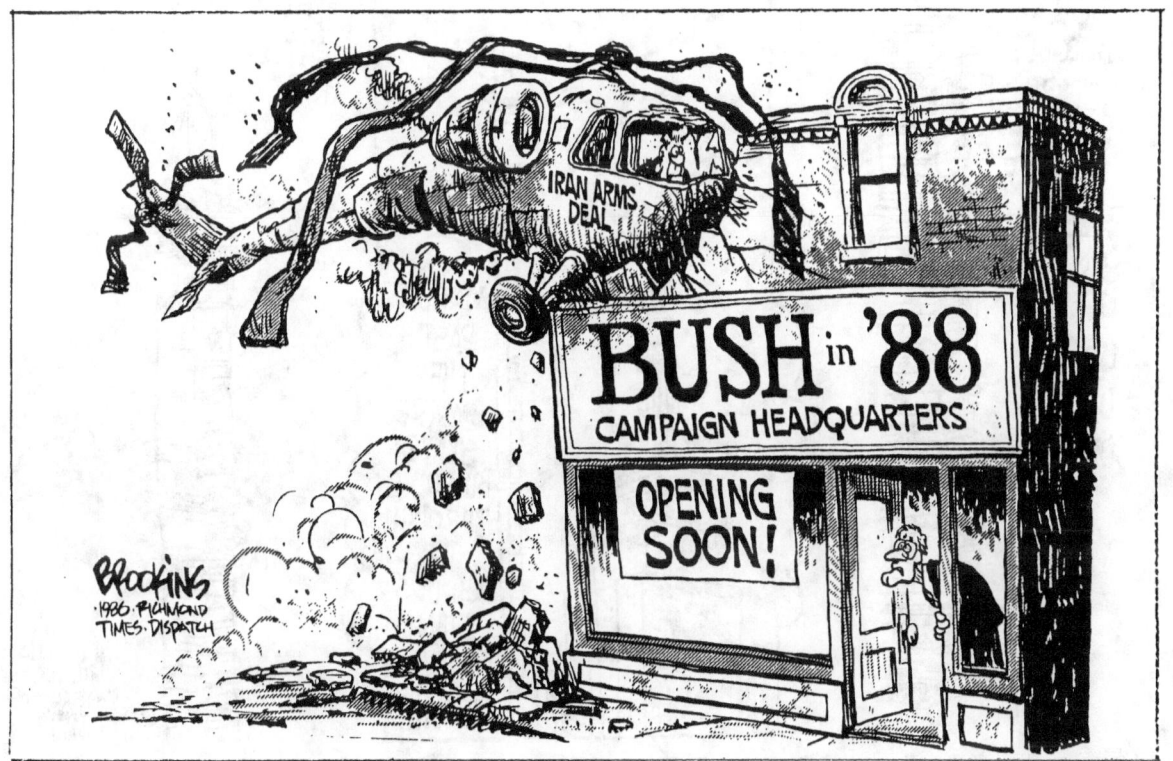

Courtesy GARY BROOKINS, (C) Richmond Times Dispatch, North America Syndicate. Reprinted with permission.

This Gary Brookins cartoon is an excellent example of how symbols can be used to clearly convey an idea. In this case, the two symbols -- the helicopter and building -- effectively illustrate the situation.

PAT CROWLY, Palm Beach Post

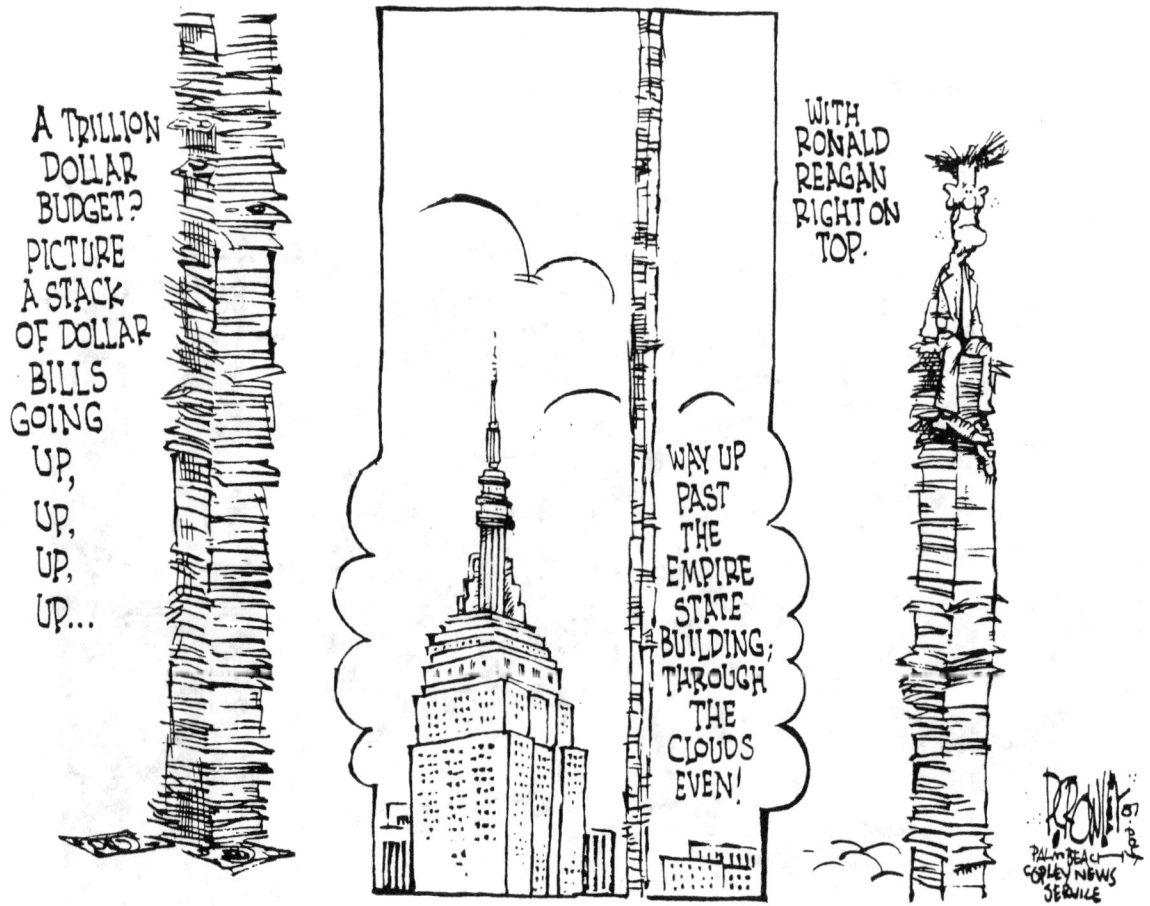

Courtesy PAT CROWLEY, (C) Palm Beach Post, Copley News Service. Reprinted with permission.

This delightful Pat Crowley cartoon gives a new twist to the trillion dollar budget situation.   Mr. Crowley has the distinction of being the only political cartoonist int he nation whose work is printed in full color, five days a week. The Palm Beach Post (of West Palm Beach, Florida) is to be applauded for their leadership in this remarkable editorial policy.

BOB GORRELL, Richmond News Leader

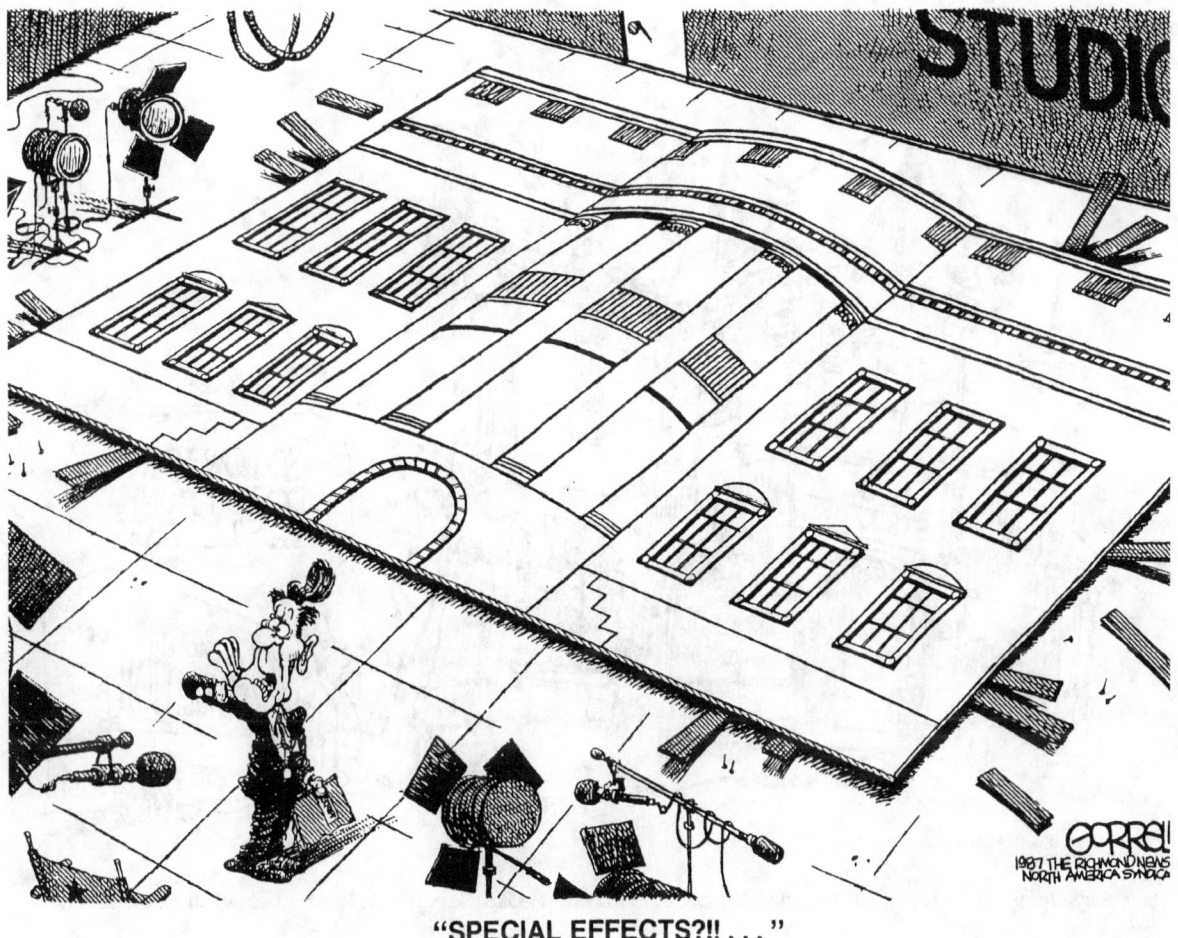

"SPECIAL EFFECTS?!!..."

Courtesy BOB GORRELL, (C) Richmond News Leader, North America Syndicate. Reprinted with permi

This Bob Gorrell cartoon clearly depicts how fragile the image of the White House can be.   IMMEDIATE IMPACT was achieved through the use of clean, uncluttered composition.

JEFF MacNELLY, Chicago Tribune

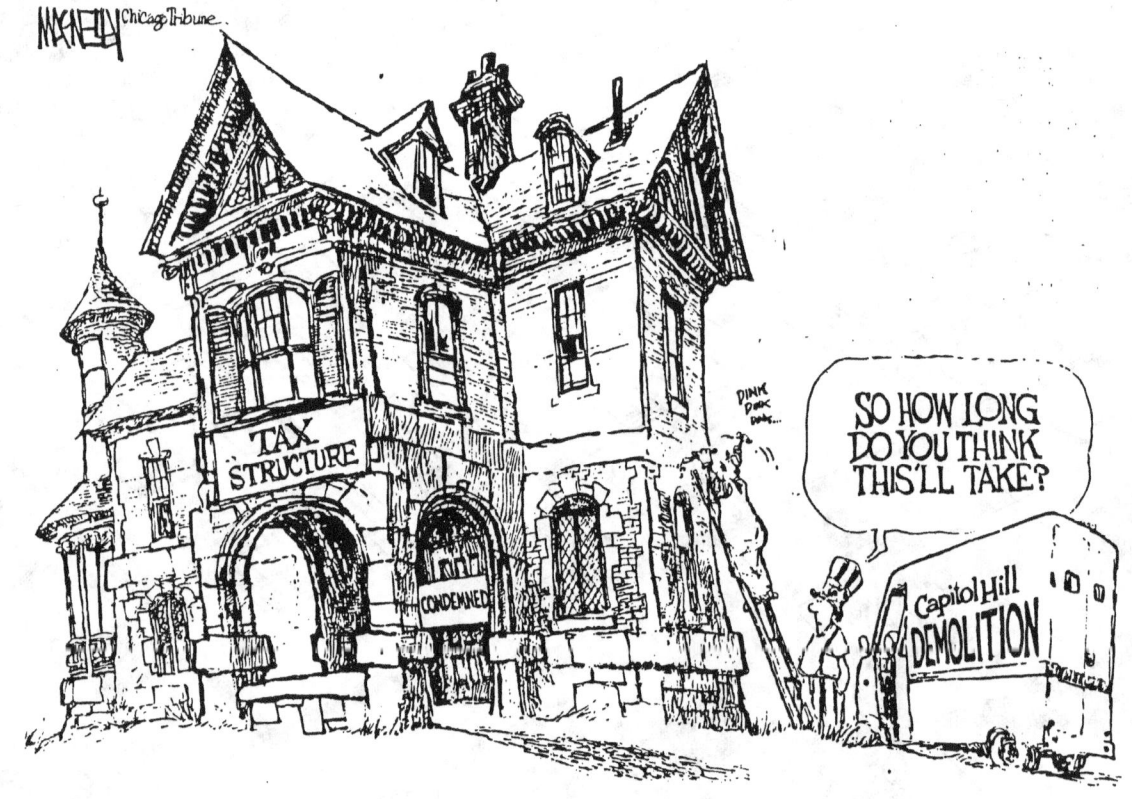

Courtesy Jeff MacNelly, (C) Chicago Tribune, Tribune Media Services. Reprinted with permission.

Jeff MacNelly consistently comes up with ideas that prompt other political cartoonists to mutter, "Now, why didn't I think of that?"　In this skillfully drawn cartoon, MacNelly uses an eerie looking building to represent the federal tax structure.

PAUL SZEP, The Boston Globe

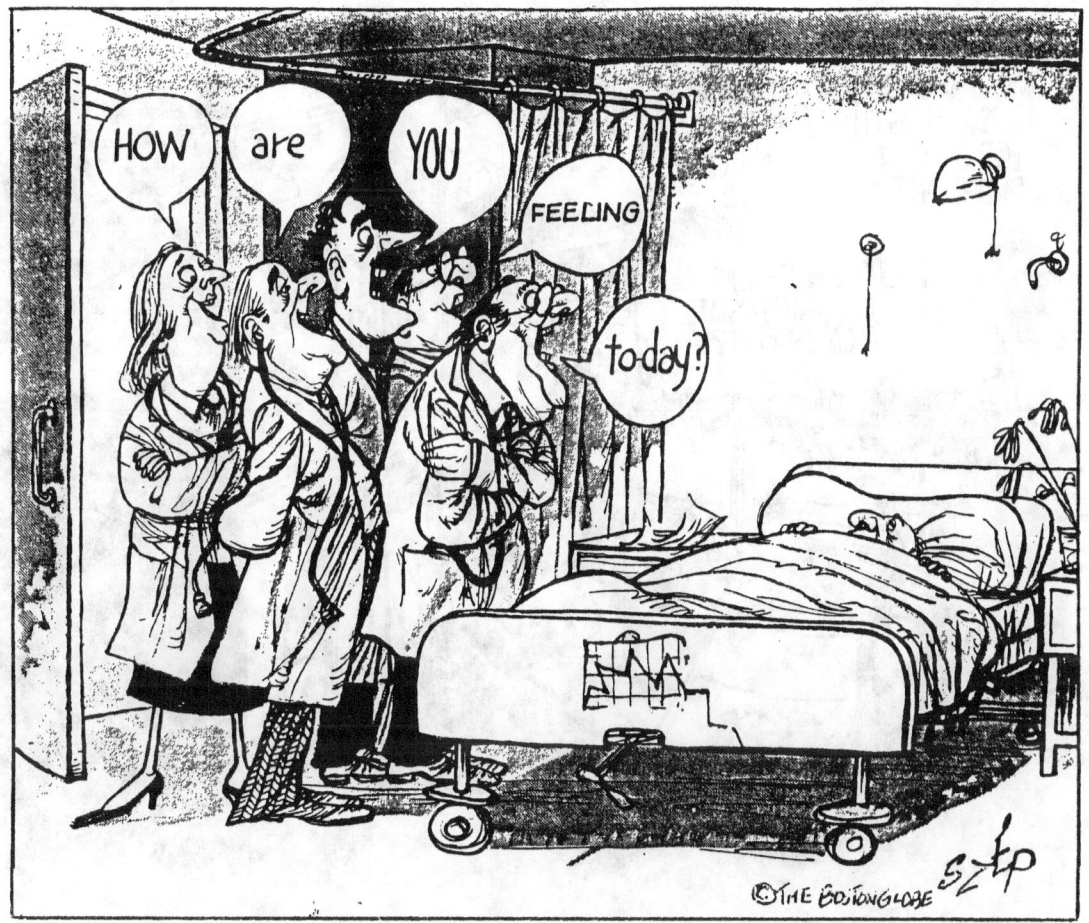

Courtesy PAUL SZEP, (C) The Boston Globe. Reprinted with permission.

This Paul Szep cartoon takes a humorous, and very truthful, look at the doctor glut which the nation seems to face from time to time. He skillfully manages to form a single unit out of the individual doctors, thereby emphasizing the loneliness and vulnerability of the patient.

DON WRIGHT, Miami News

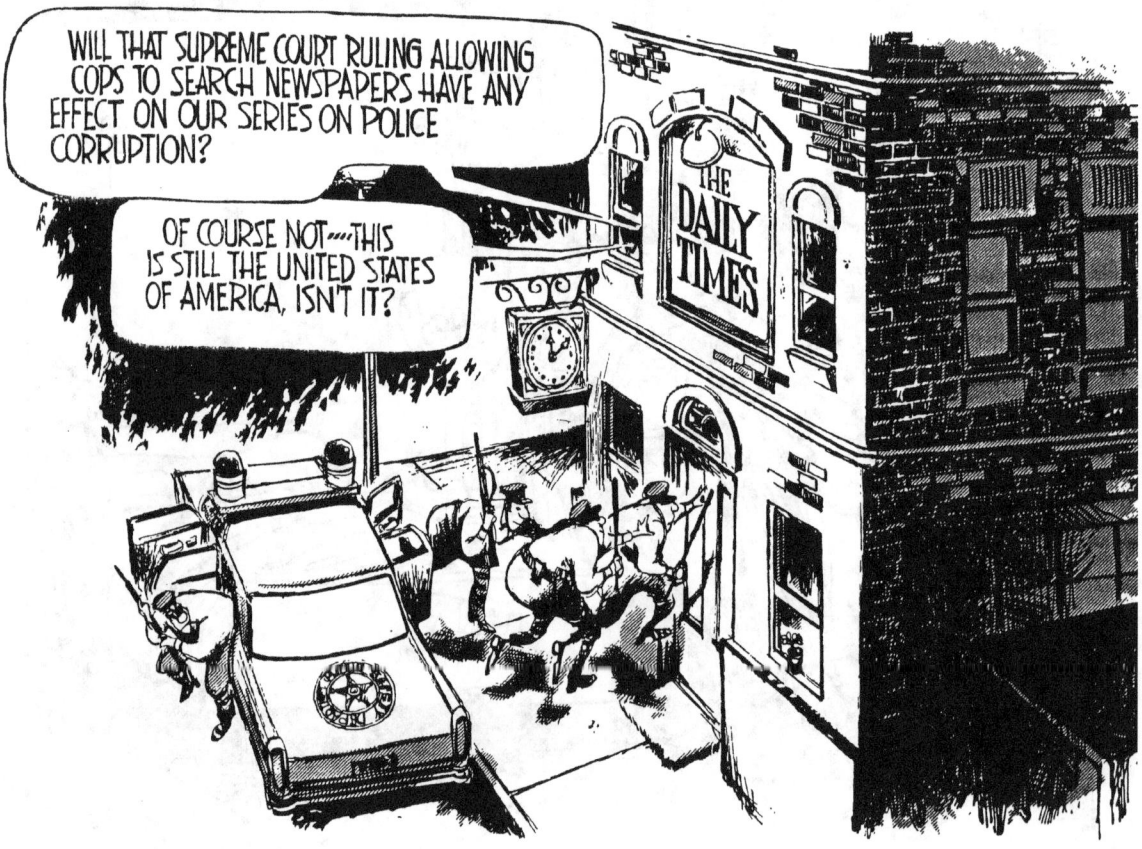

Courtesy DON WRIGHT, (C) Miami News, Don Wright, Inc., Reprinted with permis

This Don Wright cartoon illustrates the importance of neat, clean lettering, bol composition, and a thorough knowledge of the principles of perspective.   Th point is made skillfully and with outstanding draftsmanship.

QUICK-SKETCHING FROM TV NEWS & INTERVIEWS!

THE OL' BOOB-TUBE IS AN EXCELLENT SOURCE OF REFERENCE MATERIAL. AND – DUE TO CONSTANT CHANGES IN CAMERA ANGLES – IT FORCES ONE TO WORK FAST! CUTS DOWN ON DILLY-DALLY TIME!

IN MOST CASES, IT WILL BE NECESSARY TO SKETCH YOUR SUBJECT "PIECE BY PIECE" – HEAD SHAPE – HAIR – EYES – NOSE – MOUTH – CHIN, ETC. FINE! THEN ASSEMBLE THE PARTS INTO A SINGLE UNIT!!

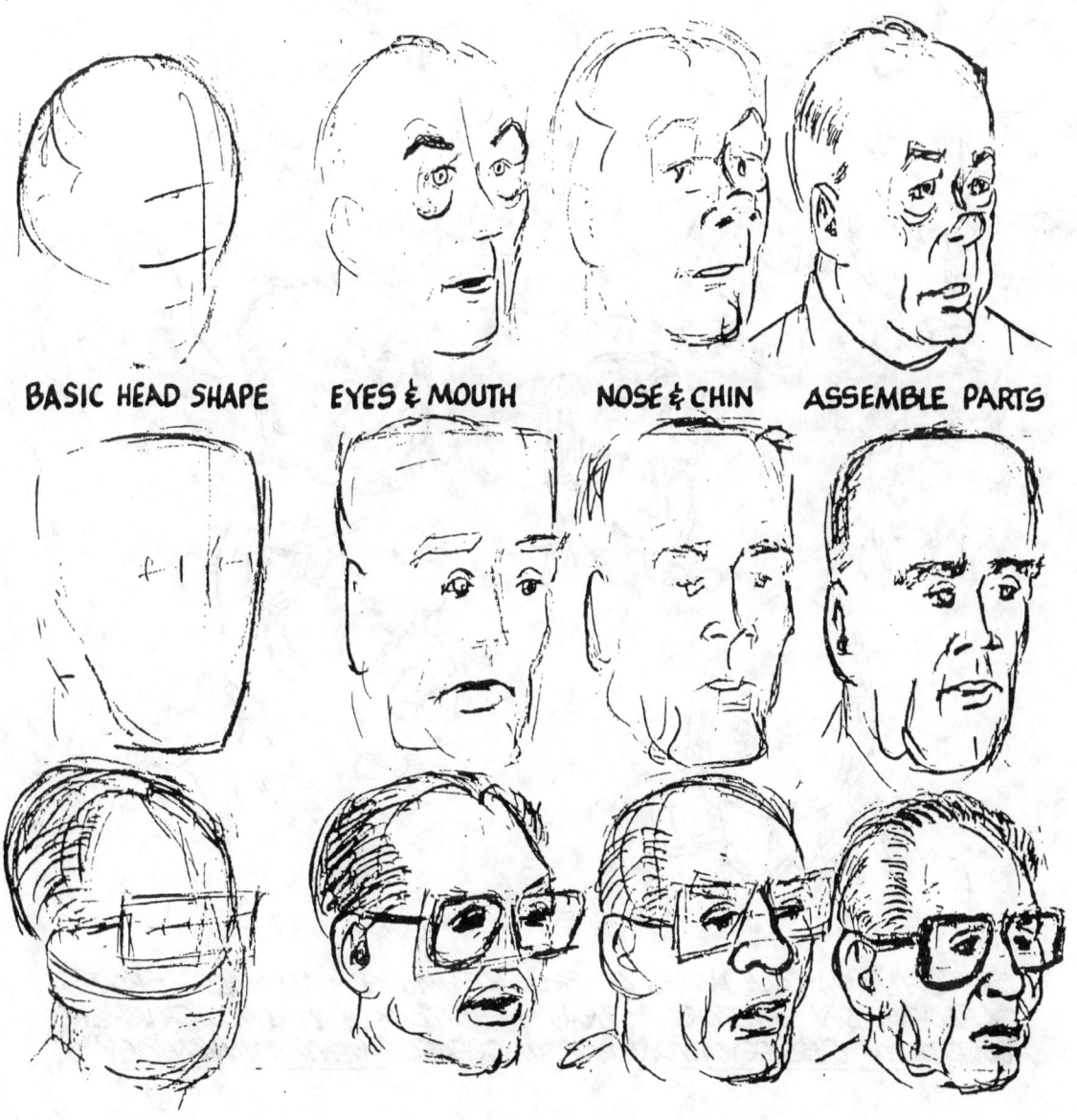

BASIC HEAD SHAPE   EYES & MOUTH   NOSE & CHIN   ASSEMBLE PARTS

THE TV SCREEN OFFERS TREMENDOUS OPPORTUNITIES TO DEVELOP "QUICK-SKETCH" SKILLS !!

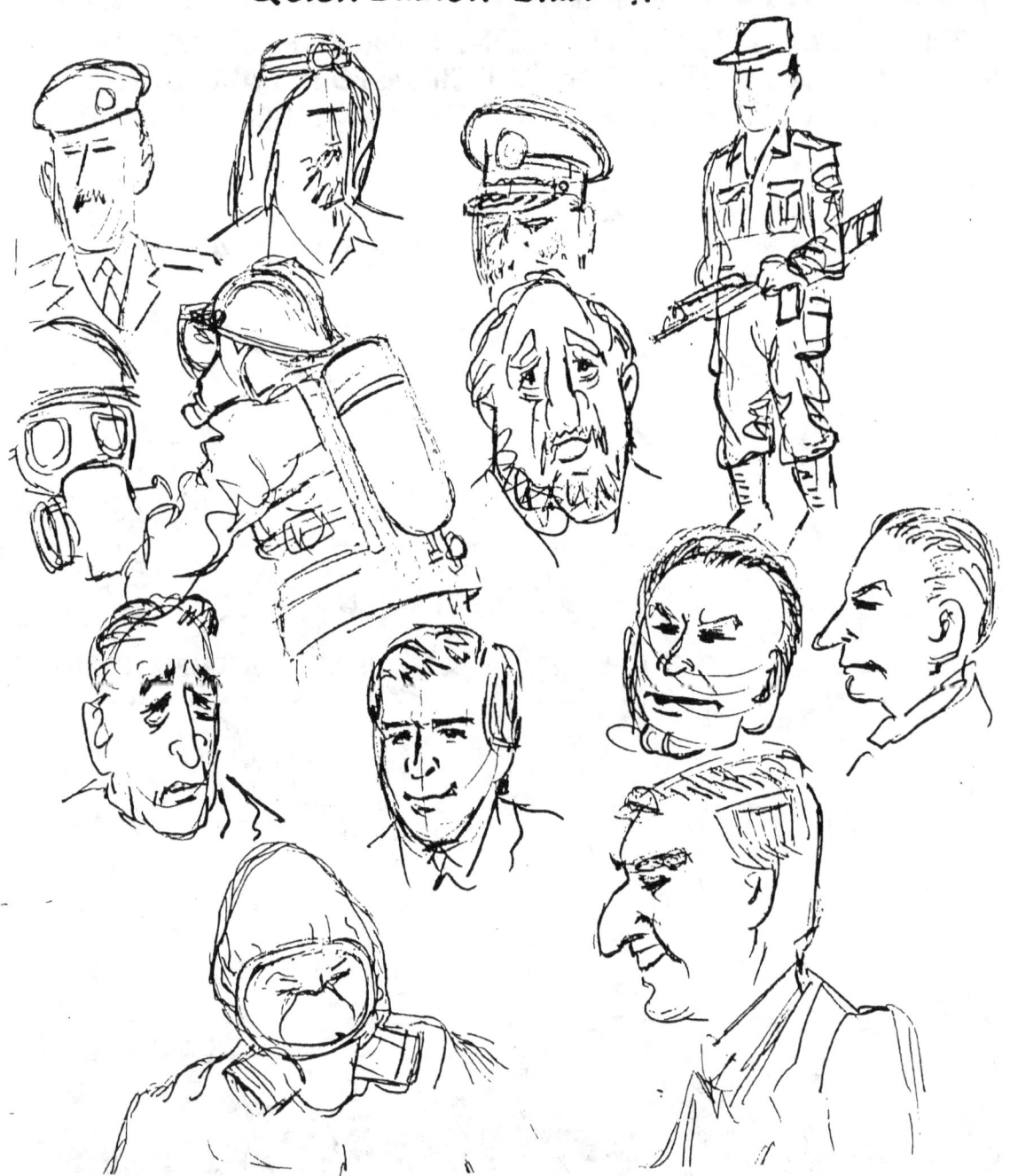

SKETCH FROM ALL TYPES OF PROGRAMMING — ANIMALS — SPORTS — EXPLORATION — HISTORIC — TRAVEL — SITCOM! IT WILL SHARPEN POWERS OF OBSERVATION AND INCREASE "MENTAL INVENTORY"!!

QUICKIE REVIEW CHAPTER SEVEN

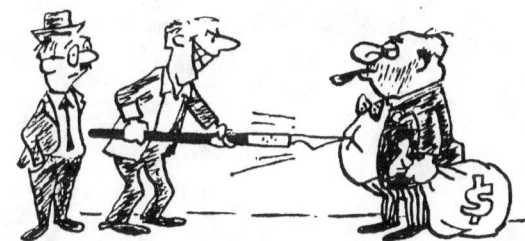

THE POLITICAL CARTOONIST'S PEN IS A FORMIDABLE WEAPON – WHETHER IT IS USED IN JEST OR WITH DEADLY SERIOUSNESS!

SYMBOLS HELP TELL THE STORY!
THEY ARE VISUAL COMPARISONS & ANALOGIES:
SOLID AS A ROCK – GROW LIKE A WEED – SMART AS A FOX – SKYROCKETING COSTS – ETC., ETC.

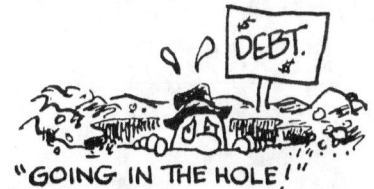

"GOING IN THE HOLE!"

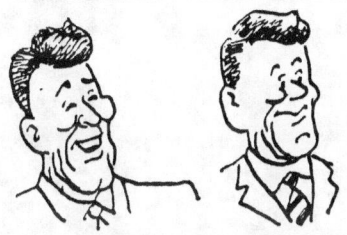

CARICATURES ARE VISUAL OPINIONS
THEY SHOULD PORTRAY CHARACTER & PERSONALITY.
THEY MIGHT BE FLATTERING, NONCOMMITTAL – OR SHOCKINGLY IRREVERANT!

NEAT LETTERING IS IMPORTANT!
SPEEDBALL PEN POINTS, CROWQUILL PENS, AND BRUSHES ARE POPULAR TOOLS

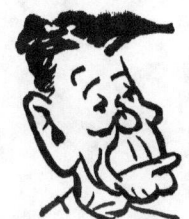

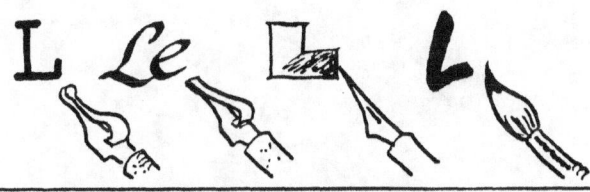

AH, HERE IT IS... A 1920 HAY BALER!

WELL ORGANIZED REFERENCE MATERIAL WILL SAVE TIME, IMPROVE DRAWING SKILLS!!

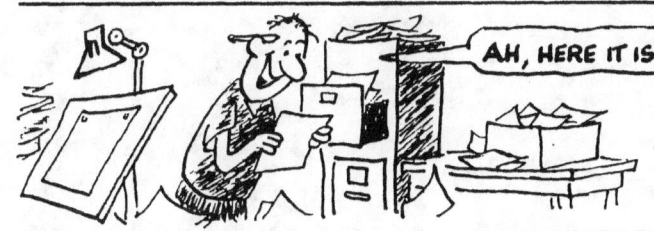

If you are an outspoken, political minded type of person, not afraid to step on some toes, a career in editorial cartooning should be considered!!

CHAPTER EIGHT
Comic Strips

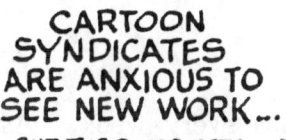
CARTOON SYNDICATES ARE ANXIOUS TO SEE NEW WORK...
BUT THEIR JOB GETS TOUGHER EVERY DAY.

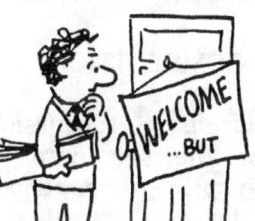
...BUT

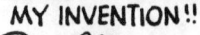
MY INVENTION!!

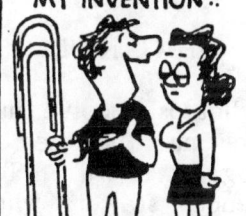
COMIC STRIPS ARE *INVENTIONS*!
DON'T RE-INVENT THE PAPER CLIP!!

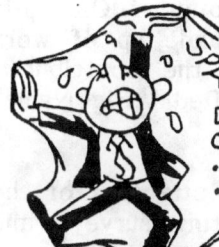
SPACE PROBLEMS
DEMAND EFFICIENT USE OF AVAILABLE SPACE
• SIMPLE COMPOSITIONS
• BOLD DRAWING STYLE

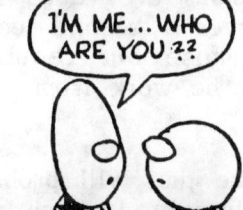
I'M ME...WHO ARE YOU??

STRONG MAIN CHARACTERS!
WILL THEY SUSTAIN READER INTEREST OVER THE LONG HAUL?

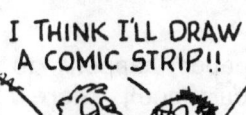
I THINK I'LL DRAW A COMIC STRIP!!

THAT IMPORTANT DECISION.
A PASSING FANCY... OR A SINCERE COMMITMENT?

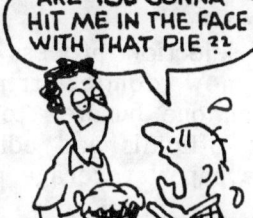
ARE YOU GONNA HIT ME IN THE FACE WITH THAT PIE??

HUMOR
GOOD OLD "ROUND-THE-HOUSE" STUFF? SLAPSTICK? WEIRD? A NEW WAVE?
...OR ALL OF THE ABOVE?

LETTERING
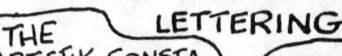
THE ARTISTIK CONSTA-NEWTY MUST BE MAYNTENANED AND DIALOG SHOULD ALLWAYS BE OF THE UTTERMOST BRIEFITY WITHOUT A LOT OF UNNES. WORDS!!

KEEP DIALOGUES BRIEF, SNAPPY, AND EASY TO READ!!

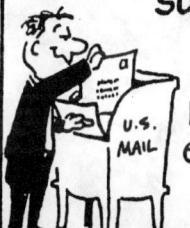
SUBMITTING WORK ...
The first strip of a submitted batch must be your best effort ... each succeeding strip should be even better!

U.S. MAIL

TOP OF THE HEAP

A successful comic strip can be worth hundreds of thousands of dollars. In some cases, that figure goes into the millions. Royalties pour in from literally hundreds of sources such as toys, games, books, advertising, endorsements, and on and on. Even in cases of less spectacular success, the comic strip provides a steady job with a darn good income. It is therefore understandable that just about every cartoonist in the country has tried, is trying, or will soon try to create - and market - a comic strip of one sort or another.

WHAT KIND OF COMPETITION?

The major cartoon syndicates receive hundreds of submissions every week. As a result, a certain system must be used or the syndicates entire operation would become hopelessly bogged down. The pile of contributors' work is reduced considerably by experienced staffers who have a set of guidelines from which to work. Any submissions that do not measure up to the initial requirements are returned to the sender in short notice.

Eventually, the submissions are reduced to, in effect, three piles. One pile contains work that deserves a second look. The next pile is made up of work that shows definite promise but requires additional work by the contributor. The third pile will likely be work from experienced, highly qualified, "Big Name" cartoonists.

This third pile is the one that will probably get the immediate attention of the syndicates' top executives and sales representatives. Marketing surveys and promotional possibilities will be discussed with several of the syndicates' top clients. Many of the "top priority" strips will fall by the wayside until only a handful remain. These will be put into a very impressive portfolio and presented to hundreds of newspapers across the country.

At this point, another selection process begins. If a newspaper happens to be in the market for a new comic strip (a very rare occurrence), there will probably be no less than one hundred to choose from. The choice will be made by the publication's top officials and editors. The selection will ordinarily be a "safe" one, aimed at the paper's average reader type.

Occasionally, a newspaper might take a chance on a "risky" strip -- one that will be controversial, very different, or extremely unusual in some way. In today's marketplace, that is the strip that will have the greatest potential for outstanding success.

GET CREATIVE

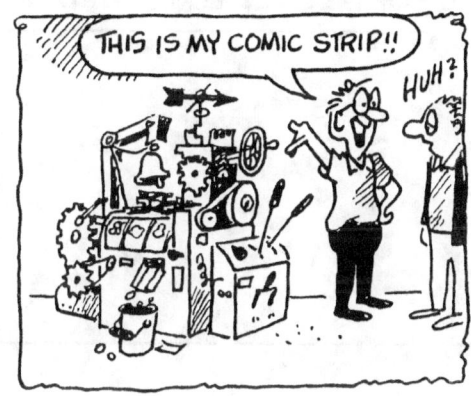

Creating a comic strip is not too much different than inventing a new device or making some vast improvements on an existing one.

A successful comic strip, like a successful invention, starts with a basic concept. The inventor recognizes a need or an opportunity for a particular device. He then enters a research phase, studies the marketplace, confirms originality, and develops expertise.

Only then will our inventor proceed to "build" his invention, adding bits and pieces, tinkering with, adjusting and testing it. Often, the final product is far different than the original idea. It will be better, more practical, more efficient.

That is how comic strips are created and developed. The characters are important cogs in the machinery, each having a particular job to do. Each is highly identifiable. Frequently, the secondary "cogs" will serve as a backup system for the central character, reinforcing the basic theme or setting up a new story line direction.

WRITING THE STRIP ... FORMATS

The majority of today's humor-type comic strips are written in what might be called a multi-panel gag cartoon format. Each individual strip has a beginning (setting up the joke) and an end (the punch line). The basic theme varies from day to day and is rarely carried over from one day to the next.

A number of other humor strips will feature a continuing story line that is chopped up into daily segments, each of which ends with a "capper." Many cartoonists feel this type of format is easier to write since a given topic provides any number of little twists and turns.

The other types of comic strips are "action/adventure" and "soap opera." These have a continuing story format. Each daily strip attempts to leave the reader anxious to see what will happen next.

A SMALL (BUT SCARY) SPACE!!
SHOW BELOW IS THE AVERAGE PUBLISHED SIZE OF THE DAILY COMIC STRIP

$135,000 to $150,000 worth of space!
NEWSPAPERS WANT TO GET THEIR MONEY'S WORTH!

The space occupied by the comic strip, in terms of advertising jargon, is about 12 column inches and represents approximately $135,000 yearly in display advertising revenue to a newspaper serving a medium-sized city.

This is not to say that it is money lost by a newspaper, since the comic pages are an important part of the paper's format. The figure does, however, partly explain why newspapers are so very selective in choosing their comic strips. They want their money's worth in terms of reader interest and potential increases in circulation. A poorly chosen strip might even result in significant loss of subscribers and advertisers.

Additionally, comic strips are purchased on a contract basis, usually from one to three years. Obviously, the syndicates and newspapers do not want to get stuck with a strip that will become dull and boring after a month or two.

The fees paid to a syndicate by a newspaper for the rights to publish a strip are based on the paper's certified circulation. Contrary to popular belief, those fees are surprisingly low -- some strips go for as little as $5 per week! Therefore, the cost of a particular comic strip rarely is a factor in the publication's decision to buy or not to buy.

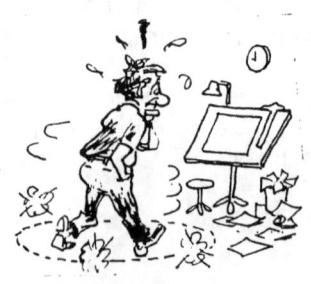

WHAT IS WANTED?   WHAT IS NEEDED?

Ask a dozen top cartoon syndicate executives what type of comic strip would have the greatest chance of success in the comic strip marketplace, and the answer would probably be one or more of the following:

* A great, totally unique adventure concept
 * A new "soap opera" type of comic strip
  * A strip aimed at the heart of low-income mid-America
   * A wholesome, upbeat strip for teenagers
    * An animal character with an interesting new twist
     * Something positive and constructive
      * Characters that are simple, harmless, and lovable
       * An entertaining strip with an educational slant

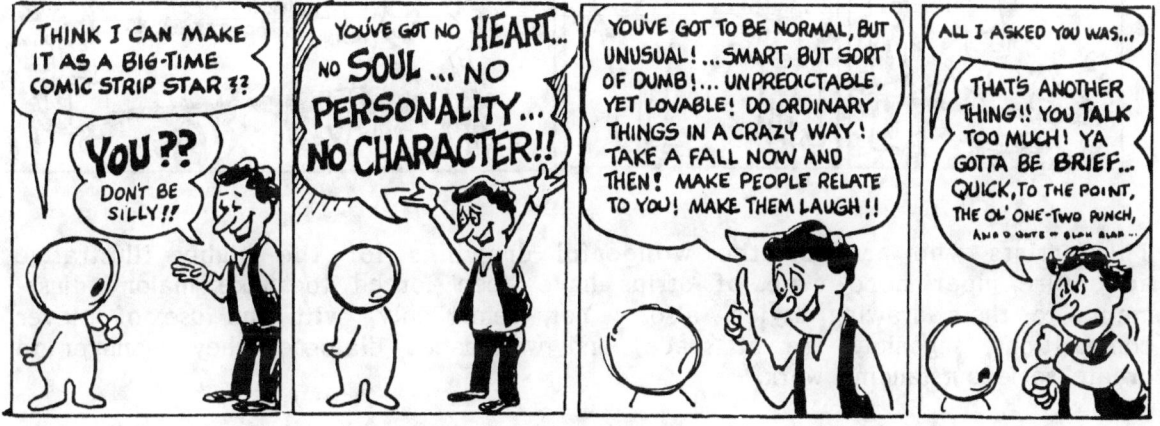

IDENTITY

Obviously, no matter what type of strip is created, the very first ingredient must be easily identifiable central characters.   This applies to their personality and character as well as their appearance.   They should be somehow almost universal in nature, yet definitely unique in some way.   The basic concept of the "star" and "co-stars" should be one that can be easily and clearly defined in 25 words or less.   For example:

* Nothing ever goes right for this overweight, uncouth but lovable Viking
* This fellow's main interests are avoiding employment and frequenting the local pubs
* This large canine is the undisputed ruler of the house and neighborhood
* Nearly every family in the world can relate to the situations in this strip
* This very imaginative kid sees things in a way no one else is able to

As we can see, each of these short descriptions set the stage for tons of material.

SPACE PROBLEMS

Many comic strips are initially rejected simply because they are too cluttered and complicated for the small amount of space available to them. Most of the strips being introduced today are based on short, quick dialogues, simplified or nonexistent backgrounds, and bold drawing styles.

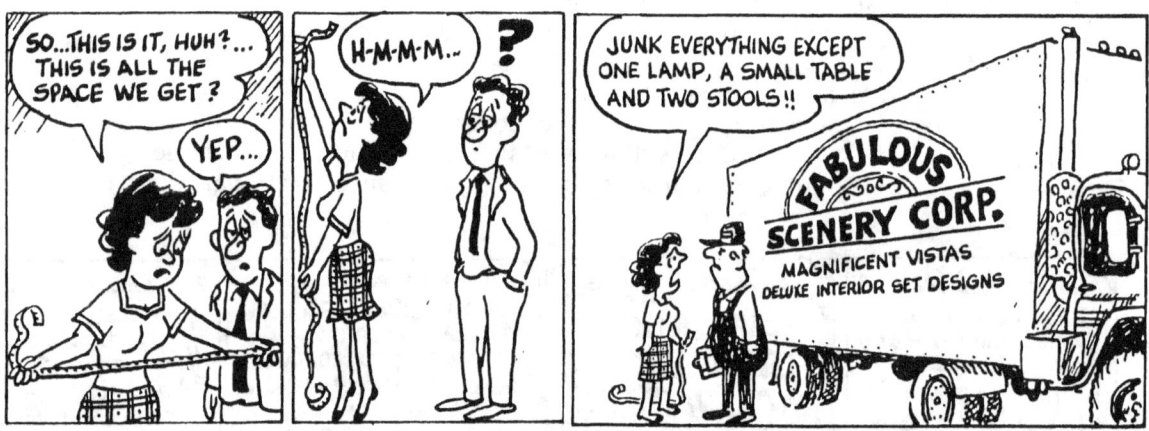

The artists who produce the wonderful drawings for the highly illustrative adventure/super hero type of strips have been forced to make major adjustments to their drawing styles, also. Yet, remarkably, with the use of clever compositions, ingenious use of space, and well-paced dialogue, they manager to create some outstanding work.

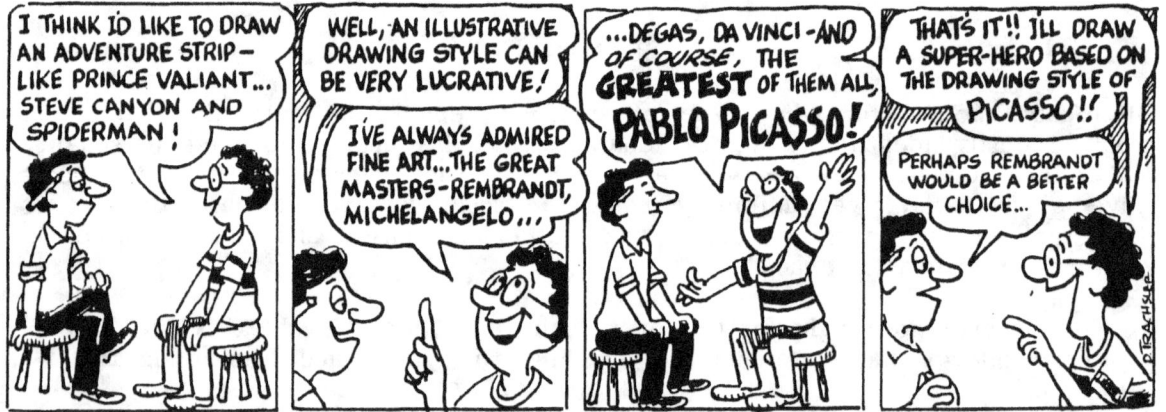

The decision to attempt to create a comic strip is an important one and should not be made on a whim or a "what the heck" attitude. Getting a strip "off the ground" can be a long and painful process that might take several years of hard work, lots of patience and determination, and more than just the average portion of good luck.

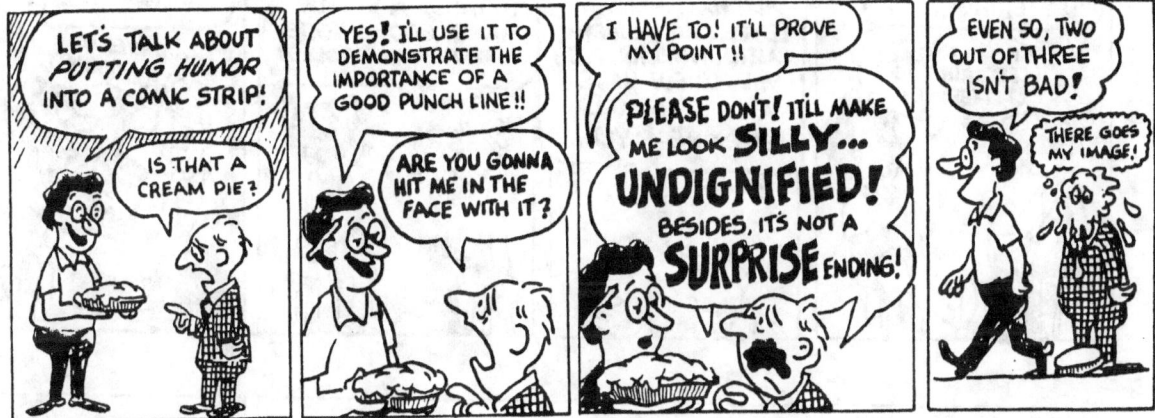

Sooner or later, the basic categories of humor, together with the three main ingredients (see Chapter 5) appear in every comic strip.   One day the characters might be involved in some heartwarming human interest stuff, and the next day the same characters might pull off some delightful slapstick.   A frequent change of pace keeps the reader interested and anxious to see more.

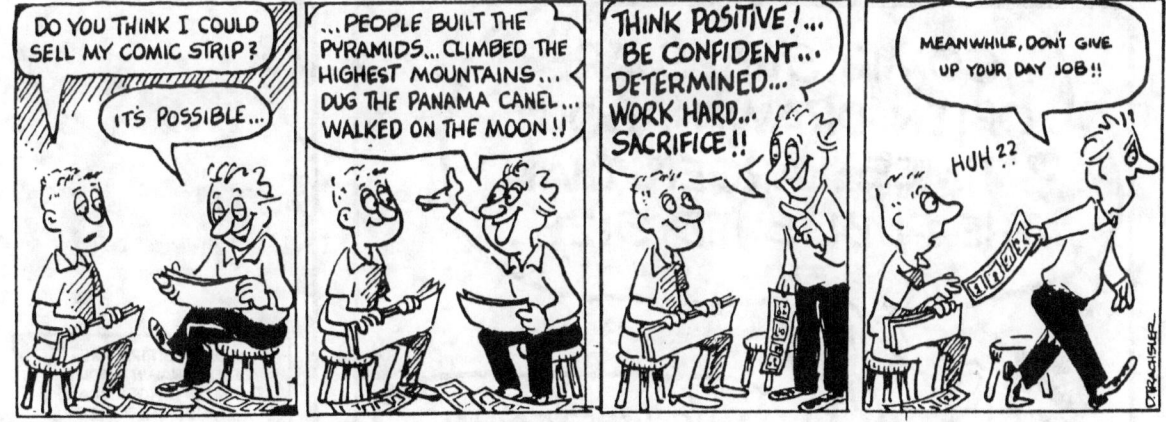

A comic strip can be based on a unique concept and still fail because the cartoonist just didn't give it his or her best effort.   The cartoonist often KNOWS that the strip isn't quite right but is too lazy to redo it ... better to make no effort at all than to make a poor one.

A considerable number of new comic strips are introduced every year.   Be assured that they are not the result of a careless attitude or a less-than-full commitment!

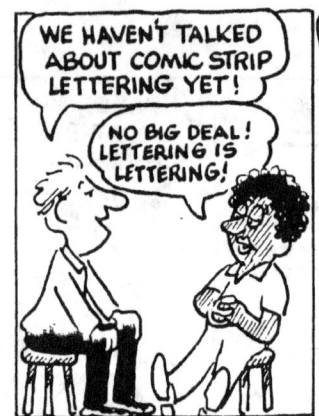

WE HAVEN'T TALKED ABOUT COMIC STRIP LETTERING YET!

NO BIG DEAL! LETTERING IS LETTERING!

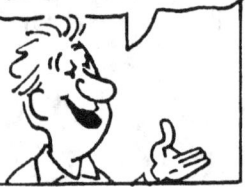

NOT SO! SOME DRAWING STYLES REQUIRE VERY *FORMAL, PRECISE* LETTERING! OTHER CARTOON TECHNIQUES WILL LIKELY HAVE A LESS FORMAL LETTERING STYLE....

THE ARTISTIK COGRANEWTY SHOULD BE MENTAYNED! IT TAKES A STEADY HAND, GOOD EYESITE AND PROPAIR TOOLES!

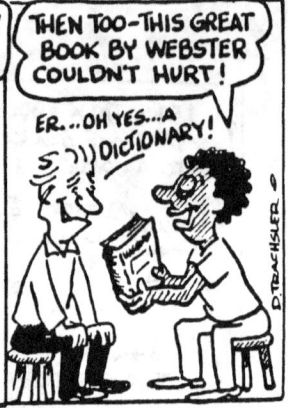

THEN TOO—THIS GREAT BOOK BY WEBSTER COULDN'T HURT!

ER...OH YES...A DICTIONARY!

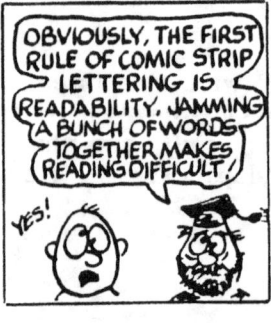

OBVIOUSLY, THE FIRST RULE OF COMIC STRIP LETTERING IS READABILITY. JAMMING A BUNCH OF WORDS TOGETHER MAKES READING DIFFICULT!

YES!

THE SPACE BETWEEN LINES OF LETTERING IS AS IMPORTANT AS THE LETTERING ITSELF! USUALLY, THAT SPACE IS ONE-HALF THE HEIGHT OF THE LETTER.

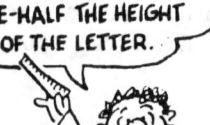

MOST CARTOONISTS USE ACCURATE GUIDELINES FOR THEIR LETTERING —

OTHERS PREFER TO SKETCH-IN GUIDELINES IN A CASUAL, FREEHAND MANNER.

POOR PLANNING CAN RESULT IN PROBLEMS!

EYE CHART

HOW SMALL CAN LETTERING GET BEFORE IT BECOMES DIFFICULT TO READ WITHOUT A MAGNIFING GLASS?

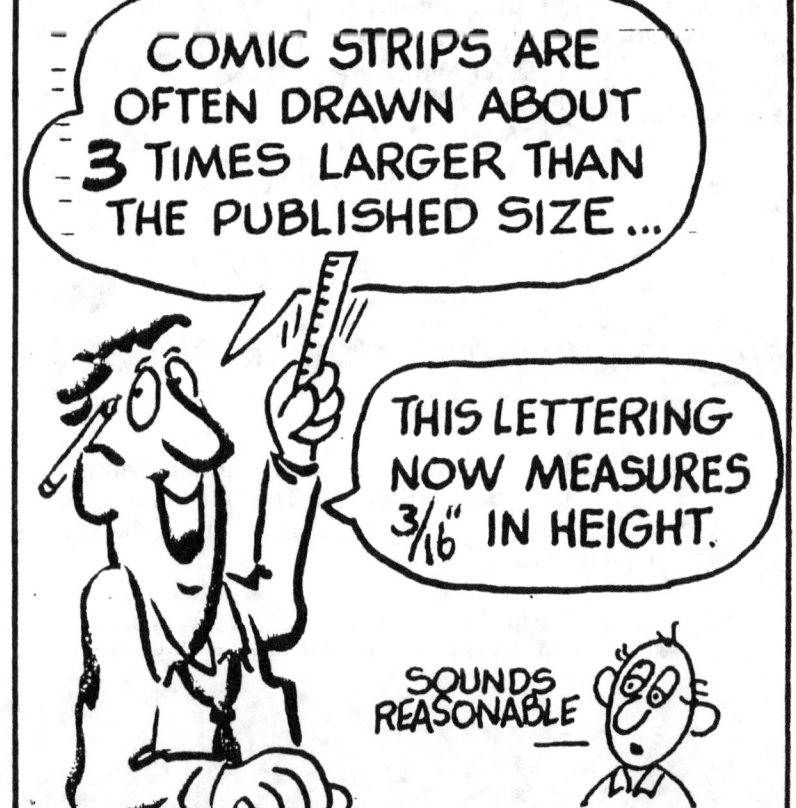

COMIC STRIPS ARE OFTEN DRAWN ABOUT 3 TIMES LARGER THAN THE PUBLISHED SIZE ...

THIS LETTERING NOW MEASURES 3/16" IN HEIGHT.

SOUNDS REASONABLE

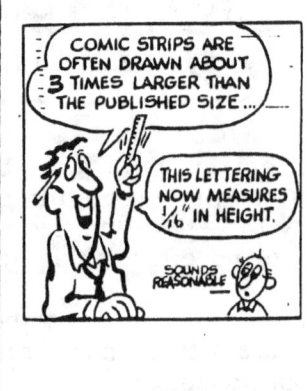

COMIC STRIPS ARE OFTEN DRAWN ABOUT 3 TIMES LARGER THAN THE PUBLISHED SIZE ...

THIS LETTERING NOW MEASURES 1/16" IN HEIGHT.

SOUNDS REASONABLE

TO MARKET, TO MARKET

Many successful comic strip artists will readily admit that their strip was sold because they happened to have the right product at the right time and place, as opposed to having the right product at the wrong place, or the wrong product at the right place. Makes a lot of sense, eh?

Obviously, the key is knowing exactly what to send where. Fortunately, their are at least two major publications that make such information available to the aspiring cartoonist.

ARTIST'S MARKET. This is a large volume published yearly by Writer's Digest, 1507 Dana Avenue, Cincinnati, Ohio 45207. This fine publication is updated yearly and lists the major cartoon markets, who to contact, the type of material currently needed, guidelines, and the whole bit.

CARTOONIST PROFILES. Post Office Box 325, Fairfield, CT 06430. This gem is published quarterly and is edited by Jud Hurd, a nationally recognized cartoonist who has more personal friends and contacts in the cartooning profession than the law allows. Each issue is jam packed with tips and stories from the top professionals in the field, whether they be working cartoonists, syndicate executives, writers, or editors. We highly recommend this publication, as we do the Artist's Market.

There are, of course, other sources of cartoon marketing information. The research department of your local public library has a listing of every major publication and syndicate. Additionally, there are numerous other books and periodicals that offer marketing information, but it has been my experience that too much information at the outset can be as much of a handicap as too little information.

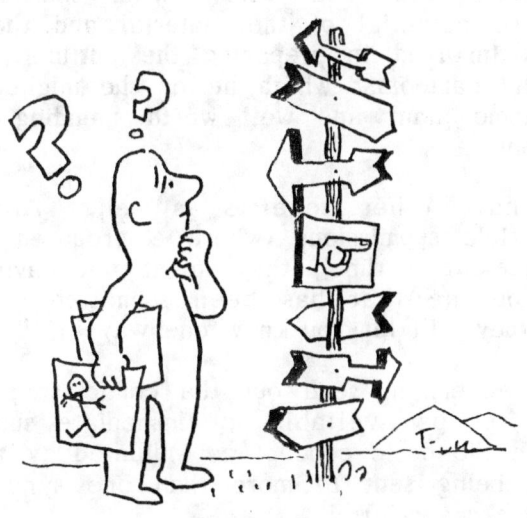

PRESENTATION

There are many things that a syndicate editor will look for when viewing a comic strip submission. Is the concept original? Has it been presented in a clear, orderly manner? Can the quality of the work be maintained over a long period of time? Will it be of sufficient interest to their newspaper editors?

The comic strip "batch" submitted to the cartoon syndicate generally consists of at least four elements:

1.   A brief but courteous cover letter (the enclosed material is respectfully submitted for consideration, etc.).

2.   An outline page introducing the central characters.

3.   20 daily strips. Photocopies, reduced to publication size, four strips nicely spaced on $8\frac{1}{2}$" x 11" paper works well.

4.   At least two Sunday strips.

Syndicate requirements for submissions frequently vary, so the contributor should seek specific guidelines either directly from the target syndicate or from the marketing information available in Artist's Market or Cartoonist Profiles. Sunday Panels should be submitted in black and white only, since the color is a separate process usually done by syndicate artists or by the publishing newspaper.

THE OUTLINE PAGE(S)

This is often the most important element of the submitted "batch," not only for the syndicate editor, but for the cartoonist as well. It should clearly introduce the central characters, their personalities, interests, ambitions, and personal habits. This will indicate that you "know" your characters well, and will demonstrate the long-range potential of the material and the sincerity of your presentation. The work involved in preparing the outline page will, in itself, suggest story ideas to the cartoonist which he or she might not otherwise have thought of. It is a "game plan" and well worth spending a lot of time and effort on in its development.

The outline page can have other benefits as well. Although most cartoon syndicates frown on multiple submissions (where a proposed strip is offered to more than one syndicate at a time), they might not have any objections to receiving an in-depth outline that has been submitted on a multi-submission basis. You may be sure they will let you know one way or t'other.

It is not advisable, however, to send out the comic strip outline unless you have at least 20 daily strips available for immediate submission, should the syndicate be interested in the basic concept as indicated by the outline. In any event, if the outline is being sent to more than one syndicate at a time, it should be made clear in the cover letter.

COPYRIGHTS

The copyright laws changed considerably in 1978. (Write to U.S. Copyright Office, Library of Congress, Washington, DC 20559 for forms and information.) It essentially states that when a work is completed by an artist or author, it is automatically copyrighted by that person and becomes his or her personal property so long as it bears the legend c , date, and name.

The work no longer requires publication prior to copyright protection, although after publication it is wise to register it with the copyright office in the manner directed in their information packet.

In the event the strip is sold, the copyright is transferred to the purchasing syndicate. This aspect of the contract should be studied closely, however, and knowledgeable legal advice should be obtained.

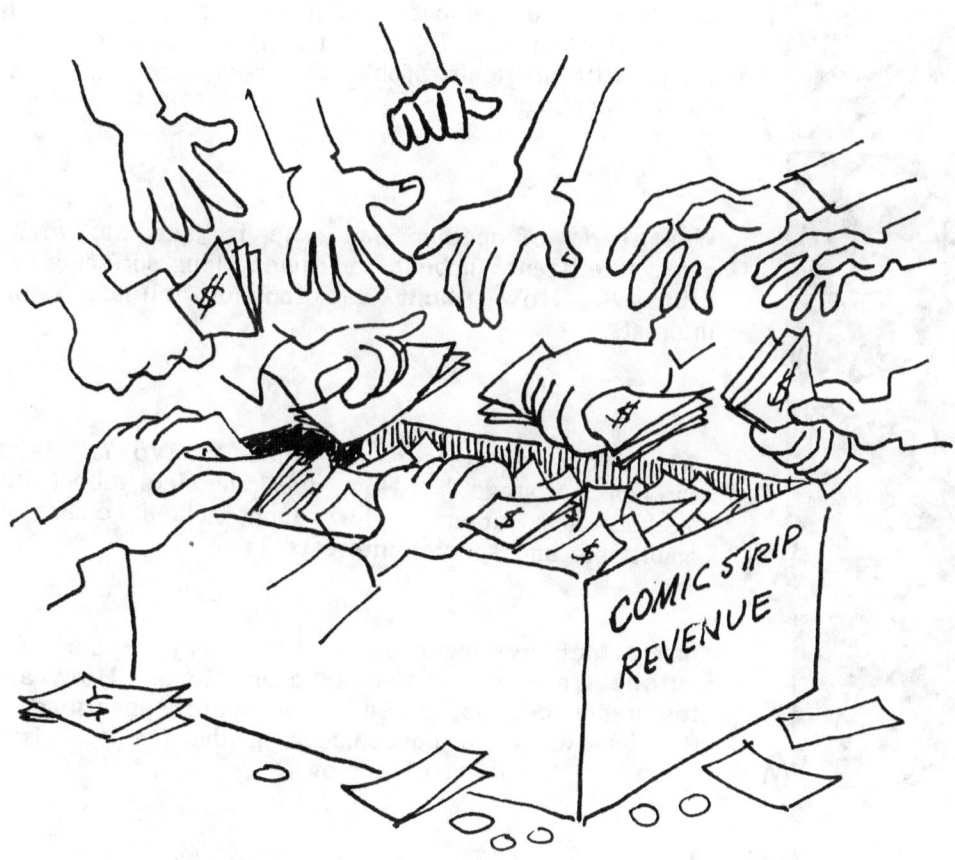

INTRODUCTORY PAGE

There are no firm rules concerning the format for an introductory page, nor is it usually a required part of a submitted strip. However, the outline, if submitted, should not be too rambling or complicated. It should be concise, yet indicate the humor possibilities and the long-range story line potential of the central characters.

Typically, the introductory page for a "family" strip might look something like this:

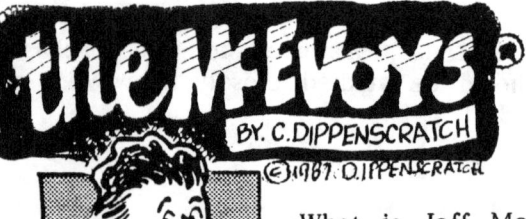

Describe where the McEvoys live. Is it an average city or town, or is there something interesting or unusual about their area?

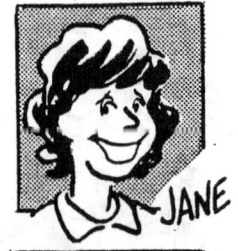

What is Jeff McEvoy's job? Is it a trade, profession, or business? How about sidelines, hobbies, special interests, and background? Is he currently working on a special project with difficult problems? What are his strong points and shortcomings?

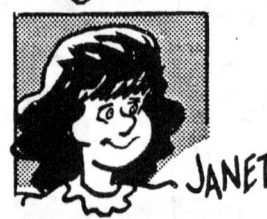

What type of mother and wife is Jane McEvoy? Is she chic, intelligent, upbeat, or quiet, long-suffering, and a bit clutzy? How about background, friends, and special interests?

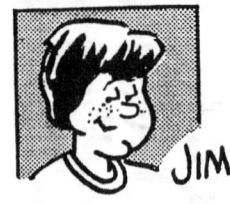

What sort of person is Janet McEvoy? Is she going through a "stage?" How does she feel about her brother, mother, and father? How about school, chums, boyfriends, ambitions, and special interests?

Jimmy McEvoy might be a typical boy or perhaps has some unique talents and characteristics. How about pets, teachers, heroes, friends, or secret ambitions? Is he a troublemaker or a peacemaker in the family? Is he clever, smart, or something of a clown?

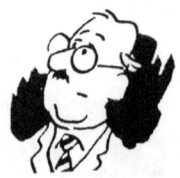

Jeff's boss
Mr. Leaver

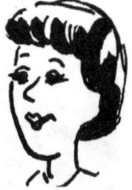

Jane's sister
"Ava"

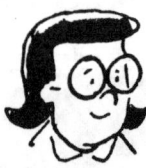

Janet's best
friend "Shultzy"

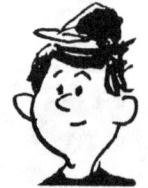

Jimmy's best
friend "Jose"

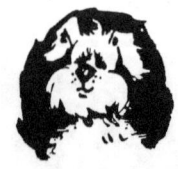

Shags
the family pet

TAKING ANOTHER LOOK AT, "NEEDED: ONE CARTOON REPAIR PERSON"
(CHAPTER SIX–SECTION 1; COMPOSITION)

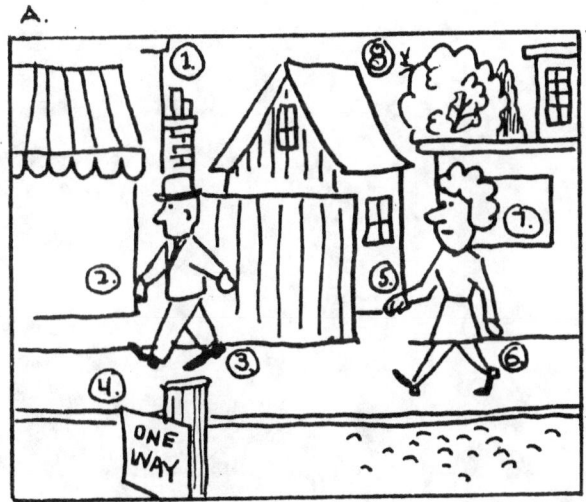

Readers quickly lose interest in the subject of a cartoon if the composition is too cluttered or complicated. It's like looking at a large handful of tangled string.

Our "problem" composition contains too many intersecting lines, as indicated by numbers at left. Additionally, the chimney, the man's figure, and the signpost are stacked in an uninteresting manner and present a disturbing vertical column. Similar lines on the house and fence also add to the confusion.

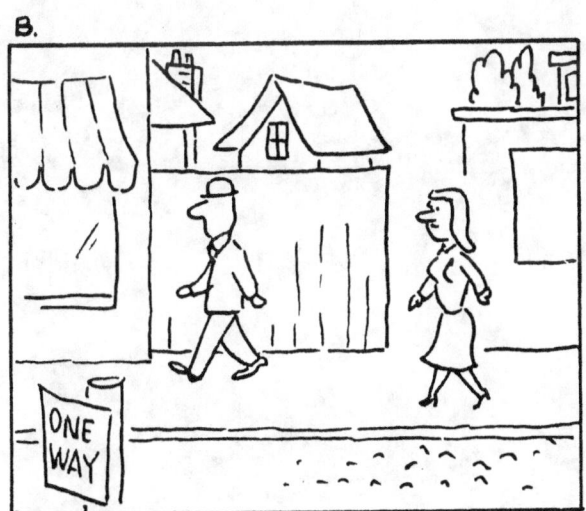

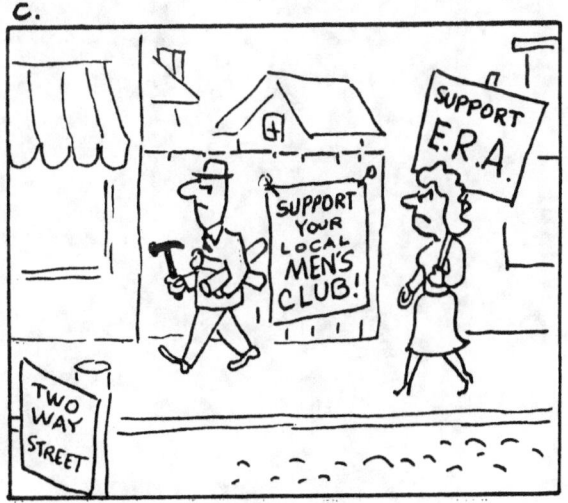

Most of the clutter and confusion has been eliminated in composition (Figure B). The situation is presented in a clear, easily understood manner.

However, we now have a drawing that cries out for something to happen, together with a situation that is loaded with humorous possibilities, one of which is suggested in Figure C.

CHAPTER NINE
Special Cartoon Markets

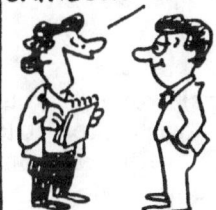

I SAW 327 CARTOONS TODAY!

CARTOONS EVERYWHERE!

They appear throughout newspapers, magazine, and the most prestigious professional journals. They are found on bean can labels and cereal boxes, as well as greeting cards, bumper stickers, and T-shirts. Clearly, the cartoon is a highly marketable product.

MAKE CONTACTS!
VISIT LOCAL PRINT SHOPS AND AD AGENCIES. CONTACT THE CLUBS AND CIVIC ORGANIZATIONS IN YOUR AREA!

DON'T KEEP YOUR TALENT A SECRET!

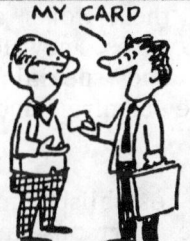

MY CARD

ARTIST'S SUPPLY STORES...
FREQUENTLY GET REQUESTS FOR NAMES OF LOCAL ARTISTS & CARTOONISTS FROM ADVERTISERS!

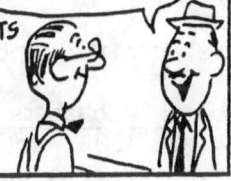

ARE THERE ANY FREELANCE CARTOONISTS IN THE AREA?

ADVERTISE!!
CONSIDER A SMALL LISTING IN THE ARTISTS SECTION OF YOUR LOCAL YELLOW PAGES —

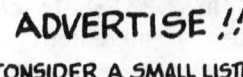

A RELATIVELY SMALL INVESTMENT, WITH BIG POTENTIAL!

CLASSIFIED ADS...
OCCASIONALLY OFFER SOME IMPORTANT OPPORTUNITIES!!

CARTOONIST needed. Freelance basis. Immediate assignments available. National publication. Call for app't. 000-1111.

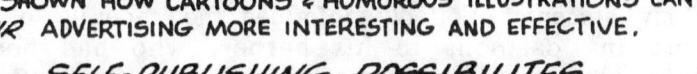

I HAVE AN ADVERTISING IDEA FOR YOU!

WORKING ON SPECULATION - RISKY BUT NECESSARY!
MOST MERCHANTS ARE NOT VERY CREATIVE. THEY USUALLY MUST BE SHOWN HOW CARTOONS & HUMOROUS ILLUSTRATIONS CAN MAKE *THEIR* ADVERTISING MORE INTERESTING AND EFFECTIVE.

SELF-PUBLISHING POSSIBILITES...
NEW DEVELOPMENTS IN LOW-COST PRINTING TECHNOLOGY MAKES IT POSSIBLE FOR THE CARTOONIST TO BECOME HIS OWN PUBLISHER!!

BUILDING A PORTFOLIO OF PUBLISHED WORK

Local hometown advertisers, organizations, printing establishments, and newspapers offer the best opportunity for the beginning cartoonist to get his work published. That, obviously, is the very first step toward a successful cartooning career. Many of today's top cartoonists in the early stages of their careers GAVE their work, free to charge, to anyone who would publish them. One published cartoon can lead to another. Like building blocks, each contact made becomes more important than the last.

POSSIBLE "GIVEAWAY" MARKETS

<u>Letter to the Editor.</u> Send in some cartoons (instead of letters) voicing your opinion on local issues, articles, or politics. A brief note along with the little cartoons might explain that you can express your views better with cartoons than with words. There is no need whatsoever to mention that you are a beginning cartoonist anxious to get work published. If the work attracts the editors' interest, you may be sure they will ask you about it.

<u>Local Clubs and Organizations.</u> Contact these folks and volunteer your cartooning services. They often send out brochures, newsletters, and flyers for their membership drives, fundraising efforts, and special events. Don't hesitate to explain your cartooning goals! People admire ambitious go-getters and often welcome the opportunity to be helpful.

<u>Local Publishers and Printshops.</u> These establishments are usually well stocked with "Clip Art" books (copyright-free cartoons and illustrations) from which they select a particular piece of artwork to fill a particular need. Occasionally, however, they have a need for a "custom" piece of art ... perhaps a simple line drawing, an advertising cartoon, or a caricature for letterheads, notepads, or business cards. Creative lettering and little "spot" drawings might help them sell a printing job that they might otherwise lose to their competitors who can provide such custom artwork. Perhaps a barter arrangement can be worked out. You supply them with cartoons and artwork in exchange for printing your business cards, letterhead, brochures, etc.

<u>Local Advertisers.</u> This can be a little gold mine for the beginning cartoonist. Be on the alert for local businesses that are in heated competition with one another. They would welcome a unique advertising campaign that might get them more attention and consequently more customers.

In my role as a private art/cartooning instructor, I have had students who sold cartoon advertising campaigns to local radio and TV stations, tire stores, car dealerships, home remodelers, garden shops, pawn shops, and furniture stores. One of my students excitedly informed me recently of having sold a series of 24 advertising cartoons to his barber, who had been running (without any noticeable results) a small display ad in a local throw-away shopper's guide publication. I contacted the barber after the cartoon ad had been running for three weeks, and he told me that business had increased significantly and that he had many favorable comments on his new advertising format. "I don't think anybody even noticed my ad until we added the cartoon bit!" he said.

Several years ago, one of my more advanced students created a series of advertising cartoons featuring animal characters and sold the series to a new car dealer, who not only used them in his newspaper ads, but likes them so well he had a local sign company paint them, large scale, on ten brand new demos that his salesmen drove back and forth to work. The results were, understandably, spectacular. This creative effort netted the student nearly $1,000! The barbershop cartoons were not nearly as profitable ($5 for each cartoon), but it gave the student some invaluable experience in creativity.

Small Town or Community Newspapers. These publications have a limited circulation and usually feature news and special articles about events that happen within their immediate area. They rarely print syndicated material of national interest, but often welcome drawings and cartoons with a local slant ... an occasional editorial cartoon based on some current political issue, for instance. Perhaps cartoons and caricatures of the local sports heroes, or even a weekly comic strip with easily recognizable backgrounds and humorous situations of local interest. The fee for such work will likely be $0.00 or, at best, pocket change, but again, it's your chance to get published! Get recognized! Building blocks and stepping stones!

Local Screen Printing Shops. For the benefit of the uninformed, screen printing is a relatively low cost method of printing "short-run" items such as posters, banners, signs, novelty items, T-shirts, limited edition art prints, napkins, and sundry other products. Visit these shops, introduce yourself, explain the services you can provide, and show some examples of your work. Get to know their range of capabilities and pricing structure. It's always possible that you might come up with a unique idea, draw it up, sell it to an advertiser, and have the silk screen shop produce it. For instance, humorous greeting cards, cartoon T-shirts, bumper stickers, or window banners.

Remember, this sort of work is not necessarily an end in itself, but a means to an end. Besides, it upsets me to hear someone say, "I can't make any money with my cartoons. Nobody will buy them." Baloney! Every place of business, print shop, local publisher, and club or organization is a potential client.

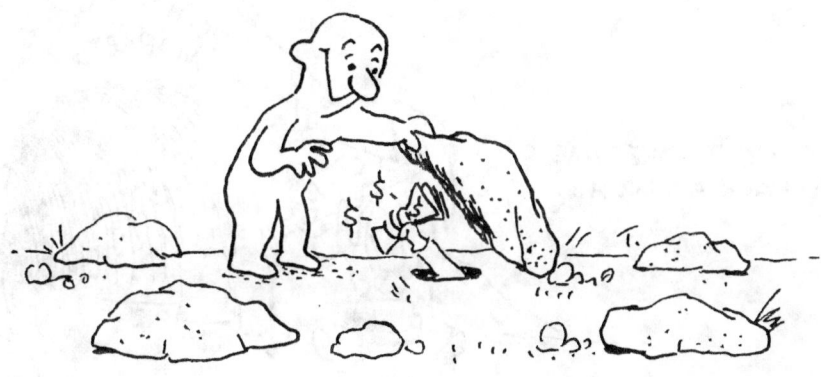

DESIGNING AND DEVELOPING AN AD CAMPAIGN FOR A CLIENT

The freelance cartoonist who sits around in his or her studio waiting for advertising clients to come knocking at the door is living a foolish dream, at least until such time as he or she has developed a cartoon character of national fame.

Most freelance cartoonists, if they are to make a living in the profession, are scrappers, scratchers, and diggers. They find their work either by knocking on doors or through the mail. Those who are interested in doing cartoons for advertising are especially good at digging up markets for their work. They study the local newspapers and "slinger" shopping guides, watching for merchants who advertise regularly.

Their first choice for a target is a small, locally operated chain store type of operations. Completely on speculation, they then create a series of 10 or 12 cartoons and catch-lines that are appropriate for the business. The cartoons might be based on the store's slogan, or certain products and services that are most often stressed by the advertiser.

I know of one cartoonist who visited all six stores of a local chain store operation and unobtrusively sketched caricatures of each of the store managers. Returning to the studio, the cartoonist put the final touches on the caricatures, created a "Meet the Manager" ad campaign, and submitted it to the main office of the operation along with a cover letter requesting an appointment with the owner. A meeting was arranged, the ad idea was sold, and the cartoonist walked out of the office with a check in hand (although he would have gladly waited the usual 10 or 30 days for payment).

SELLING TIP: Create a cartoon ad slanted toward a particular advertiser, have a photocopy made (reduced if necessary), and paste it on a full sized newspaper page, right in with a lot of other display ads. This will show the potential client how your cartoon ad literally "jumps out" at the reader.

ANOTHER TIP: Don't bother with the large, nationally operated chain stores. They have their own in-house advertising departments and seldom, if ever, consider work from outside sources.

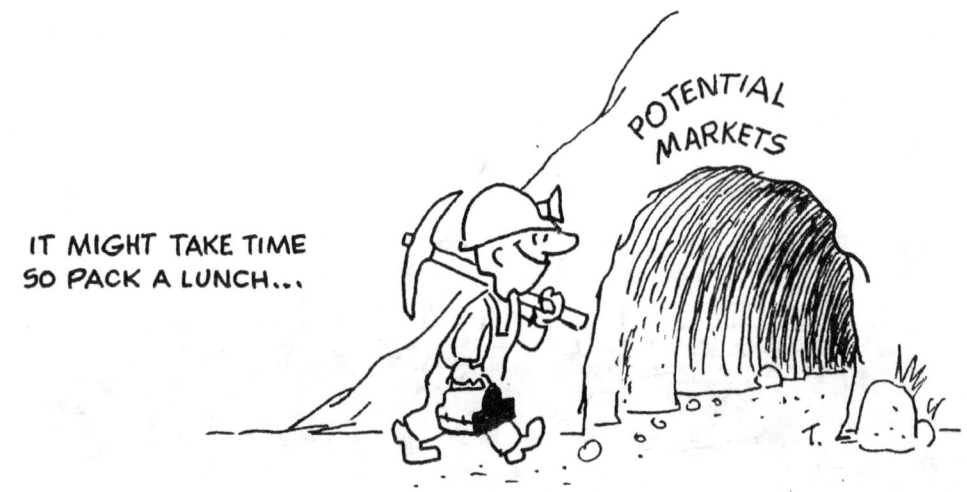

IT MIGHT TAKE TIME
SO PACK A LUNCH...

CARTOON ADVERTISING FORMATS

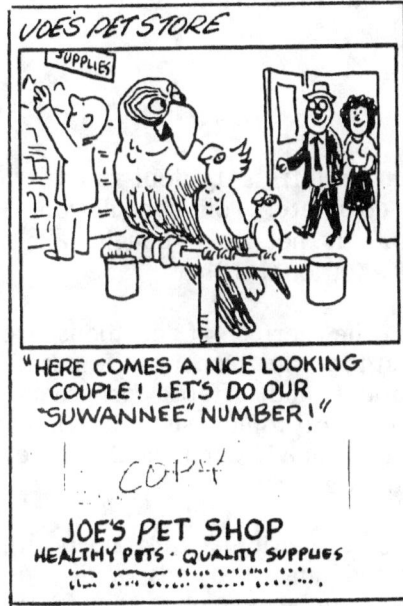

Cartoons can be used in a variety of ways to enhance a merchant's advertising message. The cartoon might be single panel or multipanel. It can be a small "teaser," an attention getter, or part of a more conventional type of ad.

Due to certain page layout restrictions, most newspapers prefer (or insist) that large display ads be of a vertical or somewhat square configuration.

Recent surveys indicated that an ad containing drawings or cartoons are up to 75% more effective than those without such eye-catchers.

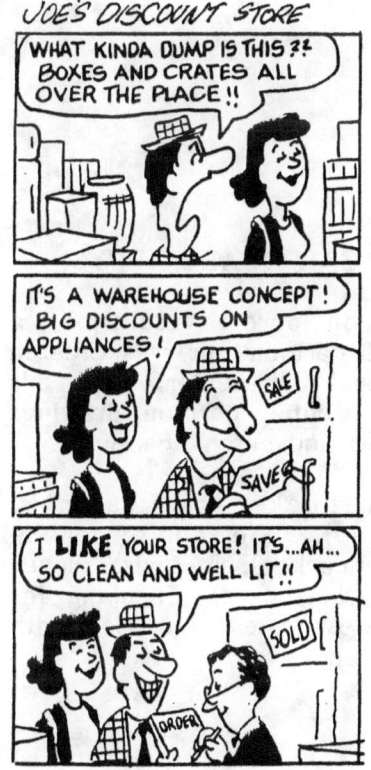

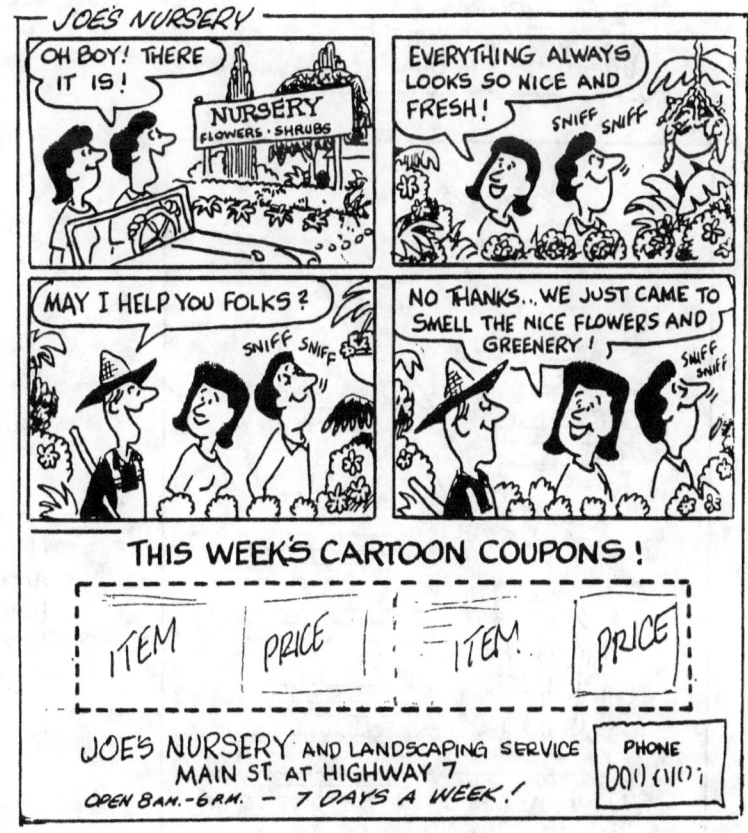

HITTING THE TARGET!

Two Advertising Concepts That Were Sold the First Time Out!

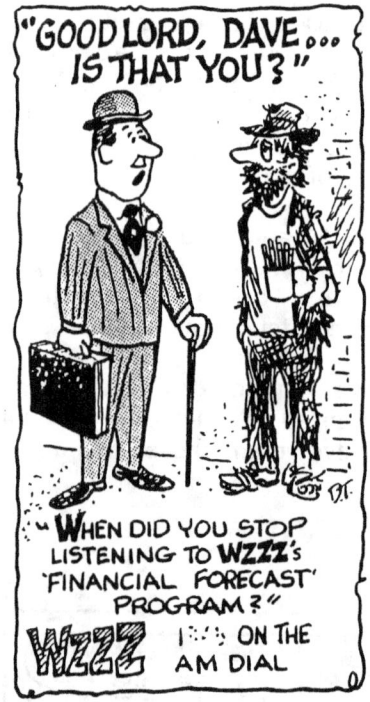

The ad cartoon at left is typical of six that were created, completely on speculation, for a radio station. It not only bought all six, but ordered an additional 18!

The ideas for the series of cartoons were no problem, since the station featured a "talk show" format and offered programming on a wide variety of topics such as finance, auto maintenance, movie and book reviews, sports, music, theater, etc.

Caricatures of the station's talk hosts were also incorporated into the ads and proved to be of great interest to the station's listeners.

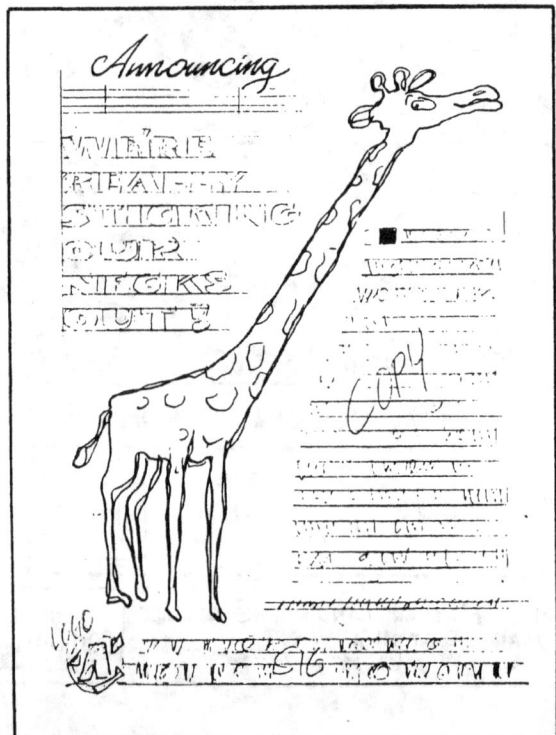

NEW CAR DEALER BUYS!

Again, on pure speculation, a series of cartoon ads was created for a local car dealer. The ads features simple cartoon drawings of animals and catchy captions.

"You'll pocket the savings" (kangaroo), "We don't monkey around" (monkey), "A wise move" (owl at chessboard), "Looking for low interest rates?" (ostrich with head in sand).

SELLING TOOLS

As mentioned earlier in this book, freelance cartooning, either part-time or full-time, is a business and should be operated in a professional manner. Neatly designed business cards, letterheads, brochures (indicating examples of work, services offered, schooling, etc.), invoices, good records, and bookkeeping are of utmost importance. Every expense directly related to the business must be recorded. Receipts and cancelled checks must be neatly filed away. During the first year or so of operation, a freelance cartooning business will very likely show a loss. When one considers the cost of materials and equipment, automobile expenses, postage, and all the other costs involved, the actual dollar loss can be significant and should be well documented for tax purposes.

BE YOUR OWN TAX EXPERT

The federal government prints hundreds of booklets on small business operation, self-employment, business use of the home, educational expenses, etc. As a business person, you should take full advantage of all the deductions allowable, so obtain these free booklets. Your public library will probably have them or will be able to tell you how to get them. Your local IRS office is sure to have them available.

Then too, there is always the possibility, slim though it might be, of obtaining a federal grant for very specialized cartoon projects, or a small business loan to help "get started." Touch all the bases. Leave no stone unturned. We want you to be successful!

RETAIN COPYRIGHTS IF POSSIBLE

An advertiser's rights to publish your cartoons should be limited to his effective marketing area only (usually a 50-mile radius). This allows for the possibility of selling the same basic concept to similar businesses in other areas of the country (self-syndication). Obviously, any portion of the ad that has been created by the advertiser must be considered to be his property and cannot be sold to clients in other areas without the written consent of the original client.

All material created by the cartoonist for a prospective customer should included the cartoonist's official notice of copyright, which is the copyright symbol c , the year, the name of the copyright holder (in this case, the cartoonist).

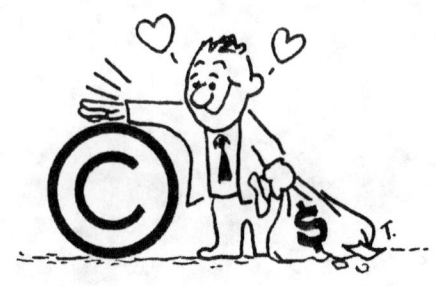

CHAPTER TEN
Cartooning on Assignment

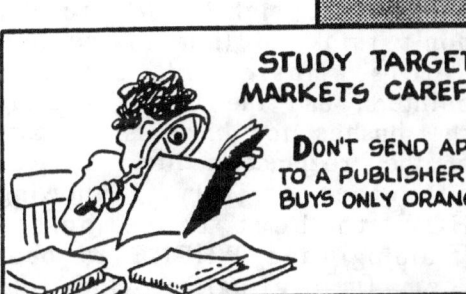

STUDY TARGET MARKETS CAREFULLY

DON'T SEND APPLES TO A PUBLISHER WHO BUYS ONLY ORANGES!

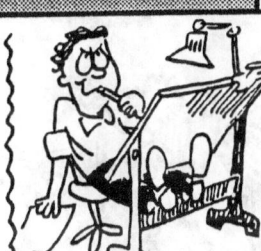

Be Creative AND UP-TO-DATE

SAMPLES OF WORK SHOULD INDICATE AN INTEREST IN NEW DEVELOPMENTS OF GENERAL-OR SPECIFIC-IMPORTANCE.

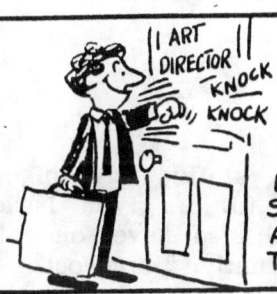

Art Directors...

NEED TO KNOW WHAT SORT OF ARTISTIC TALENTS ARE AVAILABLE IN THEIR AREA.

ROUTINELY SEND OUT "QUERY" LETTERS AND SAMPLES OF WORK.

PUBLISHERS' REQUIREMENTS VARY FROM TIME TO TIME. WRITE AND ASK. ALWAYS INCLUDE A **S.A.S.E.!**

ART/CARTOON POSSIBILITES OF A STORY OR FEATURE ARTICLE

A. Main illustration. Often illustrates a facet of the story that is unusual or unexpected.

B. Hand lettered "descriptive" title. Interprets the main subject matter in a graphic way.

C. Bold little "spot" drawings, usually in black and white with a touch of color. Effectively breaks up a large area of printed text.

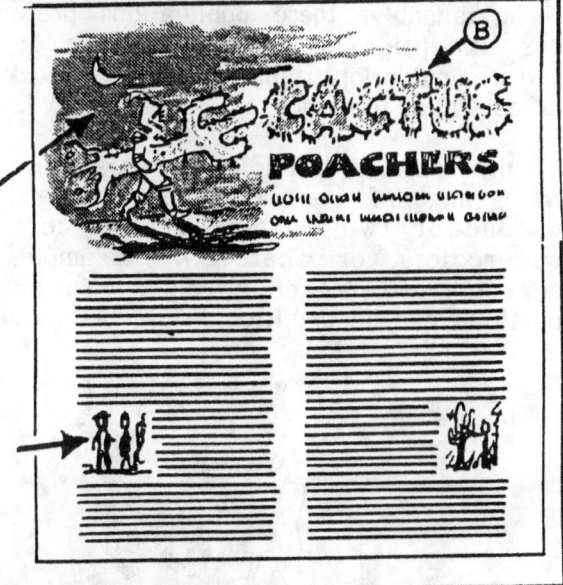

WHEN DOES THE GOLD MINE FIND THE MINER?? ... NEVER!!

... or, Is a Bird in the Hand Really Worth Two in the Bush?

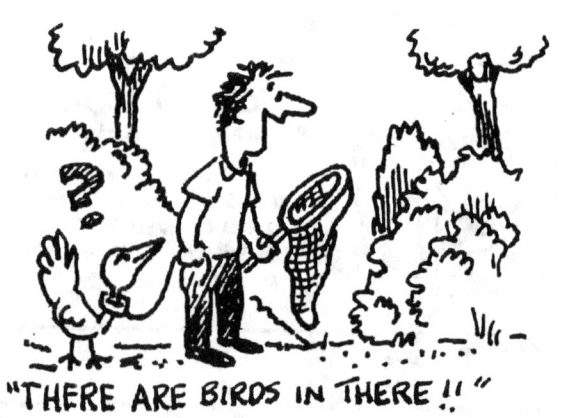

"THERE ARE BIRDS IN THERE !!"

Apparently, lots of freelance cartoonists, rightly or wrongly, don't think so (not to mention actors, musicians, authors, painters, and the like). Beating the bushes for birds is all part of the freelancer's life. It goes with the territory. Knowing HOW to beat those bushes (training) and WHERE to beat them (marketing) provides the beginner or practicing amateur with a bit of an advantage.

GET YOUR FOOT IN THE DOOR!

Most major publishers have their own art departments, staffed with highly skilled artists who do most of the artwork necessary for a given issue. However, those publications (both newspapers and magazines) also have, on call, a "stable" of freelance artists and cartoonists, and frequently "farm out" an illustrating or cartooning assignment to a freelancer whose name and examples of work are kept on file.

Understandably, these publications prefer to work with someone local, but there are exceptions. If the cartoonist happens to have the editorial offices of a major publication right in his own backyard, he has a decided advantage so far as obtaining freelance assignments (or, for that matter, a full-time job!).

In any event, a portfolio of work must be developed. This work should cover a wide range of examples ... everything from small black and white line drawings, to one or two samples of full color work (colored inks, crayons, pastels, watercolors, or whatever). Examples of black and white wash drawings and scratchboard technique might also be included. Putting together an effective portfolio can be a difficult task, but sooner or later it will pay dividends.

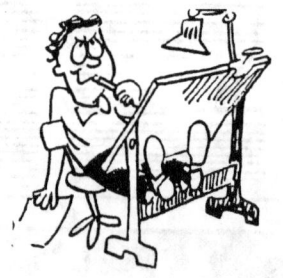

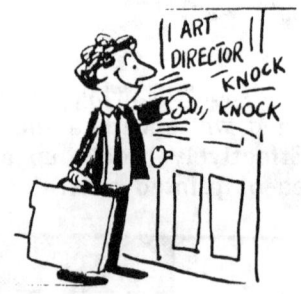

The subject matter portrayed in the examples of work is as important as the work itself. It is not wise to simply "dream up" compositions and situations that have no relationship to anything in particular. A better approach would be to search your favorite newspaper or magazine for stories and articles that have NOT been illustrated, and create drawings or illustrations for that particular story or article. This is not only a good learning experience, but lends a little more validity to the work. The story itself, or an appropriate portion of it, should be clipped out and saved for presentation with the cartoon or illustration.

Most of the foregoing applies to a portfolio of work that can be presented in person to an editor or the art director. Offering examples of work through the mail is a whole different ball of wax. Most publications have varying sets of requirements regarding samples of work that is mailed to them, so I will gain recommend the Artist's Market or Cartoonist Profiles as sources of information regarding the submission of material by mail to publishers. I must emphasize, however, the fact that the publisher's requirements concerning mailed submissions be followed exactly. They are busy people and rarely appreciate cutesy or overly creative methods of presenting work.

TECHNIQUES, DRAWING STYLES, AND INTERPRETATIONS

All major publications have their own individual format, personality, and character. Much of their identity depends on the style of artwork used for illustrations, drawings, and cartoons that are published throughout a given issue.

One publication may require innovative, unusual, or highly creative drawing styles and perhaps even bizarre, off-the-wall techniques. Another publication will use only conservative, traditional styles. Some may fall somewhere between the two. For this reason, the target publication should be studied closely. Obtain recent back issues and carefully analyze and assess the issues. DO NOT SEND ORANGES TO A MARKET THAT BUYS ONLY APPLES!

Another factor to consider is whether the publication uses illustrations that follow the text precisely and accurately. Surprisingly, some publications prefer that the illustrations be more of a teasing nature, arousing the reader's curiosity and literally forcing the reader into a story that might otherwise have been passed over.

Above all, don't be too disheartened if your first submissions are received with a less than cordial welcome by the publication. Cartoonists are a creative and inventive bunch. Drawing styles and techniques can change and improve, sometimes even on a month-to-month basis. Do not hesitate to submit a new batch of samples to a publisher from time to time. That bird in the bush isn't always found on the first attempt!

SMALL SPOT DRAWINGS AND CARTOONS AS A SPECIALTY

Thousands of small, nationally distributed trade journals and special interest magazines prefer to use small, well designed drawings and tiny little "spot" illustrations to add interest to a story or article. Because of budget restrictions, they often find it necessary to take advantage of whatever "Clip Art" books they have on hand. Those cartoons and illustrations are usually general in nature and may not be suitable for a particular story.

Therefore, it can be a good idea to submit your name and address along with some small examples of your work to as many of those publications as possible. Also include a price list of some sort. Keep the fees for your services low, or the samples, and your name, will probably end up in the nearest wastebasket. Above all, don't let the prospect of low pay for your work dampen your spirit or minimize your efforts. At the outset, getting some GOOD examples of your work published should be the main objective.

It is of the utmost importance that, when creating examples of your work, you do not select a story or article that has previously been illustrated by another cartoonist or illustrator. The freelance cartoonist must be a real fighter, but a fair one. No hitting below the belt or after the bell ends the round.

DOUBLING PROFITS

One of my students recently received an assignment to create three small drawings for an article to be published in a rather obscure magazine. After reading the article a few times, he came up with about 20 possible ideas, sketched them up, and showed them to me. We selected the three ideas that were the most appropriate for the story and, with only a little extra effort, turned the rest of the ideas into some fairly decent gag cartoons which are currently being submitted to the trade journal markets.

This is not an unusual occurrence when creating ideas for story illustrations. Several years ago, one of my students got an assignment to do a large illustration for a teenage fashion magazine. The illustration required a considerable amount of research on costumes of the seventeenth century. The student found the subject so interesting that she continued her research on the subject and not only did a fine job on the illustration, but sold 30 additional drawings to a publisher of children's coloring books which, in turn, lead to a full-time job illustrating all sorts of children's publications and instructional books.

As mentioned several times throughout this book, one idea can, and should, lead 100 others, and Idea No. 101 will lead to another hundred even better ideas.

THE BARE NECESSITIES

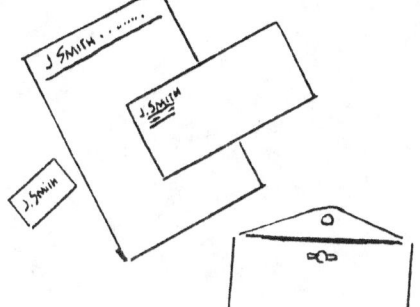

The freelance cartoonist operates with much the same sort of business stationery used by any mail business, except that the cartoonist is selling an artistic type of service, not TV repairs or plumbing supplies, and his literature should reflect that fact. Business cards, letterheads, and brochures should be neat and well designed.

The standard 3½" x 8½" brochure has proven to be an effective selling tool, and has enough room for a brief resume and several examples of the cartoonist's work.

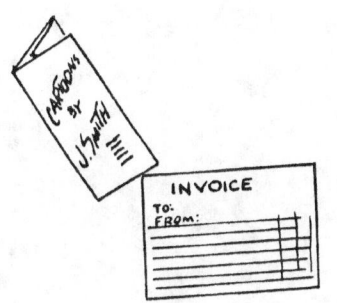

However, as the cartoonist's range of capabilities increases, it is usually a good idea to replace the brochure with a small booklet. A compact, 20-page, 5½" x 8½" booklet, when included with a brief cover letter, can make an impressive presentation. It in, examples of the cartoonist's work can be offered in a neater, more organized manner.

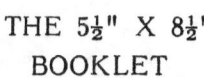

Printing costs and expertise can vary between one print shop and another. Check around and ask about the various ways in which such a booklet can be produced. In any event, the cost will be considerably more than the brochure, but GOOD WORK WARRANTS A GOOD PRESENTATION.

THE 5½" X 8½"
BOOKLET

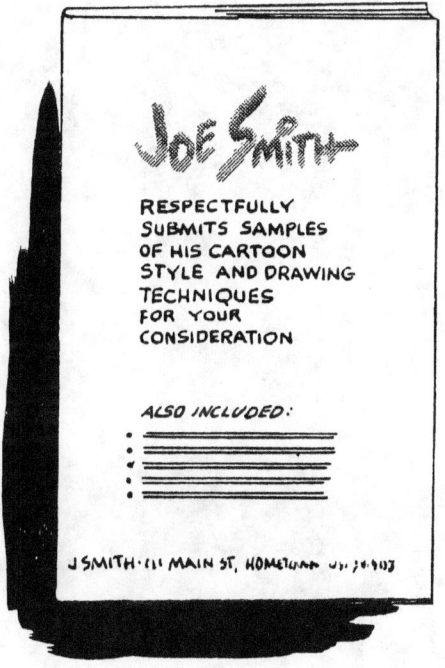

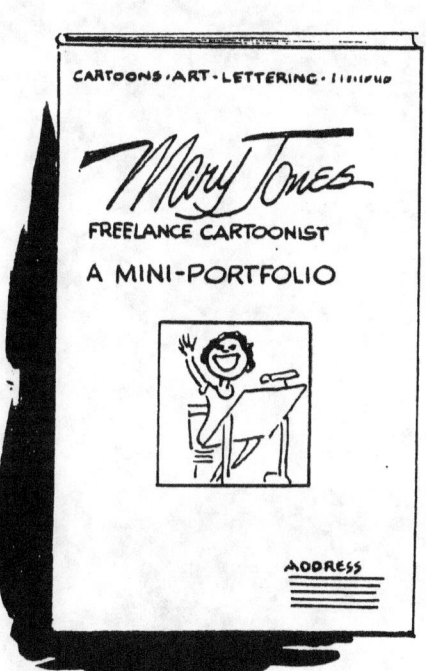

CHAPTER ELEVEN
Caricaturing

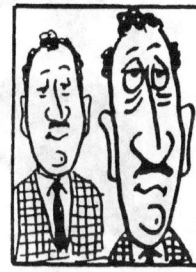
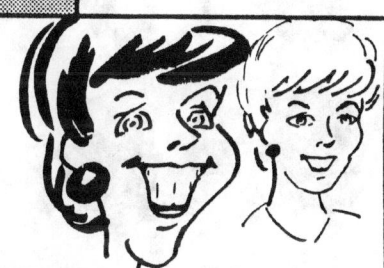

THE CARICATURE MUST INDICATE *PERSONALITY & CHARACTER* AS WELL AS FACIAL FEATURES —

THE CARICATURIST LEARNS TO LOOK AT FACES IN A MORE THAN CASUAL WAY!

THE CARICATURIST IS A "FACE DETECTIVE" —
SEARCHING FOR CLUES THAT CLEARLY IDENTIFIES A PARTICULAR INDIVIDUAL

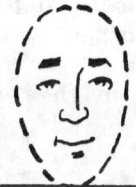 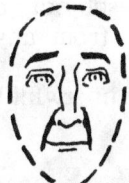 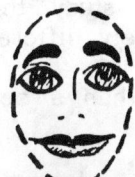 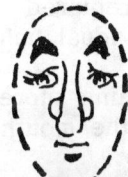 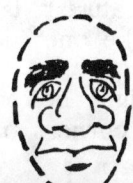 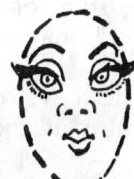 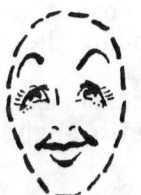

VERY OFTEN, THE <u>SMILE</u> IS A PERSON'S MOST IDENTIFIABLE CHARACTERISTIC —

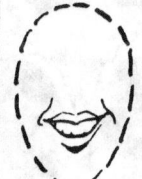 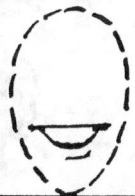 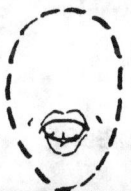 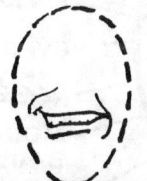 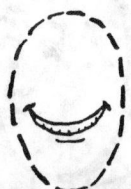 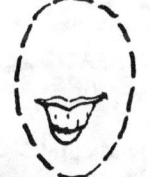 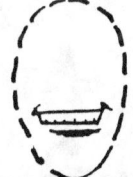

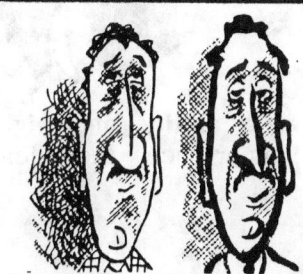
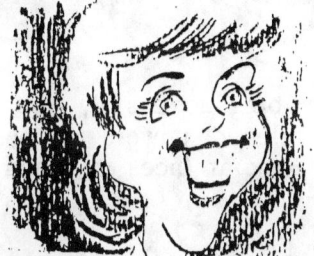

THE DRAWING STYLES & MATERIALS USED TO CREATE CARICATURES FOR BLACK & WHITE REPRODUCTION ARE NECESSARILY MUCH DIFFERENT THAN THOSE USED BY THE "SIDEWALK" CARICATURIST, WHOSE CHOICE OF STYLE AND MATERIALS IS

VIRTUALLY UNLIMITED!

CARICATURES: CHARACTER/PORTRAITURE
EXAGGERATION OF FACIAL FEATURES AND INNER PERSONALITY!
SUCCESS OFTEN DEPENDS UPON THE <u>DEGREE</u> OF EXAGGERATION

Exaggeration is the essence of caricatures. In some cases, the facial features that will be distorted for the purposes of instant recognition are quite obvious. In other case, the caricaturist is required to study the subject closely before finding the "keys" that make one individual uniquely different from any other.

Occasionally, the keys might be nothing more than a certain twinkle in the eye and a slight upturn at the corners of the mouth.

10 POINT CARICATURING CHECK LIST
ALWAYS LOOK FOR AT LEAST __3__ OUTSTANDING FACIAL FEATURES

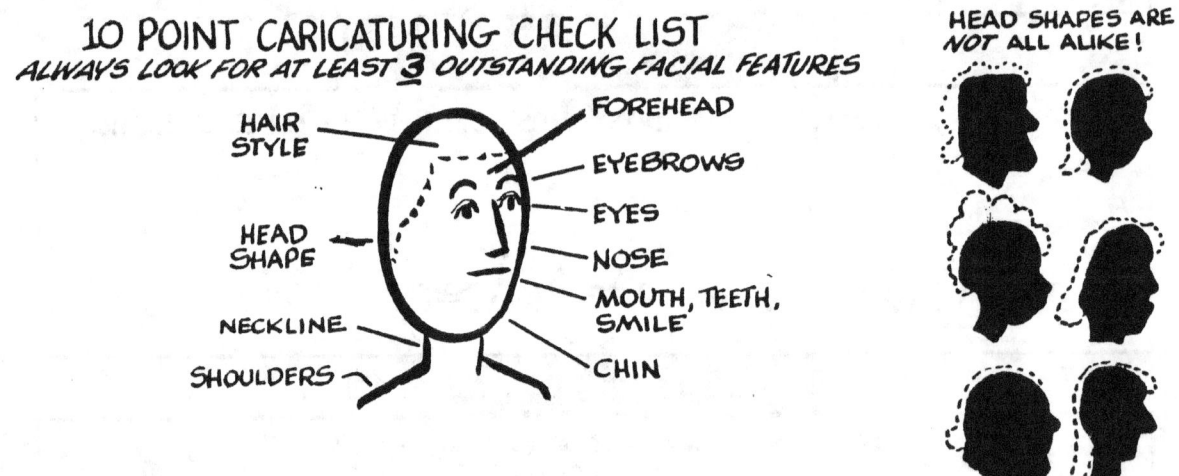

HEAD SHAPES ARE NOT ALL ALIKE!

To be successful, the caricaturist must have good drawing ability and highly developed powers of observation. Through training and experience, they learn to look at faces in a more than casual way.

THE EYES HAVE IT...

PLUS THE NOSE, MOUTH, CHIN, HAIR, EARS AND HEAD!!

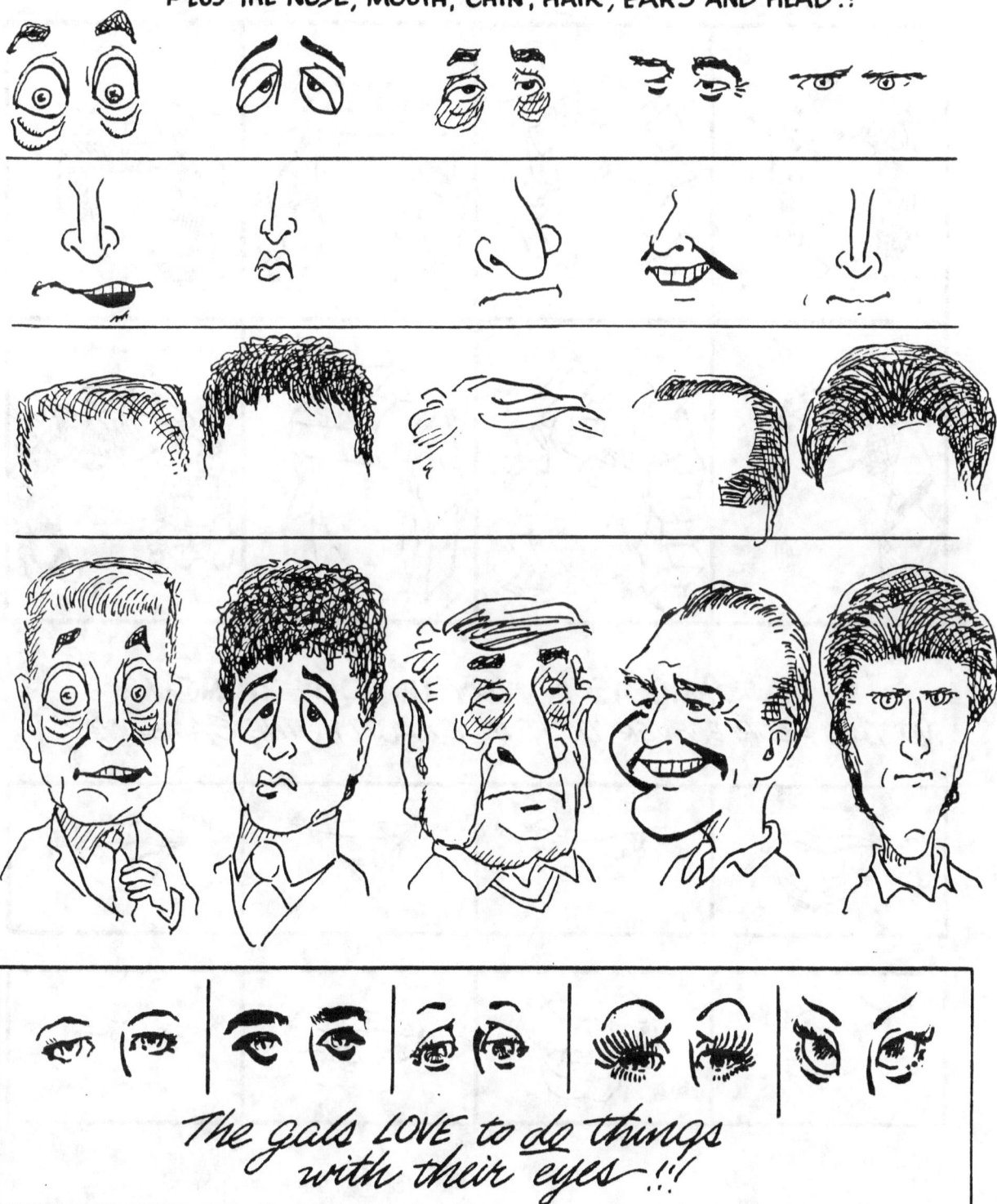

The gals LOVE to do things with their eyes !!!

THE GALS ALSO LIKE TO DO THINGS WITH THEIR <u>HAIR</u>!
WATCH FOR THE GEOMETRIC SHAPES THAT INDICATE FLOW & DIRECTION

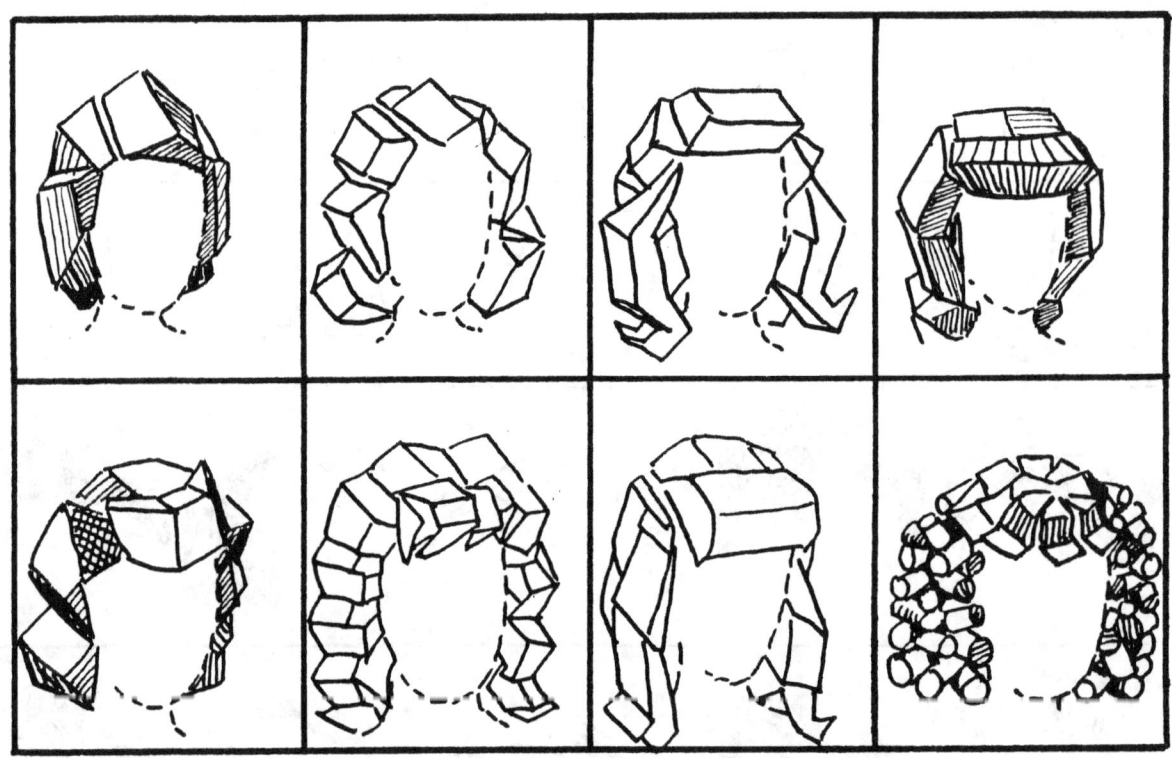

A SMILE IS A VERY UNIQUE THING!
NO TWO PEOPLE EVER DO IT IN EXACTLY THE SAME WAY.

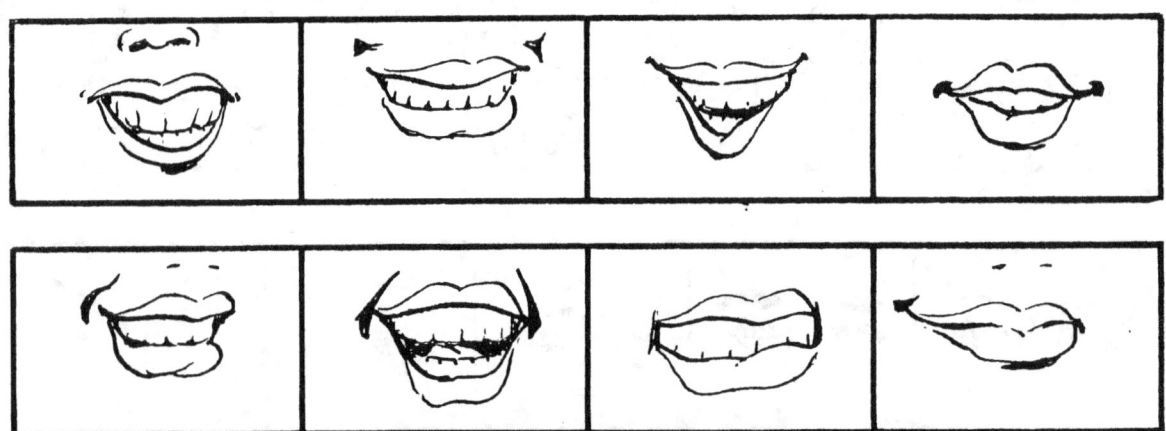

THERE'S SOMETHING _SPECIAL_ ABOUT THE LADIES! SKETCH THEM OFTEN!

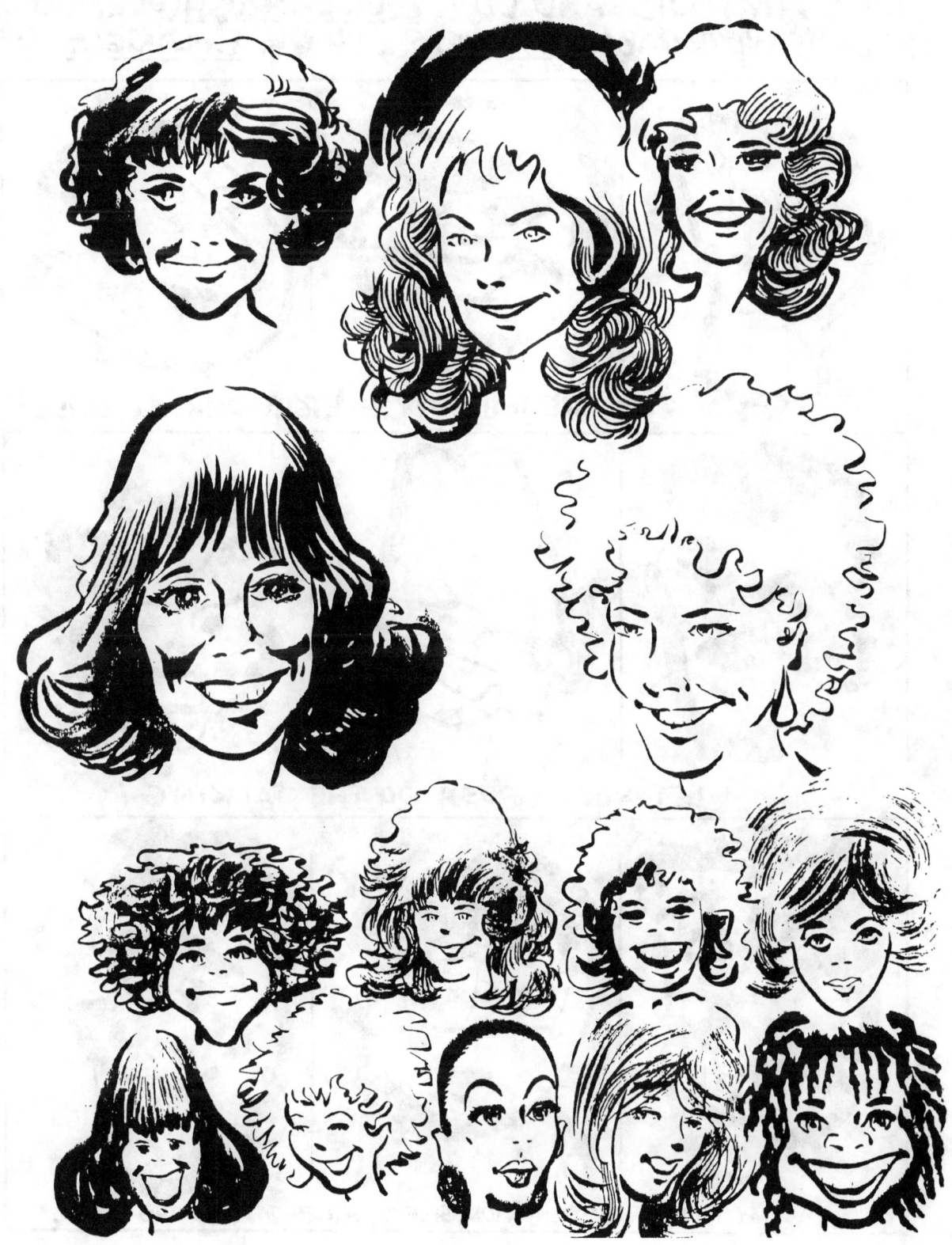

"STAY LOOSE-DON'T CHOKE" EXERCISE. SELECT A PHOTO-ANY PHOTO-AND DO A QUICK-BRUSH VERSION OF IT. DON'T WORRY ABOUT LIKENESS... THINK BOLDNESS!!

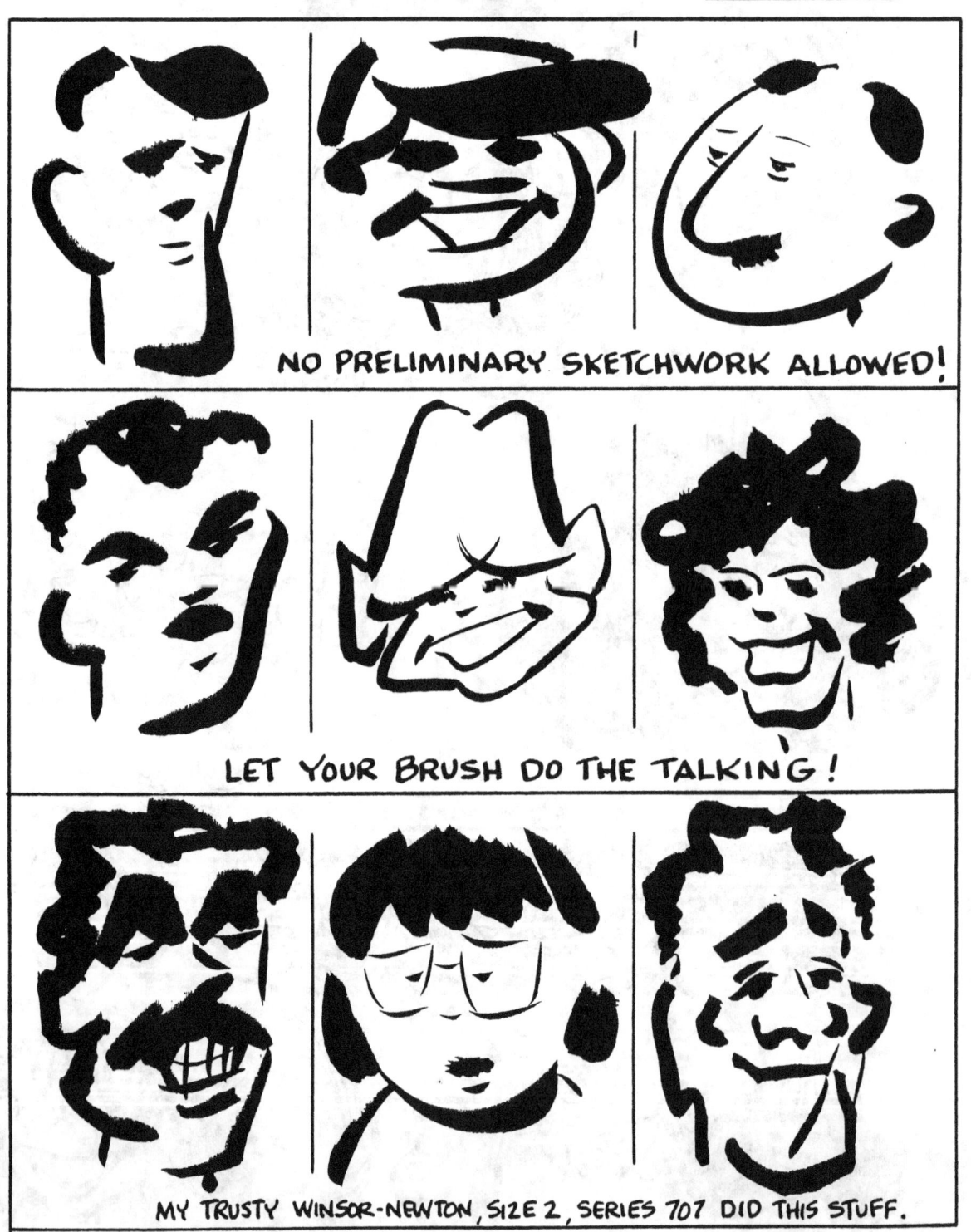

NO PRELIMINARY SKETCHWORK ALLOWED!

LET YOUR BRUSH DO THE TALKING!

MY TRUSTY WINSOR-NEWTON, SIZE 2, SERIES 707 DID THIS STUFF.

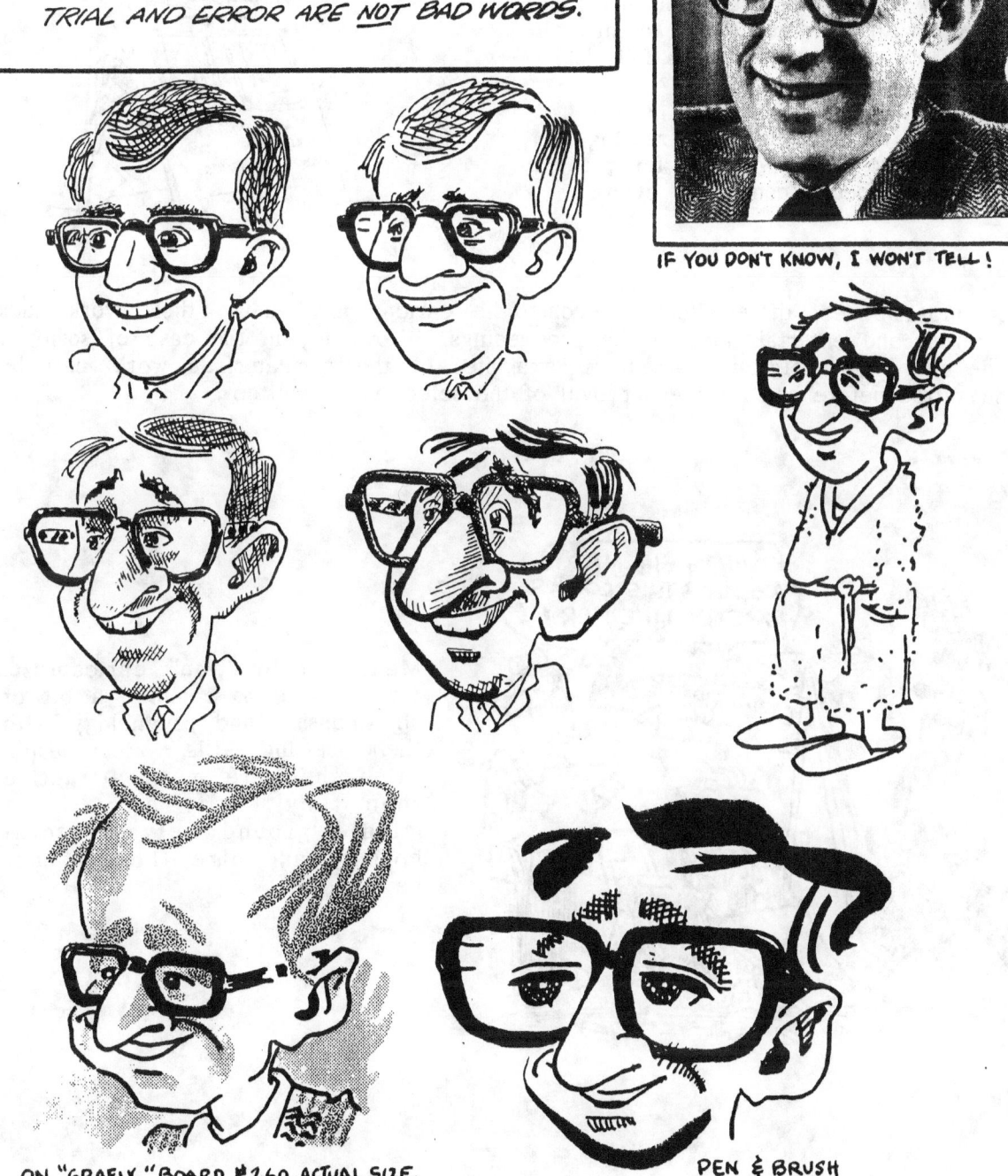

EXAGGERATING EXAGGERATIONS

A SUCCESSFUL CARICATURE CAN OFTEN BE FOUND SOMEWHERE BETWEEN REALISM AND GROSS DISTORTION.
TRIAL AND ERROR ARE <u>NOT</u> BAD WORDS.

IF YOU DON'T KNOW, I WON'T TELL!

ON "GRAFIX" BOARD #260. ACTUAL SIZE.

PEN & BRUSH

"LIVE" CARICATURING AS A PART-TIME JOB OR FULL-TIME CAREER

Many aspiring cartoonists have discovered that "live, on-the-spot" caricaturing is a way to earn a substantial amount of extra money with their cartooning talents. In fact, lots of them do it as a full time occupation.

It's usually just a matter of renting booth space at sidewalk art fairs, county fairs, and special community events.

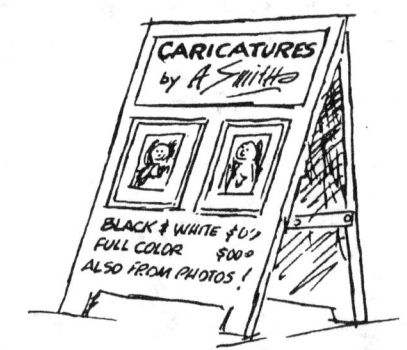

In most cases, those events welcome the caricaturist because their work adds interest and entertainment to the proceedings. However, in the case of some of the more "prestigious" art fairs, examples of the caricaturist's work must be submitted beforehand for the approval of the selection committee.

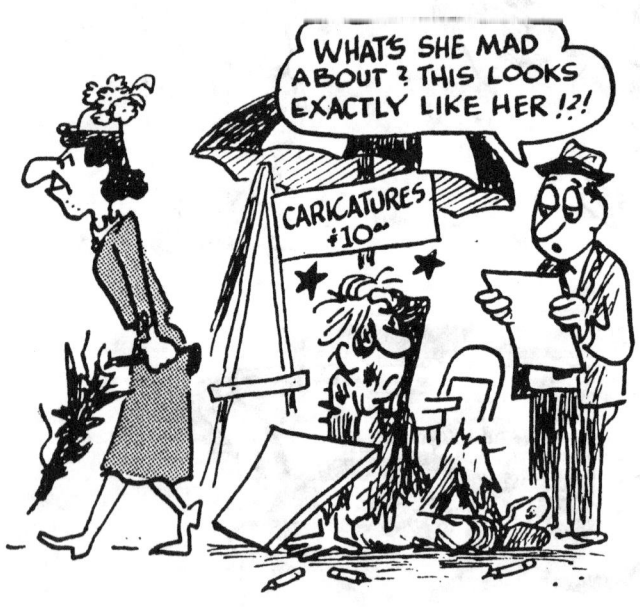

Many "on-location" caricaturists find it wise to combine a bit of showmanship and psychology with their drawing skills. Most people think they are more attractive than they really are. Some middle ground between total honesty and pure flattery must be found.

TECHNIQUES AND EQUIPMENT

There are a number of important factors that the "on-location" caricaturist should keep in mind when setting up an outdoor studio. The space, usually about 10 feet square, should appear inviting and comfortable. A small patio table and umbrella with one or two comfortable chairs will be appreciated by customers, and a small but impressive display of recent work will help sell the caricaturist's service. Small, inexpensive frames can greatly improve the drawing's general appearance and increase its value, so it might be a good idea to keep a small supply on hand should the customers request an on-the-spot framing job.

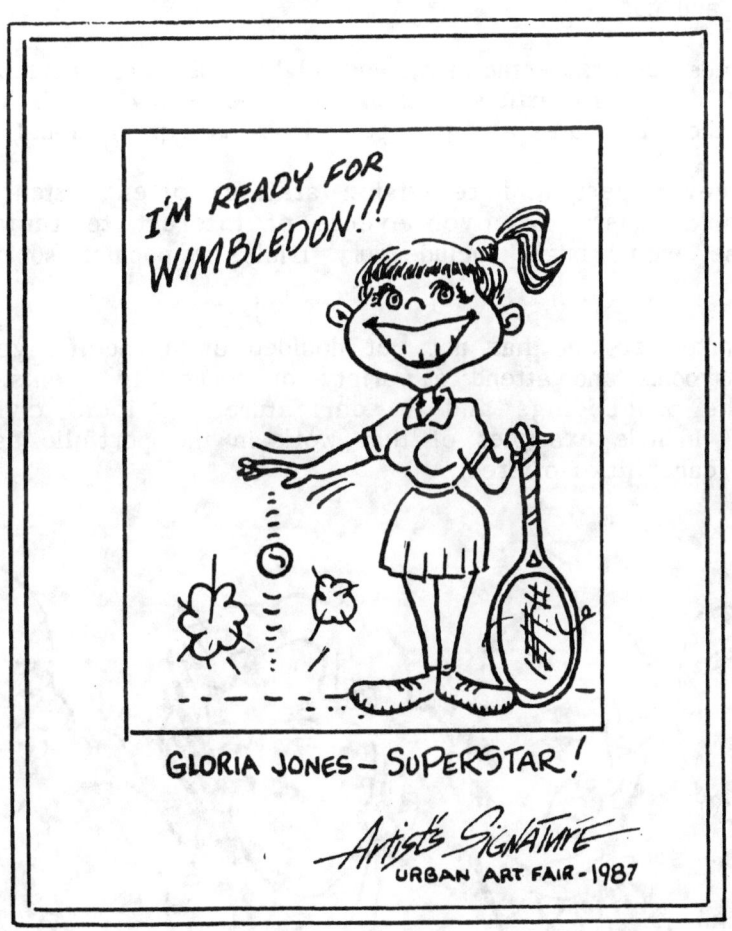

Do not hesitate to ask the customer about his or her hobbies, employment, and special interests. Include a bit of that information in the caricature, along with a cute little caption or tag line, as well as the date and location of the caricature. This makes it a souvenir as well as an original piece of art.

TECHNIQUES AND EQUIPMENT

Unlike the caricature that is created for publication, which can be done with the three-step, trial-and-error method, the "on location" caricature must be a quick, first-attempt effort. As a result, the cartoonist must develop a natural style of caricature -- one that comes easily and comfortably, yet has a definite "design" quality and a professional touch.

The techniques used in on-location caricaturing might range from simple little "quickies" in pencil, charcoal, felt tip marking pens, or pen and ink, to full color drawings in pastels, crayons, or watercolors. Prices are based on the quality of the work, the time spent, and the materials used. Prices can vary from $5 to $25 and up.

Conventions, trade shows, restaurants, and night clubs are increasingly engaging the services of caricature artists, either on a percentage basis or a flat day-rate fee where the caricatures are given to clients as a promotional gimmick.

Additionally, newspapers and television stations often assign outside sketch artists and caricaturists to cover events of interest to their readers and viewers. These events might include jury trials or popular sports and charity events.

The aspiring cartoonist who has not yet decided on a specific goal should visit the local courtrooms and attend a variety of community events. Make quick sketches of the proceedings and do caricatures of local civic leaders and political folks. Include examples of that work in the portfolio as an indication of the range of capabilities offered.

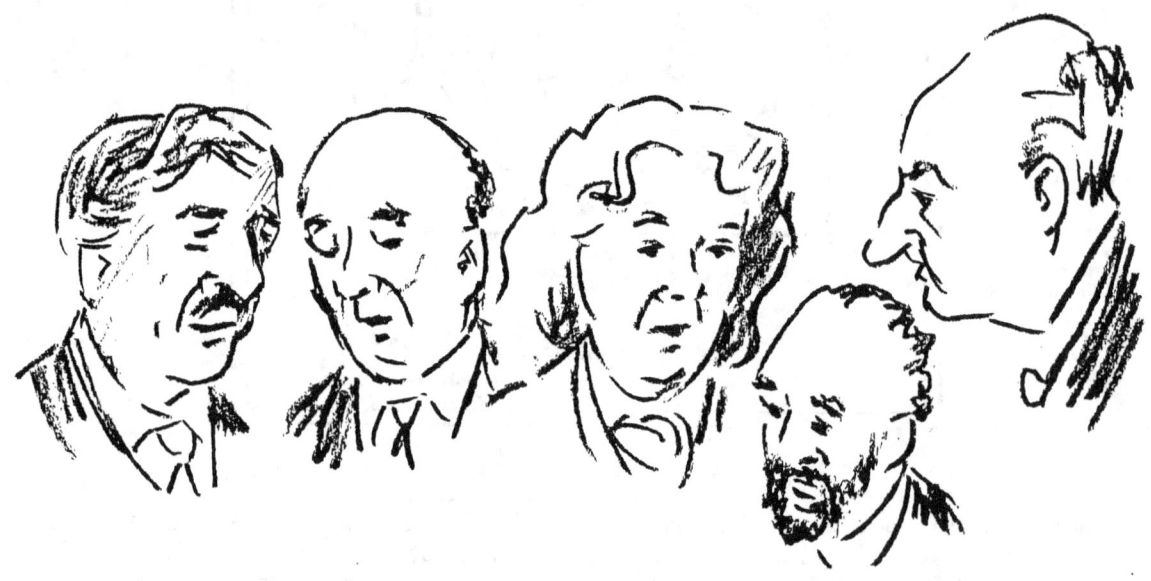

WHAT'S AHEAD?

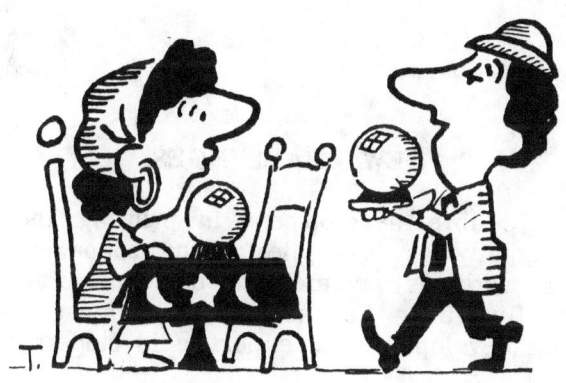

There have been at least three major developments in recent years that have had significant impact on the cartooning profession, not to mention American industry as a whole. Those developments are (1) foreign imports, (2) computers, and (3) new printing technology. Yet, the future for today's aspiring cartoonists looks brighter than ever before.

FOREIGN IMPORTS. A large percentage of today's animated video cartoons are being produced overseas. This has had a devastating effect on the U.S. animation studios, many of which have either gone out of business or have cut way back on their production staff.

This is not to say, however, that there is no future for the cartoonist interested in animation. Quote the opposite. New and more positive uses for the cartoon animated film are being developed almost daily, especially in the field of education. And while computer graphics have eliminated many of the time-consuming procedures formerly required to produce animation, the need for creative minds and talented hands will always be in demand in the industry. Computer technology has come a long way, but it hasn't yet (and never will) be able to create something out of thin air.

COMPUTER GRAPHICS. Again, the computer raises its dragon-like head, ready to gobble up anything within reach. But it is a well trained beast which feeds on nothing but the nuts and bolts of tedious work and procedures -- the kind of stuff that the talented, creative mind soon becomes bored with anyway.

PRINTING TECHNOLOGY. The printed page is now, and always has been, the primary marketplace for the cartoonist's product. With today's new printing presses, it is available to more people than ever before. Additionally, educators are voicing more and more concerns about the reading ability of students, even those at the college level. Growing emphasis is being placed on the importance of the printed page. Where there is a printed page, there is an opportunity for the skilled artist or cartoonist.

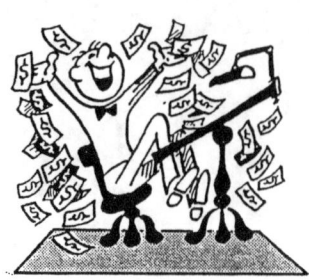

NEW CHALLENGES

Perhaps the most noticeable development in printing technology concerns full color reproduction, especially as it applies to newspaper publications. However, full color (four-color work) is an area to be considered only after the cartoonist or humorous illustrator has mastered at least the basic drawing and cartooning skills and has developed some expertise in modern printing methods.

THE "INSTANT" ERA

The hustle and bustle of today's modern living has created a need for all sorts of "instant" products, and it can be expected that the trend will soon include Instant Information, Instant Education, and Instant Entertainment. These are all areas that can benefit from the cartoonist's skill and creativity.

The role the cartoonist plays in our society today is more important than ever before. It is the universal language, easily understood by all.

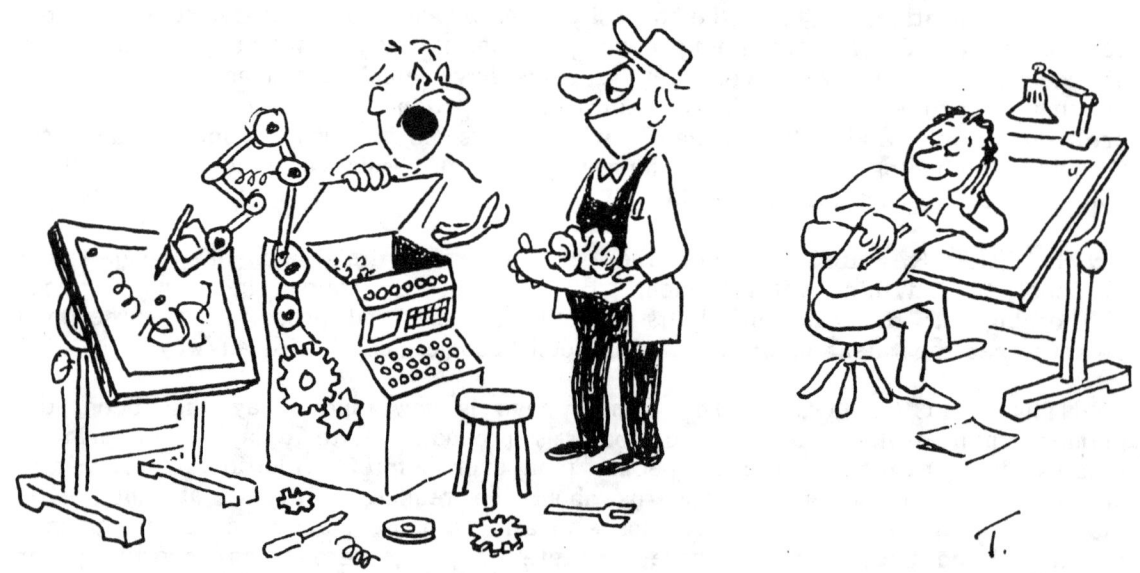

"Oh, all right, Phelps, drop it in there ... but it's not going to help much!"

About the Author

DON TRACHSLER was born in Chicago, Illinois in 1927 and studied at the Chicago Art Institute, Chicago Academy of Fine Art, Raye School of Art and was a serious student of the History of Art.

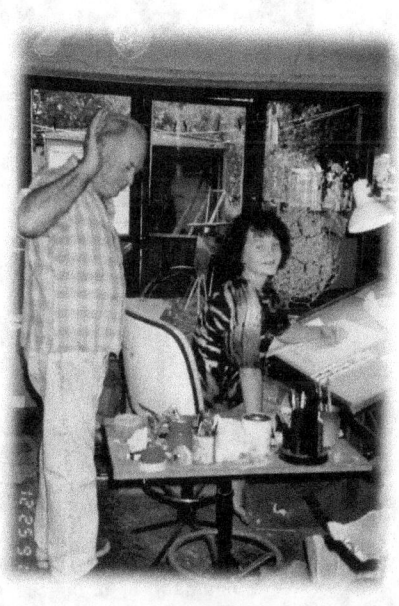

For over 60 years, Mr. Trachsler was active in art or art-related endeavors. His early drawings, in the early 1940's, were published in Boys Life magazine, he was the staff cartoonist for the Crane Tech High School newspaper and yearbook, the Director at J.A. Art Agency, Illustrator for Hi-Shopper Publishing Co. While in the Navy, he did graphic arts for the base newsletter. Later he served as art director for Kidstuff magazine and an on-assignment illustrator for the National Examiner, completing more than 300 assignments. He also created a cartoon ad series for WJNO radio, these were just some of his accomplishments.

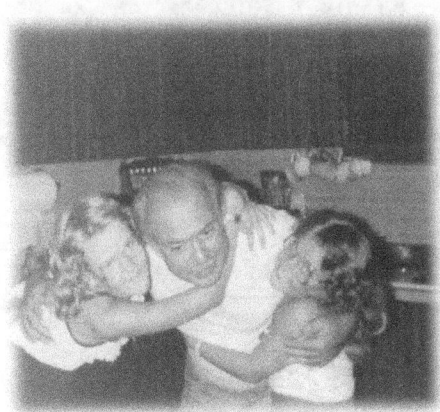

His multiple awards include the Illinois State Capital National Art Competition and the Northern Illinois Gas Corporation. Early in his career he traveled extensively displaying his sculptures and art at many festivals in the art circuit with 17 1st place awards in major group competitions around the country. He also had one of the winning submissions for the New Yorker in the National Cartoon Competition for Absolut Vodka in 1991.

His passion was Art – in any form. He dedicated his life to creating art in a variety of forms. He moved to West Palm Beach, Florida in 1970 and I'm pretty sure he was working on some project even at the time of his death in 2007.

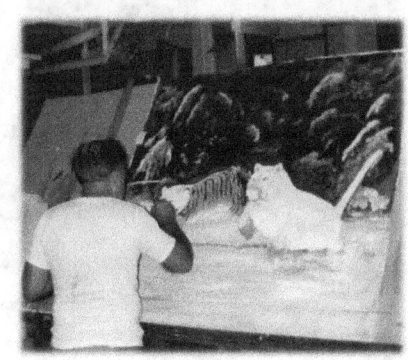

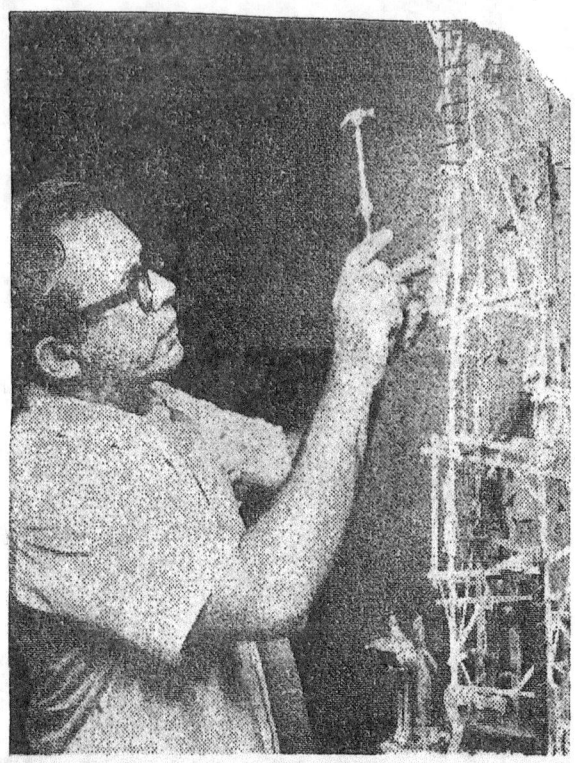

Don Trachsler of Lockport putting finishing touches to his wood sculpture, "The Committee," which he calls "a monument to organized confusion."

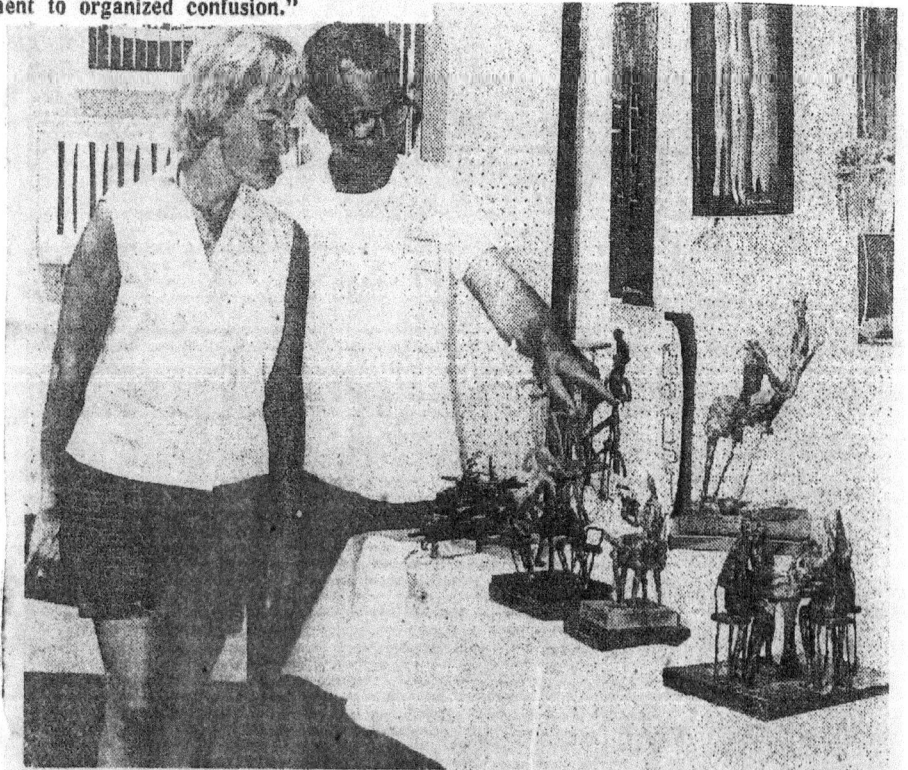

Cruz, Batavia, works on a r, Logan County, W. Va. Shayer, LaGrange Park, hangs one of his paintings. In photo at right, Mr. and Mrs. Don Trachsler, Lockport, discuss arrangement of their art works. (Beacon-News Photos).

WHATTA WHOPPER

Lying CAN get you in trouble — or win you a prize.

Take Mary Lathrop, for example.

The Garden City, Kansas, woman told a whopper of a lie, but instead of being punished for it, she earned the title of 1989's Champion Liar in the Burlington, Wisconsin, Liar's Club annual tall-tale

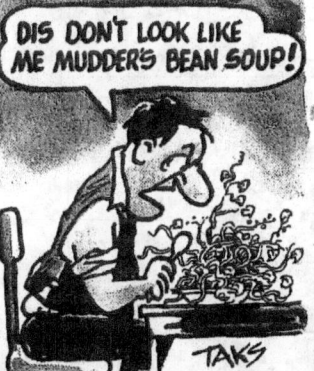

DIS DON'T LOOK LIKE ME MUDDER'S BEAN SOUP!

TAKS

slow the bean soup sprouts

Among the tall tales av mentions in the contest w stupendous story about w decided to do with its old fir chasing a new one.

"The mayor finally sett when he decided that we wi by and use it only on false stock, Wisconsin, man wr(

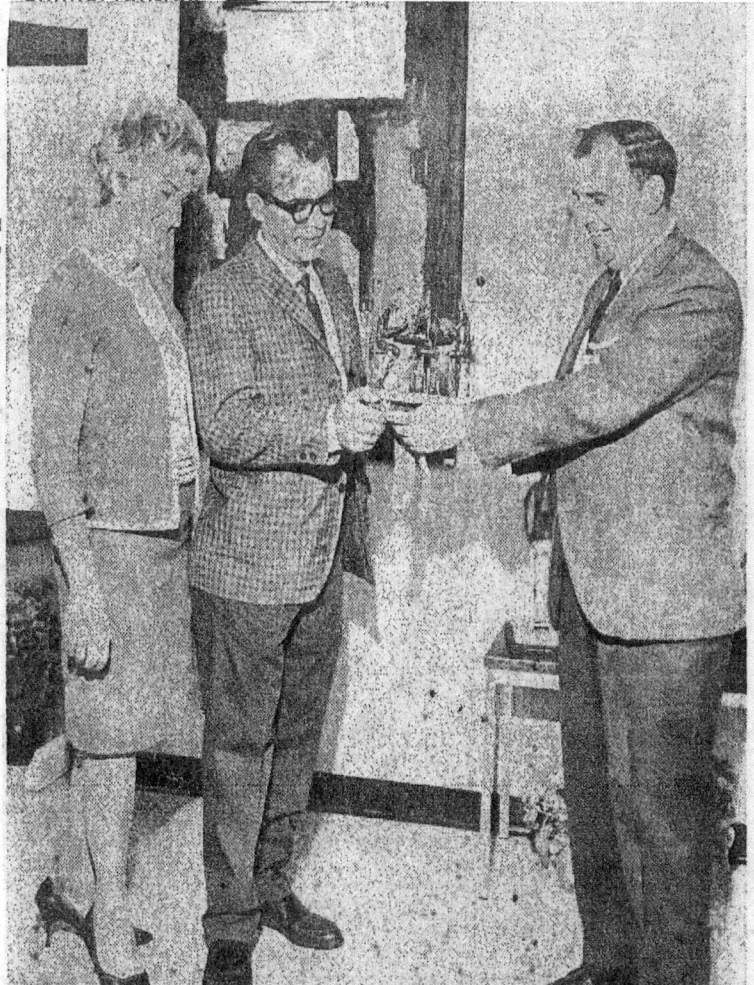

ART AWARD — Don Trachsler of Lockport (center), receives an honorable mention award for his sculpture, "High Stakes," exhibited in the art showing, "October Palette, the Best of 1966." It was sponsored by the Northern Illinois Gas Co. and the West Suburban Fine Arts Alliance. Presenting the award is Tom Kenney, chairman of the show. Mrs. Trachsler accompanied her husband to the awards ceremonies.

THE ART OF DON TRACHSLER

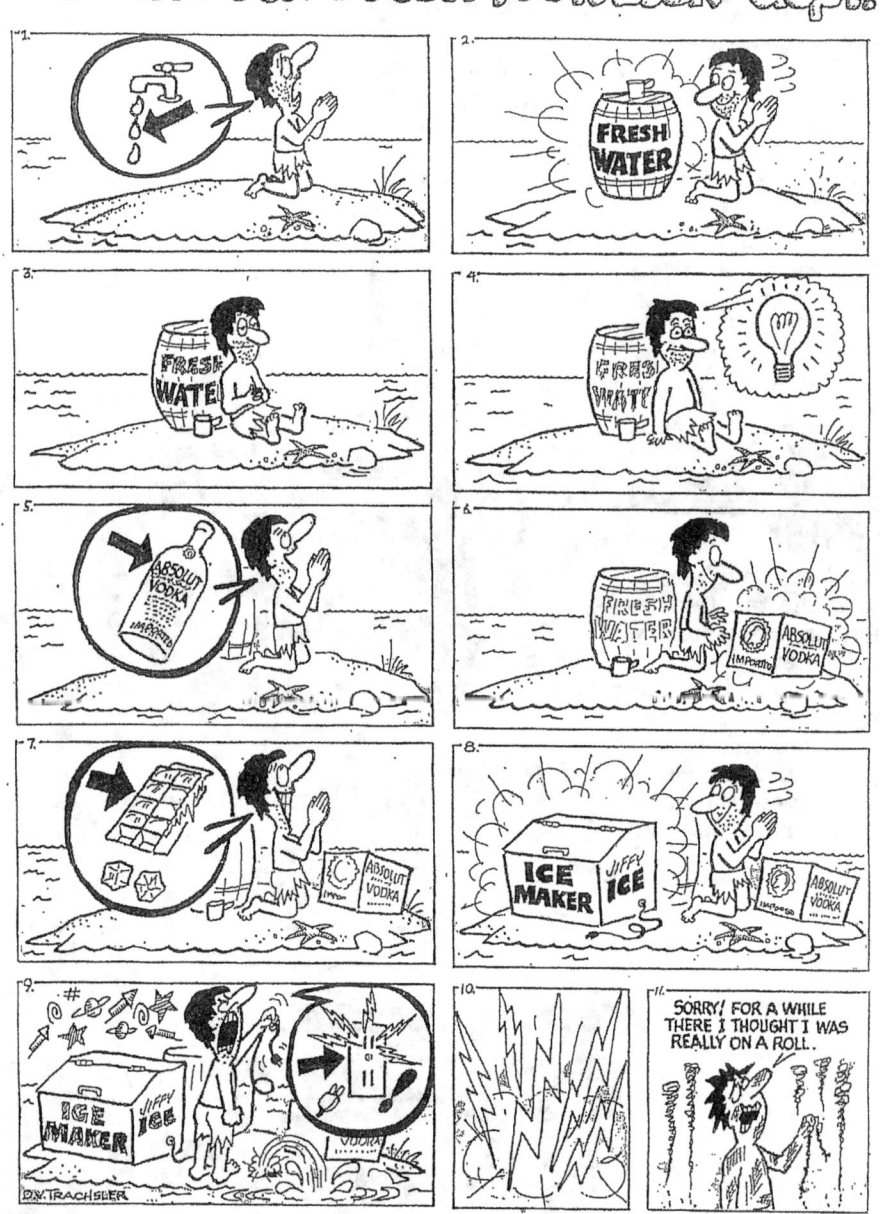

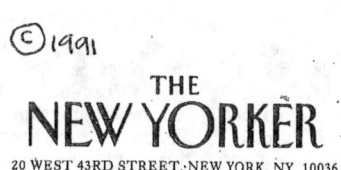

THE ART OF DON TRACHSLER

ILLUSTRATIONS FROM KIDSTUFF MAGAZINE

CARTOONS/HUMOROUS ILLUSTRATIONS

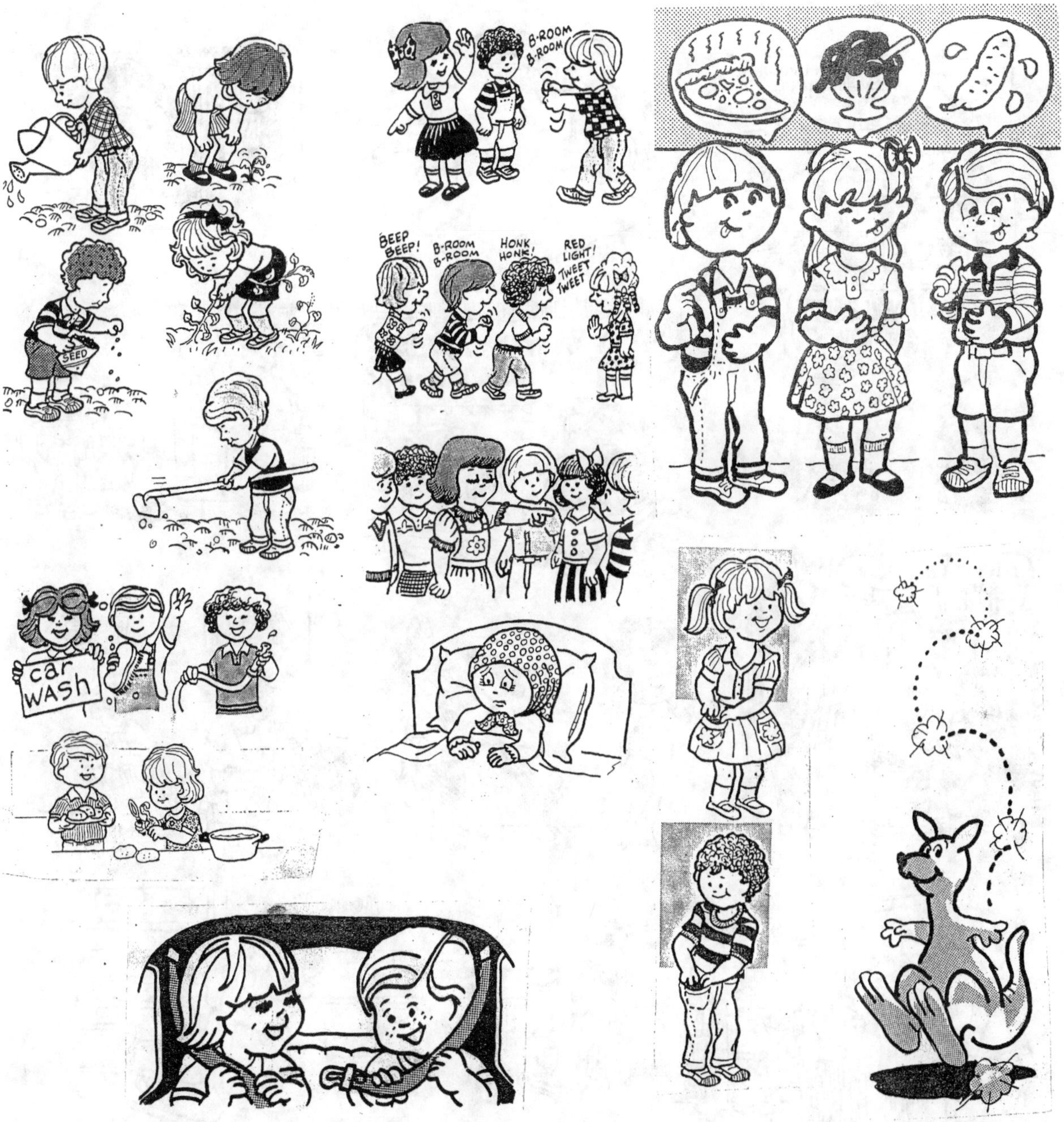

THE ART OF DON TRACHSLER

SPECIAL FEATURES ILLUSTRATIONS FROM THE NATIONAL EXAMINER

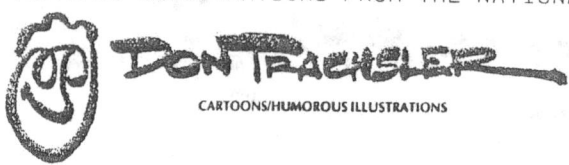

CARTOONS/HUMOROUS ILLUSTRATIONS

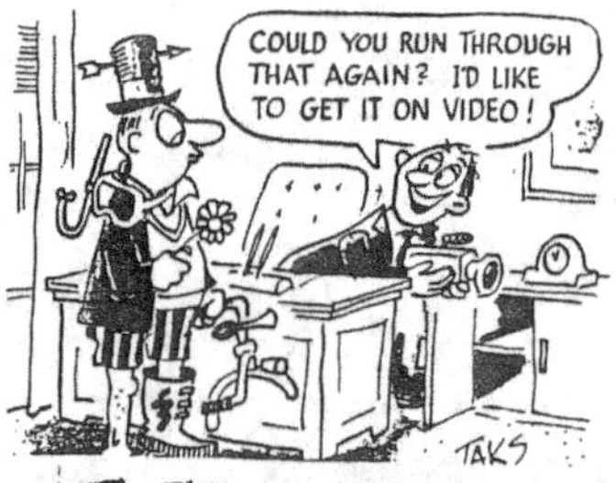

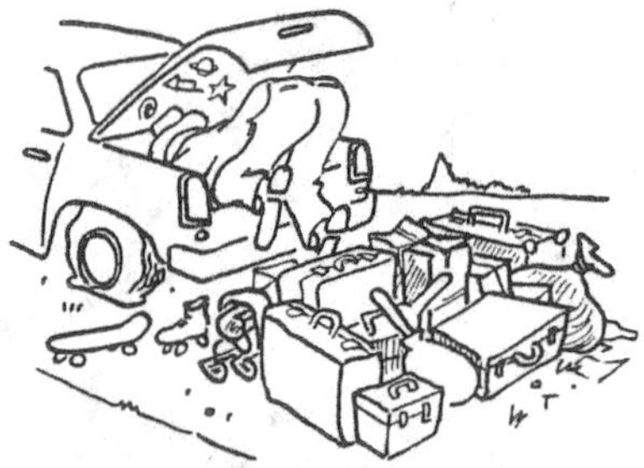

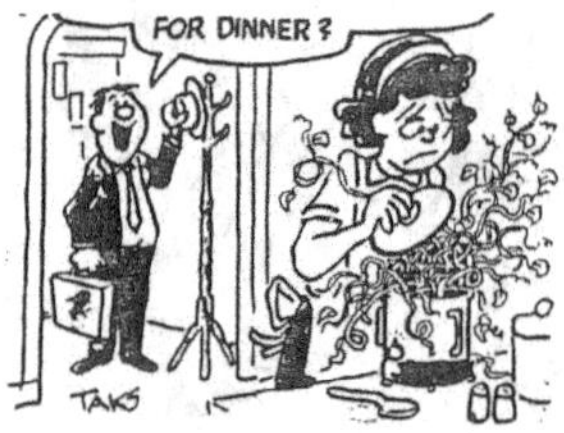

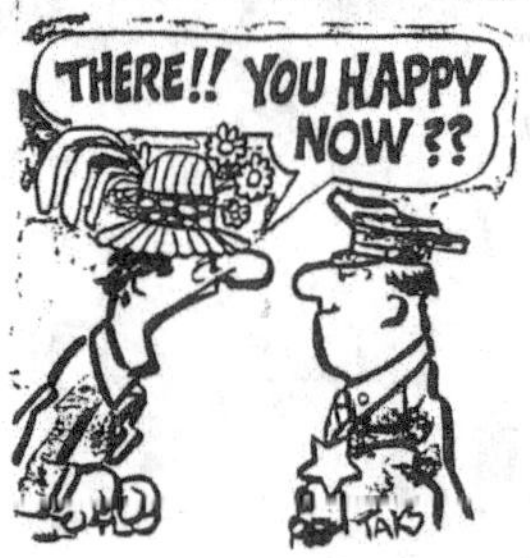

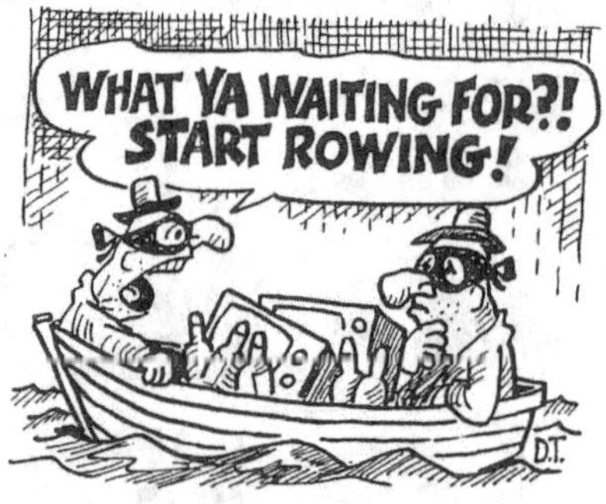

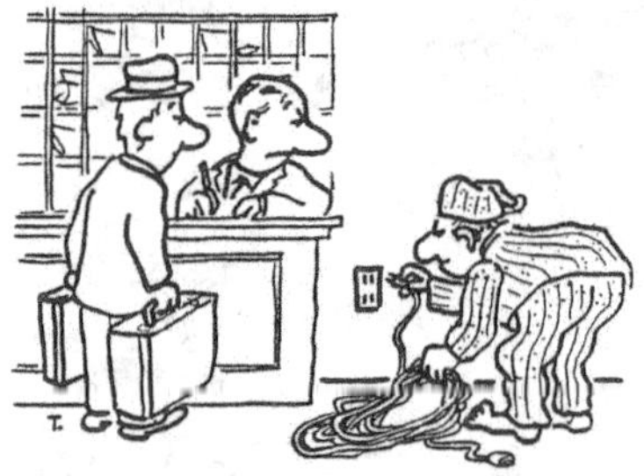

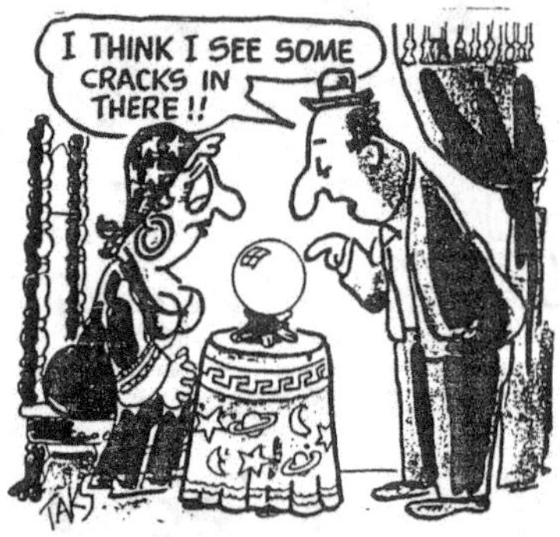

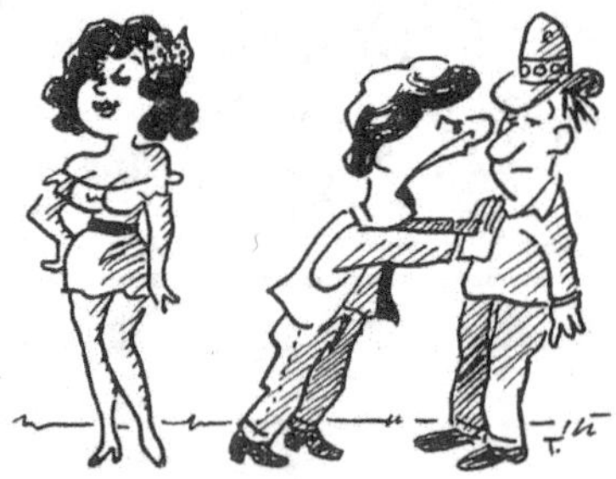

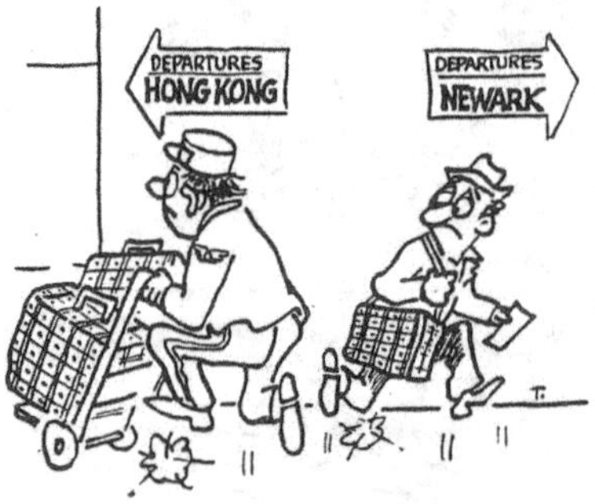

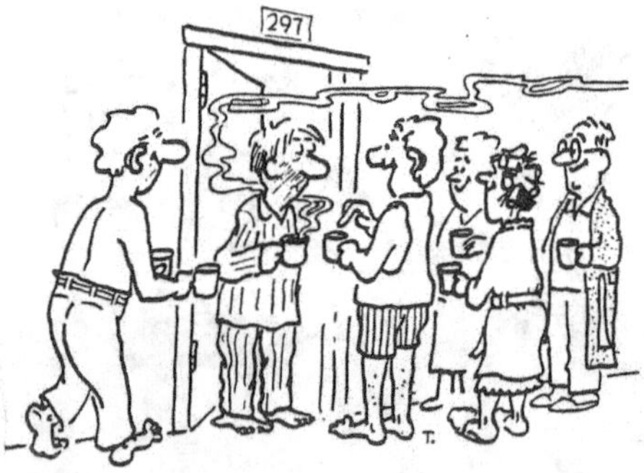

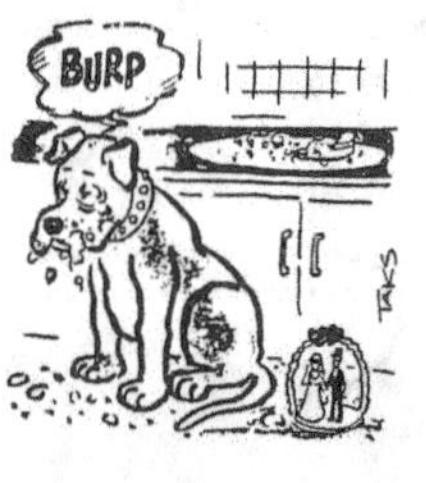

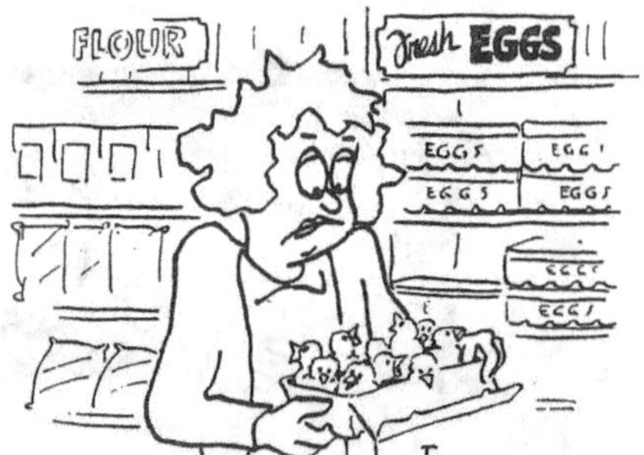

GLOSSARY

ACCENTS
Objects in a drawing that are immediately apparent.

ACETATE
A transparent plastic-like material, with either a smooth or matte finish. Used to create overlays for color the separation printing process and special effects. Also used as a protective cover over drawings.

BLOCKS
Geometric shapes drawn in perspective and used as a preliminary foundation for drawing figures and objects.

BALLOON
An outlined area containing dialogue. Most often used in comic strips and certain types of humorous illustrations.

BLOCKING IN
The rough preliminary sketch used to determine the composition of a drawing.

BRISTOL
A lightweight cardboard with a tough, durable finish on which final drawings are made. Available in smooth or kid (somewhat rough) finishes.

CLIP ART
Cartoons, illustrations, and other forms of artwork sold to printers and publishers on a copyright-free basis.

COMPOSITION
The arrangement of objects within a given space or area.

COMPREHENSIVE
A completely detailed sketch or drawing, usually just one step below the final drawing.

CONTINUITY
The presentation of a series of ideas and drawings done in an orderly manner. A progression from start to finish without interruption.

CONTOUR LINE
A line drawn in a manner that indicates form and shape.

COVER LETTER
A brief introductory letter enclosed with submitted material explaining the purpose for which the material has been prepared and submitted.

CROSS HATCH
A drawing technique used mainly in black and white line drawings to create a wide variety of shaded effects.

DESCRIPTIVE
> In lettering, the style or technique used that graphically illustrates the word or phrase used. Not necessarily limited to POW, BANG, or BOOM.

DISTORTION
> Drawing figures and/or objects in a way that emphasizes shapes and characteristics.

DRY BRUSH
> A drawing or shading technique that produces a wide variety of textured effects through the use of an ALMOST dry brush (with very little ink or paint). A course or short-hair brush usually works best.

FIXATIVE
> A clear, fast-drying liquid or spray used to protect pencil and charcoal drawings from smearing and smudging.

FLAT COLOR
> Areas that are uniform in shade and intensity without blending. Can apply to shades of gray or color.

FLOOD
> A technique using a well-loaded brush and bold, quick brush strokes. Often used over a pre-dampened area.

FRISKET
> A thin, transparent paper with a low-tack backing. Used to protect certain areas of a drawing against overspray or spatter.

FORESHORTENING
> A technique used in figure drawing and perspective establish the proper relationship between the drawing and the viewer.

FOUNDATION
> Preliminary sketch work from which figures and objects are developed.

GAG CARTOON
> A joke or funny situation illustrated with cartoon characters and usually contained within a single panel, with or without captions printed below.

GESTURE LINE
> The basic line that indicates movement, action, or emotion of people, animals, and stationary objects. Also called Action Line.

GRAFIX
> Specially processed drawing papers and bristols that have been pre-printed with invisible dot or line patterns that reappear when developers are applied

GREASE PENCIL
Sometimes known as a China Marker. Produces a dense black line similar to, but not necessarily as thick as, a crayon. Commonly used on textured papers and special drawing bristols.

HALFTONE
A printing method that produces a wide range of gray tones though the use of tiny, mechanically created dots.

HEAD LINES
Preliminary lines drawn to locate the general appropriate placement of facial features.

HORIZON LINE
A basic line drawn left to right through a composition to determine the viewing point of the observer and from which perspective is developed.

INDIA INK
A dense black drawing ink, either waterproof or water soluble. The waterproof variety is most often used, although the water soluble can be used to achieve certain special effects similar to watercolor techniques.

JOURNAL
Commonly refers to a magazine or periodical that is devoted to a highly specialized interest, trade, or profession.

LIGHTBOX
An box illuminated from the inside, with a translucent top that facilitates tracing or transferring drawings from one surface to another.

LITHO CRAYON
Also called Conte Crayon. Produces a rich black line similar to that of the grease pencil or crayon, but is not quite so soft or waxy.

LINE REPRODUCTION
A more direct printing process that does not reproduce shades of gray, such as the halftone process does.

LOGO
A design and/or special lettering style that clearly identifies a particular brand or product or name of a corporation.

MECHANICAL TINTS
A method of introducing one or more shades of gray to a black and white line drawing through the use of special materials such as films and Grafix papers and boards.

NIBS
The business end of an artist's fountain pen. Generally available in a variety of styles and widths. They are interchangeable.

ON ACCEPTANCE

A payment procedure used by some publishers wherein an artist is paid soon after his work has been approved for publication by the editor or art director.

ON PUBLICATION

A payment procedure wherein payment is withheld until the artist's work actually appears in print.

OPPOSING CURVES

A system used to enhance form and shape and to emphasize action.

OUTLINE

A brief, highly condensed version of a concept or proposed feature.

PLY

A grading system used to indicate the weight or thickness of drawing bristols.

PORTFOLIO

A collection of the artist's original drawings that adequately represents his range of capabilities, but does not become repetitious. Usually contained in a suitable carrying case. Drawings are often more impressive if matted and/or protected with clear acetate and should appear clean and crisp looking. Photocopies of previously published work (include some of the surrounding printed matter) may be included in the portfolio, but is usually more conveniently presented in a separate folder.

PYRAMIDING

Building as many versions as possible from a single drawing, idea, or situation.

ROUGHS

Quick sketches or drawings, usually in pencil, illustrating gag cartoon ideas which are sent to publications for consideration. A typical "batch" consists of 8-10 roughs. With the simpler cartoon styles, some cartoonists prefer to ink in their roughs so that, in the event of an "OK," the cartoon is available for immediate publication. The term also applies to any preliminary sketch used to represent a proposed cartoon idea.

RUBBER CEMENT

An adhesive used by graphic artists and cartoonists because of its fast drying and nonwrinkling qualities. Can be used as a temporary or permanent bonding for papers and light bristols.

SCRATCHBOARD

A form of illustration board coated with a smooth clay-like substance that can be easily scratched with any sharp or pointed instrument to achieve extremely fine lines or special effects.

SCREEN PRINTING
A highly developed form of stencil printing for reproduction on nearly anything, from high-grade papers to T-shirts and towels.

SHADING FILM
Clear, transparent film treated on the backside with a dry, low-tack adhesive and pre-printed with dot or line patterns to create a shaded effect.

SLANT
Creating material aimed directly at a specific area of interest.

SLAPSTICK
A form of humor, usually very simple, direct, and sudden. Often employs the element of surprise and ridicule.

SPATTER
A method of creating shading or special effects by dipping the tip of a bristle brush into ink or paint, and then spattering the desired area by rubbing the bristle with a finger or small stick.

SPOT DRAWINGS
Small, almost decorative drawings used to add interest and to break up large areas of text.

SYNDICATE
An organization staffed with people who have the expertise and financial ability to represent cartoonists and authors in the most effective manner possible. An agent, so to speak.

TAG LINE
The caption, punch line, or brief description used to explain a cartoon or humorous illustration.

TORNADO SKETCHING
A drawing exercise that uses circular lines to indicate the bulk and form of a figure or object.

WASH
Ink, lamp black, or color diluted to varying degrees to achieve a wide range of shades, tones, and intensities on a drawing or cartoon. Normally applied in nearly transparent consistency. Black and white washes require the halftone printing process. Colors applied in this manner ordinarily require the full color reproduction process.

WHITE TRANSFER PAPER
Similar to ordinary carbon paper, except the copy appears in white rather than blue or black. Most often used in creating the final layout on black scratchboard.

The following books are highly recommended for further study and research:

ART OF THE TIMES
Jean-Claude Suares

ARTS OF DAVID LEVINE, THE
Alfred A. Knopf, NY, pub.

CARICATURES OF GEO. CRUIKSHANK, THE
John Wardroper
David R. Godine, Boston, pub.

CARTOONING
Roy Paul Nelson
Contemporary Books, Chicago, pub.

CARTOONING FUNDAMENTALS
Al Ross
Stravon Educational Press, NY, pub.

CREATURE COMFORTS
Charles Adams
Simon & Schuster, NY, pub.

DRAWING LESSONS FROM GREAT MASTERS
Robert Beverly Hale
Watson-Guptill, NY, pub.

EARLY MORNING MILK TRAIN, THE
Rowland Emett
Stephen Greene, Brattleboro, VT, pub.

EDITORIAL AND POLITICAL CARTOONING
Syd Hoff
Stravon Educational Press, NY, pub.

GANG OF EIGHT, THE
Forward by Tom Brokaw
Faber & Faber, Boston, pub.

WRIGHT SIDE UP and/or WRIGHT ON
Don Wright
Simon & Schuster, NY, pub.

GREAT CARTOONISTS AND THEIR ART
Art Wood
Pelican Publishing, Gretna, LA, pub.

GREAT COMIC CATS
Bill Blackbears
Troubador Press, San Francisco, pub.

INSINCERELY YOURS
Dana Frandon
Charles Schribner's Sons, NY, pub.

JULES FEIFFER'S AMERICA
Steven Heller
Alfred Knopf, NY, pub.

JELLYBEAN SOCIETY, THE
Pat Oliphant
Andrews & McMeel, NY, pub.

MASTERS OF CARICATURE
William Feaver
Alfred A. Knopf, NY, pub.

MASTERY OF DRAWING, THE
Joseph Meder (Meder-Ames)
Abaris Books, NY, pub.

NEW YORKER ALBUM OF DRAWINGS, THE
Viking Press, NY, pub.

RENDERING IN PEN AND INK
Arthur L. Guptill
Watson-Guptill, NY, pub.

SMITHSONIAN COLLECTION OF NEWSPAPER
COMICS, THE
Blackbeard & Williams
Forward by John Canaday
Smithsonian Institution Press and
Harry N. Abrams, publishers

ARTIST'S SUPPLIES AND EQUIPMENT, MANUFACTURERS

Although the student is urged to become acquainted with the friendly folks at the local art supply store, it is sometimes necessary to contact the manufacturers directly for the latest catalogs, samples, etc. The following major manufacturers produce nearly every type of art supplies and equipment known to modern man. However, it sometimes takes a while for them to respond to correspondence.

General Art Supplies

M. GRUMBACHER, INC., 460 West 34th Street, New York, NY 10001

STRATHMORE PAPER CO., South Broad, Westfield, MA 01085

HUNT MFG. CO., 230 South Broad Street, Philadelphia, PA 19102

Self-Adhesive Shading Films and Special Effects

GRAPHIC PRODUCTS CORP., Rolling Meadows, IL 60008

ZIPATONE, INC., 150 Fencil Lane, Hillside, IL 60162

Grafix Shading Mediums (papers and boards)

OHIO GRAPHIC ARTS SYSTEMS, 26055 Emery Road, Warrensville Heights, OH 44128

INDEX